D1606082

Chelsea,

TENNESSEE'S CIVIL WAR BATTLEFIELDS

A Guide to Their History and Preservation

May God bless you,

Randy Bishop

10/13/12

BY

RANDY BISHOP

PELICAN PUBLISHING COMPANY

GRETNA 2010

First edition, 2008
First paperback edition, 2008
First Pelican paperback edition, 2010

The word "Pelican" and the depiction of a pelican are trademarks of Pelican Publishing Company, Inc., and are registered in the U.S. Patent and Trademark Office.

ISBN 978-1-58980-771-6
LCN: 2007901899

Cover painting: The Horse Marines, © *John Paul Strain, 2005*

Printed in the United States of America
Published by Pelican Publishing Company, Inc.
1000 Burmaster Street, Gretna, Louisiana 70053

To the students of Middleton High School, past and present,
whom I've had the honor to teach.

TABLE OF CONTENTS

PREFACE

Upon completing my first book, *The Tennessee Brigade,* I was overwhelmed at the amount of support shown by my fellow residents of Middleton, Tennessee, former and present students at Middleton High School, and other interested parties. To them another, and more proper, thank-you is graciously extended.

In addition, having been bitten by the bug to write again, I saw my thoughts turn toward future projects. Sharon, my wife and best friend, suggested the contents of this book, a work that attempts to review a number of significant battles in Tennessee in the years from 1861 to 1865. A brief description of the major occurrences of each struggle discussed, in addition to the preservation efforts at each, serves as the heart of the purpose behind this effort. If the book is found to be interesting and informative, the praises should go to Sharon for her inspiration. However, any and all blame for a lack of inducing enthusiasm must go to me.

Any open-minded individual will quickly acknowledge the loss of a large amount of what the Civil War Preservation Trust correctly labels—as did Abraham Lincoln—hallowed ground. Historians and others interested only in the period of the American Civil War cringe at the idea of the sacred sites disappearing before our eyes. It will be noted in this text that the efforts of preservationists and like organizations have met with mixed success, ranging from the existence of battlefields hardly changed since the days the soil on the fields was covered by the blood of dedicated and sacrificial men, to those areas where the existence of any signs of a vicious struggle are entirely absent.

The legislative process of saving a battlefield is a lengthy and costly endeavor. I asked an official connected with preservation what I could say to get each reader to participate in the preservation movement. His reply was to ask people to get interested and active on the local level, at an area battlefield; become aware of land that becomes available for purchase near or on a Civil War site; be available. These are goals and realistic challenges for each of us. Organizations such as the Tennessee Civil War Preservation Association, the Civil War Preservation Trust, and a host of "Friends of" organizations pertinent to various battlefields help each of us to accomplish these as well.

A simple review of the ten costliest battles of the great struggle, based upon total figures of killed, wounded, missing, and captured, will show that Tennessee contains three of the ten sites within its borders. Stone's River or Murfreesboro, at number 8, was the location of 24,645 casualties. Shiloh, at the ninth spot, had 23,741; Fort Donelson is number 10 and saw the loss of 19,455 soldiers. These almost 68,000 losses combine with other armed conflicts to rank Tennessee second only to Virginia in the number of Civil War battles taking place in a single state.

Tennessee has more than 2,900 documented and identified "sites" from the Civil War located in its borders. These include campsites, blockhouses, hospitals, battlefields, and several other types of designations. As this book focuses primarily on the battlefields and the preservation efforts at each, a brief overview of this classification should be conducted.

Fred Prouty, director of programs and the military sites preservation specialist for the Tennessee Wars Commission, defines a battlefield as the area over which two large bodies of hostile troops engaged in combat. These are divided into two categories: *small engagements* in which a small number of troops were involved, and *large engagements* where units equal to 12,000 troops or more fought.

Prouty has explained that of the 384 "principal battles" that took place in 26 states, Tennessee was the location of 38, again, second only to Virginia. By categories, Tennessee was the site of forty-one "small" battles, three in West Tennessee, sixteen in Middle Tennessee, and twenty-two in East Tennessee. Forty-three "large" battles took place in the state, with three in West Tennessee, Shiloh, Hatchie Bridge, and Parker's Crossroads; twenty in Middle Tennessee, twelve connected with Nashville, four with Stones River, two with Franklin, and one each for Fort Donelson and Spring Hill; and twenty in East Tennessee. The battles for Chattanooga comprise sixteen of the East Tennessee sites, the others being two for Blue Springs, and one each for Knoxville and Bean's Station.

With three major rivers, the Mississippi, Cumberland, and Tennessee, and seventeen principal railroads, there is little wonder that Tennessee was the location for such a tremendous number of struggles and thus, today the site of numerous efforts at preserving the related battlefields.

Preservation makes sense, not only for the sake of heritage, but also from an economic standpoint. With more than 2,900 documented sites of military actions on Tennessee soil, it's highly likely that the proclamation that no Tennessee community in existence at the time of the war was unaffected holds true to the utmost degree. However, only thirty-eight of those sites are classified as major sites, a designation given by the National Park Service as one that affected the outcome of the war. More than 90 percent of the battle sites in Tennessee are in private hands, primed for economic development for tourism or some other industry less likely to aid in the preservation of the locations.

For example, an unnamed fort at Triune was built by the hands of the same men whose sacrifices at Franklin and Nashville are largely lost to commercial and residential development. One-tenth of a mile long and on private property, the fortress was the location of fired shots, lives lost, earthen works, and now, a preservationist's dream.

In addition, it becomes noteworthy that this book is a chronological account of the Civil War in Tennessee, not a book about Tennessee in the Civil War. In stating this, I've attempted to steer clear of reviewing the number and types of military units formed for each army, the existence of Unionist sentiments in the state, or a host of other issues that presented themselves during the bloody years of the Civil War. These issues have been more thoroughly discussed by authors with much more clarity of style and expression of knowledge than I will ever possess.

In this regard, it is my utmost wish that the following pages will enlighten, educate, and entertain any reader. That is the true purpose of any worthwhile book.

Randy Bishop
February 2007

ACKNOWLEDGMENTS

To complete a book and omit the names of those individuals whose efforts made it a reality would be an utter disservice and a self-centered endeavor. I would therefore like to mention the following people and thank each for his or her worthwhile contribution to the completion of this project. Ahead of time, I also want to apologize to any group or individual I failed to mention. Inevitably there will be such an instance, and for that I am deeply apologetic.

Reed Dreaden, the Humphrey County historian, trekked over and guided me through the remains of the Johnsonville battlefield. Despite the extreme late-July heat and humidity, ticks, and poison oak, he revealed a wealth of information and did so in a professional and highly personable manner. Malcolm Wilcox of the Salem Battlefield Association did the same on a hot August afternoon. Neither of these men complained, but instead gave his respective personal tour and shared information freely. A longtime acquaintance, Herbert Wood, showed his knowledge gained in the last two decades and provided contacts for Davis Bridge, a site for which Herbert has been the driving force for its preservation. To each of these men, I am deeply indebted.

Tennessee State Representative Steve McDaniel, a businessman and well-known preservationist and advocate for Civil War sites, took a cool November Saturday afternoon to give a personal tour of the Parker's Crossroads battlefield. Mr. McDaniel's efforts and successes are as commendable as any and are eclipsed only by his level of knowledge of the battle. His words provide the bulk of the chapter related to Parker's Crossroads.

Fred Prouty, military sites preservation specialist and director of programs for the Tennessee Wars Commission, guided me in the early stages of research, met with me at the 2005 Nashville Civil War Show, and gave suggestions for the completion of the project. Individuals such as Mr. Prouty have succeeded in the area of preservation, a major purpose of this text.

Ethel Carmichael, director of the Humphrey County Public Library; Jack Wood and Robert Taylor, librarian and assistant librarian of the Tennessee Room at the Jackson/Madison County Library, and Juanita Shaw of the Old Country Store, allowed access to photos, documents, and relics that otherwise would be absent from this work. Rickie Brunner of the Alabama Department of Archives and History led me in the right direction in exploring Alabama units in Tennessee battles. Jim Cox of Reelfoot Lake State Park and Jessica Hutcherson of Fort Pillow State Park were gracious in sharing information.

Eleanor Williams, Montgomery County historian; F.B. Cain of Trenton; Faye Jacobs Owens of Bolivar; Fred Culp, Gibson County historian; James Neese of South Jacksonville, Illinois; and Pauline Cross, Giles County historian, provided information and/or leads.

Shirley Rouse, president of Knoxville Chapter 89, U.D.C., provided information and photographs related to the Bleak House or Confederate Memorial Hall. In addition, Mrs. Namuni Young of Chapter #89 U.D.C., offered a great deal of advice and material for the second edition of this book. Mr. Jim Lyle of Knoxville also gave freely of his information as a means of assisting in the preservation efforts of his city's Civil War sites. In addition, Dorothy E. (Dot) Kelly granted permission to quote from her article on Fort Sanders, the pivotal point of the siege of Knoxville, and furnished a set of excellent photos.

Ann Toplovich, executive director of the Tennessee Historical Society, was more than cooperative in allowing the use of their documents, as was Elizabeth McAulay of the University of North Carolina at Chapel Hill.

James Lewis of Stone's River National Battlefield, and Jim Jobe of Fort Donelson allowed me access to their archives, the photographing of various materials, and guidance about sites within each respective park. Mr. Jobe also supplied some wonderful photos of largely inaccessible areas of Fort Henry.

Frank Powell, editor-in-chief of *Confederate Veteran,* extended unparalleled generosity in allowing unlimited access to his publication.

Photographs and information from the magazine are noticeably present in this project.

Dave Roth of *Blue and Gray* also provided information and photographs and designed a superb set of maps to enhance each battle's understanding.

Stacy D. Allen, Historian at Shiloh National Military Park, deserves a special thank you as well. His critique of the manuscript, willingness to openly share information, and ability to guide me through the days of the bloody struggle at Shiloh are significant to the text's completion. Mr. Allen is a literal walking encyclopedia of the battle at Shiloh and a wide range of military aspects of the War Between the States.

John Paul Strain, an artist of unequaled expertise and precision, was more than generous in allowing the use of his work entitled *The Horse Marines* on the cover of this book.

Permission to use photographs of ancestors came from Darren Smith, Ron Hamilton, Joe Mode, Martha Smith, Mike Childree, Judy Patrick, Rex Gooch, and Shirley Waites. The University of Tennessee, and Margie Thessin and Angela Calhoun of Carnton were more than gracious in providing photographs for use in the book. Paul Gibson, as he was for my previous book, proved highly cooperative and encouraging in allowing the free use of images from his valuable photographic collection.

Cheryl Schnirring, curator of manuscripts at the Abraham Lincoln Presidential Library, shared the Adolph Engelmann letter, and Phyllis Smith is worthy of thanks for her cooperation related to Fort Defiance in Clarksville, Tennessee.

James D. Kay allowed the valuable Nashville information he and his board control to be used in the book. Without it, a definite hole would exist in relation to that battle's coverage.

Chris Green shared an image of his ancestor William Newlon. More significantly and unequaled by any is the appreciation extended to Chris for the use of the Newlon diary, so significant to understanding both the Shiloh and Davis Bridge battles from a first-person standpoint.

David Fraley, historian and assistant curator of the Carter House in Franklin, also provided a superior level of assistance on this project. A tour, sharing of documents and images, providing encouragement and direction as well as praise were but a few of the contributions this battle expert and preservation proponent generously provided.

Mrs. Joyce Beibers, the wife of William V. Beibers, the gentleman who first gave me the opportunity to share knowledge with the wonderful students of Middleton High School, performed perhaps the most difficult task of all and is due a special thank-you. Mrs. Beibers proofread the manuscript and did so in a totally professional and timely manner. Any errors in the text should be credited to the author and not to the lady who so meticulously carried out her requested task.

Lastly, but most importantly, my family deserves acknowledgment. My parents, Wayne and Margaret, heard my complaints and accomplishments, and offered advice, all without becoming negative at any stage of the publication process. In addition, my daddy read the manuscript several times, offering suggestions and constructive criticism. My sons, Jay and Ben, never complained when our "day trips" frequently grew into longer excursions simply for the sake of finding out some tidbit of information for the book. At long last, Sharon, my supportive and encouraging wife of eighteen years, assisted with a variety of tasks, served as "chief navigator" for a number of trips, and allotted the time I needed to complete this project and still manage to be the person—both father and son—I so strongly desire to be. She did so numerous times, usually receiving a meal as her only compensation. To each of these family members I extend my utmost love and regularly see God's presence in allowing me to spend time with them.

As an addendum to the acknowledgment section, my beloved mother, Margaret Bishop, passed away before the publication of this work was completed. As a genuine and unashamed "momma's boy," I know she would have loved to have been here and shown her pleasure and excitement over her youngest child's second book. In faith, I feel she is here and is celebrating with those she loved so dearly. I truly miss her and will always cherish the memories and love she created.

CHAPTER ONE

FORT HENRY

On February 2, 1862, General Ulysses S. Grant, commander of the Federal forces in western Kentucky and Tennessee moved his 17,000-man army from Cairo, Illinois.[1] His destination was comprised of two locations, Fort Henry and Fort Donelson.

Fort Henry, named for Confederate senator Gustavus Henry, the grandson of Patrick Henry, was an earthen fort on the Tennessee River and lay twelve miles from Donelson, situated on the Cumberland River. If these two Confederate forts could be taken, control of the Mississippi River and Kentucky would basically belong to the Union army.

Some 3,000 Confederates were stationed at Fort Henry under the command of General Lloyd Tilghman. The popular commander was a West Point-trained soldier with well-respected bravery that would eventually become more evident. From Paducah, Kentucky, Tilghman would survive the action at Fort Henry and serve a stint at a prisoner of war camp before being hit in the chest by a shell fragment at Champion Hill in May of 1863.[2]

Among the soldiers who helped build the earthen structure and manned it were the men of the Tenth Tennessee Infantry. Patrick M. Griffin of Company H would soon see action at both forts Henry and Donelson.[3]

Griffin offered this reminiscence of the Irish Tennessee regiment:

> "At Fort Henry there was no whiskey on our side of the river, but across the stretch of water was Madame Peggy's saloon. There was some mystery as to where the beverage

1

she sold was obtained, but this only added to her popularity … One night Paddy Sullivan and Timothy Tansey went over to Lady Peggy's to get some whiskey; and when they returned to the river bank, a small cloud appeared upon the horizon. They paid no attention to this, however, but rowed out into the middle of the Tennessee River … The waves got so high that the brave laddies thought their time had come. Timothy said, '… the boat will be overturned and we will lose our whiskey.' … Paddy to Timothy, '… we will just drink it and save it.' And drink it they did. The refreshment added to their courage and strength, and they reached the shore, but the boys in camp were minus their jiggers."[4]

Besides the men of the Tenth Tennessee, Fort Henry was host to a variety of artillery: eight 32-pound, two 42-pound, one 128-pound Columbiad, five 18-pound smoothbore siege guns, and one 6-inch rifle. Low-quality powder caused the fort's garrison to flirt with danger and use quick-burning fuses to achieve the desired shot distance of one mile.[5]

In addition to Grant's troops, whose approach was hampered by muddy roads, the fort's inhabitants were to shortly encounter a Federal fleet under the command of Flag Officer A.H. Foote. Included in the fleet were four well-armed ironclads, *Essex, Cincinnati, Carondelet,* and *St. Louis,* from right to left in the river.[6]

Behind the front line consisting of the ironclads, the timber-clads *Conestoga, Tyler,* and *Lexington* brought up the fleet's rear as it moved toward Fort Henry on February 6. The *Essex* contained four guns, while the other three ironclads each had thirteen. Combined, the three timber-clads had fifteen guns.[7]

The armaments of the approaching fleet and slow-moving infantry could easily overwhelm the inhabitants of Fort Henry. Having boasted a force of 1,800, the fort's manpower had largely evacuated the area by February 6. Shotguns and flintlock muskets from the War of 1812 served as the weapons for the remaining soldiers, now totally confined within the three acres of the fort's trenches. Tilghman directed the withdrawal of all troops but part of Company B, First Tennessee Artillery, and an additional fifty-five men. Each of these soldiers was to man the cannons with each gun being assigned "a particular vessel to which it was to pay its especial compliments…"[8]

Foote directed Commander Roger N. Stembel of the flagship *Cincinnati* to open fire on Fort Henry. This was done at 12:34 PM from a distance of 1,700 yards.[9] This shot ended what had been a slow and quiet descent of the river.

Rear Admiral Henry Walke, aboard the *Carondelet,* recalled the narrow width of the Tennessee River near Fort Henry and that the Confederate flag, earthworks, and barracks of the fort offered a stark contrast to the dense woods of the area.[10]

As soon as the *Cincinnati* belched out the initial shot, "the fort was ablaze with the flames of ... heavy guns." For the first hour of the fight, a steady exchange of fire sent dirt into the air around the fort. Shots also produced water sprays and dented metal on the ironclads. Inside the fort, the six-inch rifle gun burst; two of the thirty-two-pounders and the Columbiad were damaged and rendered useless for an unknown length of time.[11]

Aboard the *Essex,* a twenty-four-pound shot struck the boiler, killing acting Master's Mate S.B. Brittan, Jr. Steam and hot water filled the vessel, seriously wounding Capt. W.D. Porter, the boat's commander, who stood near Brittan when the projectile hit. Porter and others left or attempted to leave the confines of the ironclad, Porter accomplishing the feat with assistance. A total of twenty-seven men aboard the *Essex* suffered injuries from the steam.[12]

Others on board the *Essex* proved even less fortunate. James Coffey, shot man on the number-two gun, was scalded to death as he stood on his knees taking a shell from the box and preparing to pass it to the loader. Seaman Jasper P. Breas, also badly scalded, yelled that he must see the surrender of the fort before he died. Hours after Fort Henry yielded to the Federal naval assault, Breas passed away.[13]

The Confederate artillery proved highly effective. Having had the opportunity to perfect the range needed to strike approaching gunboats, their marksmanship was equal to if not exceeding that of the gunboats. The use of torpedoes was another Confederate tactic at Fort Henry,[14] yet its effectiveness was less than desired.

Prior to the accident, *Essex* had fired seventy shots before suffering thirty-two total wounded, missing, and dead. *St. Louis* suffered no casualties, fired 107 shots, and was hit 7 times. *Carondelet* also fired 107 shots and received 30 strikes from shot and shell. Damage to *Cincinnati* was substantial, with 32 strikes, compared to its dispersing of 112 projectiles. The after-cabin, chimneys, and boats were riddled, and two guns disabled.

One crewman was killed and nine wounded when a shot entered the flagship.[15]

Tilghman had been requested to hold off the Federals for one hour in order to give the remaining untrained troops enough time to make their way toward Fort Donelson. His effective leadership, command of respect among his troops, and personal manning of a gun had created a resistance that lasted almost two hours. The general saw further resistance as futile, with the gunboats approaching within 200 yards of the fort, and ordered the colors lowered. The rising waters of the Tennessee River were waist-deep where the flag stood at the fort's lower side. Tilghman notified his captors that another forty-eight hours in delaying the battle would have placed the entire works under water.[16]

The formal surrender of Fort Henry was given to the naval forces, with Lt. Commander Phelps standing in for Foote; Confederate captain Jesse Taylor substituted for Tilghman. Approximately seventy Confederates surrendered to the Federals with no shots fired by the Union infantry. General Grant entered the fort at 3 o'clock and assumed command.[17]

T.H. Merritt, Company H, Fourth Mississippi, briefly recorded his tenure at Fort Henry in writing: "We were sent to Fort Henry ... in November, 1861 ... The enemy attacked ...after a bombardment of an hour and a half, Gen. Lloyd Tilghman surrendered. We had fifty to sixty men. We had two killed, one mortally and five slightly wounded."[18]

The Federal success at Fort Henry would soon be overshadowed with the major victory at Fort Donelson. Foote's accolades at Henry would outshine those received at Donelson; his success would be far more limited at the latter. While U.S. Grant gained a name for himself at Fort Henry, the best was yet to come for the future president who—a short time before the war—had given up on his military career and was working in the civilian sector. General Halleck's announcement that the flag of the Union had been re-established in Tennessee and would never be removed had little time to circulate, as larger Federal victories within the state lay ahead.

In 1982, the graves of five members of Jesse Taylor's Company B, First Tennessee Artillery, were located and marked. These men had been killed when they had placed too much powder in their forty-two- and thirty-two-pound cannon inside the fort, causing the guns to explode. John Douglass, James Kalachau, Michael Lee, Edward McCabe, and an unknown soldier were buried in the woods around Fort Henry to prevent the Federal soldiers from pilfering their graves.[19] Today, through the work of local preservationist Carman Greenup, these men have their places of interment clearly marked.

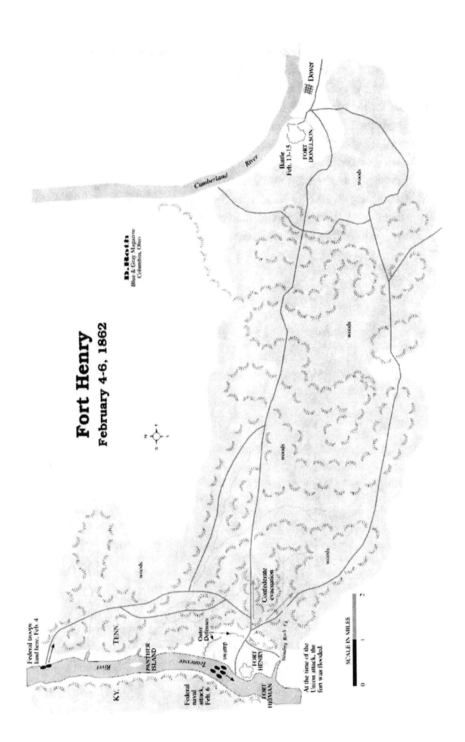

Fort Henry
February 4-6, 1862

D. Roth
Blue & Gray Magazine
Columbus, Ohio

Cumberland River

Dover

FORT DONELSON

Battle
Feb. 13-15

woods

woods

woods

woods

woods

Federal troops
land here, Feb 4

TENN.

KY.

PANTHER
ISLAND

River

FORT
HEIMAN

Tennessee

Federal
naval
attack,
Feb. 6

FORT
HENRY

Outer
Defenses

swamp

Confederate
evacuation

Kinning Rock Cr.

At the time of the
Union attack, the
fort was flooded.

SCALE IN MILES

0   1   2

Fort Henry itself is now largely inaccessible to the public. All that remains of Fort Henry are sections of the easternmost rifle pits and a road trace, sites that are difficult to find unless fortunate enough to procure the guidance of a previous visitor. A few state-furnished markers denote the approximate location of the fort and lead the visitor to the general location. Aside from the rifle pits, the rest of the fort, an obviously low-lying area at the time of the battle, lies beneath the waters of Kentucky Lake. General Tilghman saw the need to abandon Fort Henry and to take advantage of Fort Heiman, a fort under construction at that time and across the river on higher ground. However, as was the experience for the Confederates who moved from Fort Henry to face the Federal army at Fort Donelson, the preservation efforts at Fort Henry have largely been lost.

This illustration from Frank Leslie's The American Soldier in the Civil War was accompanied with the words "Bursting of a Rifled 42-Pound Gun in Fort Henry During the Bombardment." Courtesy of Fort Donelson National Military Park.

The remains of a portion of Fort Henry's easternmost rifle pits are discernable in this photo by Jimmy Jobe, Fort Donelson National Military Park Historian.

The majority of what was once Fort Henry now lies beneath this watery grave of Kentucky Lake. Photo by Jimmy Jobe.

Confederate flags mark the wooded graves of five men killed by an exploding cannon at Fort Henry. Photo by Jimmy Jobe.

CHAPTER TWO

FORT DONELSON

"No terms except an unconditional … surrender"
February 11-16, 1862

Following the fall of Fort Henry, 2,500 fleeing Confederates made their way twelve miles southeast overland to Fort Donelson. This stronghold rested on a sloping bluff 150 feet above the Cumberland River, and the enclosure contained approximately 100 acres and 3 miles of trenches on its perimeter. Fort Donelson sat just south of the Tennessee-Kentucky border and near the village of Dover, Tennessee.[1]

Dover, located in Stewart County, was comprised of a courthouse, a two-story tavern, and several houses. Nearby Fort Donelson offered a more formidable presence with twelve heavy guns and two river batteries, one being twenty and the other fifty feet above the water. Named for General Daniel S. Donelson, a West Pointer and nephew of Rachel Jackson, the fort was encircled with rifle pits, and cut trees lined the hills to the extent that the branches weaved with those of the trees to either side in an attempt to limit access to the structure. Hills, streams, ravines, hollows, oak and ash woods, and creeks such as Hickman and Indian added to the rough terrain. The Cumberland River formed the fort's northern boundary; a swampy area lay to the east and separated the fort from Dover; densely wooded ground and undergrowth lay to the south.[2]

Major J.F. Gilmer, a West Point graduate and staff member of General Albert Sidney Johnston, had worked in conjunction with brigadier generals

Bushrod R. Johnson and Gideon Pillow in attempts at completing the majority of the earthworks in the days following the fall of Fort Henry. A ten-inch Columbiad, a rifled thirty-two-pounder, and a mixture of thirty-two-pound carronades and other thirty-two-pounders served as the Confederate firepower. In addition, an estimated 18,000 to 21,000 Confederates served at Fort Donelson, where Brigadier General Simon B. Buckner, a West Point classmate of U.S. Grant, would meet the Federals in the first major Civil War battle in Tennessee.[3]

Outnumbering their enemy by as many as 6,000 troops, the Federal army, under U.S. Grant, was divided into three parts. Charles F. Smith, Lew Wallace, and John A. McClernand stood left to right, basically encircling the Confederates by the early hours of February 13, 1862. These Federal commanders—a career army officer, a future author, and an Illinois lawyer and congressman respectively—poised themselves to attack the fort.[4]

Smith's Second Division included the Seventh, Ninth, Twelfth, Forty-first, and Fiftieth Illinois; the Eleventh, Twenty-fifth, and Fifty-second Indiana; the Second, Seventh, Twelfth, and Fourteenth Iowa; and was rounded out by the presence of the Eighth and Twelfth Missouri as well as batteries D, H, and K of the First Missouri Light Artillery and Birge's Missouri Sharpshooters.[5]

McClernand's First Division was comprised of the Eighth, Eleventh, Seventeenth, Eighteenth, Twentieth, Twenty-ninth, Thirtieth, Thirty-first, Forty-fifth, Forty-eighth, and Forty-ninth Illinois. In addition, the group included batteries B and D of the First Illinois Light Artillery, as well as batteries D and E of the Second Illinois Light Artillery. Companies A and B of the Second Illinois Cavalry, companies C and I of the Second and Fourth U.S. Cavalry, joined the Fourth Illinois Cavalry and independent Illinois companies to complete the division.[6]

Wallace reported that the first of the two brigades of his Third Division consisted of the Thirty-first Indiana, Seventeenth Kentucky, Forty-first Indiana, Twenty-fifth Kentucky, First Nebraska, and Seventy-sixth and Sixty-eighth Ohio. A second brigade included the Forty-sixth Illinois and the Fifty-seventh and Fifty-eighth Illinois, but it arrived during the battle and was assigned to another command.[7]

Flag Officer Andrew H. Foote had arrived on February 12, but made no aggressive moves with his flotilla. Foote's four ironclad and two wooden gunboats were the *St. Louis*, *Carondelet*, *Louisville*, *Pittsburg*, *Tyler*, and *Conestoga*.[8]

The Federal infantry's march from Fort Henry was undertaken during unseasonably warm and dry weather along roads the Confederates had traveled earlier. Other than only minimally effective contact with Colonel Nathan Bedford Forrest's cavalry through that afternoon,[9] little had hindered the progress of Grant's army. The irony of the advance was that the Federal troops—many of whom were encumbered by and perspiring in their winter clothing—cast aside blankets and coats during the advance on the twelfth. A return of temperatures to those more consistent with winter and the addition of precipitation would soon cause the Federal troops to question the sensibility of this action.

Relying heavily upon his successful efforts at Fort Henry, General Grant planned to use Foote's fleet to pound away at the fort, causing it to surrender. All escape routes were to be blocked, yielding a large number of Confederate prisoners, with minimal Federal casualties.[10] Though the eventual Confederate surrender would occur, the bulk of the plan would be significantly altered.

While the number of Confederate defenders of Fort Donelson, as earlier noted, varies widely, a basic knowledge of those units present does exist. These included the Second and Eighth Kentucky, the First, Third, Fourth, Fourteenth, Twentieth, and Twenty-sixth Mississippi, as well as the Twenty-seventh Alabama. The Seventh Texas joined various Kentucky, Virginia, and Tennessee batteries and Green's Kentucky Battery, along with the Fifteenth Arkansas. A host of Tennessee regiments sought to defend land in their home state, including the Third, Tenth, Eighteenth, Twenty-sixth, Thirtieth, Thirty-second, Forty-first, Forty-second, Forty-eighth, Forty-ninth, Fiftieth, Fifty-first, and Fifty-third regiments. Four Virginia Regiments, the Thirty-sixth, Fiftieth, Fifty-first, and Fifty-sixth, also stood at the fort, as did Col. Joseph Drake's Alabama Battalion and Col. B.M. Browder's Tennessee Battalion. Colonel Nathan Bedford Forrest's Tennessee Cavalry and the cavalry commands of Maj. Gant, Lt. Col. George Gantt, and Major S.H. Colms rounded out the Confederates at the fort.[11]

Confederate captain Reuben R. Ross, an 1853 West Point graduate, had arrived at Fort Donelson on February 11. He led his command of the Maury County Tennessee Artillery to a position Gen. Pillow had stated was a post of danger and of honor. Clearly understanding the risks involved in manning the river batteries, Ross and his men each declared a strong desire to defend the site.[12]

In his journal, Captain Ross gave this account:

"I found the defenses were as follows: first and lowest down, an 8-gun battery of 32 pdrs with a 10 inch Columbiad on the left of them … placed in a strong but rough siege battery, with natural earthen traverses, mostly revetted [sic] with hurdles of sapwood, capped between embrasures with sandbags, the embrasures lined as usual with rawhide. There were no bomb proofs or roofs of any kind. The upper battery was a barbette battery without any traverses … This battery contained two 32 pdr. seacoast howitzers."[13]

On Wednesday, February 12, 1862, Captain Ross noted excitement in the Confederate batteries, an event caused by the arrival of a Federal gunboat. He recalled:

"Only a single gunboat engaged us that morning. She appeared above the bend, took position, and opened fire … two and one-fourth miles off, her shot and shell reached us with perfect facility. We mostly answered her with the rifle … [it] did a fine service, striking … four or five times … of the twelve or fifteen shots fired. She drew off after about forty minutes bombardment … No one was killed or … damage done by this boat."[14]

A similar story comes from a member of the Tenth Tennessee, a regiment comprised largely of Irishmen. The soldier wrote:

"… a report came … from a breathless picket that a gunboat was just around the bend … and would blow … all into smithereens … there was immense excitement. There was not much order nor discipline in those days, so the whole regiment … dropped pick and shovel … They had muskets and bayonets, but not a round of ammunition. The commander was Col. A. Heiman … a German … they were sadly disappointed that she didn't come [ashore]."[15]

The action of the coming days would yield a much higher level of intensity, casualties, and stories of valor. The battle was now inevitable.

One Confederate remembered a Federal engineer, atop a white horse, riding within 600 yards of the Confederate lines on the afternoon of the twelfth, using his field glasses to survey the fort and its defenders. A sharpshooter gained permission to move two hundred yards closer, accomplishing his intent to drive the engineer away, but failing to wound either him or his mount. Along the Confederate lines, men busied themselves that afternoon in digging trenches, throwing up parapets of logs, or resting before the fight many felt was soon to come.[16]

On the morning of the thirteenth, action increased when General John McClernand, against Grant's orders, advanced toward the fort. In his official report, McClernand acknowledged Grant's "…order to avoid everything calculated to bring on a general engagement …", yet sought to silence cannon fire from positions he noted as redan numbers one and two. He then stormed the latter, under heavy crossfire from artillery and small arms. McClernand claimed that a diversion from the gunboats would have most likely enabled the redan to be captured.[17]

Multiple phases of this attack had enabled the attacking Federals, most notably the Illinois troops of Col. Morrison, to advance within forty yards of the Confederate lines. Following the third and final assault, the wounded were unmercifully attacked by smoke and fire from dry leaves that had been ignited. Despite a number of Confederates leaving their positions to rescue their injured enemies, the retreating Federals found "their ears and souls were riven with the shrieks of their wounded comrades, upon whom the flames crept and smothered and charred where they lay."[18]

The Federal gunboat *Carondelet* made a lone attempt to assist the attacking Federals. Throughout the day, the vessel exchanged fire with the river batteries with "… elongated Parrot shells of 42 and maybe higher caliber," exclaimed a Confederate.

Captain Reuben Ross's battery had exchanged only six rounds with the gunboats when one federal round struck a thirty-two-pound cannon, dismounting the gun and sending fragments flying. A screw bolt from the Confederate gun struck Captain Joseph Dixon, mortally wounding him. J.A. Hinkle of Company A, Thirtieth Tennessee stated that a man in his parapet located next to that of Captain Dixon picked up the bomb shell and threw it out. He later exclaimed, "If it had exploded, we would have all been killed." The last command Captain Dixon gave before receiving his wound was to order his men to fire the eight guns.[19]

A northern wind accompanied the darkness of the thirteenth. The pleasant weather that greeted the warriors during the day transformed into a stormy night. Heavy rains fell upon the soldiers, and temperatures fell quickly. Sleet, freezing rain, and snow began near 8 PM and intensified the struggles of the men attempting to keep warm in temperatures that eventually fell to ten degrees. Colonel Roger Hanson's Second Kentucky possessed hooded parkas, a rarity among either army. "Great suffering and hardship" as well as "intensified winter" were two of the descriptions for the weather that pelted troops while two inches of snow covered the ground.[20]

Ben F. Loftin of the Thirty-second Tennessee was often reminded of the conditions of that night. He later explained:

> "My regiment ... supported Graves' Battery on the right, the left of the regiment being in the ditches under the guns. After completing our breastworks, I kneeled down in the ditch, with my head resting against a wheel of Graves' rifle ... I had slept long enough for my clothes to freeze to the ground, when the cannon was discharged at a sharpshooter. I jumped up, minus part of my pants ... The boys had the laugh on me." [21]

The sunrise of Friday, February 14 shone brightly on the faces of the Federal soldiers. Their sharpshooters fired from several hundred yards away toward the Confederate lines, where the cold Southerners knew the lower river battery was in range. Captain Jacob Culbertson of the Thirtieth Tennessee met with members of his command, and a consensus was reached to fire a few rounds of grape and shell at the house serving as the sharpshooter's nest. This took place just prior to 8:30 and silenced the sharpshooters in that area of the battlefield.[22]

As a piercing cold wind blew and the 9 o'clock hour approached, Federal transports were spotted below the river's bend. Using telescopes, the Confederates within the fort easily spotted disembarking Federal cavalry and infantry in great numbers, the dark uniforms in vast contrast to the newly fallen snow. Permission was sought to fire into the Federals in an attempt to limit the effectiveness of their goal to reinforce their comrades. Authority to bombard the Federals failed to arrive until 1:00 in the afternoon, by which time the Federal troops were all ashore. With only two rounds fired at the transports, they pulled away; yet black smoke farther away signaled something else was approaching.[23]

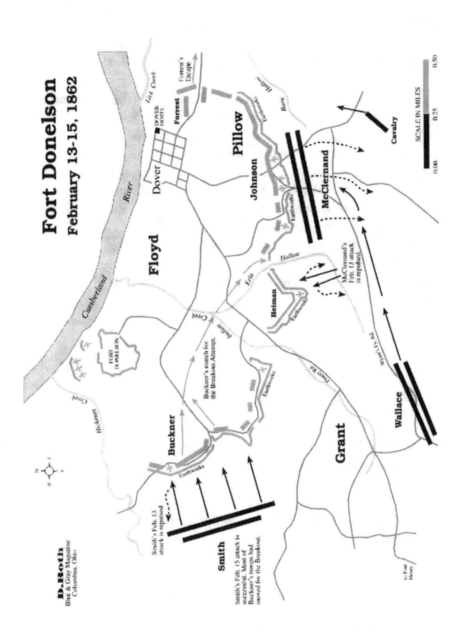

Fort Donelson

February 13-15, 1862

Cumberland River

Lick Creek

DOVER HOTEL

Dover

Forrest

Floyd

Pillow

Johnson

Forrest's Escape

Hollow

Barn

Lineworks

FORT DONELSON

Hickman Creek

Buckner

Buckner's march for the Breakout Attempt.

Earthworks

Indian Creek

Earthworks

Erin Hollow

Heiman

Earthworks

McClernand

Cavalry

McClernand's Feb. 13 attack is repulsed.

Smith's Feb. 13 attack is repulsed.

Wynn's Ferry Rd.

Smith

Smith's Feb. 15 attack is successful. Most of Buckner's troops had moved for the Breakout.

Wallace

Grant

Henry Rd.

to Fort Henry

N

SCALE IN MILES

0.00   0.25   0.50

D. Roth
Blue & Gray Magazine
Columbus, Ohio

15

Six Federal gunboats, including four ironclads, arrived at Fort Donelson. Under Foote's command, the *Carondelet* joined the *Pittsburg*, the *St. Louis* and *Louisville* with the timber-clads *Tyler* and *Conestoga* one quarter mile behind.[24] The four ironclads, one at a time, came into view and moved abreast of the others. In the Confederate batteries, tension grew rapidly. The gunboats began firing, advancing to within four hundred yards of the river batteries as they did.

One Confederate battery attendant recollected, "The four boats kept up a fire too continuous to allow screening; and when two more came into view, forming a second line, all raining shot and shell upon us, we quit hiding altogether ... they came on ... until they reached a slight undulation in the bank on the side where the boat was that I was firing at, when she turned and went to the shore." The attendant noted that shots he fired at the gunboats were merely "pointed," rather than aimed, due to the heavy fire striking his location.[25]

From left to right, the ironclads *Carondelet, Pittsburg, St. Louis,* and *Louisville* advanced while the Confederate batteries yielded a heavy toll upon the attackers. Damage to the gunboats, as well as human losses, became severe.

Commander Henry Walke, from aboard *Carondelet,* remembered:

> "... a 128-pdr. struck our anchor, smashed it into flying bolts, and bounded over the vessel, taking away a part of our smokestack. Then another cut away the iron boat davits as if they were pipestems; another went through the plating and lodged in the heavy casing; another struck the pilot house, knocked the plating to pieces, and sent fragments of iron and splinter into the pilots, one of whom fell mortally wounded; another took away the remaining boat davits, and the boat with them; still they came, harder and faster, taking flagstaffs and smokestacks, and tearing off the side armor as lightning tears bark from a tree." [26]

In spite of the damage, the gunboats initially continued their advance, eventually reaching the "blockade," located 900 yards from the batteries. Here, Confederates had placed trees in the river the previous summer but the water had unknowingly pushed the barricades away, allowing the Union boats to move closer. The Confederate guns in the river batteries had opened fire at almost the same moment and continued to fire frequently. One participant exclaimed, "The cannonade was then at its utmost, and beyond anything ever seen by any of the parties engaged ... The air above and around us was full of shot, solid, case, and shell, while the river below was almost a continuous spray."[27]

General Lew Wallace later remarked that the failure of the Federal gunboats to influence the battle's outcome early in the engagement seriously altered Grant's strategy for Fort Donelson. Wallace wrote, "There are few things connected with the operations against Fort Donelson so relieved of uncertainty as this: that when General Grant at Fort Henry became fixed in the resolution to undertake the movement, his primary object was the capture of the force to which the post was intrusted [sic] ... he relied upon ... Foote and his gunboats ..."[28]

Foote trudged forward, breaking the river's waters to move within four hundred yards of the Confederates. Shells pummeled the *Carondelet* and the *Pittsburg*. The *St. Louis*, Foote's flagship, was struck in the pilot house; the pilot wheel tore away, rendering the ship unmanageable. Foote himself was severely wounded as he stood by the mortally wounded pilot of the boat.[29]

General Wallace explained, "About the guns the floors were slippery with blood, and both surgeons and carpenters were never so busy. Still the four boats kept on, and there was great cheering."[30]

The progress of the fleet and cheering from the men aboard resulted in a steady Confederate retreat from the areas around the river batteries. The *Louisville* was hit and its tiller ropes disabled. This incident caused the *Carondelet* and the *Pittsburg* to close in on the *Louisville* to shield it from additional harm.

U.S. Rear Admiral Henry Walke reminisced of the hostile environment aboard one of the gunboats:

> "Nearly every shot from the fort struck the bow of the
> *Carondelet* ... The enemy's object was to sink the gunboat
> by striking her below the waterline. They soon succeeded
> in planting two 32-pound shots in her bow, which
> made her leak badly ... Three shots struck the starboard
> casing, four...the port casemating forward of the rifle
> gun; one ... the starboard side between the waterline
> and planksheer, cutting through the planking; six shots
> struck the pilot house, shattering one section into pieces

17

... One ... struck our casemate, passed through it ... and
burst the steam heater ... I have preserved this ball as a
souvenir ... When it burst through the side ... it knocked
down and wounded a dozen men, seven of them severely.
An immense quantity of splinters ... some of them as
fine as needles, shot through the clothes of the men like
arrows."[31]

A Confederate remembered seeing the shadow of this ball as it left its
cannon. In addition, he correctly described it as appearing to take the boat
lengthwise and pass through it entirely.[32]

From one of the river batteries, Captain Ross noted, "We had ...
no mercy on them. What a glorious thing if we could sink them! They
appeared to run backward faster than they came up."[33]

A Union officer added, "... the captains of the Confederate batteries
rallied their men ... and renewed the contest with increased will and
energy. A ball got lodged in their best rifle. A corporal and some of his
men took a log fitting the bore, leaped out on the parapet, and rammed
the missile home ..."[34]

Captain Ross recalled that the log had been procured for use in
ramming a jammed projectile from its mid-point of a cannon barrel. This
done, the gun was sponged and cleaned, presenting no problem for the
battle's duration.[35]

The gunboat attack on Fort Donelson had effectively ended, though
the Federals would occasionally fire toward the river batteries in an effort
to keep from being clearly seen through the smoke.[36]

The men aboard *Carondelet* had yet to see the last casualty at Fort
Donelson. A member of the boat recalled:

"... while we were falling back ... the warning words,
'Look out' 'Down' were often heard and heeded by nearly
all the gun crews. On one occasion ... the warning came
just in time ... as a 32-pdr. struck ... bounded on deck
and spun around like a top, but hurt no one ... some of
the young men ... disregarded the instructions, saying
that it was useless to attempt to dodge a cannon ball. The
warning words ... were again soon heard. Down went
the gunner on his hands, as the whizzing shot glanced on
the gun, taking off the gunner's cap and the heads of two

of the young men who ... were standing up ... This shot killed another man also ... and disabled the gun."[37]

The roar of the day's battle was heard as far north as Elizabethtown, Illinois. J.W. Crewdson, a teacher at Sycamore School, mentioned that all day the firing of cannon was clearly heard. His students and he knew a great battle was being fought and death, on a gigantic scale, was taking place.[38]

That night, Confederate pickets were sent out a few hundred yards; inside the fort, the men attempted to sleep. Resting on their guns in the snow, the soldiers found that the intense cold was unimaginable. The use of campfires was avoided, as the two armies were so near to one another. General Floyd, after consulting with generals Buckner and Pillow, prepared for a dawn attack on the Union right on the fifteenth.[39] The purpose of the dawn assault would be to open an escape route for the thousands of Confederates encased in the Union grip.

Moving as quietly as possible over the ice- and snow-covered ground, the Confederates moved from their rifle pits, massing to the left of their own line. One historian has noted that today it seems unbelievable that some 10,000 men from an assortment of infantry, cavalry, and artillery units could move in unison without detection by enemy forces. The most valid point for the failure of the Union army to notice this event is to recall the frigid weather and the negligence of establishing a proper watch.[40]

Major Selden Spencer of the Kentucky Battery provides a clear record of the effort in his writings of the time: "About two o'clock we were roused by marching orders ... We marched back through the town to our left wing and took our position there ... the hills slippery with ice, requiring all the strength ... at the wheels and the drivers' spurs to get the battery up one hill in an hour. It then appeared that we were to be the attacking party."[41]

The Federal unit to receive the Confederate assault on the extreme right was Col. Richard J. Oglesby's Illinois troops. Reveille was being sounded in camp when the sound of Federal pickets receiving fire brought the camp to life. Lines were formed and volleys were exchanged. Each side effectively returned the fire it received.[42]

A Confederate artilleryman recalled:

"The enemy fought gallantly, contesting the ground inch by inch, but we were not to be cool spectators at the scene.

As soon as we gained our position the enemy opened on us from a battery about eight hundred yards to our right rifled ten-pound Parrott and James rifled guns ... we had to fight them with smoothbores, except one rifled ten-pound Parrott gun ... The sharpshooters of the enemy were, as usual, very annoying, creeping among logs and timber to within four or five hundred yards of our line ... a shell wounded five of our men, one of them mortally. Their rifled shot and shells tore up the ground around us, cut off saplings and limbs around and above us, killing some of our horses and knocking off the end of a caisson." [43]

Among the Confederate dead elsewhere was Captain Frank Rogers, Company E, Fourteenth Mississippi. Rogers had served as a lawyer in Aberdeen, Mississippi before enlisting. His brother, William Rogers, a Texas lawyer,[44] would meet a similar and much more memorialized death at Corinth, Mississippi a few months later.

By 10 o'clock, the "rebel yell" was regularly heard from the attacking Confederates, who continued to gain costly ground. Oglesby's Federals were running low on ammunition and resorted to removing boxes from the dead and wounded of their army. The extreme right of the Federal line gave way, the retreating troops displaying their empty cartridge boxes. Oglesby saw one option: retreat. Meanwhile, General Grant was not to be found; he had left earlier to visit Foote aboard his gunboat.[45]

At this point, controversy rears it ugly head, for the Confederate escape route was cleared and secured. However, some two hours elapsed with no decision to abandon the area. Pillow, Floyd, and Buckner evidently entered a standoff of egotism, filled with questioning and second-guessing. Pillow sent his department commander, Albert Sidney Johnston, a telegram declaring victory for the Confederacy. As one historian explained, the Confederate soldiers, but not their leaders, were ready; and the delay shifted the momentum to the Federal troops.[46]

Brigadier General Lew Wallace, in charge of the Third U.S. Division, met regiments of the retreating Federals "... coming back in excellent order ..." Most asked for ammunition, proclaiming the lack of such, not the fierceness of the Confederate offensive, as the cause for retiring to the rear. Wallace spoke briefly with Col. W.H.L. Wallace and was informed of advancing Confederates, and the third brigade was placed in line of battle between the Confederates and the Federals. [47]

The Confederates advanced up Wynn's Ferry Road and through the trees and shrubs on either side of it. The Federals " … met the storm, no man flinching, and their fire was terrible" wrote one Union officer. [48] The Federals used this delay in conjunction with the one referred to earlier, to prepare an assault of their own.

The lull in the battle had numerous participants questioning what was to come. The answer soon came when Grant returned after riding over the icy roads to preserve victory and his own military future. Having proclaimed to his men that the Confederates fully intended to escape, Grant, at 3 o'clock, ordered Lew Wallace to attack the Confederate left and sent Major General C.F. Smith to the right.[49]

The fruitless sacrifices of the day included Captain Dabney C. Harrison, Fifty-sixth Virginia. A comrade wrote of Harrison:

> "It was his invariable custom to assemble his men for prayer … It was the last day of fighting. Capt. Harrison called up his men for worship … he repeated Psalm xxvii … With dauntless heart and drawn sword he cheered on his men. His words were, 'Follow me.' At length he fell, and the fierce tide of battle swept on, and the frozen earth trembled amid the roar of cannon beneath his prostrate form. His hat was pierced by four balls. One marred that splendid brow. A more deadly aim drove a ball through his right lung. His face was to the foe … he sunk upon the frozen ground. There he lay suffering from his wounds an hour or more … No complaint was uttered by him … he was placed on a stretcher and carried to Nashville … on a steamer, where he breathed his last as the boat was landing. He gave expression of his great desire to sleep in Virginia soil; but, amid the confusion and excitement incident to the retreat of the army, where his body was interred will never be known until the morning of the resurrection."[50]

Smith's men advanced toward the fort to the point where they were merely able to exchange fire with Buckner's troops, separated from one another by a gully. Lew Wallace's command crashed into the center, regaining control of the Wynn Ferry Road, ending all Confederate abilities of escape.[51]

Throughout the night, Pillow, Floyd, and Buckner deliberated at Pillow's Dover quarters. Conflicting scout reports of Federal reinforcements led to a great deal of indecision regarding the Confederate strategy. Buckner saw additional fighting as hopeless; his men were fatigued and low on ammunition. Pillow was in favor of attempting to escape. Floyd largely agreed with Buckner's stance.[52]

The hopelessness of the Confederate situation was perceived by others besides the conferring officers. One Confederate infantryman wrote:

> "It was evident that there was no hope for us. All Saturday evening the smoke of the enemy's transports below the fort showed that they were still landing reinforcements. They had again extended their right wing around our left, and strengthened it heavily. We were completely worn out with four days' hard fighting and four nights without sleep, exposed to the rain and sleet. It remained to ... be slaughtered or surrender." [53]

Colonel Nathan Bedford Forrest stated that he chose to leave rather than surrender. When the future "Wizard of the Saddle" asked Pillow for advice on what move he should make, Pillow replied, "Cut your way out, sir." Forrest left the house and sent word to all of his officers, explaining the situation. Almost all of the members of Forrest's regiment expressed their desire that they would go with their commander if the last man fell. Lt. Col. George Gantt's battalion and two Kentucky companies of captains Huey and Wilcox declined the invitation.[54]

Forrest took his men, opting for escape, as well as Captain T.K. Porter's artillery horses and approximately 200 men from other units, some 1,000 total soldiers "up the river road and across the overflow ... found to be about saddle-skirt deep." Forrest described the dark night's windy weather as intensely cold and added that the conditions placed more sufferings on the men, many of whom were dealing with frostbite prior to the escape.[55]

While Forrest made good his escape using the ice-covered waters around the fort, Floyd ferried his men to two steamboats on the river's opposite bank. Pillow also crossed the Cumberland, rowing a skiff to the opposite side, and headed to Clarksville. One Mississippi regiment arrived as reinforcements, only to later surrender without firing a single shot.[56]

General Buckner now held the unfortunate position of commander of Fort Donelson. He sent word to Grant asking the terms desired for surrender of the garrison. Grant's rather sudden reply was "unconditional surrender," a phrase Buckner described as both ungenerous and unchivalrous.[57] The letters U.S. in Grant's usual nomenclature became synonymous with the term *unconditional surrender.*

One shocked Confederate, J.J. Montgomery, wrote:

> "Fort Donelson ... surrendered. I could not believe it, as we had been successful in every engagement for three days, both on land and water ... Buckner said that he would surrender rather than sacrifice two-thirds of the men to save one-third. I then asked for Floyd, and was told that he had landed his men across the river and that Col. Forrest had gone also. Having no time to lose, I hastened to the river, where I found the steamer *Gen. Anderson* waiting to carry off Pillow—horses, negroes, and baggage. I went to headquarters and made every effort to get aboard, but appealed in vain, as they were afraid the boat would sink ... I returned to camp with no hope, only to submit to whatever might happen." [58]

Grant's cavalry escort had their pistols drawn as they led the Federal commander through the Confederate ranks to the Dover Hotel. Grant entered the hotel and found a number of Confederate officers and General Lew Wallace enjoying a breakfast of cornbread and coffee. A brief meeting ensued, during which Grant and Buckner discussed the situation and set the number of Confederate prisoners at no "... fewer than 12,000 nor more than 15,000."[59]

The prisoners were allowed to keep personal possessions, clothing, and blankets; the officers kept their sidearms. Two days' rations were given to the Confederates, who soon boarded trains and steamboats to prisoner of war camps at Camp Douglas, Alton, Illinois; Camp Chase, Ohio; and Camp Morton in Indianapolis. The captured officers were sent to Fort Warren, Massachusetts, and Johnson's Island, Ohio. A majority of the prisoners were exchanged later that year.[60]

Lt. John H. Davis, Company K, Eighteenth Tennessee, remarked that the defiant look on General Buckner's face as he gave Grant his sword was a manner of expression not seen before or since.[61]

J.M. Lynn of R.E. Graves's Battery, Buckner's Division, remarked of his surrender:

"As we marched on board the steamer to be transported North, Gen. Buckner was in the crowd, the Yankee band struck up 'Yankee Doodle', and a Federal officer asked ... if it did not remind him of old times, and he replied, 'Yes, it also reminds me of an incident that occurred in our camps a few days ago. A soldier was being drummed out of camp for stealing; the band was playing the Rogues March, when he said hold on, play Yankee Doodle, as half a million rogues march by that tune every day.'" [62]

T.J. Moore of Company E, 3rd Tennessee, J.C. Brown's Regiment, added:

"I was captured at Fort Donelson ... given a few crackers, and after a long delay was marched on board a boat on the Cumberland. I slept on cord wood in the hull amidst the commotion caused by crushing ice ... a week from the day of our surrender; we arrived in Chicago, and were marched three miles through mud and slush, under guard of unsympathetic foreigners, to camp Douglas. There was not a stick of wood or any straw for bedding, blankets, or fire." [63]

An estimated 2,000 Confederate and 2,600 Federal casualties were suffered at Fort Donelson, in addition to an overwhelming number of Confederate prisoners falling into Union hands. Hundreds of thousands of rations of beef, pork, rice, and other stores now belonged to the victor. Perhaps more significantly, the Cumberland and Tennessee rivers, as well as Nashville, Western Tennessee, and Southern Kentucky lay open to Grant's army.[64]

J.T. Lowry, Third Tennessee, remembered the devastation in the town of Dover the morning after Fort Donelson's surrender. Household goods of every description were scattered on the streets. He picked up a linen shirt and placed it in his knapsack. Lowry maintained possession of the garment through four months at Camp Douglas, from which he escaped after bribing a guard.[65]

The first major Union victory in Tennessee had immediate and long-term implications. Gen. U.S. Grant was now a national hero; Tennessee was primed for Federal occupation—the first Confederate state to enter such condition; and Simon Buckner's credibility was forever tarnished. In addition, the stage was set for future confrontations, many of which would be filled with destruction and casualties, within the state's boundaries.

Today's visitor to Fort Donelson can enjoy a well-preserved eleven-stop tour that includes the earthworks, a national cemetery, and the Dover Hotel, commonly referred to as the Surrender House. The three-mile-long River Circle Trail and the four-mile long Donelson Trail both begin and end at the visitors' center. Approximately 20 percent of the core battlefield is within the 560-acre Fort Donelson National Military Park that has existed since 1867. Additionally, in 2006, Fort Donelson served as the inaugural site of the Tennessee Civil War Preservation Association's "Two Flags over Tennessee" program. A "first national flag" in addition to an 1861 version of the "Stars and Stripes" is to be raised at the state's significant battlefields of the war.

The remainder of the battlegrounds are on private property, and rated as "highly threatened by development" by the Civil War Preservation Trust, but can largely be viewed in order to gain a clear sense of the terrain over which the men fought in that cold 1862 winter. As always, respect the private property rights of the individuals who own land outside the park. The visitors' center in the national park is open every day but Christmas and is accessible from 8:00 to 4:30 and can be reached in traveling one mile west of Dover or three miles east of Land Between the Lakes on U.S. 79.

Perhaps the best tribute to Fort Donelson battlefield and, more importantly, the men who fought there, comes from a poem written by W.E. Maury of the Forty-ninth Tennessee. Captured at Donelson Maury spent time as a prisoner of war at Camp Douglas, Chicago, Illinois. It was there he penned these words:

The Battle of Fort Donelson, Tenn.

The shrill whistling fife had awaked us at dawn,
The long roll was beaten, we answered the call;
The clouds lowered round us, the skies were forlorn,
While the swift falling snowflake enveloped us all.

Our knapsacks were slung, our Minies we clasped,
At morn's early dawn we had entered the fort;
'Twas February thirteenth, the foe had advanced,
With caution, the gunboats had opened their ports.

The signal guns fired, every heart was begirt,
With firmness of purpose and fixed resolve
To withstand all oppression and dye with blood
The snow-covered earth, our country to absolve.

The conflict commenced, the battle then raged,
From morning till night the cannon did sound;
Still louder the din, the foe was engaged;
With valor we met them on Donelson's ground.

'Mid clatter of musketry, and cannon's loud din,
While the swift booming shell burst high in the air;
With shouts and confusion again and again,
Our brave boys repulsed them and slew many there.

For three winter days, we withstood the attack,
Our friends they were wounded and many had died;
Still the swift, whistling bullet or Minie death-clack,
Was heard in its course as it onward had sped.

Outnumbered by foes, the white flag is unfurled;
It floats in the breeze of that calm Sabbath morn.
We are Prisoners of War! "Surrendered" the word!
As we lay on our arms most sad and forlorn.
Still Hope's beauteous star shines bright in the skies,
It illuminates our path, saying never despond
Though dark be the storm cloud that now doth arise,
Great joy will return with the brightness beyond.[66]

Modern view of the Cumberland River from the location of the Lower River Battery. Photo by author.

The Upper Water Battery. Here Reuben Ross commanded a detachment in charge of a 6½-inch rifled gun and two 32-pound carronades. Photo by author.

Modern view of portion of Fort Donelson's earthworks that once enclosed some fifteen acres. The Cumberland River lies to the right, just out of view in the picture. Photo by author.

The Surrender House in Dover. Photo by author.

Captain Reuben Ross, commander of the Upper Water Battery at Fort Donelson. Courtesy of Confederate Veteran.

Captain Dabney Harrison, Fifty-sixth Virginia. The young officer was mortally wounded at Fort Donelson soon after leading his men in morning prayer. Courtesy of Confederate Veteran.

CHAPTER THREE

SHILOH — DAY 1

"I would fight them if they were a million"
A.S. Johnston
April 6, 1862

"Place of Peace." Ironically, this phrase is the meaning of the Hebrew word *Shiloh*. The campaign that reached its climax with a two-day battle that began on Sunday morning, April 6, 1862, strangely enough took its name from a Methodist church located on the grounds of the present-day national military park. The battle is sometimes referred to as Pittsburg Landing, named for a river craft stop located on the banks of the Tennessee River. Twenty-two miles northeast of the Confederate base at the rail center of Corinth, Mississippi, the location became the scene of intense fighting on a scale previously unseen in the United States.

After the fall of forts Henry and Donelson, the Confederates were in desperate need of a victory to improve morale and boost the approval rating of one of its premier leaders, General Albert Sidney Johnston. At the war's beginning, the Kentucky native was regarded in many circles as the leading officer in the Confederacy, if not in the nation. The citizens of the Confederacy were no different from Americans of today as their moods, level of support, and opinions hinged largely upon recent accomplishments or lack thereof. Most significantly a Confederate victory was needed to preserve the very life of the western Confederacy.

The Federals were under the leadership of General Ulysses S. Grant, the hero of Fort Donelson, and seemed confident that the recently defeated Confederates were highly unlikely to attack the Union encampments at Shiloh. Seemingly aware of this mindset, General Johnston made his move from Corinth toward Shiloh on April 3, 1862 and fully intended to launch a surprise attack upon Grant's command on April 4th, yet poor roads delayed the deployment of troops and his subsequent plan of action.

The few miles between Corinth and Shiloh should have easily been traveled in the planned time, but spring rains made the dirt roads nearly impassable. The 44,000 Confederate troops, largely inexperienced in marching as well as combat, found the journey difficult to complete within the allotted time, a fact that would not only cause a major disagreement between the Confederate commander and his highest subordinate, but also result in having a clear victory transform into defeat.

Johnston's Army of Mississippi troops used one of two dirt roads, the Ridge Road and the Monterey Road, from Corinth. The Confederates were to meet eight miles from Pittsburg Landing. That location, a home known as Mickey's, would serve as the Confederate point of deployment for the attack. Some of the men of Johnston's command negotiated the narrow and curvy muddy roads that today make up Tennessee Highway 22. The Federal Army of the Tennessee's ranks slowly grew to a force of 40,000 men. Some fifty percent of Grant's men, as were almost eighty percent of those they would soon face, were largely unaccustomed to the combat that lay ahead.

Sergeant William Clark Newlon, a Union soldier of Company G, Third Iowa Infantry Regiment, recalled that his army gained a great deal of support and a number of enlistments while stationed at nearby Savannah, Tennessee. Delayed by the river's high waters that hampered their landing, Newlon and his compatriots were unable to enter camp at Pittsburg Landing until March 17, 1862.[1]

Newlon's impression of the area, aside from the willingness of local men to "fight for the old Union," was far from favorable as he wrote, "This part of Tennessee is anything but a furtile [sic] county. The country is hilly ... some cotton is raised here but the ... soil is too poor to be productive except in the bottoms. If what I have seen of Tennessee is a specimen of the state I would not give one acre of land in Iowa for 50 in this state."[2]

Many of the Confederate officers and enlisted men had the same frame of mind as their Union counterparts, in that a great battle lay ahead. Lt. Jasper Kelsey, Company A, Twenty-third Tennessee Infantry, had been awakened at 1 AM on April 3 and ordered to prepare to march with five days' rations and one hundred rounds of ammunition. A large number of his fellow regiment members were given Enfield rifles prior to the march.[3]

Several of the combat-inexperienced Confederates en route to Shiloh provided a supply department's nightmare. Requiring a wide range of ammunition, several marched with shotguns, pistols, squirrel guns, Belgian muskets, or old-fashioned flintlocks.[4] Throughout the companies of numerous other Confederate regiments, soldiers lacked the weapons Kelsey's colleagues possessed. Shotguns, hunting rifles, and limited ammunition were commonplace.

General Johnston's top subordinates included General P.G.T. Beauregard, the hero of Fort Sumter and veteran of Bull Run. General Leonidas Polk, a West Point graduate and Episcopal bishop of Louisiana, joined Braxton Bragg under Johnston's guidance. Former United States vice-president John C. Breckinridge, an 1860 presidential candidate, and Major General W.J. Hardee rounded out Johnston's command as it approached Shiloh.[5]

General Polk was in command of the first of four Confederate corps, Bragg the second, Hardee the third, and Breckinridge the fourth. Their position in battle would be Hardee and Bragg front to rear, with Breckinridge and Polk in reserve. In addition, the cavalry would guard the Confederate flanks along the two major creeks that bordered the battlefield. Hardee's Corp was composed of 4,545 men; Polk's had 9,024 troops; Breckenridge's Corp of only three brigades was made up of 6,290 soldiers, and Bragg's Corp, the largest in the army, was 14,868 strong.[6]

Owl Creek on the north and Lick Creek to the south were approximately three miles apart and ran in a northeastern direction, emptying into the wide and deep Tennessee River. With Lick Creek above and Owl Creek below Pittsburg Landing, the battlefield would resemble a triangle with the river on the east running due north. [7]

General W.T. Sherman had approved the location of the Federal camp, noting, "The ground itself admits of easy defense by a small command, and yet affords admirable camping ground for 100,000 men." General Grant added his endorsement as well in writing, "Shiloh was the key to our position, and was held by Sherman. His division was at that time wholly raw, no part of it ever having been in an engagement, but I thought this deficiency was more than made up by the superiority of the commander."[8]

Grant's command held six divisions in early April of 1862. Major General John McClernand was in charge of the First Division, with Brigadier General W.H.L. Wallace, Major General Lew Wallace, Brig. Gen. S.A. Hurlbut, Brig. Gen. W.T. Sherman, and Brig. Gen. Benjamin Prentiss providing the leadership of the succeeding numbered divisions.

A historian in the 1920s wrote:

> "The camps of Sherman and Prentiss formed the front line of Union forces about two and a half miles from Pittsburg Landing, and extended in a semi-circle from Owl Creek ... to Lick Creek ... Sherman's headquarters were at Shiloh Church ... the Union army lay in the field without entrenchment, no outposts, no defensive works, no artificial protection of any character, and no cavalry pickets to give information of the movements of a hostile army twenty miles away, with no river or mountain between them." [9]

Grant's headquarters were at Savannah, nine miles downriver. The Cherry home sat on the east bank of the river and was the location Grant chose as his center of operations. Each day he would visit the Federal camps, and return nightly to the mansion. Grant reported that his plans involved moving his headquarters "to Pittsburg, where I had sent all the troops immediately upon my reassuming command, but Buell...was expected daily...I remained, therefore, a few days longer than I otherwise should have done." Rumors circulated that Grant had also resumed his former "bad habit" of drinking excessively.[10]

The Cherry house had been built thirty-two years earlier in the early Georgian style atop an Indian mound. Brick walls eighteen inches thick, and six-inch by two-inch-thick pine floors dominated the home.[11]

Grant himself remained convinced that the Confederates would remain at Corinth. His position on this issue is more easily understood when noting that General Grant was attempting to fully follow the order of General Halleck. Explicitly commanded to avoid engaging the enemy and knowledgeable of his army's presence in enemy territory, the hero of Fort Donelson viewed the recent Confederate activity purely as reconnaissance and not as acts of aggression. Grant added, "...the troops with me, officers and men, needed discipline and drill more than they did experience with the pick, shovel, and axe."[12]

William Clark Newlon, the Iowa sergeant, explained in his journal entry for the evening of April 5:

> "It appears to be a fact beyond doubt that the enemy is concentrating a large force at Corinth, Miss. for the purpose of making one more bold stand against the Federal army at this place. On Friday evening the 4th our outposts were attacked by two regiments of the enemy, quite a brisk engagement took place, wherein several were killed and wounded on both sides ... This was a signal for a battle which I think will soon be forgot not ... If a battle takes place here between the two majestic armies the loss of life will be immense."[13]

In Confederate General Patrick Cleburne's Brigade, James A Jones of Company H, Twenty-third Tennessee, recalled the same type action as did Newlon, " ... on Friday evening ... had our first skirmish with the Federal cavalry ... we repulsed them. We camped near where we had this little fight, and so near Gen. Grant's main army that we could plainly hear the drums and their regimental bands playing at night." [14]

Another individual of the period wrote, "On April 3 and 4 there had been some skirmishing between the cavalry of both armies ... reconnoitering parties ... reported 'evidences of cavalry', but failed to find any special reason for alarm; and that very day Sherman wrote to Grant, 'I do no apprehend anything like an attack on our position'." [15]

James A. Jones recalled that on Saturday, April 5:

> " ... there were several cavalry skirmishes, and we were formed in line many times, expecting a general engagement. On Saturday night, we camped still nearer the enemy, but we had no camp fires, and made as little noise as possible. We had cooked three days' rations before leaving Corinth ... a wonder to me [is] how our army could stay in hearing of the drums and brass bands of the Federal troops for nearly two whole days and nights and the fact never be known to them." [16]

Saturday morning in the Federal camps, Sherman gave an order to cut a road from Owl Creek, in front of Shiloh Creek, to an old cotton field three-quarters of a mile east of the camp. At 2 o'clock that afternoon, when skirmishing started with the cavalry, Union officers using a glass watched a Confederate officer sitting atop a gray horse across the old cotton field. His identity was alleged to be Nathan Bedford Forrest, but the future "Wizard of the Saddle" avoided moving north of Lick Creek. This was due to the fact that entering the field where the officer was seen would have been a direct violation, on Forrest's part, of his orders. [17]

That night, Sgt. W.C. Newlon wrote from the camp of the Third Iowa, "Saturday the 5th, everything is quiet in our division but what is going on along our lines I cannot tell, but I presume that the commanding General is on the look out and will be ready for any emergency whatever. Our army here is very large, and no doubt the enemy is equally strong."[18]

Among the enemy forces Newlon spoke of, a young artilleryman of Hardee's Corps rested Saturday afternoon only a mile from Shiloh Church. His thoughts focused on the white dogwood blooms, and with the sight of them came the memory that they signaled the time to go fishing; the creeks nearby certainly held fish.[19] The peacefulness and thoughts of fishing would soon take a smaller amount of the youngster's mindset.

The now-silent Confederate army camped near the Federals, a fact, as noted, unknown and inconceivably undetected by the latter. That night, the Confederate corps commanders met to determine the feasibility of continuing the campaign. Beauregard favored a withdrawal to Corinth, explaining that the lost day, a lack of surprise, and the certainty of Federal entrenchments added to a decided defeat for the Confederates. He felt the delay and the noise of the men in gray certainly gave the Federals due notice of Confederate presence. Beauregard's vocal objection to pursuing the attack undoubtedly added weight to Johnston's shoulders. Johnston's son wrote of the incident that "Beauregard was in the full tide of popular favor, while Johnston was laboring under the load of public obloquy and odium." [20]

One Confederate recalled the existence of the element of surprise in writing:

> " ... we lay all the afternoon in line of battle and had plenty of time to look at the dogwood blooms of which the woods were full ... and heard distinctly the drums beating in the enemy's camps ... The innumerable military bands

were serenading their officers, and everybody was having
a merry time without a thought of our thirty or forty
thousand men who were listening ... " [21]

Johnston listened to the concerns of his corps commanders, offering solutions to many. Despite the firing of Confederate guns to check the usefulness of the rain-soaked weapons, the general seemed to believe an element of surprise still existed. As for the scarcity of rations among the troops—another concern of his subordinates—Johnston replied, "Let the men get them from the Union army. Gentlemen, we shall attack at dawn tomorrow."[22] Following the council's conclusion, General Johnston is said to have proclaimed to a member of his staff that he would fight the enemy "if they were a million!"

General Johnston knew that even with the element of surprise, a monumental challenge faced his army. He ordered his men to fire slow and at a distinct mark. This was likely based upon the premise that it took two men to carry one wounded man from the field, but a dead man needed no attention; so it would weaken the Union army more in wounding one of their soldiers. In contrast, Second Lieutenant Jasper Kelsey, Company A, Twenty-third Tennessee, recalled hearing an additional order, perhaps from a lower ranking officer, to aim at the knees of the enemy. He also stated that he and others of the Confederate army were to leave the tending of a wounded comrade to the infirmary corps rather than personally offering assistance. In addition, should any soldier get lost or separated from his command, Kelsey stated, he should go to the sound of the heaviest fighting[23] rather than attempt to locate his regiment and perhaps miss out on contributing to the Confederate cause.

The security Gen. Grant felt for the position his troops held was not shared among all of his officers. Col. Everett Peabody of Gen. Benjamin Prentiss's Federal command had sent a combat reconnaissance of five companies from his camp early Sunday morning. The Federal group included three companies of the Twenty-fifty Missouri and two from the Twelfth Michigan.

At 4:55 AM, members of the Union reconnaissance entered Fraley Field and made contact with 280 Confederate skirmishers of Confederate Major A.B. Hardcastle's Third Mississippi. This contact would result in a one-hour struggle and soon brought about the first known officer casualty of the day, Lt. Frederick Klinger of Company B, Twenty-fifth Missouri. The Battle of Shiloh had begun.

Peabody would receive a verbal reprimand from Prentiss at 7:30, being informed that he would be held responsible "for bringing on this engagement." An hour later, suffering from four wounds, Peabody attempted to rally his troops, but was struck by a shot that hit Peabody's lip and blew away the back of his head. He was buried the next day, but his body was removed three weeks later to Springfield, Massachusetts and placed in the family cemetery. Peabody's death ended any further allegations against him.[24]

Fraley Field was one of the occasional clearings located on the otherwise densely wooded battlefield. Rain-swelled creeks, thick underbrush, and a low number of ponds also dotted the area. One description of the battlefield explained it as being, " ... partly primeval forest, alternating with a few cleared fields, crossed by numerous ravines ... marshy margins made it difficult to bring the artillery across; the wooded heights with undergrowth forming screens and rallying points." [25]

The progression of the Confederate forces from this point of the battlefield is well-documented. The rains of recent days had yielded to a bright, clear morning. The serenity of the weather and the soft trickle of water in the swollen creeks and streams of the river would soon give way to the screams of the wounded and dying, as the transformation progressed and the woods around Shiloh Church, the place of peace, became dens of death.

The oak forest where the Twenty-third Tennessee had spent the night of April 5 had come alive with Confederates eating their cold breakfasts, an act many of their comrades failed to fully enjoy prior to the day's action. Without the sound of drums or bugles, Hardee's line, followed by the solid line of Bragg, advanced slowly toward the Federal camps.[26]

A Confederate officer said, "Every one who witnessed the scene—the marshalling of the Confederate army for the attack ... must remember more distinctly than anything else the glowing enthusiasm of the men, their buoyancy and spirited impatience to close with the enemy."[27]

The rebel yell mingled with the roar of muskets and cannon and the bursting of shells as the men in gray and butternut advanced. General Grant noted a cause for the rapid forward movement of the Confederates in writing of his own troops that "Many of them had arrived but a day or two before, and were hardly able to load their muskets according to the manual. Their officers were equally ignorant of their duties. Under these circumstances, it is not astonishing that many of the regiments broke at first fire." [28]

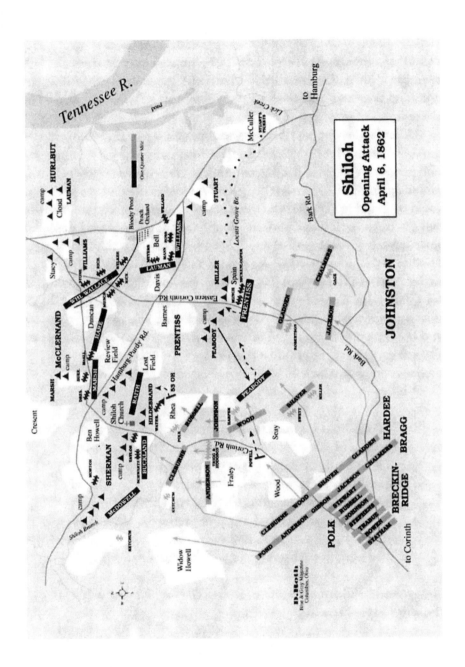

Tennessee R.

Shiloh
Opening Attack
April 6, 1862

One-Quarter Mile

HURLBUT
LAUMAN
Cloud
camp
WILLIAMS
Stacy
camp
WILLIAMS
Bell
LAUMAN
Davis
Peach Orchard
Bloody Pond
STUART
camp
MILLER
Spain
PRENTISS
McCULLER
STUART'S PICKETS
Lick Creek
to Hamburg
pond

THE WALLACE
McCLERNAND
Duncan
HARE
Review Field
MARSH
MARSH
camp
Hamburg-Purdy Rd.
KEITH
HILDEBRAND
Lost Field
Rhea
SS OH
Eastern Corinth Rd.
Barnes
camp
PRENTISS
PEABODY
PEABODY
GLADDEN
JACKSON
ROBERTSON
CHALMERS
GAGE
Locust Grove Br.
Bark Rd.

JOHNSTON

Crescent
SHERMAN
Ben Howell
Shiloh Church
camp
BUCKLAND
MCDOWELL
NORTON
TAYLOR
camp
WATER
POLK
CLEBURNE
ANDERSON
TRIGG & HODGSON
Corinth Rd.
Fraley
Wood
Scay
JOHNSON
HARPER
WOOD
POWELL
SHAVER
MILLER
AVERY
KETCHUM

BRAGG
HARDEE
GLADDEN
CHALMERS
JACKSON
BRECKIN-RIDGE

Widow Howell
Shiloh Branch
KETCHUM

POLK
CLEBURNE
WOOD
ANDERSON
GIBSON
POND
STEWART
RUSSELL
JOHNSON
STEPHENS
TRABUE
BOWEN
STATHAM

to Corinth

D. Roth
Blue & Gray Magazine
Columbus, Ohio

39

The encounters of the morning were initially sudden and decisive. James A. Jones, Company H, Twenty-third Tennessee, remarked, "… before the Federal troops had eaten their breakfasts we were upon them." General Bragg wrote, "Many were surprised and captured in their tents, and others, though on the outside, in costumes better fitted to the bed chamber than to the battlefield." Another Confederate added that the arms and accouterments in the Federal camps were "… spread around in the order … of holiday soldiers."[29]

Union soldiers began leaving the camps as some 20,000 Confederates advanced upon Prentiss's 5,000 Federal troops. To place these numbers into perspective, eight of the sixteen Confederate brigades present at Shiloh moved against just two Federal brigades. A number of Southern stragglers could be found in the overrun Union camps, where men's breakfasts were still cooking. The low and basically nonexistent amount of food devoured since leaving Corinth proved too large a basis of temptation for a great number of the Confederates, who now encountered food supplies not seen in days. General Beauregard noted this temptation became uncontrollable for some of his Confederates in writing, "…I dispatched my staff in all directions to gather reports of the progress of the battle with its exigencies and needs on our side,as, also, in quest of stragglers, whose numbers had become dangerously large under the temptations of the abundant stores of food and other articles left in the abandoned Federal camps."[30]

A retreating Federal officer added:

> "Many of our regiments were paid off just previously to the battle, and our dead comrades were robbed of hundreds of thousands of dollars. The rebels were surprised and abashed at the apparent wealth of our army. They attired themselves in our uniforms, and rifled from officers' trunks tens of thousands of dollars worth of fine clothing, toilet articles, and interesting souvenirs of every man's trunk … They seem to have gone mad with the lust of plunder." [31]

Sergeant William Clark Newlon recalled that morning in his camp of the Third Iowa. He wrote:

> "The morning of the 6th was pleasant we were preparing for morning inspection, when vollies [sic] of musketry and the roaring of cannon louder than thunder grated our

ears ... Our camps were alarmed; our outposts driven in; no time was to be lost; the long roll was beat. Fall in was the cry that met every ear. In a moment companies were formed."[32]

A member of the Twenty-third Tennessee recalled the attack upon Sherman's camp:

"Sherman hurriedly formed his line of battle in front of the camp. It was good ground for defense—a low timbered ridge, with an open valley, traversed by a small stream, in front. To attack them the Southern brigades had to cross the stream and open field. The Confederate line, which had hung for a few minutes only on the crest of the hill, like a storm cloud on the mountain's brow now burst ... upon Sherman's camps. The Rebel yell ... rose sharp and shrill from the rushing lines of Southern soldiers; their volley came pouring in, and the bayonet even was used on some whose slumbers were broken only by the oncoming of their foes." [33]

Sherman was initially reluctant to believe the situation at hand. Eventually proclaiming, "We are attacked!", the general was shot in the hand; his orderly fell. Wrapping his wounded hand in a handkerchief, General Sherman called for "...extra men for orderlies, one of mine has been shot already." [34]

A ravine fronted Sherman's position and descended rapidly to Owl Creek. Here it spread into a marsh filled with tangled vines and undergrowth. The center of the bog was impassable. [35]

A Confederate first lieutenant remarked:

"I saw Jim Wilson fall on his face ... he was shot in the eye, the ball coming out of the back of his head. A little while after I saw him roll over on his side, pull up his canteen, pull out the stopper with his teeth, and take a drink. I ... attributed his action to the effort of a dying man. We left him lying there ... and ... reported him among the killed. Several days after, in looking through the hospitals for our wounded, I was surprised to find him sitting up in bed and quite lively for a dead man. He was discharged and sent home."[36]

Another Confederate observed:

"I was lying with the men close under the bank of a creek when a twelve pound shell landed at our feet. I looked back and could see the fuse sputtering and smoking. To jump up and run and be blown to pieces or to lie still and be blown to pieces seemed to be the alternatives. I watched that fuse over my shoulder ... I saw it sputter and go out, much to the relief of ... our nerves."[37]

The early-morning struggle had caught the attention of General Grant in Savannah. Grant later recorded the incident in writing that he heard heavy firing from the direction of Pittsburg Landing while eating breakfast. Mr. W.H. Cherry, in whose home Grant was headquartered, recalled:

"Gen. Grant was thoroughly sober. He was at my breakfast table when he heard the report from a cannon. Holding, untasted, a cup of coffee, he paused in conversation to listen a moment to the report of another cannon. He hastily arose, saying to his staff officers, 'Gentlemen, the ball is in motion; let us be off.' ... in fifteen minutes he ... had embarked."[38]

The notice to Grant had come near 7 AM. Boarding the *Tigress,* Grant and his staff made their way toward Shiloh. A boat met on the way held a messenger that stated the Confederates had attacked, and that a heavy fight was raging.[39]

Edgar Cherry was a fifteen-year-old boy at the time, and his father permitted him to go aboard the boat that took Grant to Shiloh. Grant reportedly met with General Lew Wallace at Crump's Landing along the route, informing him to be prepared to march when called. Grant's 8:00 arrival at Pittsburg Landing resulted in the future president encountering commands filled with concern. With the tremendous battle raging, the general and his aides rushed ashore, leaving Edgar Cherry aboard ship.[40]

W.S. Hillyear, a member of Grant's staff, remembered arriving at Pittsburg Landing around 8:30, and that he and others with him " ... got on our horses and ... found the enemy had attacked and were engaging our right and center in overwhelming force and our troops were falling back. We met hundreds of cowardly renegades fleeing to the river and reporting their regiments cut to pieces ... soon I found myself in the midst of a shower of cannon and musket balls ... the General issued his orders and sent his aides flying over the field. While executing an order a cannon ball passed within two feet of my horse's head ... " Grant recalled that upon his arrival at the front "about 8 a.m." he realized "the attack upon Shiloh was unmistakeable."[41]

Despite Grant's arrival on the scene, the Confederate advance continued. Half a century after the battle, a historian noted that the early battle was a series of separate fights, each division commander taking care of his troops as best he could, but being outflanked, the general trend was to the rear. In his own words, General Grant explained that he spent the majority of Sunday engaged in moving from one portion of the field to the other, giving directions to division commanders. General McClernand was quoted as saying that "...he profited much by having so able a commander supporting him." [43]

A farm road with distinct ruts running on the eastern side of J.R. Duncan's cotton field served as the location where, for six hours, the Confederate advance stalled. The road ran slightly over half a mile from the historic Corinth-Pittsburg Landing Road to the north and the Hamburg-Savannah Road on the east. Today's designation of this location as the Sunken Road is a term initially applied decades after the war. No participant in the battle provided the designation of "Sunken Road" and the road was not deeply depressed until excavated by the Civilian Conservation Corps during the Great Depression of the 1930s. Near the center of the road lay an area renowned as "the Hornet's Nest." The latter term comes from a Confederate's proclamation that the Federal bullets coming from the area strongly resembled the sound of enraged hornets.

Recent archaeological work in Duncan Field and in the Hornet's Nest in addition to historic documentation has cast a large doubt that the area was the hotly contested tract oral tradition has led people to believe. The events beginning around 11 AM in the section are noteworthy just the same, as a number of Confederate assaults, piecemeal as they may have been, were directed upon the location.

Union divisions of Generals Prentiss, W.H.L. Wallace, and Hurlbut positioned themselves in the aforementioned location on the morning of April 6. From this spot on the field, as many as eight Confederate charges were repelled, with heavy losses among the attackers.

A Confederate described the Union position as a "splendid growth of forest ... in the shelter of this line of woods lay the Union lines, pouring across the open space a veritable storm of fiercest musketry."[44]

Overseeing the Confederate assault at the Peach Orchard, General Albert Sidney Johnston held the respect of his men. Confederate President Jefferson Davis had earlier spoken of Johnston and said, "If Sidney Johnston is not a general, I have none!" A witness explained that Johnston rode to a crest, calmly and as imperturbable as always, with no sign of emotion. Just in front of the Ninth Arkansas Regiment, Johnston reined in his horse with the horse standing broadside to the line of battle.[45]

The witness wrote:

> "His right arm was raised over his head, as if grasping a sword, but in the hand was only a tin cup, which he had evidently forgotten to throw aside after drinking from some of the small streams that intersected the field ... he remained motionless ... looking at our lines with a smile..." [46]

Johnston was a revered leader and the son of a doctor; he had left a distinguished U.S. military career to join the Confederacy. Atop his dappled-brown thoroughbred Fire-eater, the general was dressed in a "gray coat, old-time, black-corded pants, and a gray military cap, and had his sword buckled on." Clean-shaven except for a heavy mustache and standing nearly six feet tall, Johnston was described as one's "highest ideal of a soldier." One gentleman proclaimed Johnston as being "strong and active, and of a military bearing." General Grant described his adversary as a man of "high character and ability...officers generally...expected him to proved the most formidable man to meet that the Confederacy would produce."[47]

The charge Johnston ordered was carried out. His orderlies and staff, including Tennessee governor Isham G. Harris, had been sent away on errands. Witnesses recalled that the general rested his sword in his scabbard and that the tin cup in his right hand was a "memorial of an incident earlier in the day."[48]

According to legend, as the Confederates passed through a captured camp, an officer brought several valuable items from a tent and subsequently called General Johnston's attention to them. Johnston informed the soldier that "we are not here for the plunder." Showing regret for his stern reprimand, Johnston picked up the cup and said it would be his spoils for the day.[49]

Until the time of ordering the charge and becoming isolated from others, Johnston had passed through the day's events seemingly unharmed. His horse was shot in four places, his clothes were pierced by missiles, his boot sole was cut earlier by a ball, yet he appeared fine. Governor Harris rode back to Johnston and exchanged a few words. Johnston then requested the politician to carry a message to Colonel W.S. Statham of the Fifteenth Mississippi Infantry. Statham's Brigade was to negate a Federal battery firing from the woods to Johnston's left. This was done and Harris quickly returned to the officer's side.[50]

Meanwhile, groups of Federal soldiers had been discharging their firearms in repeated volleys as they retired from their positions. General Johnston was undoubtedly aware of the danger his men faced on this portion of the field. During this moment of triumph, the general was hit.[51]

Governor Harris returned to Johnston again, only to find the general reeling in his saddle. The governor got hold of Johnston and eased him to the ground while Major Wickham assisted. Lieutenants Baylor, O'Hara, and others hurried in search of a surgeon and ambulance. Major Dudley Hayden's attempt to get Johnston to swallow a small amount of whiskey failed as the liquid only saturated the Confederate general's chin.[52] Ironically, Johnston had earlier sent his personal surgeon to care for the wounded. Johnston's wound to the artery behind his right knee was difficult to locate due to his blood having entered his cavalry-style boot and passing through the hole shot into the sole earlier in the battle.

A witness wrote:

> "Gen. Johnston had been removed to the rear... Lieut. Baylor returned and received into his lap, to relieve Gen. Preston, the head of the great soldier. 'I looked down and saw ... a stream of blood issuing from the wound... If some one of the group had simply pressed ... firmly on the artery two or three inches above the wound, until some one could have tied a hard knot in a handkerchief and with a small stick twisted it ... but ... Gen. Johnston's staff must have been helpless in the presence of the sad and startling catastrophe. A nose bleed is more difficult to suppress. The great general ought not to have died."[53]

Ironically, an unused tourniquet was discovered in Johnston's pocket after his death. It has also been proposed that Johnston's wound could have been the result of friendly fire. Regardless, the Confederate commander began to bleed out, though only a minimal amount of visible blood existed.

Major Wickham had helped Governor Harris remove Johnston from his horse and claimed to have been with the general when the sound of a thud like that of a ball hitting its mark drew his attention. At the sight of Johnston wavering in his saddle, Harris had allegedly asked General Johnston if he was wounded; Johnston reportedly replied, "Yes, and I fear seriously." Wickham assisted a group in moving Johnston into a ravine soon after the general fainted from loss of blood.[54]

Johnston's senseless death came around 2:30 and caused an outpouring of emotion from those who admired him. His brother-in-law, General William Preston, sobbed aloud in his grief. Colonel George W. Baylor, Preston, Harris, Major Albert Smith, Wickham, and O'Hara stood around the general's body. He reportedly looked into the face of one of his attendants and then closed his eyes forever. Through the tears, Preston exclaimed, "Pardon me, gentlemen; you all know how I loved him."[55]

Dr. Yandell arrived on the scene in as few as ten minutes after the mortally wounded Johnston was discovered, but it was too late for any benefit to come to the wounded officer. Three wounds were later discovered on Johnston's body, one in the thigh, a shell fragment in the rear of the right hip, and a Minie ball that cut open his left boot sole. The doctor removed the fatal bullet from Johnston's leg that night and sent it to his family. Johnston's body was carried to Corinth, and later to New Orleans.[56]

A great deal of difficulty was involved in procuring an ambulance, and in trying to locate one, Col. Baylor met and informed a member of Bragg's staff of Johnston's death. The two men agreed that the Confederates' gaining of the ground around the Peach Orchard, the objective of Johnston's determination, was a costly endeavor to say the least.[57]

The blooms of the peach trees in the orchard of Sarah Bell were reportedly cut off by flying missiles. The petals fell on the dead and wounded, giving the impression of falling snow.

Gov. Harris found General Beauregard around 3:00 and informed him of Johnston's death. Perhaps reflecting upon his attainment of command or silently mourning, Beauregard made no comment for several minutes. He then asked, "Well, Governor, everything is progressing well, is it not?" Harris confirmed Beauregard's understanding of the battle thus far, and after offering his services to Beauregard and having the acceptance of the same, remained at the general's side for half an hour. Harris made the suggestion that he be allowed to sweep down the lines and note the progress of the battle; Beauregard replied that he would appreciate him doing so. At this, Harris rode toward the sounds of the battle.[58]

The log church where Harris visited Beauregard had been built in 1853. The church and its contents would be destroyed during the course of the battle.

Near Johnston's death site and slightly northwest of the Peach Orchard, lay the only viable water source on that sector of the battlefield. The wounded, dying, and confused of both sides used a small pond for drinking and bathing of wounds. Horses as well found their way to the waterhole, where several joined their human counterparts in death. Debris of all types mingled with bodies in and around the pond, with the blood giving a hint of red to the water and yielding the location its infamous name of the Bloody Pond.

The Confederates' struggle to gain control of the Hornet's Nest and the Sunken Road continued. As alluded to earlier, archaeological evidence disputes the century-old claim of heavy fighting and the subsequent high death rate of participants in the area. The fact remains that men under the leadership of Hurlbut, Prentiss, and W.H.L. Wallace maintained an impregnable defensive position for several hours on April 6, 1862.

The stubborn Federal defense at a number of places on the field had not come without a terrible toll. Enlisted men and officers alike fell in alarming numbers. One defender wrote, "I saw an intelligent looking man with his whole diaphragm torn off. He was holding nearly all of his viscera with both hands and arms. His face expressed a longing for assistance ... "[59]

In an effort to relieve the Confederate infantry and perhaps secure a victory before nightfall, Confederate General Daniel A. Ruggles began gathering artillery for an assault upon the Union stronghold. The six-hour attempt to gain the area would be assisted by a one-hour barrage of sixty-two cannon, the largest such assembly on the continent to that time. The 1833 West Point graduate gathered portions of eleven batteries on the southwest end of Duncan Field and began the bombardment.

While the subsequent success of the Confederate cannonade directed upon the Union position in the Hornet's Nest is well-documented, the overemphasis upon Ruggles solely accomplishing the feat of assembling the guns must be explored. Shiloh historian Stacy Allen has explained that the availability of a large number of guns from other portions of the field where action had relatively ceased accounted for their deployment and/or "movement toward the sound of the action", thus explaining the related large buildup of cannon at the site. [60]

Sgt. Newlon of the Third Iowa recalled the bombardment from the receiving end:

> "The enemy ... threw shell and shot thick and fast but many fell short while others went far above us, some exploding high in the air making quite a flash followed by a loud report. Many struck among the trees tearing them to pieces, killing birds and squirrels which happened to be upon them ... I was in a place of extreme danger, men falling upon every hand, yet I had to laugh at the action of the poor little animals ... frightened to death, running and ... apparently not knowing what to do. I have heard quite a number of soldiers remarking since that birds and small animals became very tame as the battle raged; they would come so close you could touch them. But our batteries were not silent; they placed their shot and shell with telling effect in the enemy's ranks, making terrible destruction among them. On several occasions I saw our cannon balls strike trees cutting the tops of them and they falling upon the lines of the enemy making great havoc among them."[61]

More than a century later, 115-year-old Ab Hurst, a young slave in Purdy, Tennessee at the time of the battle, vividly recalled the sound of the battle, most likely at this phase. He and a friend heard the cannon and retreated to the safety of a space under the porch of his owner's house. A passing soldier later in the day acknowledged that a battle was taking place down the Tennessee River.[62]

Ruggles's fire had enabled Polk's and Hardee's Confederates to confront Wallace's troops on the right side of the Federal line. Bragg joined Breckinridge on the Union left; Chalmers moved to the rear of the Union position.[63] The defenders soon realized their predicament, yet not before inflicting more casualties on the Confederates.

Sgt. W.C. Newlon of the Third Iowa called to mind these facts:

> "The battle continued ... with great fury along the line, but the hardest fighting was on our left wing. The enemy appeared to be trying to outflank us and force back our left wing. This they failed to do, then they rallied and made a desperate charge upon our center ... in this they failed also ... the enemy again turned on our left ... gradually did our men fall back but not without keeping up a brisk firing. Soon our right began to give ... Still we maintained our position [in the center] ... until about 3:30 ... we were near being surrounded ... an order was given to fall back, this we did for three hundred yards where we again made a stand but finding that the enemy were fast flanking us we were ordered to fall back double quick. It was not until this moment that I saw our real danger. The enemy were in full view on both sides of us coming fast upon us pouring in crossfire and one from the rear cutting our little regiment terribly, surrounding and taking many prisoners who were unable to make their escape. For ¾ of a mile we had to pass under a raking fire from our right, left and rear. We had done great executions during the day and lost ... very few men ... until this retreat began, when many of our brave little band fell on the field ... I was wounded about 4 o'clock in the right leg but not serious, as I looked around and saw hundreds with legs, arms, and bodies torn to pieces, I felt that I should be thankful that I had escaped with so slight a wound ... "[64]

Col. John C. Moore, Second Texas, noted, "The woods to our right front were full of smoke and bullets were rattling like hail among the trees." W.H. Kearney of Company L, Sixth Tennessee, estimated that his regiment suffered two hundred casualties in three minutes while assaulting the Hornet's Nest. Colonel George Porter, Sixth Tennessee, remarked that the capture of the Federals vindicated the shivering into fragments of Hindman's command, the fact that Stephen's Brigade had been swept away, Stewart's Brigade was mangled and cut to pieces, and Gibson's fine body of Louisiana troops recoiled for the fourth time from deadly shock.[65]

The Crescent Regiment had centered near the Duncan house and eventually attacked Prentiss's right. Dr. Y.R. LeMonnier was a private in Company B of the regiment. In explaining that the regiment was composed of eleven companies of Louisiana's social elite and all between the ages of eighteen and thirty-five, he lamented over the action of the afternoon. LeMonnier wrote, "It was here under such unfavorable circumstances, that our regiment in its virgin assault charged ... our baptism of fire we received in Duncan field; and our Crescent boys soon made it a crimsoned, hallowed spot ... "[66]

T.B. Anderson was a young soldier in the Twenty-eighth Tennessee during the battle of Shiloh. He said the final assault on the Hornet's Nest brought to mind:

> " ... we lost our major, Jim Tolbert. The ball that ended his life passed so near my head that I dodged ... Breckinridge rode up, carrying his hat in his hand, and said, 'Charge them, Tennesseans!' ... We did it, sweeping everything before us. In passing over that ravine, I could have walked on dead Yankees. When we gained the crest of the intervening hill, we received the surrender ... I jumped up and down, thinking the war was over on seeing all those men stack their arms."[67]

General W.H.L. Wallace had attempted to rally his men to avoid the fate that was becoming more obvious, but he received a mortal wound in the process. The highest-ranking Union general to do so at Shiloh, Wallace passed away three days later at the Cherry house. His wife was at his side with her hand on his chest. His last words were, "We meet again in heaven." Wallace would not be the last Union officer to die at the Cherry Mansion. On April 25, General C.F. Smith, Grant's replacement for a brief period following the battle of Fort Donelson, passed away from complications of a gangrenous leg injury, initially a skinned shin. The wound had occurred when Smith fell while boarding a rowboat. [68]

Union General Prentiss wrote of his capture by the Confederates:

> "I was flanked on right and left. [Confederates] came pell mell as if ... going to Pittsburg Landing in a hurry ... We fought on and on and when it seemed that absolute disaster had come ... [the enemy] killed a boy who had

been with me through the heat of that terrible battle and whose promotion I had determined upon, I ran to a tree, pulled off my hat and, I failed to be a gentleman ..."[69]

J.A. Hamby, Twenty-eighth Tennessee, remembered seeing a Federal prisoner, bound for Corinth, marching past his position on the sixth. The man was a defender of the Sunken Road and was wounded in his head, with blood dried and dripping over his clothes. Though he never learned the captured soldier's name or fate, his concern for the man remained years after the incident. The prisoner had a rope around his neck and "was being led along like a wild beast."[70]

The Federal soldiers were saved from defeat on April 6 when the Confederates failed to achieve their objective. In addition, Grant's Chief of Staff, Colonel J.D. Webster, assembled an estimated fifty guns on Grant's left line. The time needed to procure the guns was supplied by the efforts of the defenders of the Sunken Road. The line—situated today near the visitor's center— ran from the bridge over the confluence of Owl and Snake Creeks on the northwest side to the Tennessee River on the other end. This "last line" thus extended 2200 yards in length and was manned by approximately 20,000 Union soldiers, veterans of the day's fight. The tired and battered troops of Hurlbut manned the area to the right of Webster's battery, while McClernand held the center. Sherman was positioned to the line's right side or the north end of the battlefield.

Beauregard's controversial call to end the day's fighting left the Confederates victorious on the sixth and confident of the action to come with the next day's sunrise. Confederate premonitions related to revenge for forts Henry and Donelson were not to be fulfilled.

Fraley Field, the location of the beginning of the battle of Shiloh. Photo by author.

The Cherry Mansion in Savannah, Tennessee. This home served as Grant's headquarters during the Shiloh campaign. Photo by Wayne Bishop.

The plaque in the photo's left-center marks the wooded location of Gen. Albert Sidney Johnston's death. Photo by author.

Modern view from Ruggles' Battery across Duncan Field and toward the Hornet's Nest. Photo by author.

Richard Ogle, W.H. Gooch, and Thomas Gooch were three privates of Co.
F, Twenty-third Missouri Vol. Inf. to be captured at Shiloh. Photo courtesy
of Major Rex A. Gooch, USAF, Ret.

*The Bloody Pond with the Peach Orchard in the background.
Photo by author.*

*Modern view of the Sunken Road. Union resistance was concentrated to the
left with Confederate attacks coming from the right. Photo by author.*

CHAPTER FOUR

SHILOH — DAY 2

"We came here to go to Corinth, but Corinth came to us."
Gen. Benjamin Prentiss
April 7, 1862

As dusk arrived at the end of the first day's fighting at Shiloh, the signs of victory seemed destined to point in the direction of the Confederate army. Notwithstanding the loss of General Albert Sidney Johnston, the highest-ranking Confederate officer killed during the war, the day had proven successful for the Southerners. The attackers had swept through a series of Federal camps, taken some 2,000 prisoners after defeating a stubborn foe in the Hornet's Nest, and slept that night with the enemy pushed near the shores of the Tennessee River.

General Beauregard's order to cease the attack on the sixth has often been discussed and noted as a point of controversy. Proponents of his supporters and dissenters have argued as to whether or not the order came too early in the day, that fatigue was overtaking his command, or if he ignored warnings of Federal reinforcements arriving as he stopped the attack.

Many Confederates found their resting places in Federal tents. Colonel William M. Inge, Twelfth Mississippi, hurriedly passed several Federal tents when he saw one with a cot inside. Plenty of food was inside the tent, enough the officer felt, for his horse and him. Both ate plentifully and the officer slept on the cot, never dreaming of the dread issue so near. Sam Watkins, First Tennessee, held different memories of the fight on the 6th, recalling that men were lying in every position imaginable, the eyes of the dead were wide open, and the poor wounded soldiers begged for help.[1]

Joe T. Williams, Company D, Twenty-first Alabama, vividly recalled the events of Sunday night, April 6, 1862:

> "A comrade and I were searching the battlefield ... for some missing men of our company ... passing through a swampy thicket near where [we] charged the Fourth Ohio Regiment early in the morning, we heard the voice of a wounded man crying, 'Boys, boys'. Thinking it might possibly be one of our men we went to him. He begged for a drink of water ... he had rolled into the edge of this thicket in order to protect himself from being run over by the flying ambulances, artillery, and cavalry ... His left knee cap was entirely shot off and he was extremely weak from loss of blood ... His name was John Burns, of Cincinnati, Ohio, Company B, Fourth Ohio ... he begged to be carried to our field hospital where he might receive attention, and if possible get word to his loving mother, being her only son. He had a small Bible in his hand with his thumb resting inside on the fourteenth chapter of St. John. His thumb being bloody it made a bloody spot on this chapter. He desired ... this ... sent ... to his mother ... Dr. Redwood ... found his wound to be fatal ... He was eighteen ... He requested a prayer ... He handed me his Bible and requested me to hand it to Sergeant Stevenson ... The next morning I went to the hospital and learned he was dead ... I ... requested a pass to ... see if I could find Sergeant Stevenson ... He came forward to know what I wanted ... I [said] ... John Burns ... is in glory. He was visibly affected ... other comrades gathered near and heard of his death ... and expressed their gratitude to me for what I had done."[2]

Members of the Twenty-second Alabama occupied the Federal tents, ate their supper, and enjoyed comforts not seen for months. Col. J.C. Marrast was suffering from rheumatism and was unable to sleep.

The sound of someone moaning in great pain caught his attention and he stepped outside to investigate. There he found a Union officer, terribly wounded and left for dead amid a pile of his lifeless comrades. Marrast led the man to a hospital tent, where he received lifesaving care.[3]

While some Confederates began the night in feelings of confidence and safety, others were far less comfortable. Relegated to sleeping on the ground, those individuals had to do their best to gain rest as a violent rainstorm erupted. The rains saturated the field where lay "the weary to sleep and the wounded to die."[4]

Aboard *Hiawatha,* a group of Confederate prisoners spent the night en route to Savannah. Lt. Col. George Soule and E.B. Carruth had fallen captive to Prentiss's men prior to the fall of the Hornet's Nest. The duo was escorted to the river, and aboard ship joined others who shared a similar fate. *Hiawatha,* a Southern transport with five surgeons, thirteen nurses, yet no beds or medical supplies, was a Southern vessel pressed into service and was manned with Confederate sympathizers. The entourage missed the action to come and was sent to St. Louis.[5]

Several Confederate regiments, including Maney's First Tennessee, claimed to be within two hundred yards of the river's bank. On the morning of April 6, General Johnston had ridden in the regiment's front, praising them for the glories gained while in Virginia as part of what would become the famous Archer's Tennessee Brigade. Maney's regiment was given the task, with Colonel Nathan Bedford Forrest's cavalry, of initially guarding Lick Creek..[6] As the battle had progressed, the regiment's position had as well.

The Federal unit Johnston had desired Maney's First Tennessee to be wary of belonged to Gen. Don Carlos Buell. Buell's movement toward Shiloh was known, and his arrival was both anticipated and dreaded. The vanguard of Buell's Army of the Ohio began arriving as the fighting on the sixth was ending. His three divisions of McCook, Crittenden, and Nelson are usually regarded to have swelled the Federal ranks by as many as 13,000.

A captured Confederate reflected upon his time spent under guard in front of a Savannah livery stable: "There we stood looking ... at Buell's army passing, regiment after regiment, band after band, all night, and by daylight this splendid army was in line of battle to confront our depleted forces. Too many men!"[7]

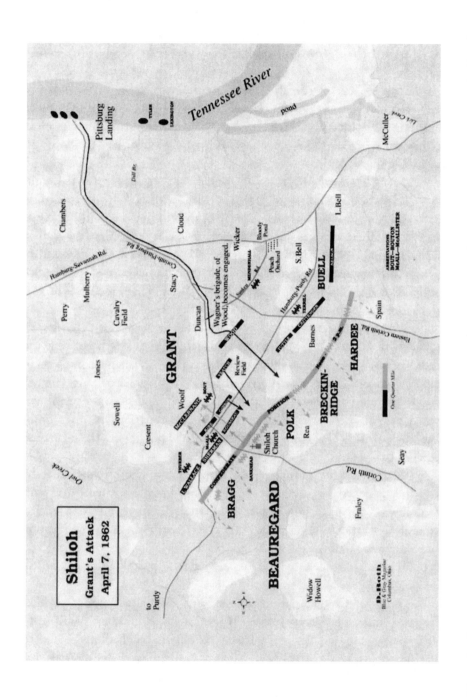

Shiloh
Grant's Attack
April 7, 1862

Tennessee River

Pittsburg Landing

GRANT

BEAUREGARD

BRAGG

POLK

BRECKIN-RIDGE

HARDEE

BUELL

Shiloh Church

Wagner's brigade, of Wood, becomes engaged.

D. Roth
Blue & Gray Magazine
Columbus, Ohio

Col. Nathan Bedford Forrest reportedly led a small group of scouts in captured Federal overcoats along the riverbank within hearing distance of Buell's army as it disembarked at Pittsburg Landing. Forrest, then a less-than-fully appreciated officer, informed a superior of the fact that thousands of Union soldiers were arriving. Forrest added that if a Confederate attack failed to begin soon, and by no means wait until morning, the Confederate army would be whipped. Generals Chalmers, Breckinridge, and Hardee received personal reports from Forrest, but he was urged to return to his camp and his plea remained largely ignored.[8]

W.B. Ellis remarked that some 20,000 Federals, "routed and utterly demoralized," were in a thirty-five-acre field lying before Pittsburg Landing. The field's owner, one Mr. Hagey, had remarked that he was certain a ramrod could not be worked up and down without striking a man, horse, or cannon due to the crowded conditions in the field. A Buell subordinate described seeing masses of Grant's army "cowering under the river bank, frantic with fright and utterly demoralized." A request was made but not granted to allow fresh Federal arrivals to fire among those refusing to be rallied.[9]

During Buell's arrival at the landing and continuing throughout the night, a duo of Federal gunboats shelled the Confederate positions. Every fifteen minutes, the *Lexington* and *Tyler* ejected shells upon the weary Confederates, robbing them of much-needed rest. While the accuracy of the shots and level of casualties these boats inflicted has been debated for generations, the fact that the firing eliminated proper sleep for the men of both sides is widely agreed upon. The Federal reinforcements, fresh and motivated, would make the difference in the fight to come.

D.C. Kelley was a member of Forrest's Cavalry at Shiloh and remembered the cannonballs from the gunboats passing high overhead and through the treetops. He felt the disorder of the Federal army would lead to surrender in the early hours of the day to come. Kelley's disgust over a lack of continuation in the fight caused him to fume inside forty years later. [10]

James A. Jones added, "... the gunboats commenced shelling us from the river. The first shot knocked down about nine men in our regiment, but I think none were killed, only shocked and stunned by the explosion." General Grant recalled that the "country was broken and heavily timbered, cutting off all view of the battle from the river, so that friends would be as much in danger from fire from the gunboats as the foe. But about sundown, when the National troops were back in their last position, the right of the enemy was near the river and exposed to the fire of the two gunboats, which was delivered to them with vigor and effect."[11]

Lt. William Gwin, the commander of *Tyler*, was eager to take part in the battle and gladly opened fire when Gen. Nelson gave him permission to do so. The five-year old wooden sidewheeler fired eight-inch shells in a twenty-five minute salvo. *Lexington* joined *Tyler*, at the mouth of Dill Branch, three-fourths of a mile above the landing, and gave valuable support to Webster's siege line.[12]

Artillery shells coupled with lightning and sent red and white streaks across the night sky. Each provided observers with glimpses of human suffering and destruction yet to be seen, but soon to become a regular event on North American soil.

Confederate hopes obviously mixed with fears. General Earl Van Dorn was on his way from Des Arc, Arkansas, but was still two hundred and fifty miles away on April 7. The roads from Van Dorn's location were in a similar condition to those from Corinth to Shiloh, causing a delay that would be unable to benefit the Confederates. Without the twenty thousand troops of Van Dorn's, the Southerners could easily lose ground earlier gained at a tremendous cost.[13]

Meanwhile, across the Union lines, word quickly spread concerning Buell's arrival. With the advance guard having joined Hurlbut in repulsing the last Confederate assault of the day, the remainder continued their arrival throughout the night. In addition, Gen. Lew Wallace, the future author of *Ben Hur*, made his arrival with some 7,000 fresh troops. Wallace had spent most of the day en route to Shiloh from Crump, but he took a long route, sometimes proclaimed as evidence of the officer actually being lost.[14]

General Grant chastised Wallace years later in writing that "his was one of three veteran divisions that had been in battle, and its absence was severely felt." [15]

With the break of dawn on Monday, April 7, 1862, the Confederate loss of land began with the initial Federal assault. W.S. Hillyear of Grant's staff recalled:

> "The first dawn of morning lighted our men onward toward the foe ... The enemy ... moving forward with the confidence inspired by their partial success on the preceding day; [the Federals] with the confidence inspired by the knowledge that we had been reinforced ... It

was the most terrible conflict I have ever witnessed ... wherever the battle raged hottest General Grant could be seen ... the rebels evidently distinguished him as a commanding general ... they opened a battery which filled the air around us with bursting shells and solid shot ... fortunately the range was a little too high, and the ricochet passed beyond us. One ball passed under the General's horse." Grant's metal scabbard was struck, Major J.P. Hawkins lost his hat, and Colonel James B. McPherson's horse was killed in the barrage.[16]

Sgt. William Clark Newlon added, "Our forces ... succeeded in flanking the enemy on our right driving him from his position toward the center ... the battle raged with great fury. The firing appeared not to cease, but a continual roar louder than thunder was heard without cessation ... bravery and gallantry was exhibited by both officers and men."[17]

Confederate Col. William Inge was sleeping in a captured tent and was brought to life by hearing the rapid fire of the advancing Federals. He jumped atop his horse and spent the duration of the day fighting, though he and others in the Confederate ranks felt their army "slowly and sullenly retreating like a wounded lion."[18]

A member of the Sixteenth Louisiana noted the resilience of the Federal troops bent on revenge:

"At dawn ... we were ordered to the right, where, judging from the firing, hard battle was being fought. On the way ... we saw some of the results of the previous day's fighting. Thousands of dead and wounded Yankees lay in our path for the space of a mile or more. The sight was a ghastly one, but it was cheerful in comparison [to] the live ones we saw a short while afterwards, for I could see long lines of Buell's men ... our shells would fall and explode among them, but the gaps were closed up and the march continued."[19]

The tenacity of the Federal troops could well be attributed to such incidents as one of their number recorded. He explained, "I saw one of our dead soldiers with his mouth crammed full of cartridges until the cheeks were bulged out. Several protruded from his mouth."[20]

A.H. Macklin, Fifteenth Mississippi, found himself appalled at the sights made more visible as the sun rose. "Patches of ground literally covered with dead heaped and piled upon each other ... Dead men were all around. One sitting against a bank and leaning his head upon his hand and knees. The position was as natural as if he had fallen asleep, yet he was dead ... wherever I turned I saw men pale in death ... faces upturned and besmirched with mud and water, hair matted with gore."[21]

A Union soldier remembered seeing masses of dead, wounded, and dying as his regiment maintained its line while it advanced. He wrote:

> "I heard a voice calling ... I went to a gory pile of dead human forms ... I saw one arm raised, beckoning me. I found there a rebel, covered with clotted blood, pillowing his head on the dead body of a comrade. Both were red from head to foot. The dead man's brains had gushed out in a reddish and grayish mass over his face. The live one had lain across him all that horrible long night in the storm."[22]

The roar of cannon and rattling muskets became so continuous that their sounds grew indistinguishable. Beginning with the opening action from Brig. Gen. William Nelson's Fourth Division of the Federal left wing, the action had grown intense. The Union center was under the command of generals McCook and Crittenden. McClernand, Hurlbut, Sherman, and Lew Wallace led the Federal right wing. Confederate opposition to Nelson came from Hardee and Breckinridge; the Confederate left was under Bragg, with Gen. Polk next to him.[23]

The Twenty-fourth Tennessee served in Hardee's Third Corps, and Lt. Col. T.H. Peebles valiantly led the group. In a letter to his wife, the officer declared, "Our brigade opened the [fight], and the 24th carried the left wing of the brigade. Our brigade sustained the heaviest loss in the army and the 24th the heaviest in the brigade. We had fifty-two men killed in the field ... and one hundred and sixty-six wounded ... .poor Buck, that had borne me so bravely through the day, was shot through the heart ... "[24]

Col. Henry George, Seventh Kentucky, recalled the day and a brief reprise from the fighting, "Lieutenant Cochran ... and I ... moved off to our right in search of water ... a running stream was discovered making its way through a small field. We ... were approaching the stream, when a heavy Federal skirmish line from the opposite side ... opened upon us. We made our way back toward our lines ... The clothing of ... Cochran was pierced by a Federal ball, and my cartridge box, and canteen were struck, my gun being ruined."[25]

Confederate Gen. Thomas C. Hindman was atop his horse when a shell burst near his ride, killing the animal. Propelled an estimated ten feet into the air, then pressed under the weight of his horse, the general was unable to see further action at Shiloh.[26]

On the Union side, Enoch Colby of the First Illinois Artillery rammed a shell into his cannon and stepped back just in time to have a Confederate cannonball pass him and go through gunner Ed Russell's stomach. Russell suffered for twenty minutes before succumbing to his wound. Russell received comfort in his last minutes from Jim Flanagan, who was ironically killed within the hour of returning to battle.[27]

Across the battlefield, the Federal forces pushed the Confederate forces back. General Grant declared, "In a very short time the battle became general all along the line. This day everything was favorable to the Federal side...The enemy was driven back all day, as we had been the day before, until finally he beat a precipitate retreat." [28]

Private Y.R. LeMonnier vividly described a portion of the day's events: "Every time we drove back one of their commands a fresh one took its place, and in turn would drive us back. We would run down to a little stream at the foot of a hill, and, lying on our faces with our muskets cocked and our fingers on the triggers ... await the enemy's coming. After surprising them with a volley, we would charge ... with our bayonets." [29]

The Confederate center began to break, and by 1:00, a number of Confederate batteries had fallen into Union hands. An estimated twenty guns the Confederates captured the day before belonged to the Federals as the afternoon of the seventh approached.[30]

Short-lived Confederate counterattacks took place at a host of locations across the field with minimal success. Early in the afternoon, Beauregard became convinced of being involved in a losing battle and sought to withdraw his army. Members of Beauregard's staff contacted various corps commanders, ordering them to begin their retreat while giving the illusion of launching an offensive.[31]

The noon Confederate counterattack at Water Oaks Pond is perhaps the most widely known of such instances at Shiloh. Brigadier General S.A.M. Wood, commander of the Third Brigade of Hardee's Third Army Corps, led some 650 Confederates through the pond's waist-deep water and into an adjoining field. The Federal troops were caused to temporarily retreat, though this attack would soon be reversed.

The Confederates so skillfully undertook their masked retreat that suspicion of such wasn't initially recognized. Fire was set to a number of Federal camps captured on the sixth, and the resulting smoke helped shield the movement of the retreating soldiers.[32]

Union pursuit was limited once the Confederate retreat was detected. Buell sent Nelson's division to the Hamburg-Savannah Road, having determined the Confederates were retreating in that direction. Lew Wallace, on the Union right, soon called off his men's pursuit. [33]

Brigadier General James A. Garfield, destined after the war to become President of the U.S., made an attempt to overtake the withdrawing Confederates. Garfield disappointedly yielded to an order to end his pursuit; his men did manage to capture forty prisoners without firing a single shot.[34]

An eyewitness to the retreat described it as such:

> "In this ride ... I saw more human agony and woe than I trust I will ever again be called upon to witness. The retreating host wound along a narrow and almost impassable road, extending some seven or eight miles ... a line of wagons loaded with wounded, piled in like bags of grain, groaning and cursing; while the mules plunged on in mud and water belly deep, the water sometimes coming into the wagons ... soldiers staggering along, with an arm broken and hanging down ... A cold drizzling rain commenced about nightfall, and soon came harder and faster, then turned to pitiless, blinding hail ... wounded and dying soldiers, without even a blanket to shelter them ... hail ... fell in stones as large as partridge eggs until it lay on the ground two inches deep ... men died during that awful retreat, and their bodies were thrown out to make room for others."[35]

Colonel Dickey's Fourth Illinois Cavalry made contact with Nathan Bedford Forrest at a location known as Falling Timbers. Forrest watched the approaching Federals and seized the opportunity that occurred when the cavalrymen crossed a small stream. Forrest led a charge into the Union lines, breaking them at one point. Dickey's command stampeded into the infantry in their rear, a number of horses becoming impaled on bayonets. It was noted that chaos reigned. Some Federal infantrymen threw down their guns and ran as Confederate shotguns and swords inflicted their damage.[36]

Forrest realized he had outrun his command and found himself surrounded as numerous Federal infantrymen attempted to drag him from his kicking horse. A Federal infantryman pushed his musket toward Forrest, the ball fired and entered Forrest's left side just above the hip, and lodged against his spinal column. Reeling in his saddle, Forrest allegedly grabbed a Union infantryman and pulled him onto his horse behind him, using the unlucky soldier as a shield.[37] The latter feat is often questioned in relation to its authenticity.

Amid shouts of "Shoot that man!" Forrest spurred his horse toward safety. Shot in two places, the horse carried Forrest to relative security before succumbing to his wounds.[38] Colonel Forrest, though badly wounded, would recover and receive a promotion to Brigadier General.

The Confederate withdrawal from Shiloh and the ensuing return to Corinth, Mississippi ended the largest battle on American soil to that time. On May 30, 1862, the Federal troops gained control of Corinth. The culmination of these events would occur six months later, when Corinth itself would serve as the location of another bloody struggle.

Shiloh itself would serve as a Federal camp for days after the battle's conclusion. About one hour after the Confederates left the field, the Federal lines of April 5 were re-established. Then the grisly tasks of caring for the wounded and dying, burning the carcasses of dead animals from across the fields, and burying the dead of both sides began. These jobs fell to Grant's troops, now in possession of the field.

A member of one burial detail explained:

> "I ate my dinner on Monday within six paces of a rebel in four pieces. Both legs were blown off. His pelvis was the third piece, and his head and chest was the fourth piece. Those four pieces occupied a space of twelve feet square ... My friend ... and myself, on the second night, looking in the dark for a place to lay down, he said, 'Let's lie down here. Here's some fellers sleeping.' We slept in quiet until dawn revealed that we had passed the night among sprawling, stiffened, ghastly corpses."[39]

It was duly recorded that General Grant's sighting of an open field over which Confederates had charged on the first day was so covered with dead soldiers that he would have been able to walk across it in any direction stepping on the dead without a foot touching the ground. The future President also stated, "Shiloh was the severest battle fought at the West during the war, and but few in the East equaled it for hard, determined fighting...On one part [of the field], which had evidently not been plowed for several years...bushes had grown up, some to the height of eight or ten feet. There was not one of these left standing unpierced by bullets. The smaller ones were all cut down." [40]

More than 3,900 Union dead are buried in the Shiloh National Cemetery established in 1866. Of these, many remain unidentified. Shiloh National Cemetery also serves as the resting place for casualties of other wars.

The dead of both sides were initially buried in trenches. Grant cited warm weather as his justification for the necessity of hasty mass burials. Today, the Confederate dead at Shiloh remain in five trenches, the largest of which holds 721 corpses stacked seven deep.

A Federal officer reminisced, "I stood ... in the woods ... and counted eighty-one dead rebels ... I saw one tree ... with thirty-one bullet holes ... one grave containing 137 dead rebels ... another grave containing forty-one dead Federals."[41]

The number of casualties at Shiloh shocked the world. The Confederate army suffered 1,728 killed, 8,012 wounded, and 929 missing, for a total of 10,699 casualties. The Union forces endured 1,754 killed, 8,408 wounded, and 2,855 missing, bringing their total to 13,047. The grand total of casualties at Shiloh for two days' fighting was 23,746.[42]

In addition to General Albert Sidney Johnston, whose death is often related to signaling the beginning of the end for the Confederacy, more than eighty officers died from wounds received at Shiloh. Georgia suffered one officer's death at Shiloh, as did the Regulars, Second Confederates. Three staff officers were also killed in the battle, as were three officers from Alabama, two from Florida, five from Texas, eight from both Louisiana and Mississippi, thirteen from Kentucky, and fourteen from Arkansas.[4]

Tennessee lost twenty-three officers, the largest number of all Confederate states involved, in defense of their home state. These included a first and a second lieutenant, as well as two captains and a major from the Second Tennessee; a captain from the Fifth, and the 154th; a colonel, two captains, a major, and a lieutenant from the Twenty-seventh. The

Thirteenth Tennessee lost a lieutenant and a second lieutenant, while the Sixth and Twenty-second each lost a captain. Another captain as well as a major were lost from the Fourth Tennessee, and the Ninth and Thirty-third lost adjutants. The Twelfth also lost a captain and one lieutenant.[44]

The Fourth Tennessee Volunteers, under the command of Lt. Col. Strahl, reported a total of 219 casualties, with 36 killed and 183 wounded in its 9 companies. The Fifth Tennessee suffered heavily as well, with 169 casualties, including 24 deaths.[45]

The Forty-seventh Tennessee had arrived at Shiloh on Monday. Composed largely of merchants and farm boys, the regiment gained rifles and ammunition, largely supplied from those captured at the Hornet's Nest. The Gibson and Dyer County regiment lost five men killed and sixty-one wounded.[46]

Mourning took place in nearby Madison County, Tennessee, when the disturbing news of the tragic deaths of its resident soldiers at Shiloh reached home. A shell blew away Jud Verser's head; Billy Cardwell died with the company flag in his hands. Another tragedy was the death of young Johnnie Midgett, killed when a minié ball entered his forehead while he lay near the wheel of a cannon.[47]

Another young victim of the battle was Allen Battle, Twentieth Tennessee, killed on the second day, and his body left behind following the Confederate retreat. His corpse was found and buried by some half dozen of his former Miami of Ohio classmates, all members of the Union army, most in the Eighty-first Ohio. The gentlemen marked the grave near a large oak in hopes of returning later for a more suitable burial. The latter never took place, though all of Battle's burial party survived the war. As a result, his grave location became one of many to fall under the category of unknown.[48]

Terry's Texas Rangers lost Clint Terry, the younger brother of the cavalry regiment's colonel, B.F. Terry. One of the least fortunate officers of all was Lt. John Crowley of company F, Eleventh Alabama. The officer had lost his right arm at Belmont, Missouri four months earlier, only to have his left arm torn off at Shiloh.[49]

A wounded survivor of the battle was future newspaperman and explorer Henry Stanley. A member of the Sixth Arkansas, Stanley received a shot to the belt buckle on the first day of the fighting and was captured during the second day's action. As a result, he spent a brief period as a prisoner of war in Camp Douglas near Chicago.

Shiloh National Military Park was established in 1894 and is one of the best-preserved battlefields in the United States. Its isolation from a largely populated area has aided tremendously in its maintaining a pristine condition. Encroachment, not from development but from the Tennessee River, has been the major threat to the park, but efforts in the last decade of the twentieth century have reasonably checked this issue. Native American burial mounds as well as the battlefield area that borders the Tennessee River have been the site of intense labor and millions of dollars of taxpayer money in an effort to eliminate the same from eroding into the powerful waters.

Open every day but Christmas, the park today contains almost 3,800 acres, approximately sixty-six percent of the battlefield, situated in rural Hardin County, Tennessee. Another 1,900 acres of battlegrounds are in the ownership of parties other than the National Park Service.[50]

A clearly marked fourteen-stop driving tour greets the Shiloh visitor and provides clear interpretation for each stop. In addition, the visitors' center greatly enhances the understanding of the battle. Shiloh is a true preservation and education success story and is a must-see for any Civil War enthusiast.

View of Pittsburg Landing a few days after the battle. Grant's command ship, Tigress, is the second ship from the right. Courtesy of Blue and Gray.

Modern view of Pittsburg Landing. Photo by author.

Major John F. Henry, Fourth Tennessee Infantry. Fighting in his home state, the Cumberland University graduate was wounded in his side at Shiloh. Henry's alumni records indicate the wound proved fatal. Courtesy of Paul Gibson.

CHAPTER FIVE

ISLAND NUMBER 10

"It was no time for faint hearts."
John Milton Hubbard
April 7, 1862

Control of the Mississippi River was an integral part of the Federal strategy to segment and eventually control the Confederate supply lines. Some forty miles south of Columbus, Kentucky, the river made a sharp double curve, resembling an inverted "S" in shape, with the bottom toward the east. In the bottom bend lay Island #10, so named as it was the tenth island in a chain running from north to south below the mouth of the Ohio River.

In the early 1820s, the island was described as being 400 acres in size, but by 1862, the main channel had heavily eroded the location. Unique among the chain of islands, Island #10 was largely immune to overflow. At the time of the Civil War, the island contained houses and barns and was in cultivation.[1]

Island #10 was in the Kentucky Bend, a point where the Mississippi River made a 180-degree northerly turn. Confederate batteries, five on the island and five on the shore, complemented a redoubt above the bend. Six heavy guns lay in the redoubt, and a battery of sixteen floating guns were anchored on the island halfway along its length.[2]

Command of Island #10 had evolved to Confederate Brigadier General W.W. Mackall, previously assistant adjutant to Albert Sidney Johnston.

General P.G.T. Beauregard had initially overseen the construction of the island's fortifications; but Beauregard's call from Johnston to proceed to Corinth resulted in the February 1862 order for Major General John P. McCown, and in late March, Mackall afterward leading the military efforts on the island.[3]

On the morning of March 31, Mackall arrived at Island #10, taking charge that afternoon. Mackall's regimental officers informed him that hard labor, the recent evacuation of New Madrid, Missouri, and the widespread belief that the island was "untenable and its defense hopeless" had broken down the men of the lower ranks and left them dispirited. Captain Sheliha, Mackall's engineer, examined the area on April 1 and 2 and found the post to be effective as long as the 30,000 Federal troops across the river were prevented from crossing.[4]

Approximately 7,000 Confederates inhabited the defenses on the island and the land batteries on the Tennessee shore. Under brigadier generals A.P. Stewart, L.M. Walker, E.W. Gantt, and James Trudeau, these included such units as the First Alabama, Tennessee, and Mississippi, the Fourth and Fifth Arkansas Battalions, Eleventh and Twelfth Arkansas, Eleventh and Twelfth Louisiana, Fifth Louisiana Battalion; Fourth, Fifth, Thirty-first, Fortieth, Forty-sixth, and Fifty-fifth Tennessee. In addition to these groups, artillery, cavalry, engineer corps, sappers, and miners were present at the river location.[5]

John Milton Hubbard served in the Seventh Tennessee Cavalry and remembered that during this time, he and his fellow cavalrymen spent on Island #10, "our hardships increased, as we were poorly supplied with tents and cold rains were falling."[6]

In the previous weeks, Union major general John Pope had isolated and captured New Madrid, Missouri. In doing so, he secured several thousand small arms, supply stores, and provided a boost of morale that propelled the Union soldiers toward an assurance of victory in the attack to occur at the island.

Above the now-isolated Island #10 were Federal gunboats under Flag Officer A.H. Foote. To the Confederates' rear lay Reelfoot Lake and its surrounding swamps, areas labeled as impenetrable. Toward New Madrid and on the Missouri shore below, Pope's army held strong positions. Escape from the island was, at that time, a virtual impossibility.[7]

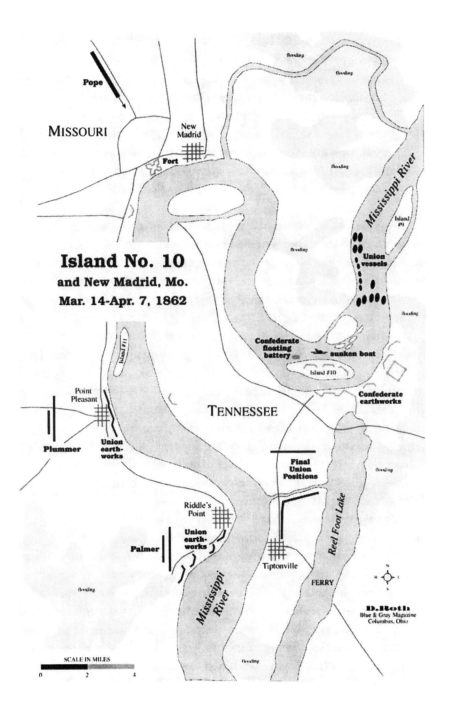

Pope

MISSOURI

New Madrid

Fort

Island No. 10
and New Madrid, Mo.
Mar. 14-Apr. 7, 1862

Mississippi River

Island #9

Union vessels

Island #11

Confederate floating battery

sunken boat

Island #10

Confederate earthworks

Point Pleasant

TENNESSEE

Plummer

Union earthworks

Final Union Positions

Reel Foot Lake

Riddle's Point

Union earthworks

Palmer

Tiptonville

FERRY

Mississippi River

N

D.Roth
Blue & Gray Magazine
Columbus, Ohio

SCALE IN MILES

0   2   4

John Milton Hubbard explained:

> "the river rapidly rose and there was a rushing current through Reelfoot Lake in our rear ... I know that our captain wished to be ordered to the main land ... we concluded that our only resource was to reach a dry spot on the lake shore and collect a few old flatboats and to reach the east side. In making our way to the lake we found much of the back water up to the saddle skirts ... As the lake here was five miles wide, and the water still rising, our crossing would surely be slow and perilous."[8]

The level of the river had risen to a point that the entire wooded peninsula that sat in the great bend was under water. The overflow was deep enough to allow transports to float to a position where troops could be moved across the river for the purpose of capturing Island #10. The logistical problem lay in the fact that the wooded area, six miles in width, eliminated such movement.[9]

At this point, a unique aspect of the capture of Island #10 came into play. Under the leadership of Col. J.W. Bissell, approximately six hundred Union soldiers, "an organization composed of twelve full companies of carefully selected workmen, chiefly mechanics, and officered by men capable of directing such skilled labor" began clearing a channel. As previously noted, the ability to escape the island was practically unrealizable, yet a number of Confederate batteries guarded a road to Tiptonville on the river's east side. A channel serving as a bypass of the island would allow Union gunboats to move within the position to accomplish such a mission with minimal damage from the island's defenders.[10]

For some two weeks, Bissell's crews progressed through the overflows, slowing when they reached the drift-heaps of the bayous. Using a variety of craft and working from daylight to sundown, the men stood on platforms and cut off the trees about eight feet above the water. Another crew followed with an arched saw set in a frame attached with a pivot, and cut the stumps four and a half feet below the waterline. Two minutes was the average time per tree, but as long as two and a half hours was devoted to one troublesome tree. Despite the rapidly running water and the slippery conditions, not a single man was killed, wounded, or listed as sick.[11]

Meanwhile, gunboats were being outfitted for the task of attacking the Confederate position. Eighty-by-twenty-foot coal barges were armed and manned. Eventually, the barges were disregarded and the *Carondelet* began the adventure on the dark night of April 4. A thunderstorm illuminated the gunboat, but its close proximity to the shore eliminated the Confederate guns on the island from being depressed to the point at which they would prove effective. Two nights later, *Pittsburgh* bypassed the island,[12] giving the Union attackers the distinct advantage.

Commander Walke of the *Carondelet* had seen his movement past the Confederate batteries made successful largely by a Union raid two days earlier; the Federal soldiers had spiked the Confederate guns of Rucker's battery. On the night of the gunboats' advance, sharpshooters were on deck for added protection. Rain and the late detection on the part of the Confederates certainly enhanced the Union predicament.[13]

The end, as evident as could be possible, was now quick in coming. Word spread throughout the Confederate ranks that each man should be on the alert to take care of himself. Four transports laden with Federal troops led to an attempted withdrawal. A few hundred Confederates managed to escape, but some 5,000 to 7,000—including General Mackall—were not as successful.

N.B. Nesbitt, Company H, Fifty-fifth Tennessee, recalled:

> "while our regiment was on dress parade, the enemy threw a shell ... scattering the dirt on the men nearest to where it struck ... we were ordered to break ranks ... and be ready to march at a moment's notice. The news was welcomed, as we had been undergoing a siege for two or three weeks, and had been shelled day and night ... While our company was thus engaged, crowded around our camp fire to the number of twelve or fifteen, a shell came shrieking through the air and struck right in our midst and exploded, leaving a hole nearly large enough to bury a horse. When the dust and ashes settled, not a vestige of fire or cooking utensils remained ... we found a skillet of corn pones in another company, the bread still in it. How we escaped unhurt is a miracle. There were some large poplars standing east of our camp, and there was a perfect stampede to them ... the long roll beat and we were ordered to march out and leave our baggage. After wandering around a day or two we were surrendered, a stupendous blunder, as every man could have gotten out in safety, as hundreds did, but our officers told us if we attempted it and were captured it

would go harder on us, consequently we had to undergo the horrors of prison life ... "[14]

The battle, as such, of Island #10 was over. The effect of its loss was felt throughout the ranks. Perhaps having its significance overlooked due to its occurrence at the same time as the bloodbath at Shiloh, the fall of Island #10 has never really received the attention it so deserves. With it, the Mississippi was taking a major step toward Union control.

John Milton Hubbard had managed to escape prior to the Union raid on the island. He wrote:

> "We had a long ride to Bolivar, and reached home just in time to hear the guns at Shiloh ... Then came the news that Island No. 10 had surrendered ... The holding of the great river became now a doubtful proposition ... A few of our men even now went to their homes to stay. The faithful set about reorganizing the company ... Our sacred honor and plighted faith to our state were involved. It was no time for faint hearts."[15]

Today, Island #10 largely rests under the waters of the Mississippi River, and the changing river channel has bonded its remains to the Missouri shore of the river. Its story is effectively recalled on a kiosk near an overlook of the island's location. The kiosk has a ramp that is currently in desperate need of maintenance. In addition, the interpretive sign that serves as the kiosk's focal point is largely unreadable. Most of the state's interpretive signs are difficult to locate. Once found, such as the one for the position of Rucker's battery, the signs are of little value. The Rucker sign, for example, refers to land that is located on private property, thus inaccessible to the interested visitor. The Cremaillere Line Fortification, built by slaves for the purpose of providing flanking fire and the only known earthwork of this type built in Tennessee, consists of sections of earthworks, some four feet tall and twenty-five feet wide. Once 3600 feet long, only 1300 feet of the works still exist. Other sections of the line are only slightly visible and water frequently fills portions of the earthworks.

The surrender of the island coincided with that of Shiloh and provided a blow to the Southern control of the Mississippi Valley from which the Confederacy would fail to recover. For the soldiers of the Confederacy, and for the interested observers of the location of such contention, Island #10 is lost forever.

The major information center for Island #10 is this difficult-to-locate and largely unreadable kiosk. Photo by author.

A poorly maintained cemetery contains the graves of those who died at Island #10. Photo by author.

Capt. Robert Isbell, Co. D, First Alabama, was one of the fortunate Confederate soldiers who escaped the island. Courtesy of Paul Gibson.

CHAPTER SIX

BRITTON LANE

"I never witnessed a hotter fight."
September 1, 1862

Under orders from Confederate major general Sterling Price, Col. Frank C. Armstrong moved his command of 3,300 troops northward from Holly Springs, Mississippi. Armstrong's assignment was to proceed into West Tennessee, and as historian James Brewer explained, conduct a task that "was classic for cavalry, raid ... along the Mississippi and Tennessee Central Railroad, harass the enemy ... disrupt the enemy's supply line, and do not become decisively engaged."[1]

This proposed action would hopefully draw the attention of Union soldiers in West Tennessee and possibly hinder Union forces strongly at work within the state's borders. Armstrong left from Holly Springs on August 27, 1862 as acting brigadier general of the following: Second Missouri, Second Arkansas, Pinson's First Tennessee, Jackson's Seventh Tennessee, Barteau's Second Tennessee, Wheeler's Sixth Tennessee, Wirt Adams's Regiment of Mississippians, Saunders's Alabama Battalion, Forrest's old regiment, and Wells's Scouts.[2]

The ensuing days found Armstrong's soldiers strongly tested in skirmishes at Bolivar on August 29 and 30, and at Medon Station on the thirty-first. In Bolivar, the Twentieth and Seventy-eighth Ohio Regiments joined four companies of the Second Indiana and two from the Eleventh Indiana, as well as the Ninth Indiana Artillery to fight the Confederates. Confederate casualties at Bolivar were reported to be an even one hundred killed and wounded; Union losses were five killed, eighteen wounded, and sixty-four missing. The Confederates began their approach to Denmark from Medon at the same time a group of Federal troops, comprised of some 1,800 men of the Twentieth and Thirtieth Illinois Infantry, two cavalry companies, and a two-piece artillery battery left Denmark for Medon.[3] The paths of these two groups would unexpectedly cross on the hot dusty morning of September 1, 1862.

Sixteen-year-old Calidonia Wilson and her father, William Wilson, a cabinet and coffin maker in the Denmark community, took a leisurely stroll that day. Arriving at Denmark Presbyterian Church, the father and daughter saw men of the Twentieth and Thirtieth Illinois regiments behind the church building, where they had camped the previous night. One of the officers from this group had been housed in the Wilson home, where Calidonia had voiced to the officer her disgust over the fact that soldiers of his command had robbed the Wilson family of sweet potatoes from their garden. The officer had assured Miss Wilson that such action would stop, yet her displeasure had only increased when she found a box of potatoes hidden in his room.[4]

The Union soldiers pulled out from the area of the church and John Taylor's nearby farm while church services began that morning. A few miles away, Armstrong's hungry Confederates roasted corn prior to the start of their march. In an effort to shorten their trip to Medon, the Union soldiers under Col. E.S. Dennis diverted their march from the main road toward their destination and entered onto a fourteen-foot-wide country road called Britton's Lane, named for a local farmer.[5]

Approximately four miles from Denmark, Captain Foster's two Federal cavalry companies leading the Union advance met Armstrong's advance troops around 10 AM. While pickets were immediately sent to inform Armstrong of the presence of Federal troops, he wasn't informed until noon, by which time he was having lunch at a local home. This friendliness of local citizens struck hard at the Union troops, at least one of whom accused the area residents of allowing the Confederates to spring an ambush upon the men in blue.[6]

Armstrong rushed his men forward with the Second Missouri in the lead and the battle at Britton Lane had begun. C.Y. Ford of Company G in the Second Missouri recalled:

> "we ... were standing by our horses, when two pieces
> of artillery let loose two charges of grapeshot into our

column at point-blank range, but with no casualties resulting. Bugles sounded, and, as soon as we had mounted, Lieutenant Brotherton, of General Armstrong's staff, dashed up and ordered Colonel McCulloch to draw sabers and charge the battery a few hundred yards down the road."[7]

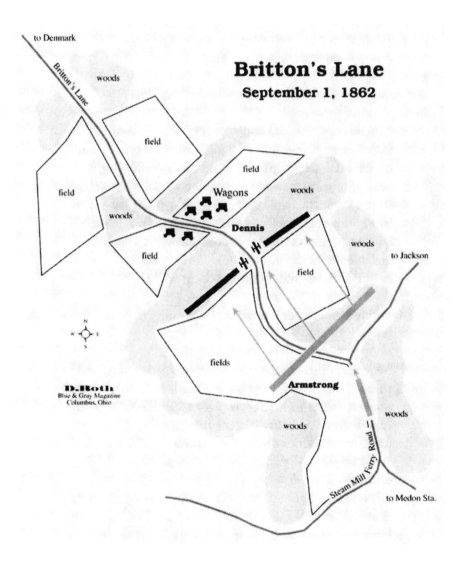

The impact of the initial Confederate charge was minimal. A Federal soldier recalled:

> "We had no sooner formed our line than the enemy sent up a hideous yell from the timber on the opposite side of the field ... They did come, to meet a sheet of flame and a shower of lead ... they were thrown into confusion ... Again and again they charged, and fought desperately ... We held our ground nobly ... the field in front of us was now strewn with horses and men."[8]

A member of Col. Wirt Adams's cavalry remarked:

> "The enemy was ... strongly posted in the woods ... In their front on one side of the lane was a cornfield, and on the other a field grown up in bushes—affording good cover for their skirmishers ... thrown well in front on both sides of the lane, while two pieces of artillery, supported by a strong infantry force, were in position directly in the lane where it entered the woods. There was a high 'stake and ridered' fence on each side ... the road was narrow, caused by deep gullies that had been washed."[9]

T.J. Dupree commanded a company of Confederates at the battle and noted:

> "We were dismounted, formed into a single line under cover of the woods near the east end of the lane ... we reached the fence and were over it ... the field to the right was in corn, that to the left in potatoes ... we were under hot fire from the enemy not more than 200 yards away, concealed by the woods ... command was given to lie down. Soon, 'Forward, charge!' and then the rebel yell was raised, and right up to within a few yards of the cannon's mouth did this little skirmish line rush; but the boys in blue gallantly stood their ground and bravely fought until the right of our line, retarded by the standing corn, swung around, struck them ... and the blue line disappeared in the woods.."[10]

Armstrong sent wave upon wave of men toward the Union lines. The strong fence stood to the Union front and Armstrong's men struggled to tear it down. Eventually, the Union line was broken and the cannon forced back. Men piled up at the fence as Confederate cavalrymen lost their horses amid the smoke and musket fire. The sound of the battle led church leaders to end services early in nearby Denmark.[11]

C.Y. Ford of the Second Missouri, Forrest's Cavalry, recorded his recollections of the struggle in an article written forty years after the event. He wrote:

> "The guns were supported by an infantry force on each side of the road, and we were supported by the 1st Mississippi on the left and the 7th Tennessee on our right. These ... were dismounted ... The grapeshot and Minie bullets cutting the dry stalks and our charging horses made a dreadful noise. We charged right up to the guns, but all three regiments were driven back. Our colonel's horse was killed, as also the flag bearers' horses ... we again rallied ... and, all dismounted, charged them again, and drove them from the field. It was a bloody battle ... and our loss was heavy both in men and horses."[12]

Upon finally capturing the Federal artillery and drawing it off, the Confederates took it to the east end of Britton's Lane. One of the cannon was rumored to have been badly damaged and thrown into a well. A wholesale assault of the Union position had been discouraged as Armstrong sent relatively small groups to each portion of the field. The criticism of this command decision is evident in the words of Pvt. John Milton Hubbard, who stated:

> "Our army could have enveloped them, and should have done so. The regiments were fought in detail ... Dr. Joe Allen of Whiteville mounted the fence and fell dead on the enemy's side ... John Bradford of Toone, and Willie Wendel, a school boy of Bolivar, were killed near the fence. D.E. Durrett of Bolivar received a wound which put him on crutches to the day of his death ... Tom Joyner and John Fortune were severely wounded. How

so many men got out of that field alive is one of those unaccountable things that sometimes occur in war ... the men were thoroughly dispirited."[13]

Another Confederate expounded upon Hubbard's recollection in writing:

"Gen. Armstrong called up Col. Adams's Regiment, which had been covering the rear that day, and ordered him to form by fours and drive the enemy from his position ... there was not a man [who] could see the death trap we were to ride into. We formed in the road ... we started on our desperate charge ... the enemy had an enfilading fire at us with their artillery, but when the clear notes of the bugle rang out ... we swung by fours into the narrow, dusty path to death, we were in pointblank range and not more than a hundred and fifty yards from their guns ... now vomiting double charges of grape and canister as fast as they could ... skirmishers on both sides poured a steady fire into our charging column ... Col. Adams ... well to the front ... was a conspicuous target for the enemy ... Close ... to him rode Sgt. Major Lee Brisco, Lieut. Montgomery, and Capt. Bondurant, the first two to give up their gallant lives a few seconds later amid the captured guns of the enemy, and the latter to fall wounded with his horse shot dead beneath him near the same spot. The fire was awful, and under the withering blast the head of our column went down. Those behind, unable to see for the blinding dust, spurred madly forward toward the sound of the guns, only to stumble and fall over their dead and wounded comrades and horses in front until the narrow land was completely blocked ... the guns were won ... but with no ammunition to use them ... Col. Adams ... seated on the cream colored mare ... with a smoking pistol in his hand and the light of a panther in his eyes ... looked down the lane to where his charging squadrons were completely blocked in a confused mass of dead and wounded men and horses ... Col. Slemmons and Col.

Pinson dismounted and came to our support, driving back
the enemy, who were again advancing."[14]

What the Confederates had in fact gained was minimal. Seven total
charges over a four-hour period had yielded slightly more than 200
Federal prisoners. U.S. Colonel Dennis reported five killed and fifty-five
wounded. Disagreements abound over the victor of this struggle, with
arguments varying from having both sides agreeing to cease the action,
to the Federals being routed. One historian argues for a Union victory in
noting that Armstrong's raiding party pulled out of West Tennessee after
the battle.[15]

A Confederate veteran of the battle exclaimed that while the "foolhardy
charge should have never been made," God saved the men in gray from
annihilation. With some 2,000 rifles and a number of artillery pieces
focused on the charging Confederates, God's grace is the only reason, the
soldier wrote, that the battle was a Confederate victory.[16]

Armstrong left the field at 3 PM with some 100 prisoners in tow. Seventy-
nine additional Federal prisoners were housed and guarded overnight in
the Masonic Hall above the Presbyterian Church before being paroled the
following morning. Between 115 and 179 dead Confederates—numbers
vary among sources—lay at Britton's Lane.[17] Most were buried in mass
graves on or near the field.

E.B. McNeil said of the interment of the Confederates:

> "Of the killed 23 were buried in one pit, and one each
> in two other graves; namely Bradford of near Toone
> and Peters of Whiteville ... The majority of those killed
> were members of the 1st Mississippi Calvary Regiment
> commanded by ... Col. R.A. Pinson ... The other killed
> and wounded probably belonged to the 7th Tennessee
> Cavalry ... W.H. Jackson was colonel."[18]

Confederate captain T.J. Deupree wrote, "I never witnessed a hotter
fight ... my company lost a little more than two-fifths of its numbers in
killed and wounded in less that ten minutes."[19]

The pro-Confederate feeling among the residents of the Denmark
area and in nearby Jackson certainly created a bad taste for months to
come in the mouths of the Federal soldiers who fought at Britton's Lane.
While conflicting decisions abound over casualties, victor, and even the

exact location of the battlefield, the humanitarian efforts of the people of Denmark are clearly noted as being genuine.

W.P. Reed was a private in Company B of the First Mississippi and the first man in his regiment wounded at Britton Lane. Initially thought to be mortally wounded, Reed lay in a field hospital with no attention for three days until Miss Mamie McBride, a local lady, carried the wounded soldier to the home of her neighbor, who shared the same name—Thomas Reed—as the wounded Reed's brother. Of his treatment, W.P. Reed recalled, "Mr. Reed was a very old man who had practiced medicine and he, with his wife and daughters, nursed and cared for me." In addition, Union surgeons from nearby federally occupied Jackson would visit Reed when making trips to check on their own.[20]

Margaret Bryant, the wife of Jack Bryant, took the wounded of both sides into her home. Mrs. Bryant lived in a cabin at the edge of the cornfield where the Confederate cavalry made its charge. Wounded soldiers from both sides crawled to her door; many were allowed inside as bullets flew. Mrs. Bryant acted unselfishly and gave aid to as many of the wounded as time allowed her to. Her husband, sick with fever, lay in bed, unable to help his wife as she tore apart sheets and clothing to use as bandages. Years later, the heroic lady exclaimed, "I didn't want no medal, but I would have been glad to get [back] the sheet I tore up."[21]

Perhaps no personal story of the battle of Britton's Lane touches one's heart more than that of Sanderson Jefferson, whose father had been killed at the battle of First Manassas. Sanderson, just fourteen years old, ran away from his Alabama home to join Nathan Bedford Forrest in an attempt to avenge his father's death. The boy's mother received only one letter from the young soldier; it stated that his uniform was largely rags.

Mrs. Jefferson made her son a uniform from the boy's great-grandfather's Revolutionary War uniform. Sanderson's ancestor had worn the uniform at Yorktown, only to die at the same location. Mrs. Jefferson used a unique-style button on the homemade uniform,[22] certain to instill pride in the young man. These buttons were to play a significant part in the young boy's future.

The teenager's body, found in front of the fence in a cornfield that Col. Duckworth's Seventh Tennessee charged through, was to be buried, yet three men of the burial party—Bill Henry, C.W. Henry, and Shedrick Pipkins—found it sad that such a young boy should spend eternity in an unmarked grave. Before wrapping the boy into a wool blanket and burying his corpse, one of the men cut a button from the boy's uniform, not for the sake of owning a relic, but to use for possible later identification of the body.[23]

Captain Guthrie had ridden with Forrest, and twenty years after the war, attended an Atlanta reunion of Confederate soldiers. One of the gravediggers had presented Guthrie with the button from the boy's uniform; the piece created a great deal of conversation. Upon hearing the story of her son from a reunion attendee, Guthrie showed her the button he had carried for years. With threads from the uniform she had lovingly made for her son's uniform still attached to he button, the lady positively identified the object as coming from her deceased young soldier's uniform. The lady traveled to Denmark, where the elderly Shedrick Pipkins showed her her son's grave. Young Jefferson now rests beside the remains of his great-grandfather, whose uniform was altered for the teenager from Alabama.[24]

Five men, three Confederates and two Union soldiers, who fought at Britton's Lane, would eventually rise to the rank of general. James D. Brewer, an expert on the battle of Britton Lane, has noted the uniqueness of a battle the scale of Britton's Lane producing such an impressive number of general officers. The Confederate veterans of the battle to gain the high rank were Wirt Adams, William H. Jackson, and Col. Frank Armstrong, Armstrong achieving the rank of brigadier general. Major Warren Shedd, commander of the Thirtieth Illinois, and Col. Elias S. Dennis were the two union participants to ultimately attain the rank of general.[25]

Today the Britton Lane Battlefield Association has set aside an area to commemorate the action of September 1, 1862 and memorialize those individuals who gave their lives on the field that hot dusty day. Memorials, a cabin, and interpretive signs line the well-manicured path that allows visitors to gain a deeper understanding of the battle. A non-profit organization, the Britton Lane Battlefield Association hosts a re-enactment every other year, alternating with Parker's Crossroads. Any assistance to the above efforts, financial or otherwise, would gladly be accepted.

MONUMENT TO CONFEDERATE KILLED AT BRITTON'S LANE IN SEPTEMBER, 1862.

In the late 1800s, Confederate veterans of the battle dedicated this monument to the dead of Britton Lane. Courtesy of Confederate Veteran.

View of the Britton Lane battlefield. Photo by author.

Denmark Presbyterian Church. Photo by author.

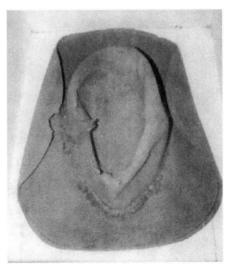

This Confederate hat was found on the battlefield two hours after the fighting ended.
Courtesy of the Old Country Store, Jackson, Tennessee. Photo by author.

CHAPTER SEVEN

DAVIS BRIDGE

"The sky was darkened with shot and shell."
Sgt. W. C. Newlon, Third Iowa
October 5, 1862

The ferocious battle at Corinth, Mississippi on October 3 and 4, 1862 resulted in what is generally regarded as a Union victory. Slightly more than 2,100 Federal casualties were suffered, with an additional 230 men missing or captured. Their Confederate foes had more than 1,400 men killed, approximately 5,700 wounded, and 2,268 individuals listed as prisoners of war.[1] Following this defeat, Confederate major general Earl Van Dorn left Corinth late on the fourth, moving in a northwestern direction.

The Confederates' planned retreat route would follow State Line Road. Van Dorn's 7,000-man force of the Army of West Tennessee was not initially pursued by Union detachments, for reasons largely unknown to this day. However, 8,000 Union reinforcements under major generals E.O.C. Ord and Stephen A. Hurlbut were summoned from their camp at Bolivar, Tennessee to move southeasterly through Hardeman County and toward Corinth. The course was set for the two forces to intersect.

Two days earlier, Van Dorn had made preparations for a safe retreat, leaving General Wirt Adams's Mississippi Cavalry at Metamora, Tennessee following the encampment at nearby Davis Bridge, also known at Hatchie Bridge, on the way to Corinth. Adams's troops spent the period from October

2 forward not only securing the Corinth-Ripley Road in the Metamora settlement,[2] but also in scouting the nearby Tennessee communities of Pocahontas and Middleton. Always mindful of the possibility of the arrival of the Corinth-bound Federal soldiers, Adams's men would experience action hours before the conflict to come in the Hatchie River Valley.

Adams's scouts spotted Ord's men as the latter passed through Middleton, Tennessee on the morning of October 4. A group of the Fifth Ohio Cavalry moved eastward to the bridge spanning the Big Muddy River. By the evening of the fourth, men of Hurlbut's camped on either side of the Big Muddy, three miles east of Metamora. From Big Muddy, the Union soldiers reported hearing the action at Corinth, and realized time and distance were minimal before "meeting a strong portion of the rebel army."[3] The prediction would soon come to be fulfilled.

Saturday, October 4 had been an extremely hot day, yet Hurlbut's command had marched twenty-six miles before bivouacking on State Line Road. After leaving Bolivar at 3 AM, the tired Federal cavalry had been "incessantly engaged" with Adams's cavalry for the second half of the journey. Two brigades, one under each J.G. Lauman and J.C. Veatch[4] composed the bulk of Hurlbut's division.

William Clark Newlon, a twenty-five-year-old third sergeant in Company G, Third Iowa Infantry Regiment, recalled the events of October 4, 1862:

> "We marched with great rapidity untill [sic] within four miles of Pocahontas twenty five miles from Bolivar where our advance met the advance of the enemy. Here we camped for the night in the face of the enemy. The two armies camped for the night on separate plantations with but a narrow skirt of timber between the two hostile Armies. Scarcely had we halted when a large body of Rebel Cavalry came dashing in the direction of our encampment. Gen. Lauman first decried the charging foe … he mounted his noble steed and … cried in a deep low voice that signalized his earnest '3rd Iowa fall in'. We were laying on the ground … Scarcely had the sound of our commander's voice died away in the distance when every man was in ranks. And in an instant a deadly wall of steel was presented to the advancing foe. Finding us prepared for their reception, they quietly fell back to their former position. Again all was quiet. Taking from our Haversacks

a portion of the food prepared the day previous for the
journey we ate our evening meal. And let me say here
that none but a weary soldier can enjoy such a meal. How
delicious to our taste was that hard bread and rusty bacon
after that day of fasting and hard marching. Our cold
and scanty meal being devoured, we lay ourselves upon
Mother Earth for night's repose with nothing to cover us
but the high Heavens and its guardian Angel to protect
us. Already had dark clouds begun to gather in the distant
west. Soon the lightning began to flash. And the peals of
thunder became louder and louder. Presently the surging
billows tossed with fury in the dark Heavens, threatening
the Earth and its inhabitants with utter and immediate
destruction. Heavy drops of rain began to fall carelessly
to the Earth. Soon to be followed by torrents of rain. Yet
all this failed to disturb the quiet and pleasant slumbers
of many weary soldiers."[5]

Veatch's brigade, with Lauman's in reserve, led the advance of the
Union army on the morning of Sunday, October 5. Historian Peter
Cozzens wrote that the approach was far from desirable as "deep hollows
and ravines bisected the road, and dense thickets and woods impeded
maneuver off it." The narrow road approaching the Hatchie River caused
Hurlbut a great deal of concern for the ambulances and artillery caissons,
as well as for the safety of their crews. These were moved into an open field
south of the road, as to not impede the progress of the column.[6]

W.R. Stites, Company G, First Texas Legion, recalled, "In our advance
... the regiment to which I belonged ... Whitfield's, Maury's Division ...
was detailed to defend the Hatchie Bridge. General Hurlbut, with his well-
equipped division of infantry, was known to be in striking distance."[7]

Around 8 AM, Major General Ord rejoined the march and took
command from Hurlbut. Ord was less than two weeks away from his forty-
fourth birthday and had been a major general little more than five months.
An 1839 graduate of the U.S. Military Academy, the Seminole War veteran
would soon gain notoriety on the banks of the Hatchie River.

The Federal lead column was "soon sharply engaged" as Confederates of
Moore's brigade, Dabney Maury's division, sent cavalry, infantry, and artillery
assaults in the direction of the advancing Federals. Colonel Hawkins's 360
Texans had assembled east of the bridge around 8:30; Confederates under

Maury stood within 300 yards of the line of blue-clad soldiers and some 150 yards to the west of the Davis home on Burr's Branch.[8]

A Confederate remembered, "Our regiment was double-quicked back perhaps a mile. Every available man in it was deployed as a skirmish line to try to make the appearance of a large force. We met their advance ... and exchanged a few shots with them until their main column came up, when we fell back slowly toward the bridge, firing as we fell back."[9]

From his vantage point on Metamora Hill, Major C.C. Campbell, the Union artillery commander, saw the Confederate line form. Eight cannon, four belonging to Capt. William Bolton of the Second Illinois Battery and the remainder from Capt. Silas Burnap's Seventh Ohio Battery, set up at the junction of State Line and Ripley-Pocahontas Road and on a knoll approximately one-half mile to the south. Two other guns of the Seventh Ohio Battery would eventually join these and be positioned slightly north of the center, toward Bolton's position.[10]

John D. Martin was a member of Company A, Twenty-fifth Indiana who recorded the events of the day at Davis Bridge. He wrote:

> "We had marched about five miles when a detachment
> of cavalry was coming back. Some of the older soldiers
> said we were going to have a fight. Sure enough when we
> got upon the hill, as our regiment was in the advance, we
> could see the Rebels crossing the Hatchie River on the
> bridge. They were about one-half mile away. The ground
> between us was clear, it being a farm. They were crossing
> their troops and forming a line of battle and running some
> artillery over and getting them into position."[11]

Veatch's Brigade, consisting of the Fourteenth, Fifteenth, and Forty-sixth Illinois as well as the Twenty-fifth and Fifty-third Indiana drew positions behind the artillery, where they were soon reinforced. North of State Line Road, the infantry troops stood in the following order: Fifteenth Illinois, Fourteenth Illinois, and the Twenty-fifth Indiana straddling the road. South of the road were the men of the Fifty-third Indiana, Forty-sixth Illinois, Sixty-eighth Ohio, and Twelfth Michigan. Near 9 AM, the Federal troops stretched across Metamora Hill, providing what appeared to be an endless line to the Confederates near the Hatchie River.[12]

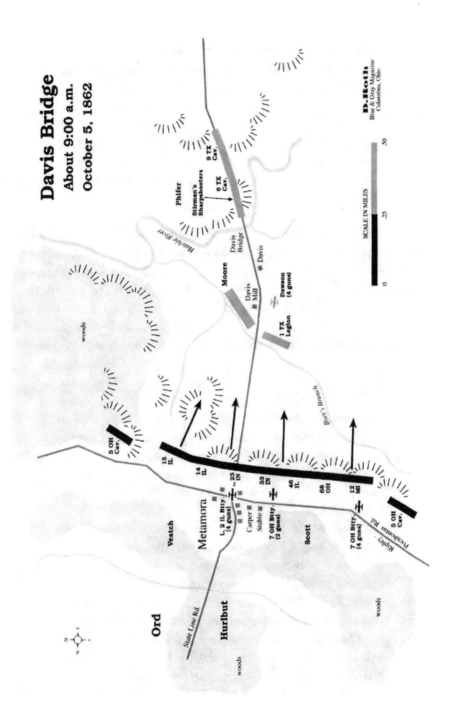

Davis Bridge

About 9:00 a.m.
October 5, 1862

9 TX Cav.

Phifer

Stirman's Sharpshooters

6 TX Cav.

Hatchie River

Davis Bridge

Davis

Moore

Davis Mill

Dawson (4 guns)

1 TX Legion

Burr's Branch

5 OH Cav.

15 IL

14 IL

25 IN

53 IN

46 IL

68 OH

12 MI

5 OH Cav.

Ripley Pocahontas Rd.

Veatch

Metamora

I, 2 IL Btty. (4 guns)

Carper

Stable

7 OH Btty. (2 guns)

Scott

7 OH Btty. (4 guns)

woods

Ord

State Line Rd

Hurlbut

woods

woods

D. Roth
Blue & Gray Magazine
Columbus, Ohio

SCALE IN MILES

0   .25   .50

N

97

One witness, serving as a correspondent, stated:

> "The first important contest was opened about 9 o'clock for the possession of the hill, whose slopes and the bottom beyond stretched three-quarters of a mile to the bridge across the river. The enemy had planted a battery of four 12-pound howitzers immediately in front of the bridge to protect the advance of their infantry, which had already been massed in the timber on both sides of the wood ... our line of battle was advancing up the opposite side, preceded by the artillery."[13]

The Confederate twelve-pound howitzers belonged to Capt. William Dawson's St. Louis Battery and stood to the southwest side of Davis Bridge. As Major William Burnett used these guns to respond to the increasing Union artillery fire, approximately 1,000 Confederates of the First Texas Legion stood to their front along Burr's Branch. While this number was a mere fraction of the advancing Union infantry, these men were all that were able to cross prior to the beginning of the Union bombardment.[14]

> A Union soldier wrote, "Bolton's Battery was quickly planted in position on the hill, which was no sooner perceived by the enemy than they started a column of infantry on their left, facing our right, to flank it, which movement was checked by throwing out Burnap's Battery to the right of Bolton's Battery some distance, which opened upon the advancing column of Rebel infantry a most destructive fire of grape and canister, which ... sent the whole mass helter-skelter back through the timber, across an open field, and into the woods beyond, so far that they were never seen afterward. Immediately afterward, both batteries were brought to bear upon that of the Rebels in front of the bridge, and, after a sharp contest, were [able] to silence it. The first line of battle had been formed by the Second Brigade, the First being held as a reserve. Gen. Veatch led on his line in gallant style. His right was speedily engaged by fresh troops which the enemy had thrown across the bridge and deployed to their left, but with little effect in stopping the onward march

of our troops. The left wing of our column, with Capt. Fox in its lead, were feeling their way through a point of timber and over a deep gully, and endeavoring to draw the fire of the Rebels posted to the right of their battery. This they did not succeed in doing until they reached an open space, when the fire of the Rebels told plainly where they were and that in numbers not to be despised. The infantry engagement which followed was sharp, short, and decisive."[15]

W. A. Lee, a member of the Fifteenth Arkansas, a regiment of Moore's Brigade, recalled, "the artillery ... opened fire ... We had no knowledge of their close presence until then. Their infantry was concealed less than two hundred yards in our front when the artillery fire began. Some sharpshooters whom we thought belonged to the cavalry ... we could not see them, began to fire on us."[16]

The cannon fire had allowed the Federal soldiers to make an advance from Metamora at noon, yet this had been met and driven back when the Confederates on the west side of the Hatchie River made a counterattack. With this eventually being driven back, the Federal forces, owing primarily to one regiment's flanking movement through a cornfield, surrounded approximately 200 Confederates. These Southerners saw no choice other than to surrender, though many of their comrades risked life and limb in gaining their escape to the east side of the bridge and crossing the Hatchie.

Confederate W.A. Lee retained these memories of the minutes in which captivity or freedom were the major aspects of his thought pattern:

> "It was reported that General Moore, seeing that he was trapped, gave orders for his men to get back to the north side of the river the best way they could; but we didn't hear his orders at the right of the brigade. The river at our back and 15,000 infantry less than two hundred yards in our front created, it may be imagined, much anxiety. The ... 15th Arkansas was on the right of the brigade. Observing considerable commotion down the line, one of our regiment ... concluded it was a charge ... We took the charge for a fact and moved forward at a rapid rate and ran over their skirmish line some forty yards from a fence

that their main line was concealed behind … a few steps farther and we realized what we should have known before we crossed the bridge. They made for us a sheet of fire from the third or fourth rail in the fence … we surprised them as well as being surprised ourselves at finding them concealed behind a fence so close to us … We lay down until their fire slackened a little, and then we made good use of time to get back to the river. We bore downstream … to find a tall sycamore that had fallen squarely across the river … It made a very good foot bridge, and all got away that made a strong effort."[17]

John D. Martin of the Twenty-fifth Indiana exclaimed that he never heard such a racket as took place during the Federal charge. The running and yelling Martin and his fellow men in blue offered to the Confederates resulted in the Rebel retreat across the bridge.[18]

A captain in the Twenty-eighth Illinois Volunteer Infantry wrote of the events:

"Many swam the river and got away and some crossed the bridge and escaped … they were pressed so hotly they did not have time to burn the bridge. A boy of 18 or 20 was just climbing the bank of the river … J.C. Howell of Company K brought his gun to bear upon him … and made a prisoner of him. An old man with silvered locks … came crawling up the bank and said, 'I will surrender but never run.'"[19]

Though he exaggerated the number of prisoners gained at this stage of the battle, one individual offered this insight: "In twenty minutes from the time the Rebels opened their fire, four hundred of them threw down their arms and surrendered."[20]

Capt. William Strong, Company K, Fourteenth Illinois Infantry, recorded his thoughts of this stage of the battle in an October 11, 1862 letter from his camp near Bolivar to the editor of the *Winchester Democrat* in Illinois. He wrote, "through wooded thickets, tangled briars lacerating the legs of barefooted boys, for some had no shoes, climbing fences or rather mashing them … I think we crossed twenty … leaping over deep ravines and gullies … through fields well stocked with stubborn growth of weeds, three feet taller than our heads, not halting until reaching the bluff on the west overlooking the Hatchie."[21]

At 12:30, General Ord, evidently in pursuit of a quick victory and a boost to his ego and morale of his troops, ordered the Federal troops to cross Davis Bridge. The pursuit of the retreating Confederates would soon cause a major problem for the men in blue and a severe wound for their commanding officer.

A member of Maury's division remembered of the Federal charge that "they had driven us back and across the river, and were in possession of the bridge before the advance of our retreating army arrived at the top of the ridge on the north side of Hatchie."[22]

W.R. Stites, First Texas, noted that he

> "saw Gen. Frank Cockrell, of Gen. Price's troops, riding up and down his line, hat in hand, speaking words of cheer and encouragement to his command ... It was here, so the story went, that General Van Dorn counciled [sic] with old 'Papa' Price that they surrender a portion of the army there; but Price, it is said, told him he would take the Missouri troops out, which he did."[23]

The escape of numerous Confederates may have been aided in the near disintegration of the Federal command at this point. Veatch's troops had just completed their capture of four Confederate guns, but confusion and personalities entered the picture, creating only problems for the Union victory at hand.

The Twelfth Michigan and Sixty-eighth Ohio regiments had joined in the Union advance. Through the misunderstanding of orders, the captain of the two leftmost companies advanced some two hundred yards ahead of his regiment. Col. R.K. Scott sent word for the captain and his command to return back to the Union line, a fact that infuriated General Ord, who exclaimed that the troops should be told to advance, not retreat. Ord, using the flat of his sword, struck Lt. George Welles, a man well-liked among his command, on the face. This action drew the attention of several nearby and less-than-impressed soldiers. By estimates, a number of these soldiers aimed their muskets at Ord as the general and Welles parted company.[24]

Bolton's battery joined six Union regiments on the east side of the Hatchie River and positioned themselves in a half-acre triangular-shaped area that one regiment could have easily filled. Aligning themselves on both sides of the road, the Union troops were pelted with fire from Confederate cannon and infantrymen. The Sixth and Ninth Texas of General Phifer's brigade fired round after round into the trapped Federals. Confederate reinforcements, including a group of sharpshooters, made deadly work of the situation. The remnants of Moore's brigade, now vengeful for their captured Confederate brothers-in-arms, joined in the melee. The Eighteenth, Nineteenth, Twentieth, and Twenty-first Arkansas regiments contributed greatly to what was reported as "a terrific power."[25]

A Union soldier noted, "During this time the Rebels opened another battery on an eminence a quarter of a mile in rear of the bridge, and commanding it, and were throwing a galling fire from it, as well as from their infantry, which lined every available point on that side of the river.[26]

John D. Martin of the Twenty-fifth Indiana added, "smoke from the musketry was so dense that we could see only a small distance. We climbed to the top of the hill; they had waited until we got in line of their cannon when they turned it loose on us ... with grape shot and canister."[27]

Col. Cyrus Hall, Fourteenth Illinois Infantry, ordered his men to seek shelter along the riverbank. He saw no support at hand and judged a further stand against "a fire so murderous" as having no purpose. The reinforcements, to Hall's delight, were soon arriving and crossed the bridge through the Confederate fire, though casualties mounted quickly and in tremendous numbers.[28]

Sgt. William Clark Newlon, Third Iowa Infantry, remarked, "the fighting commenced in earnest. Men and horses were falling thick and fast until it seemed as though we were all to be slaughtered on the ground."[29]

Ironically, among the Federal wounded was General Ord, hit just above the ankle. Confederate double-shotted canister poured into the Union ranks, creating a literal bloodbath. Dozens of blue-clad soldiers joined those of Col. Hall's and hid along the riverbank or jumped into the murky waters of the Hatchie River. These incidents undoubtedly led Ord to proclaim that Davis Bridge was "that miserable bridge." With Ord wounded, command of the Union troops immediately fell to Hurlbut.

Sgt. Joseph Ackerman of the Fifteenth Ohio fell with a wound to his head. In the Fifty-third Illinois, Capt. Charles Vaughn received a canister to his knees, crushing the bones. In an attempt to lead his men from the bridge to the safety of tall weeds located nearby, First Lt. Armand Pallisard waved his sword and screamed, "stand firm, we must not lose our ground!"

The eyes of many of Pallisard's troops were focused on him when he stopped in mid-sentence, his chest then torn apart by canister shot. The young Frenchman was a recent immigrant to the U.S. and had joined the army to fight for his new homeland when the war erupted.[30]

From the Confederate viewpoint, things couldn't have been transforming in a more positive manner. Charge after charge from the Union troops failed to dislodge the men of the South from their positions on the east side of the bridge. Casualties virtually ceased for the Confederates, while Federals dropped in increasing numbers. The Union dead and wounded piled upon the narrow bridge. Some of the unfortunate souls fell into the muddy Hatchie and simply floated away.

Col. E.L. Stirman, First Arkansas, wrote of the carnage he and others produced on the advancing Union troops. He proclaimed:

> "We would allow them to approach until we could see the whites of their eyes, then without exposing ourselves in the least we would pour volley after volley into them, cutting them down like grass. No man on earth could stand such a fire. Our men were all fine shots and nearly every shot must have taken effect. I never saw such slaughter in my life. They fell by the hundreds, then recoiled, reformed, and rushed to meet the same result. It was impossible to drive us from the position by direct attack."[31]

With the mathematical advantage on their side, the Federal troops began moving across the bridge more quickly than the Confederates, positioned on the hill above, could shoot them. A division under Gen. Jacob G. Lauman, consisting of the Twenty-eighth, Thirty-second, Forty-first, and Fifty-third Illinois and Third Iowa regiments moved down river to the north in an attempt to engulf the Confederates.[32]

One Federal participant recalled:

> "most of these troops, deploying to the left, drove the Rebel infantry from every position they attempted to maintain, and Col. Hall and Col. Rogers led their regiments up the hill to flank the Rebel battery. Gen. Veatch here received a stroke on the head of his scabbard from a passing round-shot, which for a time completely paralyzed him. The Rebel battery ... was rapidly hauled

off to another eminence, some distance to the north-west of its old position."[33]

Sgt. William Clark Newlon added:

" ... we were ordered to charge across the Hatchie. The command was given, 'Charge bayonets, forward, double quick, march'. Such a sight I never before witnessed ... The sky was darkened with shot and shell. The Earth trembled as though it would be sent in twain ... The branches of trees were severed from the body by cannon balls. The wounded, dead, and dying covered the ground, yet not a murmur was heard ... we were charging upon the enemy's last battery ... I received my ... shot. The man by my side was instantly killed a second before me, and I fell upon him."[34]

The Confederate response to the Union flanking was quickly carried out. At the 3 o'clock hour, the Confederates moved to the east and occupied the next hill where they stood staring at the Union line now on the hill from which fire had raked the blue-clads on their attempt to take the bridge. Meanwhile, during the height of the struggle, Gen. Frank Armstrong had taken two companies of the Seventh Tennessee Cavalry six miles upriver along the Boneyard Road, where they repaired a bridge at Crum's Mill.[35]

By 4:00, General Martin E. Green led the last Confederate troops in retreat. The battle of Davis or Hatchie Bridge was over. Four 12-pound bronze howitzers, 5 caissons, 650 small arms, and as many as 420 comrades were left behind. The soldiers would be moved to Bolivar and then to prisoner-of-war camps. Union reports stated that a number of small arms were thrown into the river. It is generally agreed upon that most of the Confederate losses occurred west of the bridge, yet even an approximate number is left to speculation. Hurlbut's Federal troops buried thirty-two Confederates in a mass grave on the field. The location of this place of interment remains a mystery to this day.

Forty years after the battle, Confederate casualties were only estimated among some of the participants, as a member of Moore's Brigade wrote, "I do not know how many men we lost out of our brigade ... our loss was heaviest on the left side of the bridge. Our company, F, lost Lt. Metlock killed and three or four captured. I suppose the losses of other commands corresponded with ours."[36]

The Union victory had come, as Hurlbut reported, "with severe loss." Four hundred ninety-three Federal soldiers had been wounded, many seriously. Fifty of Hurlbut's men lay dead; another seventeen were missing. The large number of wounded, noted the victorious commander, were "rapidly and successfully treated,"[37] though this term is relative.

Will C. Newlon entered into his diary his memory of the treatment he received. He wrote that despite a severe wound in his leg and fearing the possibility of a Confederate return and his subsequent capture, "I crawled to the bank of the river, some six rods, fell in, swam across and floated down some 200 yards ... I was taken out by Corporal Van Byning and Matt Boyd ... we lay upon the field until the next evening ... we were put in ambulances and wagons and conveyed to Bolivar, thirty miles distant. On the evening of the eighth my leg was amputated by Surgeon Carl of the 41st Illinois Infantry." [38]

Newlon's amputation was recorded in an undated and anonymous article entitled "The War Spirit of an Iowa Soldier." In Bolivar, Newlon joined other wounded warriors as they awaited medical care in "the large church building or ... in the spacious apartments of the wealthy disloyalists" of the town. Newlon's surgical procedure was performed on a porch of one of the homes as his "poor shattered, torn and half fleshless leg" was removed with no sigh of pain or questions arising from Newlon. Upon completion of the surgery, the patient was awakened by the sound of the band playing "Hail Columbia" in an effort to harass the arriving Confederate prisoners. Newlon had temporarily lost his sense of time as he cheered for his comrades to avenge the "fresh graves of your slain." He then laid his head back down and quietly muttered to those around, "Well, boys, good bye ... I should do but sorry fighting on a wooden leg."[39]

A significant number of the Union wounded at the struggle for Davis Bridge had come from the Twenty-eighth Illinois Infantry. While claiming to have captured a Confederate officer and a flag, the regiment had suffered heavily as the first group to cross the bridge. Among those of the ninety-seven that were killed, wounded, or missing were privates Harry Keith, George Lapham, and Frederick William of Company A, as well as Charles Bedford and James Lyman of Company C. Morris Souers of Company A would lose an arm to amputation after the battle. From Company I, Private William Neal had a leg amputated, while James Voorhes's right arm was shot off. Upon returning to camp at Bolivar, additional soldiers succumbed to wounds received at Davis Bridge. These included George Farthing, Company C, on October 8; Alonzo Felmings, Company K, October 11; George W. Rader, Company E, and Franklin Dobbins, Company H, October 18.[40]

Relating his treatment following the strain of his leg being amputated, Sgt. Will C. Newlon wrote, "Four days after the operation … the main artery broke and bled profusely … it was with the greatest care and attention that I recovered at all … I am indebted to Surgeon Reables, Fry, and Blakely."[41]

The retreating Confederates left their wounded behind and made their way toward Holly Springs, Mississippi. The defeated men suffered tremendously on this trek, noted John Milton Hubbard. Hubbard wrote, "our troops, worn out and hungry … drank the wells dry. When a beef was killed the hungry men were cutting the flesh from the carcass before the hide was off … morale of the army was not good."[42]

Various regiments of the Union army camped on the Davis Bridge battlefield, caring for the wounded. John D. Martin remembered the tasks at hand for his fellow members of the Twenty-fifth Indiana and him, "We stayed there the 6th and 7th, burying the dead and taking care of the wounded of both armies … there was a detail of men to dig graves and bury the dead, they dug great long ditches wide enough to lay each man close together until the ditch was full … We got back to Bolivar on the 8th."[43]

Among the Federal dead was young William D. Price, Co. A, Fifty-third Illinois. The acting Second Lieutenant was killed during the chaos encountered when the Confederates maintained a literal killing field in the small area of land west of the bridge. A comrade wrote that "He had risen to one knee, looking along the confederate line when a bullet entered his right side, pierced his heart, and came out under his left arm. He was killed instantly." Another wrote, "…nobly he done his duty, his last words were 'give it to them'." Price was buried in his uniform with "his blanket constituting the only envelope for him…his name and rank were carefully traced on a board at his head". A letter and accompanying map were sent to the officer's father and detailed the location of Price's grave. On the thirteenth of October, Price's father, attended by a Mr. Lewis and four soldiers retrieved the body, under a flag of truce, and placed it into a "metallic burial case". On October 18th, 1862, William D. Price's body was interred in the family plot. [44]

A member of the victorious Federal army wrote of the Confederate withdrawal, "Guns, blankets, knapsacks, haversacks, canteens, and cartridge boxes were scattered broad cast in every direction."[45]

Confederate evaluation of the performance of their enemy was less than favorable. One noted, "we were apparently in a box. Shrewd generalship on the part of the Federals would have captured our whole army ... Van Dorn drew off at the proper time and followed his trains. The Federals were not disposed to follow, as good generalship would have dictated, for our troops ... could have made little resistance."[46]

As with many battles of the great war, area legends and rumors abound. One of the most familiar tales surrounding Davis Bridge is of the existence of a cannon, left behind at the battle's conclusion, and visible only at a low level that the Hatchie River has failed to reach in decades. One former resident of the area remarked that as a young child in the 1940s, he saw a crew of timber cutters hitched to a "barrel ... barely visible above the murky waters ... all corroded and red looking."[47] Other residents of Hardeman County, the home of the battle site, have proclaimed to have jumped from the cannon's barrel while engaging in an afternoon swim in the river. As far as the recovery of the cannon and the proof of its existence goes, only time will tell.

The third day of the battle of Corinth—more commonly known as the battle of Davis Bridge, Hatchie Bridge, or Metamora—has gone largely unnoticed since its occurrence on Sunday, October 5, 1862. Second only to Shiloh as the largest battle in West Tennessee, the site was the location of a conservatively estimated 500 Union and 400 Confederate casualties. The estimated 15,000 participants of the battle have long since gone; only a fraction of their names are recorded. However, through the valiant efforts of the Davis Bridge Memorial Foundation, the battlefield is well on the way to being preserved for future generations.

Herbert Wood, president of the organization, has led a two-decade struggle to purchase several acres of core battlefield for preservation purposes. In the late 1980s, the initial $2,750 purchase of five acres provided the cornerstone for the existence today of more than two hundred acres, more than half of the core battlefield, under the ownership of the State of Tennessee. The work of Wood and fellow Davis Bridge preservationist Rex Brotherton was duly recognized in May of 2006 when the duo received recognition with the Tennessee Civil War Preservation Association's Robert A. "Bob" Ragland Award, a tribute given annually to recognize outstanding preservation efforts of Civil War battlefields. Additionally, the land east of the Hatchie River—the site of heavy bloodshed and the location of the strongest Confederate resistance—is privately owned, but negotiations to purchase this 650-acre tract have been ongoing. Currently, the Civil War Preservation Trust rates the Davis Bridge battlefield as under a "low threat" of losing its potential preservation status.

With the 2004 opening of the multimillion-dollar interpretive center in Corinth as an extension of Shiloh National Military Park, the future looks bright for the preservation of the Davis Bridge battlefield. Many proponents of the preservation of this site feel that Davis Bridge has the potential to be a true phenomenon, possibly to be linked to Shiloh and Corinth and become associated with the National Park Service. As of the publication date for this book, plans were underway to transform an early Twentieth Century schoolhouse in Pocahontas, located on highway 57, into a state-of-the-art visitor's center. The potential for such an occurrence should serve as a major catalyst for the understanding and appreciation of the battle and lead to the rightful recognition this battlefield deserves.

Davis Bridge site. No known picture of the bridge exists. Photo by author.

Memorial near bridge site. Photo by author.

View of Hatchie River bottom from Metamora Hill. Photo by author.

Sgt. William Clark Newlon, Third Iowa, was seriously wounded at Davis Bridge.
Courtesy of Chris Green.

Capt. William J. Somervell saw action at Davis Bridge. Courtesy of Paul Gibson.

William Cabell was seriously wounded at Davis Bridge. Courtesy of Confederate Veteran.

These two shells were recovered in the 1970s by a diver at the site of Davis Bridge. Photos by author.

"The path of Glory leads but to the Grave."

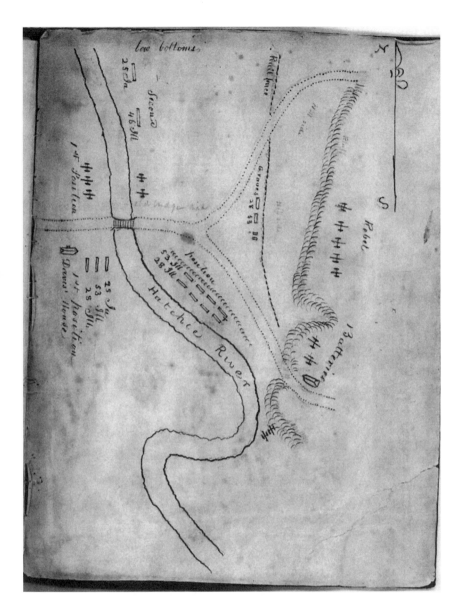

Acting 2ⁿᵈ Lieutenant William D. Price (shown on the bottom of the previous page) of Co. A, 53ʳᵈ Illinois, was killed at Davis Bridge. A letter and map were sent to his father detailing the location of William's burial. The young soldier's body was recovered from a mass grave and returned to his home town for burial in the family plot. Such events took place for hundreds of families across the nation during the tragic days of the American Civil War. (Photo and map courtesy of Paul Russinoff.)

CHAPTER EIGHT

HARTSVILLE

"We were after them ... to kill, main or
capture the whole squad."
December 7, 1862

On December 7, 1862, an incident took place in the small town of
Hartsville, Tennessee, located approximately twenty-five miles north of
Lebanon. The incident is commonly regarded as the boldest and most
successfully executed cavalry raid of the War between the States. In
addition, the outcome of the affair propelled Colonel John Hunt Morgan
to legendary status and brought about what many saw as his long-overdue
promotion to brigadier general.

Morgan's presence in the Hartsville area had been influential long
before the day of the cavalry action he so masterfully led. He had actually
begun the publication of *The Vidette*, a local paper that often served as a
means of making known his philosophies and ideals. The paper is still
under publication to this day.

One issue of *The Vidette* contained a proclamation in which Morgan
stated that an issue of the *Cincinnati Daily Gazette* had contained an article
calling for "Morgan's friends to pay for the acts of their favorite Chieftan"
[sic]. Noting that his attacks on Union soldiers, having previously been
respectful of private property of the troops, would now be comprised of
"the law of retaliation into full force." In turn, for every dollar taken from

his fellow supporters of the Confederacy, Morgan declared two would be taken "from all men of known Union sentiments."[1]

In an effort to maintain cohesiveness among the citizens in the Hartsville area, Morgan had earlier used the paper to outlaw the sale of flour or bacon to Federal troops. He also noted in an issue that the legal tender for the area was Confederate Treasury Notes, and those refusing to complete transactions involving these would incur "most severe penalties."[2]

Morgan's command eventually became based in Murfreesboro with the Army of Tennessee. Troubled by the news that a Federal garrison had been established in Hartsville and the nearby communication of Castalian Springs and Gallatin, Morgan saw an attack as inevitable. Persistence paid off for Morgan when General Braxton Bragg granted him permission for such an advance upon the Federal position in Hartsville.

R.T. Pryor, Company D, Second Kentucky, recalled the elation that Morgan's selection of his regiment, along with the Ninth Kentucky, brought to members of the group. Captain J.T. Morehead's Ninth Kentucky served with Major J.W. Hewitt's Second Kentucky in Colonel Roger W. Hanson's Brigade and would be under the command of Morgan's uncle, Colonel Thomas J. Hunt, during the Hartsville excursion. The two infantry regiments of 700 men and Robert Cobb's battery joined Morgan's men to create a Confederate force of approximately 1,300 men.[3]

Morgan's march from Baird's Mill to Hartsville was conducted under far-from-desirable conditions. An estimated four inches of snow lay on the ground, and a participant noted, "It was required for the infantry to march … over sloppy roads, and at all times to be subjected to great cold." No bridge crossed the Cumberland River in the area the Confederates desired to use in crossing, and a soldier explained that it was necessary for the cavalry to swim part of the way over. One Confederate stated, "Day and night they kept a record breaking gait" and that neither "cold nor storm had … terrors for these Kentucky Confederates."[4]

Mr. John Hinton lived near Hartsville, and three days before the battle allegedly rode through, closely following Federal pickets, stopping at the widow Kirby's home, four miles east of Hartsville. Hinton was fearful of attempting to try to reach his planned destination of Mr. Frank Kirby's home, two miles farther away and across the Cumberland River, due to his possession of a paper detailing the position and strength of the Federals at Hartsville. Widow Kirby and her teenage daughter listened to Hinton's explanation of his situation and offered assistance. Young Miss Kirby ripped a slit out of her old sunbonnet, wrapped the paper around it, replaced the slit, and sewed it up. "With a woman's wit and a veteran's courage," the young girl set out on horseback for Mr. Kirby's home; the whole time the bonnet negligently hung from her neck. The anxiously awaiting Kirby listened to his niece's story and invited her inside.[5]

Frank Kirby's son, a boy of about twelve, whistling as he walked from the house, gave the impression of driving up the family cows. Once out of sight, the lad quickened his pace and soon re-appeared with a group of Morgan's men, who reportedly received the paper from Miss Kirby.[6] The accuracy of this report is questionable, but within a few short days, the success of the alleged piece of paper's contents would be certain. Morgan's scouts reported that approximately 1,500 Federal troops—considerably less than the actual number of more than 2,000—were based in Hartsville.

Having left Baird's Mill on the morning of December 6, 1862, Morgan's men had only rumors to use as a basis for their destination. Tradition holds that the troops received notification at 2 PM that day in Lebanon that the next morning they would attack the Federal installation at Hartsville.

During the night of December 6, a portion of Morgan's men began crossing the Cumberland at Puryears Ferry. Two flat boats belonging to a local resident were used in the crossing, which was to take no more than five hours. Instead, the crossing took seven hours.[7]

R.L. Thompson of the Ninth Kentucky remembered being two miles from Hartsville and that his position was:

> " ... a thickly wooded country and close up to a ford on the Cumberland River. There in the stillness of that cold, starlit night the various regiments received their orders ... Asleep in the town was a force of ... Federals. We were after them, our object being to kill, maim, or capture the whole squad or, failing, receive a like fate. Such is ever the game of war ... our battalion began laying out the rail fence in gaps on the side of the road ... we established our base and placed guards at the ford in sight of the enemy's camp fires ... and were closing in around the enemy while they slept." [8]

Henry L. Stone, a fellow member of the Ninth Kentucky added, "We left camp after sleeping one hour and a half, and got in position in five hundred yards of the enemy at five o'clock in the morning, before it was light."[9]

Before the sun rose on the morning of December 7, the Union pickets sounded the alarm that the Confederates were attacking. Reports have the initial contact taking place between 6:30 and 6:45 AM; many of the participants agreed that a large number of the members of the Thirty-ninth Brigade were still sleeping when the contact occurred.[10]

The Thirty-ninth Brigade had spent much of its three-month existence marching and had gained a new commander in Colonel Absalom Moore just five days earlier. Since Moore's assumption of the brigade's leadership from Colonel Joseph R. Scott, warnings of Confederate presence in the Hartsville area had been issued but had largely gone ignored.[11] This seems difficult for modern students of the war to comprehend, since Morgan and his men were so well-received in Hartsville and the surrounding area.

Morgan's brother-in-law, Basil Duke, had left many of his cavalrymen on the south side of the Cumberland while he pushed the remainder of his command to rendezvous with Morgan. Some fifteen men were actually suffering from the frozen conditions, to the extent that they were left behind. In addition, Col. James D. Bennett kept the Ninth Tennessee Cavalry in Hartsville along the Hartsville-Castalian Springs Road to lessen the possibility of a Union escape. The battle would prove to be Bennett's last; the well-liked commander of troops from Macon, Sumner, Smith, and Wilson counties would die from typhoid-pneumonia in January 1863.[12]

The large number of campfires in the Federal base gave Morgan and his staff, observing the area, the first notice that the number of enemy soldiers reported by his scouts was too low. Duke informed Morgan, "You have more work cut out for you than you bargained for." Morgan replied, "Yes, and you gentlemen must whip and catch these fellows, and cross the river in two hours and a half, or we'll have six thousand more on our back."[13]

Morgan's words were near prophetic as Colonel John M. Harlan, in command of the Tenth Kentucky Infantry nine miles away in Castalian Springs, heard cannon fire toward Hartsville. Harlan had been in Hartsville for two weeks before being relieved by the Thirty-ninth Brigade under Colonel Joseph Scott. Harlan topped a nearby hill and saw smoke rising and sent for twenty-five wagons to follow him to Hartsville and salvage stores.[14] Meanwhile the battle, estimated to have lasted only one and a quarter to two hours, ended before Harlan reached the town.

The battle's commencement was marked with the explosion of a caisson belonging to Col. Robert Cobb's battery. A witness recalled that the explosion scattered "men and horses with a frightful noise ... Near this gruesome spot we found the mangled body of young Watt from Paducah. He was so shockingly disfigured from the explosion that we would not have recognized him but for the gay tinseled artillery cap we saw him so merrily smile under a few moments before ... " In fact, David Watt had been sitting atop the caisson when it exploded.[15]

The eyewitness to the caisson's destruction continued:

> "Close by lay Lieut. Ethridge ... a noble specimen of the American soldier. Little did he think of his sad fate when, on the march, he jocosely requested us, should misfortune befall him, to write his lady love on the flowery banks of the majestic Mississippi. Near the crest of the hill ... we recognized Lieut. Thomas, wounded in the left breast. At each gasping breath of the dying hero the blood spurted and besmeared his richly gilded sword belt. Near by, leaning against a large oak tree, sat his chivalric messmate, Lieut. Rogers, of Phil Lee's company. He appeared almost lifelike, so much so we called to him. No answer given, we were assured that his brave spirit had found a home among the angels. Near this hornet's nest of the battle, we found the body of Capt. Crockett. It must have been a hand-to-hand fight, for he was so blackened with powder that we could scarcely recognize him."[16]

The 104th Illinois Infantry formed in a line of battle on a hill a quarter mile northwest of town. Putting on their overcoats as they hurriedly lined up, the Union soldiers were much better clad than their enemy; a majority of the cavalrymen of colonels Cluke and Chenault had rags on their feet.[17] All the while, the snow and cold temperatures teamed to increase the misery of the Southern soldiers.

The 106th and 108th Ohio Infantry regiments filed to the right of the 104th while Nicklin's battery of the Thirteenth Indiana Artillery of twelve-pound cannon lent support. The Union right flank was quickly turned when the dismounted Confederate cavalry charged down Hartsville Ferry Road. Before fleeing and abandoning the artillery, the 106th Ohio fired only one round. The 108th Ohio joined the retreat[18] too late for many of its members, who fell captive to Morgan's onslaught.

A Confederate wrote, "The firing soon became general, and of all the fighting ever done that was the hottest for an hour and fifteen minutes. The bombs fell thick and fast over our heads, while Morgan's men yelled at every step, we all closing in on the Yankees. I fired my gun only two or three times."[19]

Cobb's battery joined the Second and Ninth Kentucky regiments in pushing the Federal left flank back into their camps. Dislodging sharpshooters and a battle line, the Confederates advanced over rough terrain and a deep ravine before capturing "two pieces of artillery and a stand of colors" at the river's edge.[20]

A participant wrote, "McDowell, Lee, Joyce, Moss, Higgins, and others, with swords in hand, rushed forward and by command and cheer renewed the charge until victory was smiling on the star-flowering banners of a band of heroes as brave as ever heard bugle call on embattled plain."[21]

Captain Nat Crouch, Company B, Ninth Kentucky, demanded the surrender of Colonel Moore on the bank of the Cumberland. Crouch asked the Federal officer, "What do you surrender?" Moore's reply was comprehensive: "My whole command."[22]

One Confederate cavalryman wrote of the battle's outcome, "There was a hot time in the old town of Hartsville ... beginning a little after daylight ... I remember fording the river several times and returning each time with a prisoner on my horse."[23]

The Confederate victory had resulted in the capture of three infantry regiments and one cavalry regiment, a total of more than 1,800 prisoners. In addition, more than 1,000 stands of arms, ammunition, clothing, stores, and sixteen wagons now belonged to Morgan's victorious men.

The significance of the captured supplies was later stated in Basil Duke's evaluation of the battle at Hartsville. He proclaimed, "The most valuable capture at Hartsville was of boots and shoes, for some of the cavalrymen ... had no other covering for their feet than rags."[24]

As noted earlier, Chenault's men were predominantly poorly shod. This was but a slight deterrent for Chenault's services in the battle caused Morgan to promise the officer a promotion to brigadier general. Morgan was only a colonel himself at the time and, although acting as a brigade commander, was unable to do so.[25]

A cavalryman supported Duke's statement in noting, "We took the whole force prisoners ... all their small arms, wagons, etc. I captured a splendid overcoat, lined through and through, a fine black cloth coat, a pair of new woolen socks, a horse muzzle to feed in, an Enfield rifle, a lot of pewter plates, knives and forks, a good supply of smoking tobacco, an extra good cavalry saddle, a halter, and a pair of buckskin gloves, lined with lamb's wool, also a cavalry hat."[26] This gentleman's recollections obviously centered on the items gained from the struggle and focused little on the captives.

The cost in casualties was significant, yet more so for the Union army. For the Confederates, 21 men were killed and 104 wounded. Fourteen Confederates were also listed as missing. For the Union forces, the number of captured is regarded to have been 1,834. In addition, 204 Federal soldiers were wounded and 58 killed.[27]

One of the Confederate deaths was that of Craven Peyton, a young blonde-haired soldier. Peyton received a pistol ball near his knee while charging a battery and initially seemed safe from serious injury. Though he received the care of a kind-hearted local lady, Peyton "fretted himself to death and died of exhaustion." In fact, the diagnosis of blood poisoning was determined as the youth's cause of death.[28]

The home of a local lady, Letty Halliburton, was used as a hospital for the Confederate wounded. Every room of her mansion was occupied by Morgan's wounded, and Mrs. Halliburton generously "bestowed her entire bed linen to serve as bandages" for the wounded.[29]

Dr. John O. Scott was the only Confederate surgeon left on the battlefield with the wounded and remarked that:

> "the circumstances of this battle were different from any I have ever known. The victorious heroes … had left the dead and wounded on the field of carnage, and for an hour or more there reigned a silence as gloomy and profound as a graveyard during the weird hours of midnight. Nothing was to be seen save here and there wounded soldiers and abandoned worthless muskets. A wagon belonging to some negroes was pressed into service and … wounded conveyed to the mansion."[30]

One wounded soldier surnamed Edwards had been shot through the right lung and was informed that death was imminent. An attendant recalled:

> "believing he was dying, he requested one of the nurses to pray for him. The nurse … rushed for the chaplain, Mr. Pickett. It was a touching scene … to see the eloquent divine on bended knees by the side of the dying hero and hear him utter a prayer to the Eternal King of heaven so earnest and fervent that the most hardened and wicked wept like children."[31]

Dr. Scott recorded the fact that kind citizens of the Hartsville area saw that the dead of the battle were decently buried "with headboards marked so plainly that in after years the resting places of these heroes could be located by friends."[32]

In the late 1800s, nine Federal casualties of the battle were discovered in a mass grave. As a reporter of the era wrote, "the greatest diligence was exercised soon after the great war ... to collect all the Union dead into national cemeteries, some were overlooked ... near Hartsville ... and recently they were discovered by grave diggers." None of the bodies was able to be identified, yet the blue cloth and U.S. buttons present in the grave caused investigators to conclude these were casualties of the December 7, 1862 battle. The nine were taken to the national cemetery near Nashville. [33]

Recognizing the achievement and valor of Morgan's men in the Battle of Hartsville, General Bragg ordered the name "Hartsville" inscribed on the banner of each participating Confederate regiment. Morgan gained his commission to brigadier, and his men were the recipients of cheers and praises in their return march to Murfreesboro. Though he would be killed later in the war, Morgan narrowly escaped death or injury during his move from Hartsville. Cannon fire from Colonel Harlan's troops arriving after the fight hit a tree above Morgan and his staff, sending wood fragments into the air.[34]

Today the Hartsville battlefield is fortunate to have a thorough seventeen-stop driving tour that adds understanding of the conflict. Located near the junction of highways 141 and 25 north of Lebanon, Hartsville allows visitors to pay homage to "The Thunderbolt" John Hunt Morgan and others who bravely risked their lives at this small town in Tennessee.

The reward for these efforts is that Hartsville is considered to possess a "low-threat" status in the Civil War Preservation Trust's rating system. The Battle of Hartsville Preservation Association gladly accepts any assistance in continuing and furthering their efforts, ones that have yielded results and garnered recognition for Mr. Tim Heath of the association. In 2004, Mr. Heath's work related to the driving tour and a book on the battle resulted in his receipt of the Robert Ragland Award from the Tennessee Civil War Preservation Association. This award, given to a high contributor of preservation related to Civil War sites, is one of the many accolades certain to come for this individual, group, and the Hartsville battlefield.

Dr. John Orlando Scott was the only Confederate surgeon left after the battle. Courtesy of Confederate Veteran.

This was the location of Letty Halliburton's home. A yellow flag flew above her home as a sign that wounded could come there for help. Every room of her house and all bed linens were used for the care of the wounded. Courtesy of Tim Heath.

Location of Cobb's battery. Courtesy of Tim Heath.

Location of Maj. Robert Stoner's battery of two Mountain Howitzers. Courtesy of Tim Heath.

With four inches of snow on the ground and bitter cold weather, Morgan's men crossed the river at this location. Courtesy of Tim Heath.

View of the Hartsville battlefield. Courtesy of Tim Heath.

A bloodstain resembling a man's face can be seen on the floor of the Averitt-Herod House. Courtesy of Tim Heath.

CHAPTER NINE

SALEM CEMETERY

"A ... spirited little brush with the Confederate forces"
Leander Stillwell, 1920
December 19, 1862

In December 1862, Jackson, Tennessee served as a major link for Union-controlled railroad and telegraph lines. General Jere Sullivan commanded the Jackson district for the Northern army and feared an attack on the area was certain. Sullivan believed, as did other Federal officials, that Nathan Bedford Forrest would lead the Confederate assault, and thus Sullivan called for the buildup of Federal defenses in the area.

By mid-December, Forrest had entered West Tennessee, and on December 18 captured 2 artillery pieces and more than 150 prisoners in a struggle at Lexington, a short distance east of Jackson. Union colonel Adolph Engelmann was sent to Jackson that evening to take command of Federals retreating from Lexington. With him were the men of the Forty-third and Sixty-first Illinois regiments under the leadership of Lt. Col. Dengler and Major Ohr respectively.[1] In the early stages of the march, Engelmann met factions of the Eleventh Illinois Cavalry, Fifth Ohio Cavalry, and the Second West Tennessee Cavalry.

Engelmann's forces reached the area of Salem Cemetery and established their camp in a field near the burial ground. The location on the outskirts of Jackson had been used since 1800 for a host of activities: revivals, a campground, public park, and, of course, a cemetery. At the time of the battle, an iron fence enclosed the area. Pieces of the structure, partially destroyed on December 19, 1862, are still found occasionally in the area.

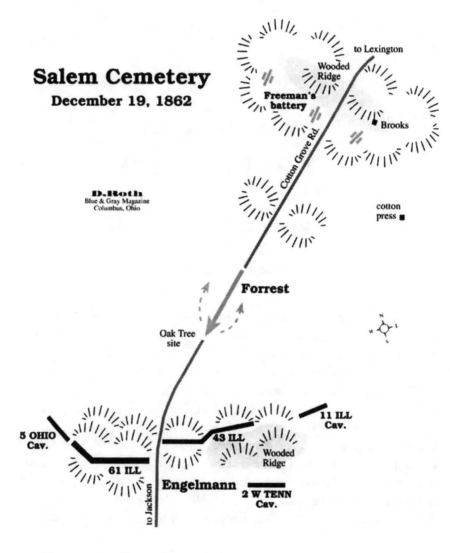

Having initially understood that the venture toward Jackson was merely a scouting trip,[2] many of the Union soldiers had made the trip without carrying blankets. The unusually cold night magnified the misery of these men, who were discouraged from building campfires that would likely give away their location. When one group of soldiers in the Sixty-first Illinois attempted to start a fire, Engelmann, wearing cavalry boots and jumping into the flames with both feet, extinguished the fire and urged the men to "keep cool" in his heavy German accent.

Meanwhile, the Confederates had established their camp approximately one and a half miles to the east of the Union bivouac. Unaware of the close proximity of the Federals, Forrest's men lit fires in their camp located on both sides of Cotton Grove Road. The chilled Northerners could see the Confederate fires from their camp.

Engelmann briefly entertained the idea of attacking the resting Confederates, but was convinced otherwise in a conversation with Col. Dengler of the Forty-third Illinois. Dengler noted the Union troops' lack of acquaintance "with the lay of the land and that night attacks were risky at best."[3] Engelmann heeded the colonel's words.

As daybreak approached on December 19, the cold soldiers of Engelmann's command "presented a doleful appearance-all hollow-eyed, with blue noses, pinched faces, and shivering." Allowed to build small fires to use for cooking breakfast, one member of the Sixty-first Illinois recalled, "I made a quart ... of strong, hot coffee, toasted some bacon on a stick ... with some hardtack, had a good breakfast and felt better."[4]

Engelmann ordered his men to position themselves on the slightly elevated ground of the cemetery. Union soldiers hid behind headstones, trees, and fences as Col. Engelmann, atop a black horse, awaited the Confederate approach. The signal to fire upon the men in gray would come from Engelmann dropping his raised saber.

Almost a half mile of open ground lay in front of the Union soldiers. The crackling sound of rifles came from this area as a group of blue-clad cavalrymen, earlier sent as scouts over a hill in the distance, fired and retreated in intervals. The purpose of this action was to draw Forrest's men into the trap set for them at Salem Cemetery.

The Confederate's Alabama Cavalry Corps and the First Kentucky Cavalry, lined four across, approached the cemetery in pursuit of the Union scouts. As the southern cavalry closed within firing range, Major Ohr of the Sixty-first Illinois gave the order to fire by file. His regiment, on the west side of the road, and the Forty-third Illinois to the east side, opened fire upon the Confederates,[5] taking them largely by surprise.

A member of the Sixty-first Illinois explained that "the effect of our fire on the enemy was marked and instantaneous. The head of the column crumpled up."[6]

Another Union soldier wrote, "like the Lyon waiting his prey we laid still they was thinking all was rite ... we waited until we could see them wink and then rose up and fired one of the most-deadly fires in their ranks ever fired."[7]

From the Confederate perspective, the situation began to go awry as the wormwood fence that aligned both sides of the road was knocked down in a number of places, and riderless horses ran in all directions. One Confederate lieutenant and two privates became pinned down by Federal gunfire, at least one of them under his dead or dying horse. All three, fearing the worst, used their horses as shields.

The exodus of the Confederate horses caused Engelmann's horse Bragg to panic. The animal ran down the middle of the road some distance before the officer was able to regain control of the steed. With this done, Engelmann returned to the site of the action.[8]

Forrest ordered Captain Freeman to set up his artillery to saturate the position beyond the trapped Confederate cavalrymen. Among the cannon placed on both sides of the road approximately one mile northeast were two recently captured Union pieces. Issued in January of 1862, the rifled guns had been captured hours earlier in the skirmish at Lexington. In the course of the war, some half dozen of these cannon, dubbed "Bull Pups," would fall into the hands of Forrest's men.

The unfamiliarity of Freeman's battery with the recently acquired guns resulted in shells flying beyond, into, and falling short of the Union position. This phase of the battle caused the three pinned-down Confederate cavalrymen to shudder in fear. They were rescued when Col. Dengler[9] moved forward and rescued the now-imprisoned Confederates.

Freeman placed a six-pound smooth-bore Napoleon to the west of Cotton Grove Road. One rifle gun sat in the middle of the road, another in the yard of the Brooks' farm to the road's east side. Twentieth- and twenty-first-century archaeological work has determined the exact location of these guns in precisely measuring the distance from the location where a host of friction primers were found.

Additional archaeological work has pinpointed the locale of the death of one of only two Union soldiers killed at Salem Cemetery. Pvt. Elisha Stout, a member of the Sixty-first Illinois, was decapitated, and six others of the same regiment were wounded when a shell landed at the location of the modern-day welcome center. South of the cemetery, Adam Kehl, Company A, Eleventh Illinois, was killed when a shell exploded near him while he held a number of horses.

As the Confederate infantry had closed to within 100 yards of the Union position—still concealed at this point—a barrage of fire erupted from the

Union infantrymen. An undetermined number of Forrest's men were killed or wounded at the spot marked by a large oak tree. Today a marker occupies the former location of the tree where the bulk of an estimated sixty to eighty of Forrest's men were killed or wounded at Salem Cemetery.

The effectiveness of the Federal fire can largely be attributed to the position Engelmann's troops held. To the west of Cotton Grove Road and having the protection of headstones and a variety of trees were the men of the Fifth Ohio Cavalry and the Sixty-first Illinois. Slightly to their front and to the right of the road were the men of the Forty-third Illinois and Eleventh Illinois Cavalry. A wooded ridge stood near the center of these two units and fronted the Second West Tennessee Cavalry, protecting the rear of the Federal position.

As the precision of the Confederate artillery fire improved with the quickly growing familiarity with the captured Federal pieces, Engelmann felt it to be in the best interest of his men to withdraw. The retreat toward Jackson was "done in good order and according to all rules and regulations."[10] The battle of Salem Cemetery was over.

Approximately 1,000 to 1,500 men participated in the battle, which lasted between one and four hours, depending upon the source being consulted. The most authoritative source, the Salem Cemetery Battlefield Association, describes a duration of two hours.

Caught unaware, Forrest again proved his ability to escape defeat and obtain victory from a superiorly manned and better-positioned foe. Forrest's objective in moving into the area had been to keep the Union army in Jackson, enabling two of his subordinates, colonels Russell and Dibrell, to make additional raids in West Tennessee. With this being accomplished at Salem Cemetery, Forrest would become able to focus on the towns of Humboldt and Union City.

On the night of the battle at Salem Cemetery, a skirmish took place a few miles to the south near the modern-day junction of Hart's Bridge Road and Perry Switch Road. Major Nicholas N. Cox led his troops of the Tennessee Battalion to fulfill Forrest's orders to "destroy bridges and culverts on the railroads from Jackson to Corinth and Bolivar."[11]

Aware of Confederate activities in the area, Captain David Hassleton Harts and eighteen men in command, Company C, 106th Illinois Infantry, spent the frigid night keeping a vigilant lookout for such near their location. Harts's men occupied a blockhouse on the Harrison Trestle along the Mobile and Ohio Railroad. From the blockhouse, the Federals saw a group of crouching figures walk onto the railroad track. This caused

Harts to order the lights inside the blockhouse to be extinguished and for preparations to be made for action.[12]

The shadowy figures belonged to Confederate Captain Whitwell and the men under his command, including James Coble, John Bates, Dave Mathis, Green Leeper, and Egbert Shepard. Seeing the lights of the blockhouse extinguished and realizing the danger of the situation, Mathis jumped from the track as he told the others to do the same. The request was made too late, as it came within seconds of the command to fire from within the blockhouse.

A Federal volley poured from the blockhouse as the Confederates jumped from the trestle. One of the invaders failed to escape the fire and was seen falling. John Bates crawled to his fallen comrade and, though unable to discern the victim's facial features, felt a moleskin cap on the man's head. Such a head covering belong to James Coble. Bates and the other survivors retreated to safety. The next morning, the Federals emerged from the blockhouse and discovered the corpse of a red-haired Confederate where he'd fallen.[13]

The body was hastily buried in a nearby field, in an unmarked grave. A short period later, another group of Union soldiers, witnessed by a local woman, began uncovering the body, possibly thinking it belonged to one of their own. Realizing otherwise, they reburied the soldier.[14]

For fifty-one years, Coble's grave remained unmarked and largely forgotten. In March 1914, the *Commercial Appeal* and the *Jackson Sun*, two West Tennessee newspapers, published a letter from Captain Harts, asking for assistance in finding the grave and identifying the soldier killed in the fire his order initiated. A lady surnamed Harris read the plea and recalled seeing the removal and reburial of the body. Coble's comrades, not knowing what had happened to his body, provided additional fact that lead to the identification of the soldier. Harts personally paid $300 and had a monument erected at the site.[15]

The inscription on the monument is written as:
James Coble
10th Tenn. Forrest's Cavalry
Grave unknown for 51 years,
Killed Storming Federal Blockhouse This Place,
Night, December 19, 1862

The monument is located on private property and should be respected as such.

A modern-day visit to Salem Cemetery finds much of the area largely unchanged from the day of the battle. Cotton Grove Road is in its same location, yet it is paved and provides easy access to the cemetery from Jackson. The Salem Cemetery Battlefield Association, under the leadership of tireless individuals such as Malcolm Wilcox, has done an outstanding job in erecting monuments, an information center, cannon, markers, and in restoring graves. It is due to Mr. Wilcox's generosity in sharing his knowledge of this conflict that the bulk of information is provided. Unless cited differently, Mr. Wilcox is the source of information in this chapter.

Among the graves in Salem Cemetery is that of Adam Huntsman, the gentleman who defeated Davy Crockett in his 1836 bid for Congress. This event caused Crockett's departure for Texas and eventual entry into folklore. Huntsman's headstone and numerous others dating to 1862 bear bullet marks, many from the Confederates firing at Union soldiers hiding behind them. Other marks on the headstones have been attributed to twentieth- and twenty-first- century vandals.

With the planned purchase of 300 acres in the area and the display of a host of artifacts from the battlefield, the preservation of this location should be secured for years to come.

View of Salem Cemetery. Photo by author.

Ground Zero Pavilion at Salem Cemetery. Photo by author.

North view from cemetery. Forrest's initial contact was at the top of the distant hill. Photo by author.

From this location, Engelmann gave his order to fire on Forrest's troops. Photo by author.

Forrest's campsite the night before the battle. Photo by author.

CHAPTER TEN

PARKER'S CROSSROADS

"Charge 'em both ways."
December 31, 1862

Nathan Bedford Forrest stands among the premier military leaders of the American Civil War. As the pages of this chapter testify, no analysis of battles occurring within the state of Tennessee could or should be compiled or completed without the devotion of a great deal of space to the man whose rise from private to brigadier general is unique in its own right. Perhaps in no situation are his capabilities of military strategy and coolness under fire made more evident than in the action on the last day of the war's second year at a West Tennessee town known as Parker's Crossroads.

Located approximately thirty-five miles east of Jackson, Tennessee at the junction of Interstate 40 and Highway 22, the battlefield is a well-preserved and effectively interpreted series of stops owned by the State of Tennessee and under the maintenance provisions of the City of Parker's Crossroads. The Parker's Crossroads Battlefield Association has worked diligently since its formation in October of 1993 to preserve an amount of land now nearing 200 acres in size. In spite of the successes, the battlefield is considered by the Civil War Preservation Trust to have "some threat" to its preservation, primarily due to the location its prime real-estate holds.

The major catalyst in this successful endeavor—as most projects tend to rely heavily on one person or small group of individuals—is Tennessee state representative, Civil War enthusiast, and Parker's Crossroads businessman Steve McDaniel. It is Mr. McDaniel, unless otherwise noted, who provided the bulk of information for this chapter during an interview in November 2005. His unselfishness and deep devotion to his admitted "pet project" has reaped benefits for the community of Parker's Crossroads and for untold visitors past and future. McDaniel will quickly note that without the multifaceted efforts of a number of local, state, and federal agencies and volunteers, the June 2006 dedication of the Parker's Crossroads National Battlefield would be far from a reality. This was the first such event in Tennessee since 1971.

Visitors at Parker's Crossroads today are greeted with two walking trails, a northern loop and southern loop, a seven-stop driving tour, interpretive signs, well-groomed fields, several cannon, and a host of improvements brought about to enhance the understanding and appreciation of this location in respect to the conflict of 1861-65. An authentic log cabin serves as the park's information center and houses educational facilities and a bookstore. More than 1,400 acres of the battlefield are on the National Register of Historic Places. While the park itself is open to the public, it is imperative that each visitor notes the boundaries and respects the rights of private ownership of property in the area of the battlefield.

Parker's Crossroads—or Cross-Roads as it was known at the time of the battle—was named for the Reverend Dr. John M. Parker, a resident of the area. The locale's namesake was both a Baptist preacher and a physician. While the battle to come would be associated with Parker's label, the area would also be referred to as Red Mound for a natural feature south of the crossroads.

Parker, his wife, and their children lived in a house on the northeast side of the junction of the east-west Rock Springs Road and the north-south Huntingdon-Lexington Road. The house is no longer standing, but it is a generally accepted fact that it faced west, toward the Huntingdon-Lexington Road. While no photograph of the home is currently known to exist, descendents noted and historians recorded its exact location. To the north of the house, an orchard stood at the time of the battle and has recently been replanted. The area must have been rather impressive, as a census some dozen years before the battle valued Parker's holdings at $50,000.

Forrest's first raid into West Tennessee had been highly productive, with numerous gains and minimal casualties. From mid-December 1862, two Union brigades under Jeremiah Sullivan had been pursuing Forrest in an attempt to halt his movement across the Tennessee River. Col. Cyrus Dunham, in charge of a brigade comprised of Indiana, Iowa, and Illinois troops, had arrived at Parker's Crossroads on the morning of December 31, 1862 to assist in hindering the elusive General Forrest from reaching safety across the river.

Forrest's soldiers had arrived at a site known as Flake's Store on the twenty-ninth of December, spending that night and the thirtieth at the location, resting from their exploits of the previous weeks. Located on the McLemoresville Road, approximately four miles from Parker's Crossroads, the store belonged to a gentleman whose son was in the Confederate army, a not-so-common occurrence in the Parker's Crossroads area. The store sat atop the dividing ridge of the Mississippi and Tennessee rivers and was only 100 yards from a natural spring. Archaeological evidence shows that the Confederate camp extended some distance from the store, a fact solidified with the large number of men, horses, and equipment Forrest had with him at this stage of his campaign.

Around 4 AM on New Year's Eve, Forrest's men were awakened and ordered to prepare to march. They made their southeast move toward Parker's Crossroads at the same time the Federal forces approached from the southeast. With Forrest's Cavalry Brigade were the men of Col. George G. Dibrell's Eighth Tennessee Cavalry, Col. James Starnes' Fourth Tennessee Cavalry, Col. Jacob B. Biffle's Ninth Tennessee Cavalry, and Lt. Col. Alonzo Napier's Tennessee Cavalry Battalion. As well, Lt. Col. T.G. Woodward's Kentucky Battalion joined Major Nicholas Cox's Tennessee Cavalry Battalion and Col. A.A. Russell's Fourth Alabama to create a formidable force. Capt. Samuel L. Freeman and Lt. John W. Morton added their respective batteries to the fine collection of soldiers.

Col. Dunham's Federal command of the Third Brigade, Sixteenth Army Corps, Army of the Tennessee was a well-worn group of soldiers, having slept but a few hours on the night of the thirtieth. The men had taken part in a skirmish prior to sundown, adding to their fatigue. Three dead Confederates had been left on the field as Dunham's men awaited contact with what was reported to be 8,000 men and twelve pieces of artillery under the leadership of General Forrest. With some 1,554 men at his disposal, Dunham's command consisted of Lt. Harry Lee's 30 men and 3 pieces of the Seventh Wisconsin Battery, Col. H.J.B. Cummings' 405 men of the Thirty-ninth Iowa, 529 men of the Fiftieth Indiana Volunteers under Lt. Col. Samuel Wells, and 65 men of companies A and E of the Eighteenth Illinois Volunteer Infantry of Captain John Davis.[1]

Before daybreak, Col. Dunham sent forward Lt. Judy's Company A, Fiftieth Indiana as an advance guard. Confederate pickets made contact with this detachment near Parker's Crossroads. Dunham had the Fiftieth Indiana and Eighteenth Illinois move up the McLemoresville Road in pursuit of the rebel pickets.[2]

General Forrest's men were enjoying breakfast on the property of Hiram Britt. The troops were scattered about the heavily wooded lots of Britt's when a sentinel fired a shot from a hill near the Britt house around 8:30 on the morning of the thirty-first. The soldiers ended their meals and hastened toward Hicks Field.[3]

Dunham's pursuit continued past the home of Dr. Williams and to a point approximately one mile northwest of the physician's residence that would play an integral part in the battle's activities. The Federal soldiers now stood on a small rise facing north, toward Hicks Field. The modern-day roadbed is in close proximity to the location of the war-era route, enabling any visitor to obtain a true feel for the movements of December 31, 1862. Three cannon of the Seventh Wisconsin Battery stood to support the Federal battle line, formed and faced north toward what was initially assumed to be "a large company or two small ones" of Confederate troops. The men of the battery had earlier encountered the Confederate pickets in the initial contact of the day.

S.L Halstead recalled, "we drove the rebels from their breakfast table with the grub smoking hot. Having been on half rations and no rations for the past five days, I availed myself of the opportunity and partook of a well got up Southern breakfast. In the meantime gun No. 1 was feeding those for whom the breakfast was prepared shot and hard shell."[4]

Another Union soldier wrote, "we were a little waked up by hearing our battery that was ahead thunder a few saucy toned notes at some foe invisible to us. Twas a calm clear cool morning, and the thunder tones of the cannon rang defiantly over the West Tennessee hills and we stood behind the hill awaiting any subsequent turn of affairs in a very unconcerned manner."[5]

Facing south toward the Federals just 400 yards away was Sgt. Nat Baxter's twelve-pound bronze mountain howitzer, a gun of Freeman's Battery. The gun had been moved into its position on the northern edge of Hicks Field along a sunken road. General Forrest had personally directed the placement of Baxter's howitzer and, according to Baxter, left the gun with the support of fewer than two hundred Confederates.

To the northwest side of the Confederate position, hidden in a ravine, the horses of the supporters Baxter mentioned were being held. Reportedly, a short distance eastward in a location known as Hick's Hallow, Confederate horses were being shod at a blacksmith's shop minutes before Baxter's gun opened fire.

The first shot from Baxter's howitzer was immediately effective, as it hit one of the three Federal guns, rendering it unusable. The exchange of fire from the remaining Federal cannon with that of Baxter's and the subsequent addition of five cannon to the Confederate battery created tense moments for the men of the Seventh Wisconsin, as well as for local residents such as Dr. Williams. A cannonball entered the roof of his two-story home and exploded, fortunately without injuring any of the occupants.

A member of the Seventh Wisconsin Battery recorded this series of events. In a letter, S.L. Halsted wrote:

> "The battery was then ordered to take a position at the end of the lane heading north ... to feel the strength of the enemy ... The first gun fired was answered by four batteries of two guns each, from the surrounding hills, so arranged as to bring a perfect crossfire on our boys, yet they stood firm to the guns and replied with the utmost energy. The first damage done was to kill my horse ... .At this place Sergeant Minott J. Marsden was struck with a shell across the back and side, leaving his right lung bare."[6]

Confederates of Col. George Dibrell's Eighth Tennessee Cavalry and Col. A.A. Russell's Fourth Alabama Cavalry effectively delivered the crossfire Halstead recalled. In turn, the Federal casualties mounted quickly. Relying primarily on the artillery fire, Forrest's men killed or disabled several horses and gunners.[7]

In the fury of the early minutes, S.L. Halstead struggled to carry the wounded Sgt. Marsden to safety. Halstead explained:

> "it was with much difficulty that I could get the infantry to come and help me take him off the field ... I carried

him three rods before they would assist ... The shell from eight guns all concentrated on the two doomed pieces. Yet the boys stood firm till ordered to withdraw ... poor Marsden, knowing he had but a short time with us, saw us retiring, and asked why we were falling back. I replied, to take a more commanding position. He answered, 'Tell the boys not to leave the guns till the rebels are whipped, and I and my country are avenged.'"[8]

The Union soldiers began a retreat from the field south of Hicks Field, rallying at a house slightly northwest of Dr. Williams's home. The Confederates followed the blue-clad troopers as the two forces traded possession of the area of land twice. Captain Davis's Mounted Eighteenth Illinois joined Lt. Col. Wells and his men of Company F, Fiftieth Indiana in this task. Artillery fire was exchanged as "the fire for a little while was intense on both sides." Seeing the Confederate formation on a nearby ridge, Dunham sought neither an additional rally nor bombardment. He ordered his command to cease fire and return to the crossroads where the rest of the Federal troops awaited them.[9] During this Union retreat to the south of the crossroads, no organized line of battle took shape, nor were any shots exchanged. Archaeological examination of the area has revealed few artifacts to offer proof otherwise.

Forrest's troops followed the Federals toward Parker's Crossroads. A feint charge was mounted, giving the illusion of an attack to come from the east. Instead, the Confederates moved to the point where their main assault would come from a northerly direction. This would create havoc in the Federal lines where artillery positions were established to meet the phony attack and were caught in the main attack trying to reposition their guns. One Federal quartermaster noted that there was so much confusion at the crossroads at that phase of the battle that if the Confederates had actually moved into the intersection rather than make the move they did, a quick and certain victory would have been Forrest's reward.

The rapidness of the Federal movement is impressive to modern historians when taking into account the fact that a detachment of Major Attkisson's Fiftieth Indiana had moved one cannon by hand following the killing of the horses intended for such purposes. Dunham sent the wagon trains to the rear of the newly established Federal line where one company each from the 39th Iowa and 122nd Illinois guarded it.[10]

Two companies of the Fiftieth Indiana were moved forward to check the Confederate advance as soon as Dunham detected the existence of the counterfeit assault. Lt. Col. Wells of the Fiftieth Indiana sent Company G, under Captain Caruthers, and Company B of Lt. Davis, in a double-quick manner to the lane and along the edge of a wooded area. Company G met what one participant recalled as "a galling fire" in the lane and the result was a retreat to the woods, where they joined Company B.[11]

A "vigorous attack" ensued as the Confederates approached the newly established Federal line. On the Federal left stood Company G of the Fiftieth Indiana, recently forced to retreat from the Confederate force they now prepared to meet with additional troops. Furthermore, Dunham's 1,500-man line, from left to right, included the 39th Iowa, 122nd Illinois, a detachment of the 18th Illinois, and the 50th Indiana.[12]

Col. Dunham had the initial plan to place the Federal artillery between the 39th Iowa and the 122nd Illinois for an effective bombardment of the Confederate batteries. The Confederates' intense cannon fire had negated this strategy while their musket fire pelted the left side of the Federal line. Dunham saw his artillery being placed at this point of the Union line and rode to the spot, ordering the guns to be moved between the aforementioned Iowa and Illinois positions. To his self-proclaimed "utter astonishment" Dunham was informed that, with the ammunition of the Federal batteries nearly depleted, any change of position would be highly unproductive.[13]

The ferocity of the action, as well as the pride in accomplishing one's mission, is shown in the words of a member of the 122nd Illinois in a letter written three days after the battle. He stated:

> "Here it was before our line was quite formed, before we had fired a gun at them, that Andy was wounded by a musket ball through the leg below the knee. He fell like a dead man and I thought at the time he was killed ... Shells were bursting around so thick ... Our Co. was marched along in the timber some 75 or 100 yards from where Andy fell and we were halted, ordered to a fence, and the word given, then the 122nd fired its first round in battle. For one hour from this time the roar of battle was tremendous and the 122nd won its name as a regt of more than common bravery."[14]

The Confederate artillery was arranged in a half-moon shape, the left flank of which heavily struck the easternmost side of the Union lines. Captain Freeman's Battery was divided with half on either side of Morton's guns at center. The effectiveness of the Confederate fire was no less than tremendous.

A Union infantryman recalled, "The Rebs had all their guns posted on a hill or a chain of hills bearing down on our line … almost impossible for a man to stand up and not be hit by all the most incessant storm of shell shot & other tricks brass 12 and 6 pounders are in the habit of chawing [sic] up and spitting out."[15]

Noting the deadly barrage coming from the Confederate left, Col. Dunham decided to capture the position "at all hazards." In addition to the withering cannon fire, Dunham's men faced the southerly musket fire from Forrest's dismounted cavalry, whose horses were being held in the orchard to the rear of the Parker house. Two unsuccessful Federal charges brought Dunham's troops within eighty yards of the Confederate battery on the extreme Federal right, but double canister shot eliminated any prolonged stay on the part of Dunham's aggressors.[16]

The Federals positioned themselves behind a rail fence where the Confederate barrage continued to inflict casualties. Without orders from or the consent of General Forrest, Lt. Col. Thomas Alonzo Napier seized the opportunity to launch a charge upon the Federal position held by the Thirty-ninth Iowa. Napier reached the fence line, reportedly climbing upon the rails, where he was mortally wounded. Napier's life, along with those of several of his command,[17] was lost through this reckless endeavor and lack of discipline. Napier's mindset could have been altered through the rumored situation of his intoxication at the time of his self-initiated attack. Recently discovered evidence disclosed in an eyewitness account proposes that Napier may have actually been on horseback rather than climbing the fence, as has been the accepted scenario for years.

Confederate colonel V.Y. Cook expounded that "Col. Thomas Alonzo Napier … who … fell … at Parker's Crossroads while gallantly leading his regiment to a charge in the very face of enfilading Federal fire … a gallant but unnecessary sacrifice and unauthorized by General Forrest."[18]

At this stage of the battle, Forrest sensed the weakness and discouragement of the Federal troops. Near midday, the Confederate general sent word to Col. Alfred A. Russell and his Fourth Alabama Regiment to move with Lt. Col. T.G. Woodward's Kentucky cavalry eastward. Col. Starnes's Fourth Tennessee Regiment, moments earlier arriving on the field from near Huntingdon, was sent to the west. The purpose of these two deployed units was to encircle the Federal position and attack the Union lines from the rear.

This movement left a weakened Confederate line now facing a superiorly numbered Federal force. Forrest moved several pieces of Freeman's artillery to positions that enabled the Confederates to produce an effective crossfire, should the Federals choose to advance. No sooner had the artillery been repositioned than Dunham's command moved from the safety of the fence line and advanced toward Forrest's center, now manned only with Col. George G. Dibrell's Eighth Tennessee Cavalry. Grape and canister discharged into the advancing Federals, again inflicting heavy casualties and pushing Dunham's men back to the safety of the split-rail fence.[19]

One Federal soldier explained the carnage in his area of the field: "While we lay by the fence ... a shell came thru the fence and burst directly under the legs of Geo Finch ... John Hagler ... was wounded in the left arm and leg while laying by my side ... Finch was not more than 5 feet from me when he was killed. Alex Jemison of our mess was struck by a piece of shell making a slight wound in the calf of the leg."[20]

J.H. Anderson added his thoughts from the Confederate aspect of the battle:

> "When shot and shell were flying thick ... Lieutenant Baxter ... walked among his men, encouraging them with his manly bearing and words of cheer ... part of Dibrell's Regiment was supporting our battery ... they moved a little farther to our right. Not being aware of what the move meant ... Baxter ran up to them and said, 'Boys ... don't leave us. We will whip them.' They soon convinced him that he need have no fear of their leaving him, and then they poured the shot into the Yankees thick and fast."[21]

A Federal participant recalled:

> "The enemy showed twelve guns ... the shell, hard shot and grape fell in uncomfortable proximity to us. Our horses, one by one, dropped. Sergeant Alford Walworth fell dead at his post, after having been wounded. Louis Kohnkie was knocked off his horse with a shot through the shoulder. Corporal John Abraham received a shot

through the thigh and scrotum while sighting his gun; died January 8, 1863. Private O.L. Clark received a fatal shot through the head; Liet. Samuel Hays ... shot in the hip ... Barret a shot in the leg that disabled him ... Wright ... shot through the lower thigh ... Isaac Dewey was made perfectly deaf from the near bursting of a shell; Gen. McCready was severely scratched and clothing badly torn with shell and bullets, yet did the boys right nobly stay to their guns ... and having no support from the infantry spiked their guns and stood with arms folded biding their time for an easy capture."[22]

The Fiftieth Indiana's bayonet charge made against the Confederates was exemplary. Col. Dunham remembered it as "a style never surpassed and seldom equaled." The regiment forced its way through the weakened Confederate lines before being pushed back.[23]

Forrest ordered the Confederate center forward as Starnes, Russell, and Woodward moved northward from their positions into the Union rear. Starnes's command charged up the Lexington Road, entering the left flank of the Federal position where the Thirty-ninth Iowa stood. These untested green troops were little match for the veterans of Forrest's command.

In his report to Lt. John R. Simpson, Col. H.J.B. Cummings wrote of this stage of the battle:

"After fighting an hour or more in this position, some officer came down to my right and gave an order which several of my officers say to me was, 'Rally to the rear.' ... my command ... being raw troops and imperfectly drilled ... mistook the command for an order to retreat, and commenced breaking for the rear ... I hastened towards the right of the retreating men and gave the order to halt and the command to form, and had done much towards reforming when we were opened upon by a heavy fire of dismounted men. They then in more confusion fell back towards the fence and received standing the fire of the enemy's artillery ... Under this fire, so unexpected from front and rear ... about the half of my regiment broke to the left of our line as formed in behind the fence and crossed the road into the cornfield upon the opposite side."[24]

The movement into the cornfield had followed the last Federal offensive of this stage of the battle. Forrest's men had moved southward toward Red Mound, there surrounding and capturing many of the counterattacking Federals. With the latter was William Peter of the 122nd Illinois. He and his brother Samuel had each worn an iron bulletproof vest that day; yet, as William wrote his parents, "It was while we were passing through the strip of timber that Sammy fell. I did not know of it till we were formed on the other side of the timber. Then one of the boys came up and told me that Sammy was wounded in the leg." Samuel's leg wound, caused by an artillery shell, would prove fatal.[25]

L.B. Corbin, a friend of the mortally wounded Samuel Peters wrote:

> "we turned to the Rebs in our rear, when we had got a little way from the fence, a shell burst right before and nearly severed both legs of Samuel Peters, he died soon after— both legs were broke ... Our Col. is badly wounded, struck by a musket ball in the leg below the knee. While one of our company ... was holding up the Col's head a ball took off his arm at the elbow."[26]

The ability of the Confederates of Starnes, Woodward, and Russell to envelop the Union lines is a superb example of the effective use of terrain in a military engagement. A modern-day survey of the system of ravines used to infiltrate the Federal right makes it clear to see how dozens of men could be secretly moved within rock-throwing distance of an otherwise superiorly positioned foe. Add smoke and undergrowth to the scene and Forrest's achievement becomes even more understandable.

In addition to encompassing the Federal lines, the Confederates had managed to capture a wagon train. The train had moved into a hollow, seeking shelter, when the encircling movement by Maj. John P. Strange, Forrest's adjutant, led to the discovery of the train. The wagons and attendants would not spend the entire day as captives, though, as Forrest's men were themselves about to be placed on the defensive.

In Forrest's words, "We drove them through the woods with great slaughter and several white flags were raised in various portions of the woods." With the Union forces now divided into two distinct groups, one near Red Mound, three-fourths of a mile southeast of Parker's Crossroads, and another behind the split-rail fence, the battle entered a stage of cease fire.

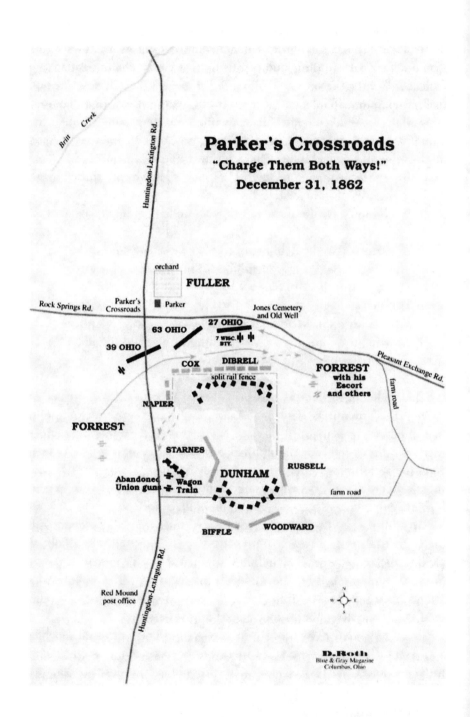

Parker's Crossroads

"Charge Them Both Ways!"
December 31, 1862

orchard

FULLER

■ Parker

Rock Springs Rd.

Parker's Crossroads

Huntingdon–Lexington Rd.

Britt Creek

Jones Cemetery and Old Well

Pleasant Exchange Rd.

63 OHIO

27 OHIO

39 OHIO

7 WISC. BTY.

COX

DIBRELL

split rail fence

FORREST
with his Escort and others

NAPIER

FORREST

farm road

STARNES

Abandoned Union guns

Wagon Train

DUNHAM

RUSSELL

farm road

BIFFLE

WOODWARD

Huntingdon–Lexington Rd.

Red Mound post office

N
W E
S

D. Roth
Blue & Gray Magazine
Columbus, Ohio

General Forrest sent an aide with a flag of truce toward Col. Dunham's position. Dunham rode toward the aide, demanding his directive. When the aide replied that Forrest was under the impression that Dunham had surrendered, the Federal officer brashly replied that the Confederate general was mistaken, and that if any surrender had taken place, it had done so without Dunham's knowledge or permission.[27] The aide left Dunham and returned with the news to Forrest.

Gen. Forrest had the aide return to Dunham and demanded an unconditional surrender. Dunham met this request with a challenge for Forrest: "If he thinks he can take me ... come and try."[28] The aide once more returned to Forrest with less-than-victorious news.

Forrest had thrown a body of cavalry to the rear of the enemy; others of his troops were flanking the Union troops. Little choice other than surrender seemed logical. The white flag of the Federals was then displayed; "the order to 'cease fire' came from the Confederate officers, and the day seemed won" wrote one young Confederate.[29]

During the truce, generally regarded as an hour in duration, Confederates counted prisoners and began attending to the wounded and preparing the dead for burial. Nat Baxter, whose artillery had effectively cut into the Federal lines, conversed with his counterparts in blue. Men of each army struck up conversations with those of the enemy. Rumors exist today of Federal guns having been stacked near the Parkers' woodpile.

As the heated negotiations progressed, Col. Charles Carroll, a member of Forrest's staff, sprinted on horseback toward the Confederate commander. Pulling his horse alongside Forrest's, Carroll stated, "General, a heavy line of infantry is in our rear. We're between two lines of battle. What'll we do?"

Forrest's response, now legendary, was "Charge 'em both ways!"

James Martin Metcalfe was a member of Freeman's battery and gave his recollection of the incidents: "Heavy columns of infantry, supported by cavalry, were soon seen coming rapidly in Forrest's rear. It was he who was hemmed in. The trapper was trapped. To cut his way out seemed hopeless, but it must be done. It was Forrest's way."[30]

The predicament the Confederates found themselves in was predicted minutes earlier by an older soldier, who reprimanded his younger counterpart for pilfering through the personal effects of a dead Federal soldier. The older man rebuked the youngster in saying, "you may be in the same fix as that dead Yankee before night. Forrest is going to get the worst licking a soldier ever got."[31] Given the fact that the Federal position was almost surrounded, the elderly man's premonition certainly brought stares and chuckles from those who heard it. That would change in the near future.

Forrest's request for a two-front assault had to have come at a time when the Wizard of the Saddle was baffled at the possibility of Federal reinforcements arriving at the battlefield. Forrest had sent four of Captain McLemore's companies to Clarksburg for the purpose of protecting the Confederate rear and preventing such an incident from taking place. McLemore hadn't seen the approaching Federals, but had heard the cannon fire in the direction of the crossroads. Taking a different route to Forrest's location than did the advancing Federals, McLemore's arrival came too late to have any impact upon the battle's outcome.

The Federals arriving on Britt Hill were members of the Twenty-seventh Ohio under the command of Col. John W. Fuller. Fuller's Ohioans had gained a respected name for themselves weeks earlier at Corinth and now seemed destined to trap the elusive Forrest. Fuller had heard the sounds of battle, even noting the change in location as he neared Parker's Crossroads.

The recorded history of Fuller's Ohio Brigade noted this in its coverage of the incidents at Parker's Crossroads:

> "The firing was first heard to the right of the point where the road from McLemoresville crosses that leading from Huntingdon to Lexington; in half an hour it was directly in his front; in half an hour later it was all to the left of the crossing, thereby rendering it certain that the enemy, who approached from McLemoresville, was rapidly driving Colonel Dunham's Brigade before him."[32]

Less than two miles from the battle, Fuller was informed by an orderly to halt his movement toward Parker's Crossroads until General Jeremiah Sullivan, now three miles behind Fuller, caught up with him. Fuller dispatched Capt. Dustan, a brigade assistant adjutant general, to ride to Sullivan, explain the situation, and request a countermand to the order to halt. Moments later, another courier, who had been ordered to inform Col. Dunham of the arrival of reinforcements, informed Fuller of his inability to reach Dunham. Fuller felt assured that he must move forward to relieve the entrapped Federal forces.[33]

Some 200 yards from the position where Fuller would gain an overview of the battlefield, General Sullivan arrived to assist in the relief of the surrendering Federals. To the left of the Huntingdon-Lexington Road, Col. Zephaniah S. Spaulding's Twenty-seventh Ohio positioned themselves with two pieces of artillery from the Seventh Wisconsin at their front. To Spaulding's right, or west of his position, stood Col. John W. Sprague's Sixty-third Ohio. Straddling the Huntingdon-Lexington Road and positioned to its right was the Thirty-ninth Ohio of Col. Edward F. Noyes.[34]

General Forrest rode to the area of the peach orchard at the rear of the Parker home in an attempt to evaluate the situation. The Federal reinforcements had taken this area, and Forrest was only eighty yards from the enemy's lines before realizing this. A Union officer saw Forrest as he neared the orchard and yelled for him to halt and surrender. The wily Confederate general replied that he had already done so and was merely intending to round up more of his command to do so.[35]

Capt. J.C. Jackson witnessed the incident and stated that Forrest said, "All right. I'll go back and get what few men I have left." The general then rode off "as deliberately as a farmer going from his plow." When Forrest reached his escort, located nearby, he notified them that a charge would take place.[36]

Forrest returned to the Confederate main line and immediately began a recruitment process of individuals to assault the northern Union position. Nat Baxter was actively requested to join in the attack, and informed General Forrest that he had no weapon to use in the attack. Forrest replied that this didn't matter, as he only wanted to make as big a show as possible.

While Forrest readied a group of men for the attack upon the newly arrived Federal troops, Company F of the Twenty-seventh Ohio was gaining accolades that are duly noted in the company muster roll for November and December of 1862. "The Regiment took part in the Battle of Parker's Cross Roads, charging upon and capturing a Rebel battery of 7 guns and retaking a second brigade composed of the 37th Iowa, 122 Illinois, 50th Indiana, 7th Tennessee and two companies of the 10th Illinois that were completely surrounded, two pieces of their artillery spiked and the brigade making terms of surrender."[37]

Approximately 250 Confederates, 4 caissons, 6 cannon, 400 horses, and a large amount of small arms fell into the possession of the Union soldiers in the orchard and the area around the Parker house. Seventy-five thousand rounds of ammunition, five wagons, two ambulances, and their teams were also captured. Drivers and artillerists lay killed or wounded in great numbers. Major Cox of Forrest's command was among the captured officers.[38] In addition, the captured Federal train would soon be retaken at the site of its earlier fall to the Confederates.

N.N. Cox recorded the events following his capture at this juncture of the battle:

> "... a number of ... men were captured—J.P. Strange, Forrest's adjutant general, Gen. R.P. Neely, of Bolivar, and myself ... we eventually reached Cairo, Ill ... While there ... a detachment of Federal soldiers with fixed bayonets came into camp and called out five of us ... We had seen a newspaper threatening to retaliate on some of General Forrest's men for something he was charged with having done. We were marched to a horrid dungeon, or jail, in the town of Cairo, and locked in a loathsome, filthy cell. No explanations were given or a word said that furnished us any information as to what it meant."[39]

Freedom eventually came to Cox and others of his party, who escaped captivity while later being moved to another site.

Following the recapture of the Federal wagon train, one of the Union soldiers witnessed these events: "Co. G ... of our Regt and Co. A of the 37th Iowa were guarding our baggage train ... Henry Wilcox received a ball through his brain, relieving him from further toil and pain in this world ... Poor Wilcox died bravely at his post."[40]

The newly arrived Federals fought relentlessly against Forrest's men as Confederates were showered with shots from the Federal cannon, now with replenished ammunition. General Forrest and his approximately one hundred "volunteers" threw themselves at the Federal artillery, scattering gunners, infantry support, and horses from three Union caissons. The horses fell captive to the Confederates,[41] a small recompense for the number the butternuts had lost.

During this charge, Forrest's hat was shot through. Having already lost a number of horses to shots in earlier brawls, and being no stranger to personal wounds, the general slowly evaluated the incident. Briefly slumping in his saddle, Forrest declared, "Came pretty close, didn't it?"—though his exact quote had no less than one expletive added.

Among the members of the Thirty-ninth Ohio, several were less fortunate than their enemy's commander. Lieutenant Colonel Redfield was severely wounded in the left shoulder, Major Griffiths in the head. Other severely wounded officers included Captain Browne and Lieutenant Rawls. Redfield, Colonel Cummings would note in his report, "retired only when his wound compelled him to do so."[42]

Forrest's idea to charge in both directions had paid off. The Union offensive now transformed into a defensive mode, and Forrest was able to lead his command from the field as the Federals pulled back, awaiting a suspected Confederate assault. Near Clifton, Tennessee, Forrest's command re-crossed the Tennessee River on New Year's Day 1863. Casualty estimates regarding the battle of Parker's Crossroads vary for each army. With both sides claiming victory, the battle marked the end of a chapter on Forrest's West Tennessee campaign. Forrest claimed to have seen dead Federal soldiers "piled up around the fences" and estimated as many as 1,000 Union dead and wounded compared to 60 killed and wounded and 100 captured among his own men. One of three cannon captured days earlier in the struggle at Lexington was lost to the Federals as well.[43]

One severely wounded Confederate was the nineteen-year-old former flag bearer of the Fourth Alabama, Arthur Hopkins Beard. The young man had recently been promoted to captain of Company I, but the wounding and eventual amputation of his left arm caused his resignation from military service.[44]

General Sullivan, estimating Forrest's force of 1,800 to have been 7,000 strong, reported that as many as 200 Confederates lay dead on the field. Union losses were reported to be 27 killed, 140 wounded, and 70 missing.[45]

Among the Union casualties listed in regimental reports, the Thirty-ninth Iowa Volunteer Infantry had several entries. The three men killed in action, Corporal Jacob Koontz, Waggoner Dimmick Layton, and Private Jonah C. Stearns had their names memorialized. Dying of wounds received at Parker's Crossroads, the same regiment listed four privates: Edward Brown, William H. Chamber, Benjamin P. Chase, and Solomon Pontius. Those wounded and surviving from the Thirty-ninth Iowa totaled thirty troops.[46]

The Seventh Wisconsin Light Artillery had borne the brunt of the initial contact with the Confederates at Parker's Crossroads and, while the actual numbers aren't as high as in other units, the percentage is certainly greater. Three members of the Badger State Flying Artillery, Second Lieutenant Samuel Hays and sergeants M.I. Marsden and A. Wallock were killed in action on the last day of 1862. Three additional men died of wounds received that day. All holding the rank of private, they were Orrin L. Clark, John Graham, and Minot J. Marsden. In addition to these six, four other members of the group were wounded.[47]

The 122nd Illinois Volunteer Infantry had the highest casualty total at Parker's Crossroads with seventeen men being killed in action, three succumbing to their wounds after the fight, and two men surviving their wounds. Dying of their wounds were privates John Brown, Philip Eglehoft, and William Snyder. Those killed in action at Parker's Crossroads included privates Joseph Crossgrove, John Davis, Henry Opperman, Evan Richmond, George Finch, Samuel Peter, John Baird, Henry Wilcox, Jesse Bryant, James Gibson, Samuel Hicks, Ernst Russell, and Roswell Briggs. Corporals Reuben Fletcher and William Moore and Second Lieutenant Pleasant L. Bristow were the additional names reported for the 122nd.[48]

Following the carnage of the thirty-first of December 1862, care for the wounded of both sides began. As noted in the number of individuals in this and other battles who later succumbed to their wounds, the severity of the wounds and often a lack of proper care increased the death rate. W.R. Britt, a resident of a home just north of the crossroads, recalled holding lamps inside his house as surgeons, particularly one with long whiskers, worked on the wounded in the house's hallway. In one corner of the crossroads sat a home whose well was a reported dumping ground for amputated limbs. In the yard of this same house, an unexploded three-inch Hotchkiss shell was uncovered more than 100 years after the battle. Dr. Williams's two-story house, a structure that played a prominent part in the battle, served as a field hospital after the battle. Local legend has bloodstains being visible on the floors of the home until its destruction by fire decades after the battle. Around the Parker house, minié balls and a host of other relics were recovered generations after the struggle on and around the home's grounds. While the Parker house has long since been destroyed, the name of its proprietor lives on. One particular story is noteworthy.

As Fuller's Brigade pursued Forrest near the battle's end, three Union cannon were placed in the yard of the elderly Parker, a known Unionist. Parker realized fire returned from the Confederate artillery could easily damage or destroy his home, and he demanded the Federal cannon be moved. When asked which was more important, the Union or his house, Parker replied to a Federal officer, "My house!" In 1864, Parker died and was buried in a nearby cemetery. He and his wife have graves that face north-south, different from all other graves in the burial grounds. The reason, locals state, is that Parker wanted to be able, upon Gabriel's blowing of his trumpet, to "kick the Yankees back north." Without a doubt, the intrusion of his home changed Parker's stance on the war's outcome.

Taking a strong stance opposite Rev. Parker's, an elderly lady of the vicinity allegedly held a level of contempt for "Mr. Forrest and his hoss critters." For "forming a streak of fight" in her backyard and destroying her garden fence and only ash hopper, the lady claimed to never be able to forgive "the General for this carelessness."[49]

Mass burials were not unique to Parker's Crossroads, yet a Union burial site is clearly marked today along the fence line where the Federal troops made their valiant stand. A recorded but unmarked mass Confederate grave lies south of the crossroads, along the old Huntingdon-Lexington Road, near modern-day Interstate 40. At the time of the battle, the area of the gravesite was a picked cotton field.

One of the most unusual grave discoveries took place in late 1993. Tennessee state archaeologists and Representative Steve McDaniel unearthed a skull, bones of an arm crossed on the chest, and buttons with blue wool attached. The identity of the soldier may never be known, yet theories abound. One possibility is Reuben Ross Fletcher, a member of the 122nd Illinois, whose left leg was shattered at the fence when cannon fire hit nearby. The leg was amputated after his brother carried him to the field hospital, and soon Reuben began complaining of the cold. Explaining that he wished he had listened to his parents and stayed at home, Fletcher complained of a pain in his stomach, the pain of death. Within fifteen minutes, young Reuben Fletcher died and was buried on the field.[50]

While not on the same scale as many of the better-known conflicts of the war, the Battle of Parker's Crossroads was the site of destruction, heroism, and death. The preservation efforts have succeeded at the location and are examples for countless other such sites to follow. Through effort, perseverance, and dedication, the same given by the thousands who fought and the hundreds who became casualties at Parker's Crossroads will last for generations.

Col. Cyrus Dunham, Fiftieth Indiana. Courtesy of P.C.B.A.

Sgt. Nat Baxter. Courtesy of P.C.B.A.

Location of Flake's Store. Forrest's camp was in field at the left center of the picture. A natural spring is in the trees to the right side of the picture. Photo by author.

Rep. Steve McDaniel points to the location of the cannon that fired the battle's first shot. Photo by author.

Hicks Field. The view is in the direction from which the Federal troops advanced. Photo by author.

The remnants of the Huntingdon-Lexington Road lie to the right of the trees. Col. John W. Fuller's men approached the crossroads from the direction faced in the picture. The location of the W.R. Britt home, a hospital in the days after the battle, is in the center background and is the site of a modern dwelling. Photo by author.

The Parker house sat in this vicinity where an orchard has recently been planted in the location of that of the Parkers. The crossroads sat to the extreme right of the picture. Photo by author.

The fence line where Union soldiers made a strong stand. The Union burial site is to the right, just outside the picture. Photo by author.

Union burial site. Photo by author.

In this field, Forrest ordered his men to charge both ways. Photo by author.

Rep. McDaniel points to the hill where Forrest's men stood and fired into the surprised and surrounded Federal troops. Photo by author.

View from Parker's Crossroads toward Interstate 40. Photo by author.

Rep. McDaniel standing at the Confederate cannon position. The crossroads are at the far left of the picture. Photo by author.

Freeman's Battery Monument, the battlefield's first. Photo by author.

Pistol remains recovered from the battlefield. Photo by author.

Graves of Rev. Parker and his wife. Note the different direction they face. Photo by author.

CHAPTER ELEVEN

MURFREESBORO (STONE'S RIVER)

"The onslaught was sudden and the slaughter so great ..."
December 31, 1862–January 2, 1863

In October of 1862, Union major general William S. Rosecrans replaced General Don Carlos Buell in an effort to attempt to crush Confederate resistance within the borders of Tennessee. Seen as too cautious and spending unnecessary time gathering in Nashville, Rosecrans was soon threatened with having his newly gained command taken from him. The general's reply to Henry Halleck explained that an advance upon the Confederate positions would be made only upon the point at which Rosecrans felt adequately prepared to do so. With no further pressure from Halleck, General Rosecrans left Nashville on December 26, 1862 with plans to accomplish the aforementioned objective.

Under his command, Rosecrans had just over 43,000 men of the Army of the Cumberland, also known as the Fourteenth Army Corps. His subordinate officers included, among others, major generals Alexander McCook and George H. Thomas, as well as brigadier generals Richard Johnson, Philip Sheridan, James Negley, Thomas Wood, John M. Palmer, and Horatio Van Cleve.[1] On December 30, the Union army reached Murfreesboro, where they camped less than half a mile from the Confederate base.

Almost 38,000 Confederate troops in the Army of Tennessee were commanded by General Braxton Bragg, a veteran of the Mexican War, who reportedly held mixed levels of esteem among those in his command. This situation possibly arose from Bragg's reputation of ordering the shooting of soldiers exhibiting insubordination. Bragg's reputable corps commanders included lieutenant generals William Hardee and Leonidas Polk, with major generals B.F. Cheatham, John C. Breckinridge, and Patrick Cleburne among his division commanders. Succinct Brigadier General Joseph Wheeler led four cavalry brigades and played a significant role in the days prior to the battle at Murfreesboro.

Wheeler's cavalry had gained the rear of Rosecrans's army on the twenty-ninth, attacking Starkweather's brigade of Rousseau's division near Jefferson at daylight on the thirtieth. Despite an assault that "was handsomely repulsed," Wheeler's men managed to engage the Union wagon train for two hours and, in turn, destroy twenty wagons. The reported Union losses totaled 122 killed, wounded, and missing in this engagement. Wheeler moved to LaVergne and at noon on the same day, attacked and captured McCook's supply train. The damage inflicted upon the Union army in the two encounters was the loss of approximately a million dollars in property and seven hundred prisoners.[2]

B.L. Ridley was a seventeen-year-old boy who heard the struggle at LaVergne. In his first sight of battle, Ridley recalled, "the zipzip of Minies and the basso interlude of the shells beat upon the air ... It sounded like the breaking of millions of sticks, and the cannons boomed like a trip hammer sounds over a stubborn piece of heated iron. Then followed the woo oo oo ing of the solid shot, the whizzing howl of a shell as with a shuck tied to it."[3]

Wheeler arrived on the Confederate left flank at Murfreesboro at 2 AM on the morning of December 31. The smiling cavalryman had "made the entire circuit of Rosecrans's army in forty-eight hours ... bringing back to camp a sufficient number of minie-rifles and accouterments to arm a brigade."[4]

A woman wrote of Wheeler's adventure:

> "At sunset the troops filed onto the front lawn with clanking and rattling accouterments. A small gentleman stepped forward, saying, 'My men have strict orders to touch nothing, sir'. Then, turning to my pale ... mother, he said, 'We have had nothing to eat ...' She called to the

cook, 'put on both ovens and have them ready quick ... she filled the old fashioned bread tray and deftly made dough which she rolled into ... cakes. When the first were done, she said to General Wheeler to call the men ... they received from my mother's hands the fresh warm light bread, while tears fell from her eyes and her lips moved in prayer. As fast as the cakes were cooked she gave them to the men ... no doubt some of the noble band died before their bread was eaten. It was a holy sacrament."[5]

Wheeler's arrival in the Confederate camp occurred only hours before the assault upon the Union position was scheduled to begin. Bragg's memo to his general and staff officers established the line of battle of the Army of Tennessee as such:

"in front of Murfreesboro ... left wing, in front of Stone River, right wing in rear of the river. Polk's Corp ... left wing, Hardee's Corps right wing. Withers' Division ... first line in Polk's Corps, Cheatham's the second line. Breckinridge's Division forms first line, Hardee's Corps; Cleburne's Division, second line ... McGown's Division to form reserve opposite center on high ground ... Jackson's Brigade reserve to right flank ... Two lines to be formed from 800 to 1,000 yards apart, according to the ground. Chiefs of artillery to pay especial attention to posting of batteries and supervise their work, seeing that they do not causelessly waste their ammunition. Cavalry to fall back gradually before the enemy, reporting by couriers every hour when near our lines. Wheeler will move to the right and Wharton to the left ... All quartermasters, commissaries, and ordnance officers will remain at their proper posts, discharging their duties."[6]

Another participant offered this explanation from the Confederate perspective:

"Hardee's Corps, consisting of Breckinridge's and Cleburne's Divisions, were in line of battle to the right of Stone River; Polk's Corps, Cheatham's and Withers's Divisions, were formed to the left of that stream, the

Nashville and Murfreesboro Pike passing through the right division of the corps. General Rosecrans had made a rapid concentration of his forces by various turnpikes leading to Murfreesboro and massed a large force under General McCook on the extension of the left of the Confederate army. That caused a rapid movement of Cleburne's Division from the right of the army to the left of Polk's Corps, leaving Breckinridge's Division on the right of Stone River. General Hardee was given McCown's Division supported by Cleburne ... Hardee in command of the ... left wing." [7]

P.R. Jones, Company I, Tenth Texas Cavalry, served in Ector's Brigade, McCown's Division at Murfreesboro. Not held in reserve as the above memorandum requested, Jones found himself near the left of the advance Confederate line. He wrote of the night of December 30, 1862, just prior to the beginning of hostilities:

"we ... were in a lane with rail fences on each side, about four hundred yards from the main line of the enemy. Orders were to speak only in a whisper, as the enemy's pickets were not more than one hundred yards in front, the plan of battle being to take them by surprise next morning. We took down one of the lines of fence and spread the rails out over the ground next to the opposite string, which was left for breastworks. On the rails we passed the night without fires, most of the men sitting down watching the camp fires of the enemy ... We passed a most disagreeable night ... at times pelted with heavy showers ... I fortunately had a good wool blanket that I had brought from home ... with a hole in the middle large enough for a man's head. I stuck my head through, pulled my hat down, took my loaded gun under the blanket, and thought of what would take place tomorrow."[8]

Joseph Hutcherson, Co. C, Third Georgia, was positioned next to Jones's regiment and on the extreme left of the Confederate line. In Rains's Brigade, McCown's Division, Hutcherson explained:

"spent the night in a large cornfield, the corn still on the stalk, with stacks of fodder here and there from which we drew bundles to rest upon as we listened all night long to the sound of the axes of the enemy, who were felling trees for breastworks. An all night drizzle ... added much to our discomfort as we bitterly thought of the morrow."[9]

Emory Sweet, Ninth Tennessee, Maney's Brigade, Cheatham's Division, added:

"we were placed in a line of battle on the north bank of Stone's River, and although the ground was frozen hard, we were not allowed a spark of fire. The Yankees ... their line of pickets and sharpshooters only three hundred yards in our front. We had orders ... to watch for the skyrocket that would go up in the middle of Murfreesboro the next morning for Cheatham's Division to open fire and advance on the enemy."[10]

The Federal deployment on the night of the thirtieth had Major General Thomas L. Crittenden on the left, with Brigadier General Thomas J. Wood's division occupying the extreme left. Maj. Gen. George H. Thomas held Rosecrans's center with Maj. Gen. Alexander McCook's command standing on the Federal army's right wing.

A self-proclaimed historian of the period wrote of the night's events:

"Rosecrans reported, 'My plan of battle was to open on the right and engage the enemy sufficiently to hold him firmly and to cross with my left at McFadden's Ford, consisting of three divisions, to oppose which they had only two ... the enemy attacked the whole front of our right wing ... which was partially surprised, thrown into confusion, and driven back.' Gen. Bragg says it became apparent that the object was to flank on his right, and he determined to assail him on our left ... For this purpose he moved Cleburne's Division ... "[11]

As dawn approached, a member of the Ninth Tennessee stated seeing a skyrocket fired to signal the battle's commencement.[12] Both the

Confederate and Federal armies' intentions were the same: attack the enemy's right flank; but the Confederates drew first blood.

Whether or not the Confederate attack upon the Union right was a surprise is—as are innumerable aspects of the great war—a topic of debate. Several individuals admit to partially being surprised by the Confederate assault, but the disagreements abound. Lt. Col. G.C. Kniffin of Crittenden's staff downplayed the prospect of being hit without expectation, yet he noted in his analysis of the action that the "first movement was a rush as of a tornado." The Federal divisions of brigadier generals Jefferson C. Davis and Richard W. Johnson were preparing breakfast when attacked at their positions on the right of McCook's line.[13]

Kniffin noted that the steady retreat of the Federal skirmishers did little to relieve the fury of the assault the Confederates soon hurled at the main line of the blue-clad defenders. Major General J.P. McCown's Confederates moved slowly westward as they advanced upon the Union positions; Major General Patrick Cleburne's division stood to his right with Major General James Whithers's further eastward still.[14]

Lt. J.T. Tunnell, Company B, Fourteenth Texas, Ector's Brigade, McCown's Division, somewhat supported Kniffin's claims in stating:

> "When we struck their skirmish line ... we drove them back on their main line so rapidly that we got to within easy gunshot of their main line before they knew it. My regiment confronted a battery of six guns ... but they fired only two or three shots with artillery until we were among them. Many of the Yanks were either killed or retreated in their nightclothes." [15]

To the left of Tunnell's berth stood the brigade of General M.D. Ector. P.R. Jones, a member of this unit, was a young boy who only two days earlier had seen his first dead man, a Confederate struck in the chest by a shell. In the near future, Jones was destined to see many dead of both nations poised to battle at Stone's River.[16]

Prior to the attack on the morning of the thirty-first, Jones recalled that whiskey had been passed down the line where he stood and that:

> "more than half of my company did not drink a drop, but others imbibed freely. It was not given to the soldiers to inspire courage, but to warm them up after their long

exposure to the rain and cold weather. Just about fairly good daylight, orders were given to move forward. The boys went over the rail fence and soon encountered the enemy's pickets, driving them back into their camps, which were well lit up with fires, around which they were cooking breakfast. Many were still in their 'pup' tents asleep and were killed ... The onslaught was so sudden and the slaughter so great that they retreated in great confusion, every fellow for himself and the devil take the hindmost ... we noticed that they had abandoned everything in order to get away ... one of their dead some two hundred yards to their rear ... had been killed still holding firmly to his pot of coffee."[17]

On the extreme Confederate left, Brigadier General James E. Rains had ordered his men into the attack with a ringing command. A member of his brigade wrote, "We swept everything before us for miles. We struck the enemy ... while arms were in stack and breakfast was being prepared." Another added, "The signal was given, we caught the Yankees asleep and got some of their good coffee and ham."[18]

As the Confederate attack advanced, corresponding Federal casualties and prisoners mounted. Cleburne's division found itself heavily engaged with stiff Federal resistance and additionally hampered by thickets and fences.[19] In turn, the rate of Confederate casualties also began to steadily increase. In a succession of Confederate assaults, the result was a level of carnage seldom surpassed in this or other wars.

Colonel John C. Burks, Eleventh Texas Cavalry, had seen the first line of Federals break and shouted, "Forward, boys!" to his regiment. The idol of his regiment, Burks almost immediately put his hand to his chest and fell from his horse, having received a mortal wound. Others in the regiment, proclaimed one member, pursued the Federals until themselves falling from loss of blood as had the "noble, true, and brave" Colonel Burks.[20]

Captain Meredith Kendrick of Rains's brigade received a severe wound to the thigh and propped himself against a tree while growing pale from loss of blood. Pvt. W.D. Dark of Kendrick's command, Company C, Thirtieth Arkansas, offered to carry Kendrick to the rear, but the captain declined the offer. Seconds later, a bullet struck Dark's jugular vein; the private fell dead at Kendrick's feet. Destruction reigned as others attempted to assist Kendrick. Arm and foot wounds were inflicted upon individuals such as Joseph Hutcherson and W.B. Allen before Kendrick could be safely removed.[21]

P.R. Jones of the Tenth Texas found his comrades and himself in a dilemma. He recalled:

> "a battery or two some distance in the rear ... turned loose on us about this time and killed a number of our men. It was here our company had its first men killed. Joe Reynolds ... was the first to fall. Then Thomas Dement and J.A. Holmes and one or two others. We had by this time become badly scattered, every fellow being his own general, keeping up a running fight for two and one-half miles to the cedar brake."[22]

The roar of cannon fire from the struggle was heard by Mrs. Katharine Hubbell Cumming, the wife of a Confederate captain on the staff of Brig. Gen. John K. Jackson. Mrs. Cumming and her two-month-old son were in route to meet the captain when "the booming of those cannon ... broke the stillness of our peaceful abode ... every dull boom ... represented so many lives gone ... so many hearts broken."[23]

The Confederate advance was assisted greatly when Federal units fell apart and retreated into the stationary lines of their fellow men in blue. Friendly fire undoubtedly resulted in additional Union casualties in this phase of the battle.

Meanwhile, the struggle between Cleburne's troops and those of the Federal division of Brigadier General Jefferson C. Davis continued. Only after heated exchanges of fire and a series of charges were the Union soldiers on the west side of the line pushed from their position.

A member of Company H, Twelfth Tennessee, Preston Smith's Brigade, and Cheatham's Division wrote:

> "The Federals were on a hill in the woods. The Alabamans had to go through a field to attack. The fighting was terrific for some time, and our men had to fall back. They were cut to pieces terribly when we were ordered forward to the edge of the field to lie down by an old hedgerow. The enemy cheered like a lot of little schoolboys. Cheatham gave orders for every man to be ready, and at the command

... for each one to rise on his right knee and shoot under the smoke of the enemy's guns. Then we were to load and fire as we advanced ... The enemy advanced downhill. We fired all at once, and rose yelling ... when we fired on them there was a blue line of dead Yanks across the field. We kept as close to them as possible, firing as we advanced. I saw a large ash tree in the edge of the woods, and made for it. When I reached it I was so nearly exhausted that I could scarcely get my breath. I took a swallow of water, and then reloaded my gun. Soon the Yanks' battery at our front in the woods opened on us with grape and canister, and then their infantry too ... We raised a yell, sent a volley into their lines ... and never stopped until we got the battery of six guns."[24]

One-fourth of a mile to the right of Post's brigade that stood facing the Franklin Road, Colonel Philemon P. Baldwin's brigade, joined by Captain Peter Simonson's battery on its right, realigned itself behind a fence near woods. Brigades of Colonel William Carlin and William Woodruff stood with the command of Brig. Gen. Joshua W. Sill to meet the quick advance of Lt. Gen. William Hardee's seven brigades. An estimated 10,000 Confederates began a series of attacks that a member of Crittenden's staff noted as signifying the second distinct stage of the battle on the right.[25]

Confederate brigades of brigadier generals Evander McNair, S.A.M. Wood, Bushrod Johnson, St. John R. Liddell, L.E. Polk, and colonels J.Q. Loomis and A.M. Maginault engaged in heated contests that initially routed Baldwin's brigade. Baldwin entered the woods at the rear of the front line and made an unsuccessful attempt to hold off the advancing Confederates. Major General John P. McCown, leading McNair's brigade, and Liddell found great difficulty in breaking through the portion of the line held by Federal colonel P. Sidney Post's brigade, a location reinforced by an angle where Post's and Carlin's brigades joined.[26]

Not until the third Confederate assault did Hardee's left succeed in forcing Post's withdrawal. The second charge had Brig. Gen. George Maney and Col. A.J. Vaughan replacing Loomis's and Maginault's commands, with little more success than their predecessors had achieved. Col. Frederick Schaefer's brigade of Sheridan's division had met the initial Confederate charge and driven Loomis back to his original position. The order for Schaefer's men to charge was given by Sill, who was soon killed when a bullet hit his upper lip and exited the base of his skull.[27]

The initial Confederate success and subsequent standoff was remembered in John M. Berry's memoir. He wrote:

> "we captured some of the Federal outposts, who pleaded for mercy. Gen. Liddell swore at them, telling them they were fine fellows, invading our country and then asking pardon. Old Jake, the bugler, whacked one of them over the head with his saber ... On we went, and in an open field we found ourselves face to face with the Federal force stationed behind a rail fence. I thought they would kill us all. We laid down ... firing as best we could, we would roll over on our backs and load, then turn back and fire."[28]

By 11 o'clock, the Federal resistance to the initial Confederate advance had virtually ended with casualties again mounting and artillery being abandoned. Rosecrans formed a new line on the Nashville Pike in hopes of making another stand against the Confederate assault. Again unable to fire with their fellow Federals between them and the Confederates, the Union soldiers seemed to be facing disaster. Rosecrans's chief of staff, Colonel Julius P. Garesche, accompanied the general as he personally directed the formation of the line. Standing at Rosecrans's side, Garesche was decapitated when a cannonball hit his head. Blood and brain fragments hit Rosecrans's coat, a somber moment for the commanding general who had heard the ball pass his own head moments before, decapitating his trusted subordinate.

A Confederate first lieutenant wrote of the Federal position:

> "at the south side of a small open field beyond which was a heavy grove of timber, mostly red cedar ... They had concentrated a very strong force of fresh troops and planted ... six batteries of artillery near the Nashville Pike. After resting a few minutes we sent forward a line of skirmishers and then followed in line of battle. We encountered the enemy at the edge of the cedar brake. The ground was level, but overspread with large lime rocks with many lime sinks from a foot to two or three feet deep. The timber was principally cedar, interspersed with

large white oaks and other trees. For some distance we drove them, as we had been doing; but about this time the artillery opened on us and cut the timber off over our heads ... Our men sheltered themselves as best they could behind trees, ledges of rocks, etc. Their front line of battle ... seemed to take fresh courage and began to advance on us, walking a few steps, then firing and falling down to load."[29]

The Round Forest served as one of the most highly contested and fought for segments of any battlefield of the American Civil War. Also dubbed "the slaughter pen," the area became renowned for its violence and bloodshed.

Captain S.F. Horrall, an ordnance officer and inspector on Brig. Gen. John Beatty's staff, recalled the desperation he and other Federals felt during the struggle. "In the cedar woods my brigade fought five hours, being obliged three times to 'change front to rear' to avoid the Confederates' flanking movements. At last the order came late in the day to fall back, and we did with more or less confusion, under fire yet."[30]

General C. Irvine Walker of the Confederate army wrote, "Well do I remember that thicket ... Our effort was to prevent their development of our main line of battle, and at one time half the brigade was on the picket line to prevent this, which was successfully accomplished."[31]

S.R. Etter of the Eleventh Texas added, "There I got wounded in the haversack ... a piece of bomb shell tearing off the bottom of my sack, and I lost my bread which I had baked the night before while in the big white house that stood in the old field where we made the attack in the morning, did not have time to eat it."[32]

Lieutenant J.T. Tunnell, Fourteenth Texas, remarked of the difficult position he and his comrades faced:

"I saw Colonel Andrews, of the Thirty-second Texas ... coming down the line from the right, running from one large tree to another waving his hand to the rear, which I knew meant retreat ... A retreat just then was as dangerous as an advance, but was our only salvation from death or capture; so we retreated out of the cedars and across the open field, where we again re-formed our lines. We left several officers and many good men in that cedar brake, many of them killed and wounded and some captured." [33]

P. R. Jones, Tenth Texas Cavalry, offered a summation:

> "this cedar brake ... proved to be well known as the turning point of the battle. The cedars were very dense, making it difficult to keep an alignment while going through to open ground on the opposite side. Those who got through were met with such a volley of grape and canister from ... cannon that had been hurriedly placed by General Rosecrans that they beat a retreat back through the dense cedars as best they could ... Ector's Brigade had several men captured among the cedars ... The cannonading ... appeared to completely demoralize the men. Littleton Fowler ... took refuge among these cedars behind some rocks and said that the cannonading was so terrific that he could have caught birds that were so benumbed they could not fly."[34]

A Confederate advance of major generals Benjamin Cheatham and Jones Withers began focusing on the Union center. Here four Federal brigades, two each of Negley and Rousseau, stood poised for the Confederate advance. Charges and countercharges were conducted; Negley only ordered the retreat of colonels T.R. Stanley's and John Miller's brigades when almost all of the available ammunition, including that taken from the pouches of the dead and wounded, had been used.[35]

A Confederate wrote of the situation:

> "a young man from the Ninth or Tenth Mississippi ... was unpleasantly situated, as the Minie balls were hurled at him thick and fast. Seeing a large tree a short distance in his front, he decided to make for that protection. Drawing himself up into as small a compass as possible, he made for the tree, but upon reaching it found behind it a Yankee soldier, who readily placed the Confederate under arrest, disarmed him; and the two struck for the Federal line. On their way the batteries began a furious

cannonade, with shot and shell ... the Mississippian suggested to 'Mr. Yank' that they lie down and wait for the cannonading to cease. This was readily consented to, and as soon as 'Mr. Yank' had stretched himself upon the ground 'Mr. Reb' jumped on him and disarmed him, and soon, regardless of shot and shell, the two were in ... the Confederate lines ... the account given by the Confederate of his capture and of capturing his captor caused no end of laughter ... General Bragg ... gave the soldier a thirty day furlough."[36]

Eleven Confederate brigades eyed the enemy across the Franklin Road and centered their efforts on the men in blue. Controversial piecemeal attacks across a cotton field led to few positives for the Confederates. Artillery blasts and continuous musket fire greeted them with each failed advance.

Oscar Pinney, Fifth Wisconsin Light Artillery, U.S.A., remarked that the noise of the battle was so terrible that Confederates were often seen stuffing their ears with cotton to protect their hearing. An awful crescendo, Pinney noted, was created by "rifle and cannon fire, shells bursting, men yelling, horses neighing and wounded screaming."[37]

Hammett Dell, a slave in Murfreesboro at the time of the battle, exclaimed that the roar of the battle was continual, with tin pans rattling in the cupboard. In addition, Dell felt the house shake and the earth quiver as he was certain that the day of judgment had arrived.[38]

Captain S.F. Horrall, Fourteenth Corps, Army of the Cumberland, deduced that the Federal success at this juncture was due to the right and left of the Federal line forming a "horseshoe" in the line. He remarked, "To reinforce any part of the line that might be attacked by our force, the Confederates would have, being the outside of the new line formation, to travel any way from one to three miles, while [we] could meet the same emergency by reserves moving one-fourth of a mile or less, being inside the half circle, the Confederates the outside."[39]

In an assault on the Cotton Field, Brigadier General James E. Rains joined many of his comrades in death. A witness wrote, "he occupied the extreme left of the Confederate line, and led his command with a noble daring in the memorable charge ... a Minie ball struck him in the breast, and he fell near the colors, uttering his last words, 'Forward, my brave boys, forward.'"[40]

Murfreesboro

(or Stones River)

Dec. 31, 1862-Jan. 2, 1863

Hord

Remnants of
McCook's Corps
(Johnson's and Davis'
divisions) from the
Initial Confederate
Attacks

Cav.

The climax of the battle
occurs at McFadden's Ford
on January 2, where a heavy
concentration of Union
artillery helps turn back
Breckinridge's attack.

Stones River

McFadden's
Ford

NASHVILLE & CHATTANOOGA RR

Nashville Pike

Rosecrans

Asbury
Church

Widow
Burris

Crittenden

Wood

Palmer

Van Cleve

Thomas

Breckinridge

Cav.

Cleburne

Rousseau

Overall Creek

Cosart

Hardee

Negley

McCown

Cheatham

Asbury Lane

Blanton

Sheridan

Polk

Gen. Smith

Wilkinson Pike

Gresham

SCALE IN MILES

0.00   0.25   0.50

Harding

Withers

Bragg

D. Roth
Blue & Gray Magazine
Columbus, Ohio

180

Additional praise for General Rains came from a subordinate who was quick to explain that, "The sound of cannon and rattle of small arms were as inspiring to General Rains as the first sounds of ballroom music to the lover of dance, and when a battle was in ... his flashing eye and graceful horsemanship were the admiration of his command." The individual also proclaimed that Rains met his fate while at the front of his troops, "encouraging his men onward by the most daring example and patriotic words, when pierced by a bullet that sent that knightly soul back to the God who gave it."[41]

A captain standing nearby remarked, "I saw ... Rains fall from his horse, mortally wounded; and as I turned to mention it to one of my men, a Minie ball penetrated three of my ribs, paralyzing my right leg."[42]

The first day's fighting, for all practical purposes, then came to an end. The bloodshed of the day would cause Murfreesboro or Stone's River to enter the history books as one of the costliest in American history. Unfortunately, another day's fighting, preceded by limited action, lay ahead.

Col. W.D. Pickett, assistant inspector general to Lieutenant General Hardee, recalled the night the last day of 1862:

> "As it was to be expected, there was great rejoicing in the army and throughout the South on the result of the first day's fight at Murfreesboro ... The right wing and right center of a superior army in men and artillery had been forced back for about three miles and double-backed on its center and left wing. At this time ... General Hardee directed me to parole all prisoners that were not dangerously wounded at a large Federal field hospital ... that had been swept over by the Confederate lines, four or five officers being assigned to help me. There appeared to be about one thousand wounded in the house upstairs and downstairs, in outhouses, and on the grass surrounding the house. When the gruesome job was finished ... the inspector general of the army, Colonel Beard ... reported about six hundred officers and men ... in various stages of vitality, from the slightly wounded ... cheerful and talkative, to the mortally wounded. There was no groaning ... at no time ever heard a groan, much less the shrieks and moans of the dying ... Federal litter bearers brought in

the body of an officer ... clothed in a somewhat worn ...
uniform without insignia of rank. He was of slight build,
rather thin ... face, full sandy whiskers. The wound was
from a Minie ball just below the cheek bone, the blood
from which had slightly flowed down on his whiskers ...
It was the body of Brig. Gen. Joshua Sill ... from whom
afterwards was named one of the most important posts on
the Southwest frontier."[43]

Ed Abbott, Fourth Indiana Light Artillery, was with Sill when both
were wounded. He recalled the incident in 1880: "I fell behind the wheel
of the gun with a hole through my left thigh ... Sill ... was shot and killed
not over ten feet from where I lay ... I thought of my mother's last words
on her death bed, to be a good boy, and meet her in a better world." Abbott
spent the next nine days after receiving his wound lying unattended on
the battlefield.

Private James W. Ellis, Company E, Fourth Arkansas, Evander
McNair's Brigade, McGown's Division, was severely wounded just prior to
sunrise on the first day's fighting. His arrival at a hospital in Murfreesboro
was far less than comforting to the soldier:

"So many soldiers were there that I received no
attention. One of the surgeons said, 'Don't fool with
him now. In the morning we will take that arm off.' ...
soon after dark I crept out, took up an empty bucket,
put my blanket over my wounded arm, and passed the
guards as if ... going to the pump out on the street ...
I reached the depot and left on the first train going
southward. I had relatives ... at Shelbyville ... The
ladies of the neighborhood, hearing that a wounded
soldier from Arkansas was at Uncle Joe Green's, came
to see me ... my arm was saved."[44]

Lieutenant R. A. Miller, Company B, Twenty-fourth Mississippi
Volunteers, was wounded shortly after capturing a sword early on the first
day. Inscribed upon the sword was the name "I. Abernathy, Lt. 37th Reg.
Ind. Vol." Still in possession of the sword more than forty years later, Miller
unfortunately had received a wound that necessitated the use of crutches
for the remainder of his life.[45]

Dr. F.G. Hickman, a surgeon in McCook's corps, gained fame for his service to wounded Confederates at Murfreesboro. Though serving his fellow man, regardless of the uniform worn by the wounded, Hickman was not given the same level of respect. He recorded one such instance:

> "I had selected for my regimental hospital a house which had been vacated ... on the Wilkinson or Manson pike ... General Kirk, of Illinois ... would not allow us to remove him from the ambulance, and said to us, 'Boys, get out of here as soon as possible, or you will all be captured.' His ambulance was driven on at once and escaped. I gave orders for the ambulance drivers to follow ... but ... the Confederate cavalry soon overtook them ... I did not follow, but went across the fields. One of the ambulances contained all of my surgical instruments, my valise and surgeon's sword. The surgeon's sword was a Christmas present ... In my valise ... was an ambrotype of my brother in law ... I regretted the loss of the picture more than all ... "[46]

G.B. Moon of Unionville, Tennessee visited the area of the battlefield on the night of December 31, 1862 with a group of friends, all hoping to catch their first glimpse of a battlefield. What Moon found, or failed to find, haunted him thirty years later as he wrote this recollection of the visit:

> "Upon reaching the battlefield ... we pressed on toward the smoke of the battle. Near the edge of a small field, where many had fallen, I discovered a saber bayonet stuck up between two dead soldiers one a Federal and the other a Confederate, lying close together, as if they had been placed in that position and marked ... for future recognition. I took the bayonet ... though I have often regretted doing so. Both of these soldiers may have been lost to relatives by my thoughtlessness ... at sunset went to the hospital, in a church near the town. Here I saw more horrible sights, if possible, than I had already seen. The groans and cries of suffering soldiers rang long in my ears ... Wandering over the battlefield that night, we reached the field hospital of the Twenty Third Tennessee Regiment

... I learned that my brother Richard had been wounded that evening, but I could not learn how severely ... I spent most of the [next] day searching for my fallen brother, but all in vain. He sleeps among the unknown dead."[47]

On New Year's Day 1863, the two armies stood facing one another while the wounded and dying suffered, many without help. As one Confederate officer wrote, "Neither commander deemed it advisable to attack, but each was watchful of every movement of the other."[48]

A wounded Confederate called to mind a somber incident of the day in writing:

"with arm in sling I strolled over the yard, where lay in rows hundreds of Federal dead, with narrow aisles between along which one might walk and read the name, company, regiment, and state of each. Oftentimes, the simple word 'unknown' was pinned upon the dead soldier's breast. On the outer edge of this yard a long ditch was being dug the size of a large grave, but of great length, to receive these unfortunate victims of war. While they were our enemies, my heart went out in sadness for their bereaved loved ones."[49]

Another stated, "Those of us who survived unhurt were ordered to take the wounded back to our field hospital. We had suffered fearfully. We built fires that night and slept on the frozen ground."[50]

The cold weather took its toll on many of the wounded. James Cooper, Twentieth Tennessee, wrote of his fellow Confederates and their enemy that the frigid night caused numbers of the wounded to perish.

In spite of the suffering and destruction, acts of thievery occurred. J.B. Mitchell, Thirty-fourth Alabama, C.S.A, remarked months after the battle, "There was a great deal of pilfering performed on the dead bodies of the Yankees by our men. Some of them were left as naked as they were born, everything in the world they had being taken from them. I ordered my men to take their fine guns and canteens if they wished, but nothing else."[51]

The need for food became too strong for acquaintances of C.T. DeVellin, Seventeenth Ohio Infantry. DeVellin remembered that the scant rations of two spoonfuls of molasses and a half pint of beans the soldiers received were supplemented with flesh cut from horses and mules killed earlier.[52]

That day, the first of 1863, Katharine Cumming received a telegram from her husband, temporarily relieving the worries caused by the sounds of the previous day's cannonade. The message told of her husband's horse being shot and killed while the officer sat upon it. A message Mrs. Cumming received the next day added anguish to her emotions as her husband told of two of his comrades, Col. W.T. Black and Ed Ansley, being killed at Stone's River. In addition, Ed Hall, an acquaintance of the captain, had died from his wounds.[53]

Col. W.D. Pickett, Hardee's assistant inspector general, spent January 1 listening to plans of how Rosecrans could be forced to evacuate. To his surprise, the Federal general and his troops stood firm when dawn arrived on the second.[54]

Another participant added, "after Wednesday the aggressive work stopped ... Thursday came, and every moment's delay was death to the ultimate success of Southern arms. The suspense made us restless about the result ... But the charge of Breckinridge came on the 2nd, causing that awful slaughter."[55]

The incidents that were to take place on January 2, 1863 were precipitated in a meeting and following events described by Colonel Pickett of Hardee's staff. In a vivid account of the day's events, Pickett discussed an interrupted meeting of Confederate officers, the alignment of troops of the two opposing armies, and the Federal battery that annihilated the advancing Confederates on the banks of Stone's River.

Pickett wrote:

> "On the 2nd of January General Hardee, with myself, passed ... to the crossing of Stone River, and there met Gen. Leonidas Polk alone ... the party ... crossed the river, and very soon ... met ... Breckinridge ... it appeared to be the design of these officers to make a reconnaissance with a view to a movement on the Federal left flank ... Before much had been accomplished ... a staff officer overtook General Polk and informed him he was needed on his lines ... proceeding a short distance, General Hardee was recalled hurriedly to his line ... he said, 'I must return, but will leave Pickett here to represent me.' ... [We] moved forward through open timber to the picket line ... in charge of Capt. Joel Higgins, of the 2nd Kentucky Regiment of Hanson's Brigade ... on the picket

line was a two-story farmhouse occupied as a picket post. There was some … picket-firing going on, not enough to interfere materially with the reconnaissance. In front of this farmhouse was an open cultivated field extending … four or five hundred yards and … about the same distance in width back from the river. On that side of the field it was bordered by an open woods [where] Breckinridge formed his division for the attack … on the left flank of the Federal army, extending from Stone River back about the length of a brigade front … [a] hill was on the left flank of the Federal army … could it be taken and held … would necessitate the evacuation of the Federal position or otherwise force a general engagement … The fact that a picket line was in front, and the apparent importance of the position from a strategic point of view was … evidence of … a force being ready to defend it … Bragg's orders to Breckinridge were that a vigorous attack on the position just reconnoitered should be carried, held, and strongly fortified, having in view positions for four field batteries … The hour of attack was to be about four o'clock, the signal being a discharge of four pieces of artillery in quick succession … The balance of the army at the signal [was] to make demonstrations with artillery and otherwise along the whole front … General Breckinridge took advantage of the cover afforded by the strip of woods … which fronted the position which was the object of the attack and was on the edge of the open field through which the charge was to be made. At his orders I formed the two right brigades, Pillow, in command of Palmer's Brigade, in front; supported by W. C. Preston's Brigade in the second line. On the left of Pillow was Hanson's Kentucky Brigade, supported by Adams's Louisiana Brigade … commanded by Col. Randall Gibson. The four batteries of artillery were in the rear at a proper interval, and were to go into action at the proper time.[56]

Pickett relied on Col. W.R. Milward, Twenty-first Kentucky Infantry, U.S., for his information concerning the Federal deployment. He noted that Van Cleve's division of three brigades, Price's, Fiffe's, and another, were formed in three lines from the right of the battery line, with the right resting on the river. Major General Crittenden reported that Grose's and Hazen's brigades, in positions hidden from Confederate view, supported these three brigades. Less than three hundred yards to the rear of the position that would be the Confederate object of attack were situated fifty pieces of Federal artillery that would play "such havoc with Breckinridge's Division." Colonel Mendenhall, chief of the Federal artillery, had placed the cannon in anticipation of such an attack.[57]

Pickett explained:

> "At the expected signal about 4 p.m. ... the Confederate front line, Pillow and Hanson, advanced out into the open, followed ... by the second line ... As Breckinridge, in the rear of the center of the second line, emerged from the woods, the front line had reached about the center of the field ... The front line ... was exposed to a destructive musketry fire from the infantry on the top of the ridge. About this time the whole line charged ... with the bright barrels glistening in the daylight. It was a magnificent sight, seldom seen on Western battlefields on account of so much timber."[58]

A Federal soldier remarked that the Confederates marched from the woods in three distinct lines. "Never did troops move or drill more steadily than these men."

The Confederates were soon to encounter a destructive fire from the Union artillery. Reminiscent of the Federal stronghold at the Hornet's Nest at Shiloh, and in a prelude of events to transpire at Gettysburg, the barrage directed upon the charging Confederates tore holes in the ranks.

A Federal officer wrote, "When at close artillery range, the order to fire was given. The lanyards ... struck and the deadly contents rained into the Confederate ranks, almost entirely decimating or mowing down the advancing line. But another and yet another pressed forward until within short rifle range of our line."[59]

A Confederate recalled:

> "Soon after the charge had commenced the enemy's massed artillery of fifty-eight pieces began ... at first shooting over the heads of their own men ... After a fierce contest on

the crest of the position, they swept over ... and down the opposite slope, closely following the retreating Federal troops. After getting beyond the crest on to a slope next to the river, they were out of reach of this artillery fire, as it could not be so far depressed. The Federals were followed to the water's edge." [60]

The position Bragg had ordered to be taken had been acquired. The objectives now lay to hold and fortify the location in order to drive the Federals from the field. Heavy Federal reinforcements arrived on the Union right wing, and the Confederate lines slowly retired to the crest of the recently won ground.[61]

A witness recalled that:

"then it was that this mass of fifty-eight pieces of artillery ... got in most of its work, with a range of about three hundred yards, with a discharge, estimated by its own officer, of one hundred shells per minute, at first with canister and grape and then shrapnel shells fired with leaden bullets. It can be imagined what havoc was made in the ranks of this gallant body of soldiers." In crossing the knee-deep river soldiers soon found their pants frozen and that they "rattled like rawhide."[62]

One inspection of the field indicated that most of the Confederate dead were located on and slightly to either side of the crest. On the rise above McFadden's Ford, the area where Mendenhall had massed the Federal artillery, the accepted toll in less than one hour's action is regarded to be some 1,800 killed or wounded Confederates. With no alternative other than seeking shelter in the woods where they initially formed, the Confederate troops largely ignored attempts from Major Graves and Col. Pickett to rally. A participant exclaimed that the Confederates were not panic-stricken, but readily rallied under the shelter of the woods. With the arrival of reinforcements under Gen. Patten Anderson, the Confederates were now prepared to make a stand. The expected Federal advance failed to occur.[63]

With the arrival of darkness, the forty-five-minute to an hour-long action of Friday, January 2, 1863, as well as the Battle of Stone's River itself, came to an end.

Thus began the count of casualties for the armies. Col. Thomas H. Hunt, commanding the Ninth Kentucky Infantry, had kept his troops in reserve throughout the second day. Tragedy struck the unit when artillery fire placed a six-pound shell near the officer, killing him at his post.[64]

Earlier that day, General Roger W. Hanson of the famed Orphan Brigade had allegedly offered to shoot Bragg rather than send his troops into certain doom against the Federal stronghold. Ironically, Hanson was struck just above the knee and died two days later from his mortal wound.

An eyewitness recalled the scene moments after Hanson received his wound:

> "That wounded man was 'Old Hanson', and beside him was his bosom friend and distinguished commander [Breckinridge] ... the fire of these fifty-eight pieces of artillery was in full swing. Presently an officer rode, followed by an ambulance, with tears streaming down his cheeks. It was Captain Helm, General Hanson's brother-in-law and his brigade commissary. It was a sight indelibly impressed on my memory, the dying hero, his distinguished friend and commander kneeling by his side holding back the lifeblood, his kinsman with tears of affection streaming from his eyes. All this under the fiercest fire of artillery that can be conceived."[65]

The Confederates learned from General Wheeler that considerable reinforcements had arrived, increasing the already one-sided Federal numbers. General Bragg issued an order to retreat, and with no follow-up from Rosecrans, the campaign of 1862 came to an end. Rosecrans's army entered winter quarters near Murfreesboro, and the Confederate army did so near Tullahoma, only thirty miles from Rosecrans.[66]

As is noted in the National Park Service guide for Stone's River, the battle was "tactically indecisive." With Bragg's withdrawal, Rosecrans claimed victory and gave a needed boost to Northern morale and provided the Union army a base to use for controlling Middle Tennessee and supplying the eventual drives to Chattanooga and Atlanta. The casualties show a slightly different result, though, with the Union figure reaching 13,249 and the Confederate casualty number usually regarded as being 10,266.

Confederate prisoners were to be difficult, if not impossible, to replace. One group of approximately forty fell into Federal hands during the artillery barrage on the second. Having gone twenty-four hours with little food, the group was offered food when inside the Federal lines. Passing a group of Federal stragglers, the detachment was asked, "Johnny Reb, where are you going?" The reply that caused Federal soldiers to continue hits toward their otherwise cowardly counterparts was, "Down to the front, where you're afraid to go."[67]

Other reports of the battle's aftermath were far less humorous. From across the nation, personal recollections and newspaper accounts disclosed the losses among local fighting units.

J.E. Manson reported the wounding of Major Frank B. Ward of the Fiftieth Pennsylvania Cavalry. On the first day of the battle, the mortally wounded officer had been carried to the home of Manson's father, Dr. J.E. Manson. Weeks later, on the day of Ward's death, his brother, a member of the Confederate army, paid a visit to his dying brother. Manson stated that "they held each other by the hand and recited the Lord's Prayer just before the major expired." It was also to Manson's home that the body of Major Rosengarten was brought. The home was used as a hospital for several weeks after the battle.[68]

Dr. F.G. Hickman tried to comfort the mortally wounded Captain Peter Bramlett of the Second Kentucky Infantry. The young officer had been shot through the chest and in the leg and inquired of the Federal surgeon if the wounds were fatal. Lacking the ability to mislead the soldier, Hickman told Bramlett that "the chances were greatly against him." Bramlett was near death when a female attendant offered to replace his coarse blankets with neater ones. The lady was stopped by Bramlett, who told her, "No, do not remove those blankets, for they saved my life at Stone's River. They were placed over me that cold night by the hand of an enemy, but a brother. You may come across him some time ... tell him I died under the blankets he placed over me." Following Bramlett's death ten days after the battle, the blankets were sent to his parents in Paris, Kentucky.[69]

Dr. W.A. Lowe, a native of Saulsbury, Tennessee, was more fortunate than many of his fellow Confederates wounded at Murfreesboro. Previously wounded at Shiloh, Lowe was seriously shot at Murfreesboro, with a bullet hitting his right eye and exiting near the base of his brain. The doctor recovered, but never regained the use of his eye. His brother, who attempted to carry him to the rear for medical attention, survived the struggle at Murfreesboro, but was mortally wounded at Missionary Ridge.[70]

Captain W.W. Carnes reported that the Eighth Tennessee Regiment entered the fight at Murfreesboro with 425 members. With a slight variation according to two different sources, Carnes stated the casualties of the unit were 306 to 310. Of the thirty-seven commissioned officers in the regiment, thirty were killed or wounded, including the colonel and seven of the ten captains.[71]

Robert H. Graves was twenty-two years old at the time of the battle at Stone's River. A member of the Second Kentucky Infantry, Graves was killed in the Confederate charge on January 2. For "gallantry and meritorious conduct," Graves was posthumously awarded a medal by the Confederate Congress.[72]

In 1908, General Breckinridge's son, C.R. Breckinridge, wrote a letter to Mr. T.S. Weaver of Nashville, detailing the losses of Breckinridge's Kentucky Brigade at Murfreesboro. Quoting his father, C.R. Breckinridge explained that 1,763 members of the command were "shot in about twenty minutes ... the position ... was found to be utterly untenable ... the enemy had fifty eight guns ... far too great for our small force ... It was an ill advised charge ... even if we took it, as we did, it was useless, for it could not possibly be held."[73]

Fox's *Regimental Losses in the Civil War* showed a number of Tennessee regiments whose casualties at Murfreesboro were among the heaviest of the war. These included the Eighth Tennessee, with 41 killed and 265 wounded; the Twelfth, with 164 total casualties; and the Seventeenth, with 207 casualties. In addition, the Eighteenth lost 145 men at Stone's River; the Nineteenth, 127. The percentages reveal an even more fascinating fact: The losses of the Eighth Tennessee equaled 68.2 percent of their fighting force. The Twelfth lost 56.1 percent of its active enlistment at Murfreesboro.[74]

An interesting and touching casualty of the battle involves Hugh McGuire, a one-time resident of Bangor, Maine. McGuire enlisted in the Confederate army without his family's knowledge and was killed at Murfreesboro. Only in the early twentieth century did McGuire's family learn that he met his fate in the winter battle at Stone's River.[75]

An untold number of residents in Murfreesboro and the surrounding area found their homes transformed into hospitals in the months following the battle. James W. Robert was a young boy in Murfreesboro and remembered a Mississippi lieutenant named Kelly, suffering from a shattered thigh bone, being brought to his home for care. Informed that the leg needed to be amputated, Kelly refused, instead lingering in pain for two months before succumbing to his wound.[76]

A member of the Seventh Pennsylvania Cavalry wrote to his home newspaper, noting that in the first day alone, sixty-one of his lifelong friends had become casualties at Murfreesboro. A January edition of the *Boston Journal* proclaimed that the Federal losses were fewer than 10,000, while noting "Rebel Loss Double Ours." Similar headlines were issued in the *New York Daily Tribune,* in which the statistics for the battle of Murfreesboro hailed "Union Loss not over 7,000; Rebel Loss from 12,000 to 15,000."[77]

Southern papers projected a different outcome of the battle, noting Bragg's defeat of Rosecrans with 4,000 prisoners being taken; another estimated that Confederate casualties could reach 5,000. A mid-January issue of the Columbus, Georgia *Daily Sun* held hope for a Confederate declaration of victory, claiming "the loss of the abolitionists at 20,000 ... our own at 5,000.[78]

A bright spot following the battle came in an incident involving Katharine Cumming, the wife of a member of Confederate general John Jackson's staff. Her husband had not been heard from for three days following the struggle. On the fourth day, a celebratory moment occurred that she vividly recalled more than forty years later in her reminiscences:

> "I was wandering ... aimlessly and restlessly about the grounds when I saw a horseman approaching the house ... a gaunt and travel-stained-looking soldier who wearily dismounted, and not till he spoke did I recognize my own husband. How rejoiced I was ... to see him alive, literally out of the jaws of death ... yet he was whole and well."[79]

Like the elation of Mrs. Cumming and the tragedy faced by hundreds of other families, the preservation of Stone's River Battlefield has met with mixed results. Only 700 of the 4,000 acres of battlefield are within the National Park Service's possession; a majority of the remaining land has fallen victim to development. Zoning of commercial and residential areas is common in the area and threatens to claim hundreds more acres of the bloodied soil.

Visitors to the park and newly reconstructed visitor's center today can view the Stone's River National Cemetery, the Cotton Field, the Slaughter Pen, and McFadden's Ford. Hardly altered since the battle, the final three provide visitors with a great sense of the conditions faced in two of the battle's most pivotal locations. The Hazen Brigade Monument, hailed as the oldest Civil War monument, is easily viewed, yet across the Nashville and Chattanooga Railroad, to the rear of the monument, industries and commercial institutions dominate the horizon. A six-stop driving tour, capable of being enriched by an available audio tour, carries visitors through the hallowed fields that the National Park Service proudly notes are still outlined by cedar thickets as on the days of the battle.

In addition to these features of the battlefield, a location rated as "highly threatened" on the Civil War Preservation Trust's scale, visitors may also choose to view Fortress Rosecrans, a 200-acre earthen fort named for the Union commander at the battle and intended for use as a warehouse. Approximately 3,000 feet of the earthworks remain for viewing.

The city of Murfreesboro is a fast-growing community of more than 80,000 citizens. Its location near the heart of Tennessee and serving as a feeder community for Nashville has improved its economic status in recent years, yet this same progress may signal additional troubles for preservationists in the area. As with so many other sites in Tennessee, Murfreesboro warrants the action of concerned individuals and organizations.

McFadden's Ford, from a picture made soon after the battle. Union cannon located on the far hill sealed the victory. Courtesy of Blue and Gray.

Stone's River at McFadden's Ford. Photo by author.

Abandoned cannon in the area where Sheridan's and Negley's divisions lost fourteen Union cannon. The difficult terrain is clearly visible in the picture. Photo by author.

The Cotton Field. To the left is the visitors' center, and the cemetery is to the right. Photo by author.

Chicago Board of Trade Battery. Six Union cannon on this ridge repelled a Confederate attack on December 30. Photo by author.

The Hazen Brigade Monument, built in 1863, is possibly the oldest such Civil War monument. Commercial development is evident in the background. Photo by author.

Gen. Roger Hanson: K.I.A. at Murfreesboro. Courtesy of Confederate Veteran.

Newton Mitchell, Co. I, Forty-first AL, lost his right arm in a P.O.W. camp after being wounded and captured at Murfreesboro. Courtesy of Judy Patrick.

Andrew Hudson, K.I.A. at Murfreesboro. Courtesy of Confederate Veteran.

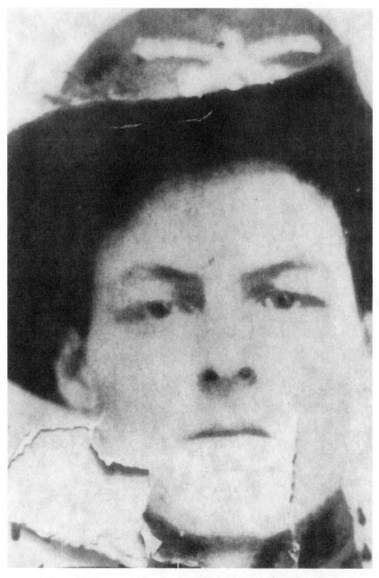

James Hamilton, Second Indiana, died of smallpox at Murfreesboro and is buried in the smallpox cemetery. Courtesy of Ron Hamilton.

CHAPTER TWELVE

THOMPSON'S STATION

"Boys, a woman has your flag!"
March 5, 1863

Following a time of heavy battle losses and a period of extreme weather, Brigadier General Nathan Bedford Forrest sought rest for his men and himself at Columbia, Tennessee. Forrest was under the command of Major General Earl Van Dorn when the latter reached Forrest in early March after marching from Mississippi. Russell's Alabama Regiment had recently been detached from the brigade and was replaced by the battalions of Lt. Col. D.W. Holman and Douglas, consolidated to form the Eleventh Regiment Tennessee Cavalry. Likewise, Col. N.N. Cox's and Napier's battalions had been combined into the Tenth Tennessee.[1]

Some 4,500 Confederates resided in the area of the rain-swollen Duck River and its tributaries in early March 1863. The soldiers had crossed the river on February 23, gradually moving nearer to Franklin, where a large body of Federal troops was stationed. On the night of March 4, Confederate scouts, weary from ten days of skirmishes in the area, reported a heavy body of enemy troops on the Franklin-Columbia Turnpike.[2]

Leading the Federal detachment was Col. John Coburn. The officer was under orders from Brigadier General Charles C. Gilbert to move south from Franklin, forage the area, and gain knowledge concerning Confederate strength and activities in the area.[3]

Coburn's firsthand knowledge of these activities would soon become overwhelming. From Columbia, Forrest and Brigadier General Red Jackson moved north with similar orders from Van Dorn. Coburn was rather prophetic as he sent a message to Gen. Gilbert noting that he had encountered a significant force "of about 2,000 to 3,000 rebel cavalry," fought it off, yet felt certain it was flanking him to the left.[4]

In fact, seven miles south of Franklin and four miles from Spring Hill, a suspected destination on Coburn's journey, lay Thompson's Station. Having been settled in the late 1700s, the community had gone through a series of names, such as Whit House and Littleberry. In 1856, Dr. Elijah Thompson gave land to the town and became its namesake. The interest and ability of Dr. Thompson in lending his town to the Nashville and Decatur Railroad for a shipping center added to the prosperity of the town, as well as to Williamson County.[5]

Running east to west and at a right angle to the north-south-running Columbia Pike, a series of hills stood near Thompson's Station. On the morning of March 5, 1863, the Confederates positioned themselves on one of these hills that overlooked a narrow valley. This hill ran perpendicular to the railroad and several highways in the area.[6]

On the extreme right stood Forrest and his 2,000 men. To his left was Armstrong's Brigade of 1,600 soldiers, situated at the high point of a narrow ridge divided by the railroad and the Columbia Turnpike to the east. Whitfield's 1,800-man Texas Brigade stood to their left. Col. S.G. Earle's Third Arkansas Brigade quickly appeared and reinforced Whitfield's position. Four pieces of King's Battery stood to the right and left of the Columbia Turnpike.[7]

Five Federal regiments, accompanied by 600 cavalry and a field battery of the Eighteenth Ohio, moved into the Confederate snare on the turnpike at 9:30 in the morning. The battery assumed a position on the right-hand ridge, with the infantry straddling the railroad. The Confederate artillery fired at the Federals, officially beginning the Battle of Thompson's Station.[8]

Col. Coburn had earlier requested reinforcements, knowing the large number of Confederates he'd be facing should an engagement take place. With the order to move forward with the troops present, Coburn carried out the command. The Thirty-third and Eighty-fifth Indiana and a battery section stood on the Federal right, positioned on a hill to the right of the road, while the other portion of the battery joined the Nineteenth Michigan and the Twenty-second Wisconsin stood atop the left hill. With the 124th

Ohio Infantry in reserve guarding the wagon train, Coburn's additional troops at his disposal were from the 9th Pennsylvania, 2nd Michigan, and various regiments of the 4th Tennessee Cavalry.[9]

From King's Battery grape and canister fell "like hail" upon the Federals, who pushed forward within 150 yards of the Confederate lines and attempted to overtake King's Battery. In response to the Federal advance, Armstrong and Whitfield's brigades moved forward to meet the challenge. A sharp exchange of musket fire between the two armies went on for half an hour before the Federal line moved back into its original position. Col. Baird of the Eighty-fifth Indiana wrote that old soldiers on both sides had never seen "hotter work" while it lasted.[10] The depot itself was destroyed, yet would be rebuilt after the war.

Forrest felt certain the Federals would mount a cavalry charge and ordered Starnes's Fourth Tennessee forward to erase the effect of such a charge. Command of Starnes's Fourth belonged at that time to Major McLemore, an officer born approximately one and a half miles from the battlefield. Being extremely familiar with the area, McLemore gave the Confederates a decided advantage.

Col. Thomas Jordan's Federal cavalry was driven from its location in a cedar thicket through the combined efforts of the Fourth Tennessee and Freeman's Battery. The battery had been moved to the front of the Confederate line and, as Col. Jordan wrote, "In a moment, a battery of the enemy, of four guns, which had heretofore been masked, opened upon our flank, completely covering the ground upon which our infantry and cavalry were placed."[11]

Van Dorn wrote that Forrest caused the Federal cavalry to leave the field. Col. Coburn recorded that the retreat of his Federal cavalry, without orders to do so, "was a contingency against which all human foresight could not provide."[12]

While Forrest's movement may certainly have provided the catalyst for the Federal cavalry's exit, it also drove a large number of their infantry to gain shelter behind a stone fence. The Confederates charged the Federal position, only to be driven back. The flag of the Fourth Mississippi and four of its regiment members were captured.[13]

A second Confederate charge was ordered under the leadership of General Forrest, atop his horse Roderick. The horse was shot and put under the care of a Confederate soldier. As Forrest, now on foot, rejoined the assault, Roderick broke free in an attempt to follow the general. Another shot hit Roderick, giving the horse a fatal wound.[14] Forrest continued ahead on foot.

A third charge provided the battle's—if not the war's—most inspirational act. Sixteen-year-old Alice Thompson, the daughter of the town's namesake, had begun the morning with a walk toward a neighbor's house. When sharpshooters of both sides began their work, young Alice took refuge in the cellar of a house belonging to Lt. Banks, a local who fought in the battle.[15]

The events that followed were duly noted:

> "as they passed the cellar ... their color bearer was shot down. When Alice Thompson ... saw this, she sprang out of the cellar, caught the flag, and waved it over her head. Col. S.G. Earle of the Third Arkansas Regiment saw her and shouted, "Boys, a woman has your flag." ... the Rebels raised a yell and drove the Yankees back. While she upheld the flag, a bombshell fell within a few feet of her, throwing dirt all over her, but fortunately did not explode. The soldiers pushed her back into the cellar. She took her skirts off and gave them to bind up the wounds of the Confederates.[16]

In the charge, Second Lieutenant R.C. White, Thockmorton's company, Ross's brigade, originally from Waverly, Tennessee, was shot through the breast. Initially thought to have received a fatal wound, White survived the war.

In one of the trio of efforts to dislodge the Federals, a member of the Fourth Tennessee had a premonition of his demise. D.M. Stegall, a fellow regiment member of Capt. A.A. Dysart, recalled the vision: "While waiting for orders to move forward our captain, A.A. Dysart, came back to me and said, 'Dug, I'll be killed today and I want you to take my watch and pocketbook and give them to Uncle Jim Dysart.'" Dysart died that day, the only man in his company to do so. A cedar tree marked the spot where Dysart met his fate.[17]

The Nineteenth Michigan and Utley's Twenty-second Wisconsin stood to the right and left of the Eighty-fifth Indiana on the end of the Union line. The Federal battery was out of ammunition and pulled from the field. The third charge, as Utley feared, proved the Twenty-second

Wisconsin too few in number to sustain another assault, and the Federal left flank fell.[18]

Forrest's foot charge had cut off routes of escape for the remaining Federal troops. Forrest leveled his revolver at Coburn and demanded his surrender. The request was quickly granted. Forrest led Coburn to General Van Dorn and introduced the two men before returning to care for the wounded.[19]

The five-hour fight had officially ended with the surrender at 4:00. The Confederate forces had grown to 6,000 by the battle's end, though almost 1,000 had arrived too late to provide much assistance. With fewer than 2,000 men and officers, and 600 cavalry, the Federals of Col. Coburn mathematically had little opportunity for victory.

Federal casualties were estimated to be 1,600, with 48 killed and 1,500 wounded or captured. Van Dorn reported the Confederate losses at 357 killed, wounded, and missing. Most of the Confederate casualties occurred during the final charge, a productive yet costly maneuver. Captain Montgomery Little, commander of Forrest's escort, fell mortally wounded at the general's side. Major Edward Buller Trezevant, commander of Cox's regiment, also met his destiny in the third assault.[20]

Col. Samuel G. Earle of the Third Arkansas Cavalry, Captain William Watson of General Armstrong's staff, Rev. Crouch, a brigade chaplain, and Lt. John Johnson of the Ninth Tennessee attest to the fact that the battle was not fought in leaderless assaults. Johnson died carrying his regimental colors, Crouch while inspiring his men.[21]

Pvt. Clay Kendrick caught the flag of the Ninth Tennessee as it fell from Johnson's hands. Almost immediately, Kendrick's right arm was shattered when a bullet hit as he waved the flag. The brave young man shifted the flag to his left hand and completed the battle.[22]

John F. Dexter of the Fifty-third Alabama recalled the significance of Col. Earle and the Battle of Thompson's Station:

> "Col. Earle led this squadron in the engagement and paid them a high compliment. Earle was the commander of this [Third Arkansas] regiment. Gen. Forrest had tried two or three crack regiments, but they failed to move the Yankees. Then he said, 'Give me the Third Arkansas, the best regiment the sun shines on.' Col. Earle was killed out right in the field."[23]

Gregory L. Wade offered an analysis of the battle in writing: "While not a critical action strategically ... Thompson's Station was important in serving notice ... that the rebels in Middle Tennessee continued to remain a dangerous ... Van Dorn and Forrest ... helped tie up many Union resources for months to come."[24]

Today, a different battle is being fought at Thompson's Station. A significant amount of the battlefield has been consumed for the cause of development. The Civil War Preservation Trust rates the battlefield as "highly threatened" by development. A lone historical marker provides information of the events of the battle.

A host of organizations seeks to protect much of the area's battlegrounds, yet soaring land prices in the area limit their effectiveness. The appearance of a Saturn assembly plant in nearby Spring Hill, and commuters from Franklin, Murfreesboro, and Nashville seeking refuge in the area around Thompson's Station have brought about many changes to this once largely rural district. The 2000 census indicated a population approaching 1,300, a significant rise from fewer than 800 in 1990, the year the town incorporated.

The area of Thompson's Station bears attention as it lends itself to either preserving the sacrifices of those who fought there or simply seeing the memory of their sacrifices become lost forever.

The state marker for the Thompson's Station Battlefield sits on the edge of this field. Photo by author.

Across the road from the marker, commercial development is clearly evident. Photo by author.

207

Alice Thompson. Courtesy of Confederate Veteran.

CHAPTER THIRTEEN

KNOXVILLE

"The attack ... was bound to fail ..."
November 1863

By November 1863, Knoxville had seen its fair share of activities from the ongoing war. Located in East Tennessee, the city was within the parameters of a virtual pro-Union stronghold, but guerilla activity and the conduct of soldiers Union and Confederate limited the level of sentiment freely expressed among residents.

Assigned the task of controlling Knoxville was Major General Ambrose E. Burnside's U.S. Army of the Ohio. Claiming a command of 12,000 effectives,[1] Burnside had at his disposal two corps of infantry and one cavalry corps. These soldiers were responsible for fortifying and defending the city that the Confederates had partially barricaded before leaving the previous August.

The significance of Knoxville rested largely in the fact that both the Tennessee River and one of only two east-west railway lines for the Confederacy passed near the city, the river to the south and the tracks to the north. These factors contributed to the city's early Confederate occupation and eventual Federal takeover. As noted in the text of dozens of pro-Union citizens of the era, as well as historians, past and present, the economic, geographic, and political ramifications related to Knoxville's possession were, to say the least, astonishing.

Burnside's arrival in Knoxville in early September brought about instructions for his chief engineer, Brigadier General Orlando M. Poe, to improve the earthworks partially completed during the Confederate occupation. Poe's plans, with Burnside's approval, called for the construction of two works: one, "an insignificant line ... thrown up on the hill northwest of the college," another to the east on Temperance Hill. The former would eventually gain the name Fort Sanders, the latter became Fort Huntingdon Smith.[2]

Confederate movements in the direction of Knoxville necessitated Burnside's deployment of troops. On October 10, an engagement at Blue Springs resulted in a temporary Confederate withdrawal. A skirmish soon followed at Sweetwater, and upon the arrival of Federal reserves at Philadelphia, resulted in the Federal movement to and concentration of troops in Knoxville.[3]

The Confederate advance gained momentum, but by mid-November, the Federals as well saw the need to control the Concord Road that intersected the Knoxville-bound Kingston Road in the village known as Campbell's Station. Burnside was challenged by Lt. Gen. James Longstreet's command of two Confederate divisions and 5,000 cavalry. Burnside's arrival at the intersection came only an estimated fifteen minutes before Longstreet's arrival.

J.W. Minnich was in the Sixth Georgia as it approached Campbell's Station. He recalled:

> "meeting no opposition until we arrived within sight of the large brick house ... we found our rapid advance checked ... For some time we engaged them with artillery, as the range was too great for rifles to be effective. After a short exchange of pleasantries they disappeared behind a ridge, and we saw no more of them that day ... we had two men wounded in my company ... one on the forehead, which raised a bump the size of a pigeon's egg and a severe headache, and the other was struck in the pit of the stomach ... which made the boy very sick for a while. At a much shorter range ... both would have proved fatal."[4]

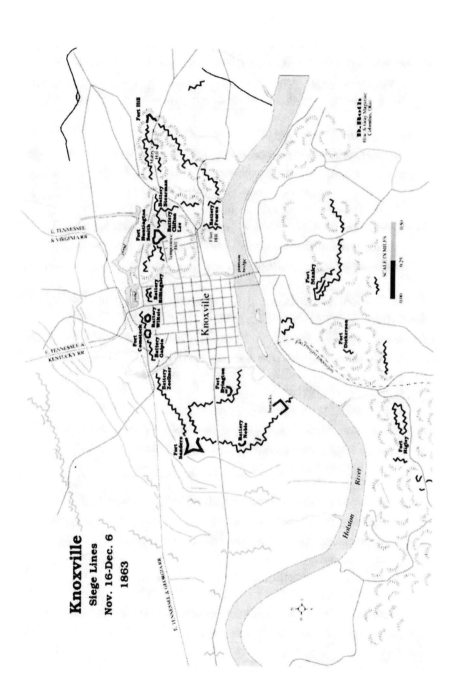

Knoxville
Siege Lines
Nov. 16-Dec. 6
1863

Having suffered an estimated 300 casualties, Burnside's skirmishers made their return to Knoxville, a trip of some 14 miles. His entry into the city had been hastened by the frequent shedding of blankets, overcoats, or other items the Federal troops saw as cumbersome and hindering their movement.

J.W. Minnich reveled in the Federals' unloading of supplies as he wrote:

> "we found what was far more important to us just then than a batch of prisoners would have been, and that was a batch of fresh-baked dough—2,000 loaves of good wheat bread—something we had not seen or tasted for a month or more, probably more, as our wagons could not keep up with our rapid moves, and more often than not we were dividing rations with our horses."[5]

The Confederate arrival at Knoxville was recorded in the words of John Coxe:

> "we marched to a point in sight of the city and halted. The railroad entering the city was near by on the left, and the Holston River was about the same distance away on the right ... Our brigade stopped in front of a fine brick mansion, then locked up and deserted ... afterwards Pete Turpin got some goodies for our mess from the cellar of this house. In front, on the left of the road, a little less than a quarter of a mile away, was a small hill, on which we could make out a line of Federal infantry lying behind a fence-rail breastwork. Beyond this ... we saw a college building and ... a large fort frowning with cannon. This fort was said to be the key [to] the city and would have to be reduced or captured before the city could be taken."[6]

After arriving in Knoxville, General Longstreet established his headquarters at the Bleak House, the home of Robert Houston Armstrong, located on a bluff above the Holston, now the Tennessee, River. Longstreet's sharpshooters, known as the "Elite Twenty", were armed with Whitworth telescopic rifles, weapons accurate to a distance of 1,500 yards. The Twenty were positioned in the tower and in the windows immediately below the structure as well as in the second floor's ballroom. The Union line lay some 750 yards to the east of the house. General Burnside had asked General William P. Sanders to hold this critical Union position, until the earthworks defending the city could be suitably completed. With only 700 troops at his disposal, the twenty-nine-year-old Sanders, a Kentucky native and a West Point graduate, held his line along the Kingston Road for more than twenty-four hours before he was mortally wounded. On the morning of November 18, Longstreet's sharpshooters were wreaking havoc on the enemy lines when General Sanders sent a message to Lieutenant Samuel Benjamin to fire a 20-pound Parrott shell into the tower as an attempt to dislodge the sharpshooters. The distance from Fort Loudon to the Bleak House was approximately 2,500 yards. Dubbed by Captain Orlando M. Poe as being the "prettiest shot of the war", the shot hit the second level southeast corner of the house, directly below the tower. Three sharpshooters were mortally wounded. Early in the afternoon, and after two hours of fighting, Captain Stephen Winthrop, riding with General Porter Alexander, mounted his horse and rode through the crossfire in an attempt to rally the Confederates. His horse was killed; Winthrop was wounded, but survived. Behind the Federal lines, General Sanders joined Major R.E. Lawder in watching Winthrop's action. While attempting to return uphill, General Sanders was hit by a sharpshooter's bullet, supposedly fired from the Bleak House, and died later that night at the Lamar House. Orlando Poe had witnessed the conversation in which Burnside's request to Sanders had been made and dutifully acknowledged. He exclaimed that the officer's wound took place just after two o'clock on November 18 and that "every spadeful [sic] of earth turned while Sanders was fighting aided in making our position secure."[7]

From the earthworks soon to be named for Sanders, a shot from a twenty-pound Parrot was fired at the sharpshooter nest atop the Bleak House. At least one of the sharpshooters in the tower is rumored to have been killed in the fulfillment of a request to destroy the origin of the shot that mortally wounded the young Federal officer.

Aside from the initial buildup and skirmishes of the area, the siege of Knoxville would prove largely uneventful for almost two weeks. Other than strengthening their defensive position, the most time-consuming portion of the day for a majority of the besieged Federals was the acquisition of food. William H. Brearly of Company E, Seventeenth Michigan Volunteers, remembered that only a small piece of bread and an occasional piece of pork served as daily rations. Corn and wheat were sometimes placed on rafts and floated down the river by pro-Union East Tennesseans, yet Confederate intervention quickly ended, or certainly curtailed, this source of foodstuffs.[8]

A private in the First Alabama Cavalry detailed an adventure he and a comrade had on what he proclaimed to be his one incident as a straggler. Their foray in an attempt to scout the area for food almost turned deadly. He wrote:

> "I left Bill with his old horse ... and went to the house and hailed. A portly old lady came out in the yard, followed by three grown red-headed girls, barefooted and ugly ... I began my grub speech ... she said, 'your sort can't get anything here, so you can just move on ... I have some fat shoats in an old field that the road runs through ... I want you to let them alone.' ... I went back to where I left Bill, thinking all the time of the fat shoats in the old field ... When we came to the field, sure enough there was a bunch of shoats ... it did not take long to dispatch one of them by putting a bullet between its eyes. We dragged it to a branch ... took out its entrails ... and were making preparations to move on when we heard a clatter of hoofs coming down the road ... that bunch of red-headed women armed with pitchforks and weeding hoes ... I grabbed the hog and dived into a dense thicket ... leaving Bill to look out for himself and the old horse ... They ... both fell into the hands of the enemy ... they did not hurt Bill nor carry him away ... we had lost our Barlow knife ... and I had also lost the gun and hog. We finally found the gun and hog, but not the knife ... Bill had a pair of scissors in his pocket ... we broke the blades apart, sharpened them ... skinned the hog ... made a hearty meal ... without bread or salt."[9]

A truly amazing fact lies in the Union army's ability to overcome their shortage of a host of basic supplies. Lacking proper diet and cover, the Federal soldiers were able to construct several earthen forts and batteries during the siege. Among the former were: Fort Sanders to the city's west, batteries Zoellner and Gulpin to the northwest, Fort Comstock and Battery Wiltsie to the east of these, Battery Billingsley north of town,

Fort Huntingdon Smith to the east of Billingsley, and batteries Clifton Lee and Stearman still further east. Forts Hill, Stanley, Dickerson, Higley, Byington, and Battery Noble eventually completed the string of Federal defenses.[10]

Fort Dickerson was the strongest of the four Federal forts south of the river. Named for 112th Illinois Mounted Infantry Captain Jonathan Dickerson, who died in a Cleveland, Tennessee skirmish, the fort was the main point to repel an attack by General Joe Wheeler. No more than six guns were in the fort, but some twenty-five embrasures existed and allowed for free movement of the guns within. Wheeler took this fact into account, noting the steep terrain and heavy defenses making further attacks against the position too costly in manpower and time. Wheeler joined Longstreet to the west of town,[11] where additional delays would ironically prove costly before an eventual assault upon the Federal positions.

By the afternoon of November 23, the Confederates had made an attack upon Fort Comstock and moved within 600 yards of Fort Sanders. A trench was dug and extended some 300 yards to the left of the fort; this was attacked and briefly held by the 169 men of the Second Michigan Infantry. "With lamentable results," the Federals were driven back after losing almost half of their number.[12]

Corporal John Watkins, Nineteenth Ohio Battery, wrote to a friend, describing the events that followed the assault. After the Confederate attack upon the Federals in the trench, a truce was called for the retrieval of the dead and wounded. Watkins proclaimed, "you had ought to have seen the rebel brutes rush out of the pits and strip the dead."[13]

A member of Confederate general Lafayette McLaws's division noted that the Federal pickets at Fort Sanders were driven back nightly. From his position, this soldier, J.B. Boothe, made the following description of Fort Sanders:

> " ... regarded as the key to the enemy's position ... the fort was built upon an irregular quadrilateral. The south front was one hundred and fourteen yards, east front eighty-five yards, north front one hundred and twenty-five yards, and west front ninety-five yards. That part of the structure assaulted was finished. The high and almost perpendicular embankment there had at its base a ditch twelve feet wide and eight feet deep. From the fort toward our rifle pits there was a very perceptible slope, from which the trees

had been cut and used as an abatis, and a network of wire was stretched between the stumps."[14]

The wire Boothe saw was telegraph wire given by one Mr. Hoxie, the caretaker of the nearby railroad property. The wire was wrapped around eighteen-inch-high stumps created, ironically, when the Confederates had cut down a host of five-inch-diameter pines during their occupation of Knoxville. U.S. general Poe noted in his memoirs that the significance of the wire was overrated and that it may have delayed the Confederates long enough during the assault on the fort to enable the Federal defenders to fire two extra rounds.[15]

In addition to the wire entangled on the stumps, the Federal defenses around Fort Sanders were numerous and effective. Abates protected the fort's front and a ditch surrounded the walls. With a width of seven feet and depth six to eight feet, the ditch would slow any attempt to scale the walls that in places had an estimated slope of forty-five degrees and a distance of twenty feet from the top of the work to the ditch in some places. Recent rains left the fort's walls slippery and practically unable to be scaled from the Confederate vantage point.[16]

A ninety-five-yard western wall was the lone one completed in the fort. The north and south walls each ran 125 yards and were near completion. The eighty-five-yard eastern wall was open. Some 440 men of New York, Massachusetts, and Michigan occupied the garrison in late November, and not only relied upon the batteries inside the fort for protection, but also lay assured in the range of other Federal batteries nearby.[17]

The Confederate plan of attack upon Fort Sanders was to be made in two columns against the fort's northwest angle. Fixed bayonets were to be used, as the determined assault was to be made without firing a shot or expelling the infamous "rebel yell."[18]

At 6 AM on the clear and cold Sunday morning of November 29, Confederate cannon fire signaled the beginning of the attack. The advance met the aforementioned entanglements but only a small amount of initial Federal fire. Inside Fort Sanders, Corporal John Watkins estimated that the air was filled with bursting shells sent from at least five positions. From his position thirty-five miles away, J.W. Minnich distinctly heard the cannonade.[19]

Confederates who had skirmished with the Federal outer defenses late Saturday began their approach from various locations around the fort. Sgt. Major J.A.H. Cranberry of the Twentieth Georgia remembered:

" ... my regiment ... by daylight had dug and occupied the rifle pits ... while our picket line was advancing we were heavily shelled from the fort, but the shells passed over us. Some of the shells exploded as many as three times like skyrockets, such as we never encountered before. Before sunrise the assault upon the fort was made by ... I estimate three brigades. The heavy picket line kept up a constant fire upon the walls of the fort, though not a Federal was seen above the rifle pits. Neither was a cannon or a small arm fired upon the advancing column."[20]

With Cranberry's regiment were the men of the Twenty-first Mississippi. J.B. Boothe, a member of that command, added:

" ... the lines had already been formed, and they were almost as silent as a funeral procession. Nothing could be heard except the suppressed commands of 'Attention, battalion! Order arms! Fix bayonets!' Then there was a rattle of steel against steel as the bayonets were adjusted and then again ... 'Shoulder arms! Forward! Guide, center! March!'"[21]

As the Confederates began entering the area filled with entanglements, the advance, by design, slowed dramatically. Additionally, the ditch surrounding the fort became a virtual killing field.

J.B. Booth remarked:

"Soon there came the terrific rattle of musketry and the deafening reports of artillery and the shriek of the shrapnel from the enemy's lines ... Confederates were determined and ... capable of accomplishing anything within the range of possibility. Some ... fell forward when the unseen network of wires at their feet was struck, but quickly arose and again rushed forward. The lines of gray encircled the fort, leaped into the ditch, and endeavored with all their might to climb the steep embankment, but without avail. Some were killed and wounded in the ditch by hand grenades thrown from the bastion. Only a few reached the top by getting upon the shoulders of their comrades and climbing by the aid of their bayonets thrust into the embankment, but they were immediately shot down by the riflemen in the fort."[22]

Lieutenant Colonel McElroy of the Thirteenth Mississippi Regiment used his sword to carve hand- and footholds in the outside wall of the fort. Successful in doing so, he reached the top of the fort but was shot down immediately.[23]

J.A.H. Cranberry, Twentieth Georgia, criticized the battle plan in stating:

> "no provision was made for crossing the ditch around the fort ... columns could go no farther. Hand grenades were then thrown over the walls of the fort into the ranks of our men, their explosion causing a panic and a retreat. Then the enemy appeared above the walls of the fort and fired one volley into the fleeing columns, and there was one discharge of the artillery."[24]

Another member of the assaulting Confederates, A.J. Cone of the Eighteenth Georgia, remarked:

> "We soon got to the fort, but an impassable ditch prevented our getting over it. The men soon filled the ditch and began to help one another on the parapet, but we were subjected to an enfilading fire from both sides of the fort. No attack was made on the lines of breastworks on each side of the fort, and had that been done, we could have taken the fort and captured Knoxville and the entire enemy's force. Our loss was eight hundred gallant sons of the south. Col. S.Z. Ruff ... only shortly before advanced from lieutenant colonel ... was killed."[25]

Criticism of the strategy again arose as one Confederate participant wrote, "The attack was ill-conceived. His [Longstreet's] men had the utmost confidence in his able generalship, but the manner of the assault was a dismal failure."[26]

One Confederate recollection noted Private Robert Thompson of the Eighth Georgia grabbed a tossed hand grenade "that seemed to have a long fuse" and threw it back into the Federal position inside Fort Sanders, and there, the grenade exploded.[27] No estimate or proclamation of the damage inflicted was offered.

The effectiveness of the hand grenades caused J.A.H. Cranberry to remark, "our forces broke in retreat from the explosion of the hand grenades thrown into their ranks ... just one volley was fired into our retreating lines."[28]

J.B. Boothe explained that Major Goggin of McLaw's staff rode to Longstreet and informed him of the situation; an immediate recall of the Confederates resulted. The assault on the fort, noted Union general Poe, had been gallantly made but repulsed in less time than describing it would take.[29] The attack had, in fact, lasted just twenty minutes.

Though the attack on Fort Sanders was over, the Confederate siege of Knoxville continued until trains transported them on the third and fourth of December. J.B. Boothe recalled:

> "On the 4th ... the men ... were informed that a detour of Knoxville would be made that night. A great many did not have shoes, and they were instructed to provide for themselves rawhide moccasins ... I was a luckless barefooted boy ... who had never before undertaken to construct a pair of rawhide moccasins. But necessity is said to be the mother of invention; and after I had incased my feet in the warm plush of a piece of Tennessee ox or cow-hide made into moccasins ... I was highly complimented ... on the neatness of my job."[30]

Almost immediately, blame for the Confederate failure to capture Fort Sanders and regain control of Knoxville became a frequent topic of conversation. Many of the issuers of blame and complaints directed their energy to General Longstreet.

A.J. Cone of the Eighteenth Georgia wrote:

> "Longstreet blundered in waiting about ten days for Burnsides to intreach [sic] himself, and then again by assaulting the fort at all. The main attack should have been directed to the wings of the fort, and these we would have captured easily, which would have made the fort untenable ... and more than two hundred gallant

men killed would have been spared. It was pitiable to see the spirits of those men after we were forced back under the hill. They knew they had not had a fair chance, and demanded to be led against the breastworks, that they might redeem themselves from failure because of our commander's blunder, but it was not allowed, and, crestfallen, we were forced to retreat."[31]

Another Confederate participant simply proclaimed, "Longstreet decided on the fatal error of assaulting Fort Saunders [sic]"[32]

One of the more complete and lengthy criticisms of Longstreet, his ability, and decisions, came from J.W. Minnich in his 1913 memoirs:

"I felt that he had his 'limitations' and that as commander of a large and independent force, he was not a 'success' ... the query among us of the cavalry was, 'Why didn't he walk right into Knoxville?' We all felt ... it could have been taken without much greater loss than we suffered when the attack was made. Our troops had forced Burnside into Knoxville ... and had followed the enemy so rapidly that he could not offer any protracted resistance to our advance. The soldiers were enthusiastic and eager to try conclusions with the enemy and were in high hope of capturing the town and its defenders, or, at least, driving them out and into the open country ... We fully expected Longstreet would move to the assault on ... the 18th, and great was our surprise and chagrin when the day passed so quietly ... Instead ... Longstreet sat down to a siege of the place, thus giving Burnside time to strengthen the light defenses which our troops had previously built. When, on the 29th, the assault was made, twelve days had elapsed, and then, with only half or less of the troops that should have been employed, the attack, under the circumstances, was bound to fail, as it did ... because of Longstreet's slowness."[33]

Supporting Longstreet and his decision, a Mississippi infantryman wrote, "Circumstances over which the commanding general had no control and which are now well known history compelled him to abandon any further attempt to capture Knoxville and its garrison."[34]

Sgt. Major J.A.H. Cranberry reported in 1910 that:

"The East Tennessee campaign was a failure. General
Longstreet must have thought that Gen. LaFayette
McLaws, commanding a division, and Gen. E.M. Law,
commanding a brigade, were in some degree to blame for
the failure, for they were not permitted to remain longer
in his command, yet by their own men no officers were
ever more popular or more highly esteemed."[35]

McLaws himself stated, "The main cause of the failure was the
slipperiness of the parapet, upon which it was impossible for any large
body of men to gain a foothold and the severe fire from the north side
of the fort, which drove the men from the most accessible point of the
assault." [36]

Regardless of the source of blame, Knoxville was permanently lost
to the Federals. Inadequate supplies and unusually cold weather negated
Longstreet's hopes to regain the city and avenge his losses. Confederate
general E. Porter Alexander reported Longstreet's losses at 129 killed, 458
wounded, and 226 captured, for a total of 813. He correctly estimated the
Union losses to be around twenty.[37]

The sight of the Confederate dead caused mixed emotions in an Ohio
defender of Fort Sanders. Corporal John Watkins recalled:

"As soon as the firing stopped I went up and got on the
parapet to look ... such a sight I never saw before nor do I
care about seeing again. The ditch in places was almost full
of them piled one on top of the other ... They were brave
men. Most of them Georgians. I would give one of the
wounded a drink as quick as anybody if I had it. That is
about the only thing they ask for when first wounded. But
at the same time I wished the whole Southern Confederacy
was in that ditch in the same predicament." [38]

Among the wounded was James Williams of Company C, First Texas
Regiment. Williams lost a leg in the action at Knoxville and survived the
war to become a county treasurer in Austin, Texas.[39]

J.A.H. Cranberry, Twentieth Georgia, recalled the aftermath:

"a flag of truce was displayed from the fort. The Federals swarmed out of the fort, and our men met and mingled with them between the fort and our picket line, where the dead and wounded lay. The Federals claimed the wounded, but those who could walk paid no attention to the order, but returned to our lines. Our dead were collected and we buried them, ninety seven in number, in one grave. A few were mortally wounded. Among these was a Colonel Ruff ... Captains Moore of the Eighth Georgia ... and Robert Wellburn, of the Ninth Georgia ... were also killed. Private Moon, of my regiment, was killed. He left our regiment and went with the attacking troops as they passed by and was shot in the retreat."[40]

Though the siege is, as earlier noted, generally regarded to have ended on December 4, a number of the Confederate troops left Knoxville in the hours after the attack on Fort Sanders. For most, the retreat increased their demoralized state.

Cranberry expounded:

"General Longstreet in his work says we remained [at] Knoxville four days after the assault. Some of the cavalry might have done so. My command marched till ten o'clock next day before halting ... On the night following our movement east we waded a stream, and our clothing froze upon our bodies as soon as we emerged from the water."[41]

J.B. Boothe, Twenty-first Mississippi, graphically explained his plight with his homemade moccasins:

"misfortunes never come singly ... the rain came down in torrents and continued to fall until the creeks and rivulets west of Knoxville ... were full and overflowing. There were no bridges, but these streams had to be crossed ... with rawhide moccasins it may be revealed that such footwear is not adapted to wet weather ... Before crossing the second stream mine were large enough to be pulled upon the feet of a good-sized elephant, and while fording

the third stream my footwear and my feet parted company
... during the night the temperature fell rapidly ... the
ground became frozen ... my feet were cut and bruised
by the stones and ice, and it was no better when the sun
came out during the day and the ground began to thaw.
It made me look for the deepest mud to walk in ... passed
a piece of artillery stuck fast in the mud up to its axles.
An officer on horseback galloped up and ordered us to
pull the cannon out of the mud. We paid no attention to
the order ... A ... dwelling was located on the roadside
... A lady was standing ... looking at the soldiers as they
passed ... The good woman asked the size of my shoe ...
she called to one of her daughters ... she took off the shoes
with apparent willingness, and I was told to put them on
... After supper the lady asked me where I was from and
said, 'I would not fight for any government on earth that
did not furnish me with shoes.'"[42]

Gen. E. Porter Alexander recalled a similar situation involving footwear.
Gen. Longstreet had given permission for his soldiers to "swap" shoes with
any prisoners taken during the retreat. A standing joke soon evolved as
it was noted that Longstreet's requirement entailed each man having to
have something to actually "swap." Humorous comments, in spite of the
situation, came from those losing and gaining better shoes.[43]

John Coxe noted the events of the retreat, primarily the scavenging
for food: "We marched rapidly, without rations, all night and at 8 a.m.
halted ... during the night, I picked up two apples on a side road, but we
had parched corn for breakfast ... the third day out from Knoxville ... a
furious snowstorm struck us."[44]

The Knoxville Campaign's conclusion is usually considered to be
signified by the Battle of Bean's Station on December 14, 1863. Longstreet's
desire to capture the town and Union Brigadier General J.M. Shackelford
would lead to a daylong battle that resulted in heavy casualties for both
the Union and Confederacy.

John Coxe recalled the events of the day:

"we found two of our batteries unlimbering behind a rail
fence, and ... was ordered to support these batteries ... we
saw the extensive and pretty plain of Bean Station ... over

which were to be seen a Federal army of all arms moving about ... our two batteries opened on them, and a lively artillery duel ensued ... General Kershaw rode up and said there was a line of Federal infantry creeping up through the cemetery as if to charge our batteries and ordered us to charge upon them. We ... broke up their line, but only after a sharp fight. Several of our men fell in the cemetery. The Federals fell back over the bottom and into ... woods on higher ground, but they continued to fire back at us as they went."[45]

The Bean's Station site, in Grainger County, is now submerged. With the Tennessee Valley Authority's damming of the Holston River, the waters of Cherokee Lake covered the battlefield. At certain times of the year, portions may be seen, but the majority of the area remains under water. A Federal hilltop redoubt is still able to be visited and plans are in existence to use this site as an interpretive area for the battle. In using a walkway to the island that is occasionally seen, and establishing a suitable pull-off, preservationists hope to preserve a portion of the heritage the area holds for future generations.

The Knoxville battlefield today has all but disappeared to the frequent enemy of Civil War sites: urban sprawl. The numerous Federal trenches that connected their forts, as well as the forts themselves, have been replaced with various businesses and subdivisions. Signs with sayings such as "Save Ft. Higley," the Federal fort closest to the Confederate lines, can be clearly seen. The city General William T. Sherman entered after the siege and declared it to be the best-fortified city he'd viewed, has seen most of these fortifications vanish forever.

As if prophesying the struggle to come, a reporter for Knoxville's *Morning Tribune* made this analysis of the fortifications on the thirty-third anniversary of the battle, Sunday, November 29, 1896:

"A third of a century has passed and where that eventful Sunday showed the dead and wounded soldiers whose life blood colored the clay there are on the site of the fort and that bloody slope the homes of some of the best citizens, on the plain that the army quickly marched over are homes, church[es], schools, beautiful streets and a factory ... on the site of the fort of Longstreet is a college

224

... On that bloody slope of Fort Sanders trees do not seem to have grown ... then the carnage of war, bloodshed and death—today homes, life and happiness."[46]

The major proponent in the effort to save the remaining Knoxville-area battlefield landmarks is the Knoxville Civil War Roundtable. The organization was formed in 1983 and has seen its membership approach 200. Its Web site, regular meetings, and newsletter have successfully led to the preservation and interpretation of the city's Civil War sites. In addition, various period relics, signs, and a driving tour brochure have increased awareness of Knoxville's treasures. The sole remains of Fort Sanders are signified by a sign.

The roundtable's director of membership and past president is Jim Lyle. Mr. Lyle provided an informative list of the 1863 Knoxville Civil War defenses and their locations. Two of the landmarks, forts Elstner and Milhalotzy, have unknown locations. These two establishments were not present at the time of the battle. The other sites of the area include: Fort Byington, Fort Sanders, Fort Dickerson, Fort Stanley, Fort Hill, Fort Huntingdon Smith, Fort Higley, Fort Comstock, Battery Fearns, Battery Billingsley, Battery Wiltsie, and Battery Zoellner. Of these, Fort Sanders was the only one to be named at the time of the battle; the others received names from Gen. Burnside in memory of officers killed in the East Tennessee campaign.[47]

The unending support of conservation and preservation efforts in Knoxville is long overdue. Appealing to local and state officials for such efforts is one way to ensure the reclamation of these locations for the future.

Called Asylum Hospital or General Hospital #1, this building served as a hospital for both armies during Knoxville's occupation. Courtesy of Dorothy Kelly.

This monument to the 79th New York Infantry (Highlanders) is located at the corner of Sixteenth and Clinch streets. Courtesy of Dorothy Kelly.

Entrance to Ft. Dickerson in Dickerson Park, located off Chapman Highway. It is one of only two remaining forts across the Tennessee River, (called the Holston River during the war), from Knoxville. Courtesy of Dorothy Kelly.

Interior of Ft. Dickerson with one of the three cannon placed by the Knoxville Civil War Roundtable. Note the eroded magazine and embrasures. Courtesy of Dorothy Kelly.

Ft. Sanders shortly after the siege. Note the tree stumps and steep approach to the fort. Library of Congress

This drawing in the tower of the Bleak House proclaims to hold the images of three men shot in the location. This is a superb example of preserved Civil War art. Courtesy of Shirley Rouse, President, U.D.C., Chapter 89.

Gen. William Price Sanders. The Natchez, Mississippi resident and West Point graduate chose to fight for the Union and was mortally wounded in Knoxville on November 18, 1863. U.S. Army Military History Institute in Carlisle, PA.

Strawberry Plains area near Knoxville. Courtesy of University of Tennessee Libraries, Special Collections.

The Bleak House, prewar photo. The Armstrong family resided in the home and chose to stay during the siege as soldiers camped around the house. From the tower, Confederate sharpshooters used British Whitworth rifles, accurate to 1,000 yards, to pick off Federal personnel such as Gen. William Sanders. Courtesy of Shirley Rouse, President of U.D.C., Chapter 89.

Pvt. Andrew Owen, Co. D, Second Tennessee, U.S., was captured in Rogersville, Tennessee near Knoxville on November 6, 1863. He died of diarrhea at Andersonville Prison on June 9, 1864. Courtesy of Darren Smith.

Wade Greene, Co. A, Eighth Tennessee, U.S. was a veteran of Knoxville, Nashville, Strawberry Plains, Franklin, Spring Hill, and Chattanooga. During his absence, three of his sisters were physically abused, likely due to his pro-Union sentiments. Courtesy of Joe Mode.

CHAPTER FOURTEEN
CHATTANOOGA

"The whole face of the mountain was lurid with bursting shells."
November 23-25, 1863

Mid-nineteenth-century Chattanooga was a major rail center and thus a key possession for the opposing armies of the Union and Confederacy. Situated in a bend of the Tennessee River and on its south bank, where the river ran nearly due west, Chattanooga would soon become the focal point of a series of events that would draw the attention not only of the participants in the battle, but the entire nation as well. The climactic event, in November of 1863, would lend the struggle for the control of the area the title of "The Battle Above the Clouds."

Confederate general Edward C. Walthall, a prominent figure in the famous struggle for Chattanooga, said of this oft-used nickname, "The explanation of this poetic name ... is found in the fact that during most of the day in question a dense fog enveloped the sides of the mountain and hung above the valley, so obscuring the view from below that nothing could be seen of the occurrences above except the flashes from the guns which gleamed through the darkened space around the scene of the conflict."[1]

Another quote from a participant elaborated that "the so-called 'battle above the clouds' was not a battle in the common acceptation of that word; and, borrowing an expression from a writer in the *New York Tribune*, 'there were no clouds to fight above; only a mist, which settled down and enveloped the base of the mountain.'"[2]

A description of the area from a period writer stated:

> "Lookout Mountain abuts on the Tennessee River
> opposite Moccasin Point. The declivity is so abrupt at the
> water's edge that it was a great triumph of engineering
> skill to make room for the track of the Nashville and
> Chattanooga railway between the mountain and the
> river. Considerably above the railroad a wagon road runs
> westward from Chattanooga across the northern slope of
> the mountain ... about midway between the river and the
> mountaintop, is a comparatively level space ... "bench of
> the mountain" ... and on the western end of it stands the
> ... Craven's house ... This bench extends, with the cliff
> on one side and the steep and rugged descent to Lookout
> Valley on the other, from the north end of the cliff
> around the mountain on the western side, with enough
> open space upon it for a garden and a small field west of
> Craven's house. A road ... very rough ... from Craven's
> house around the eastern side of the mountain intersects
> ... Summertown Road, leading from Chattanooga to the
> summit. Lookout Mountain extends southwestwardly
> from the river across the northwest corner of Georgia
> and into Alabama, and Raccoon Mountain lies west of
> it and parallel to it in its general direction. Between the
> two is Lookout Valley. On the eastern side of this valley
> is a succession of hills, and between these hills and the
> mountain runs Lookout Creek, which empties into the
> Tennessee at the northern end of the mountain opposite
> Moccasin Point ... so called because of its resemblance to
> an Indian's shoe ... a peninsula formed by a loop which
> the Tennessee makes in reversing its southward course ...
> The ankle of the Indian shoe represents the neck of the
> peninsula at its narrowest point, the distance being about
> a mile across from Brown's Ferry."[3]

U.S. Grant expounded on the matter in noting that Lookout Mountain,
at a height of 2,200 feet, sat to the west of the valley, Missionary Ridge,
above Chattanooga Creek, on the east. East of Missionary Ridge flowed

South Chickamauga River; on the west of Lookout Mountain sat Lookout Creek, with Raccoon Mountain farther west of that."[4]

After the battle of Chickamauga, the Union army was retired to Chattanooga and formed in front of the city. Federal troops under Rosecrans, Crittenden, and McCook, followed later by Major General George H. Thomas, entered the city seeking refuge. General Braxton Bragg's Confederates soon followed, taking control of the high ground that surrounded the Federal position in Chattanooga Valley.[5]

Bragg's army of approximately 30,000 would face a Federal force of as many as 60 to 70,000 men. Major General George H. Thomas led the Army of the Cumberland with the Fourth Army Corps under Major General Gordon Granger; Major General O.C. Howard led the Eleventh Corps, Brigadier General John W. Geary the Twelfth Corps, and Major General J.M. Palmer the Fourteenth Corps. Major General William T. Sherman's Army of the Tennessee, with Major General Frank P. Blair, Jr. in command of the Fifteenth Corps and Brigadier General John E. Smith leading the Seventeenth Army Corps, would join them before the battle's conclusion. Engineer troops, cavalry, and artillery reserves also swelled the Federal ranks.[6]

Bragg's Confederates included the men of Lieutenant General William Hardee's Corps and Major General John C. Breckinridge's Corps. Hardee's subordinates included the likes of brigadier generals John K. Jackson and States Rights Gist, as well as major generals Carter L. Stevenson and Patrick Cleburne. Brigadier generals J. Patton Anderson and William Bate joined Major General A.P. Stewart to round out Breckinridge's corps commanders. Artillery and cavalry joined these to complete the Confederate forces at Chattanooga.[7]

Confederate brigadier general E.C. Walthall, a brigade commander in Cheatham's Division of Hardee's corps, recorded the location of the opposing forces as:

> "The right of the line, on the left bank of the river, rested northeast of Lookout Mountain, but on the opposite side the Union forces occupied Moccasin Point and planted batteries there and picketed the stream down to Brown's Ferry and beyond. The defenses at Chattanooga, already strong, were improved, and when the Union line had been covered by rifle pits the position seemed so secure against assault that when Bragg came up he decided not

attack General Rosecrans, but to besiege him. For this the topographic conditions seemed favorable, and, with the dispositions ... Bragg made of his force, the investment for the time seemed complete and effective. His right rested on the river above Chattanooga; his left ... at a point on the river west of Lookout Mountain and below Brown's Ferry ... Rosecrans could not supply his army by ... the railroad, the river, or the wagon roads along its banks on either side."[8]

The Confederate siege of the Union forces under Rosecrans, prior to his replacement by Thomas, caused Rosecrans to give a strong impression for the inclination toward retreating from the area. U.S. Grant later wrote of this proposal that this "terrible disaster" would have lost the strategic point to the Confederates and would have resulted in a loss of all the artillery in the Army of the Cumberland as well as the demoralization or capture of the Union army itself.[9]

Grant was quick to note, "The artillery horses and mules had become so reduced by starvation that they could not have been relied on for moving anything ... more than ten thousand animals had perished in supplying half rations to the troops."[10]

Another Union officer reported that the receipt of half rations had necessitated troughs of artillery horses to be guarded as a deterrent to soldiers attempting to take the animals' corn. The limited arrival of supply wagons often resulted in their being followed by hungry troops who picked up grains of corn as small additions to their scant rations.[11]

Bragg's possession of Lookout and Raccoon mountains on the west of Chattanooga, along with the aforementioned river, railroad, and the shortest and best wagon roads south and north of the river between Chattanooga and Bridgeport, Alabama had brought about these conditions for the Union soldiers. The two locations were just twenty-six rail miles apart, but Rosecrans saw Bragg's position as necessitating the use of a route over the mountains. This new route increased the distance between the two communities to more than sixty miles. The limited amount of poor-quality beef the soldiers received caused the frequent declaration that the troops were sustained by "beef dried on the hoof." Wood became another scarce commodity and created the practice of cutting trees a great distance upstream, creating rafts of them, and floating these downstream using poles as paddles.[12]

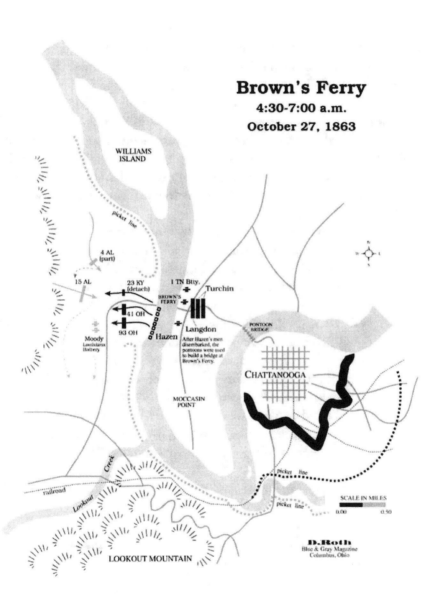

Brown's Ferry

4:30-7:00 a.m.

October 27, 1863

WILLIAMS ISLAND

picket line

4 AL (part)

15 AL

23 KY (detach)

1 TN Btty.

Turchin

BROWN'S FERRY

41 OH

93 OH

Moody Louisiana Battery

Hazen

Langdon

After Hazen's men disembarked, the pontoons were used to build a bridge at Brown's Ferry.

PONTOON BRIDGE

CHATTANOOGA

MOCCASIN POINT

Lookout Creek

railroad

Picket line

Picket line

LOOKOUT MOUNTAIN

SCALE IN MILES

0.00   0.50

D. Roth
Blue & Gray Magazine
Columbus, Ohio

Despite these conditions, General Thomas was informed upon his assumption of command of the Army of the Cumberland that Chattanooga must be held at all costs. In addition, he learned that Grant would come to his relief as soon as possible. Grant met with Rosecrans, who was returning north, and listened carefully to what he regarded as excellent suggestions on the part of Rosecrans. Grant wrote that he only wondered why Rosecrans "had failed to carry out these ideas."[13] Many of these would serve as points of Grant's strategy and would affect a positive outcome on the part of the Federals in Chattanooga.

Meanwhile, Confederate attacks by Joe Wheeler's cavalry destroyed hundreds of Federal wagons bound for Chattanooga along the sixty-mile trail from Bridgeport. In addition, those wagons running the gauntlet were subject to attack from Confederates closer to Chattanooga. One later incident was recorded by a member of the Ninth Tennessee, who wrote:

> "One day a foraging party of the enemy came in sight with thirty or forty wagons and about one regiment of infantry. All of the wagons but seven passed on, when the regiment halted and stacked arms, and the men were soon busily engaged in gathering a field of corn ... Every available man of our seventeen ... was soon in line, and going down a narrow trail we soon reached the creek below, where deployed as skirmishers ... the order was given, 'Fire' ... drivers dismounted, left their teams, and all rushed pell mell through the corn to where the guns were stacked ... We had captured thirty-five mules and six wagons, one mule having been killed in the fray ... This is my experience as picket on Lookout Mountain."[14]

The Confederate infantry fared little better than their besieged enemy. An officer recalled:

> "I reported the almost helpless state of my command on account of ... worthless arms, and was assured the matter would be attended to at once; but it was not done, and on the following day I received orders to proceed with my command to the eastern slope of Lookout Mountain and relieve the brigade on duty at this point. We were without tents, having been ordered to leave these in our

first encampment, near the foot of the mountain. Many of the men were scantily supplied with blankets, as well as provisions, which consisted principally of rice and beans. During the three weeks we occupied this position the men were frequently exposed to a cold north wind, the ground being sometimes covered with snow. When we secured ammunition we found the cartridges either too large or too small for a number of the guns. When too small they could at least be inserted in the barrel and held in place by ramming leaves on top as wadding; but when a snugly fitting cartridge was inserted into a gun with a worthless lock spring the soldier frequently discovered it had become permanently lodged in the barrel."[15]

In late October, General Grant, perhaps knowledgeable of the Confederates' weapon plight, ordered an attack upon the road to Bridgeport, a successful operation that opened a supply route that Federal soldiers deemed the "cracker line."[16] The surprise move down the Tennessee River had surprised the Confederate pickets and lessened the suffering of the Union troops and doubtless led to demoralization of the Confederates.

A Confederate wrote:

"by a skillful movement, perfect in conception and execution, the Union forces seized the hills covering the outlets by Brown's Ferry, and held them, and bridged the river at that point, as well as at a point on the opposite side of the peninsula next to Chattanooga. Thereafter the army in Chattanooga had uninterrupted communication with Stevenson and Bridgeport and a much shorter route by which reinforcements could be sent to Lookout Valley than the Confederates had, and the siege was ended; but for some reason the partial investment was kept up."[17]

Other battle assignments from Grant immediately followed. In addition to a successful movement to Brown's Ferry, General Palmer moved down the river's north side to hold the rear of Hooker's troops; 1,800 men of Hazen's command, used 60 pontoon boats to capture Confederate pickets.[18]

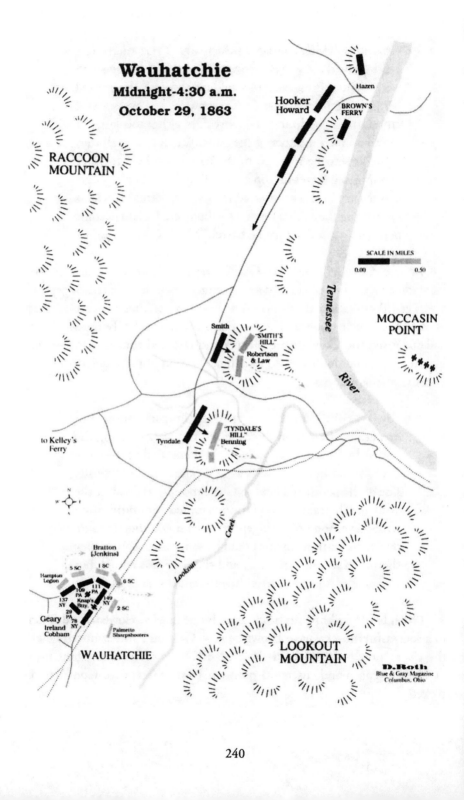

Wauhatchie
Midnight-4:30 a.m.
October 29, 1863

Hooker
Howard

Hazen

BROWN'S
FERRY

RACCOON
MOUNTAIN

SCALE IN MILES

0.00   0.50

Tennessee

MOCCASIN
POINT

Smith

"SMITH'S
HILL"

Robertson
& Law

River

"TYNDALE'S
HILL"
Benning

to Kelley's
Ferry

Tyndale

N
W   E
S

Creek

Bratton
(Jenkins)

5 SC   1 SC

Hampton
Legion   6 SC

109   111
PA   PA

137   Knap's   149
NY   Bttty.   NY

29   2 SC
PA   78
NY

Geary
Ireland
Cobham

Palmetto
Sharpshooters

WAUHATCHIE

Lookout

LOOKOUT
MOUNTAIN

D. Roth
Blue & Gray Magazine
Columbus, Ohio

With the subsequent securing of Kelley's Ferry, eight miles from Chattanooga and connected to the town by a good wagon road, a host of provisions found their way to the Union soldiers. Shoes and clothing that had been previously lacking for the oncoming winter were now present.[19]

Brevet Major General William Farrar Smith, U.S., proclaimed that the completion of this task "gave at once to the army food; clothing, with forage for the animals which were yet alive, and ... ammunition ... From being an army in a condition in which it could not retreat, it became an army which, [as] soon as it was reinforced by the troops with Sherman, assumed the offensive."[20]

On November 15, W.T. Sherman arrived in Chattanooga. Though Grant feared for the safety of Ambrose Burnside and his command at Knoxville, the battle plan he had devised for Chattanooga could effectively be implemented. It included Sherman attacking the Confederate right flank and crossing it in order to threaten or hold the railroad to Bragg's rear. Hooker was to perform the same task on the left flank of the Confederates, and Thomas, at the center, was to assault the enemy while most of its members were engaged on the flanks. Hooker's orders were changed when it was determined that Lookout Valley had little value to the Union army and was sent to the right toward Rossville.[21] The number advantage fell to the Union and the stage was set for their advance upon the Confederates.

On the night of November 22, a Confederate deserter reported that Bragg was withdrawing his troops from Chattanooga. A letter sent under a flag of truce from Bragg to Grant two days earlier led to the same understanding in stating, "As there may still be some non-combatants in Chattanooga, I deem it proper to notify you that prudence would dictate their early withdrawal."[22]

General Thomas was directed to establish the validity of the deserter's report by attacking the Confederate pickets. The Confederates were driven from their first line and the Federal troops secured an eminence sometimes referred to as Orchard Knoll. During the night, this position was fortified with artillery and it was also determined that a division of Buckner's corps had left the Confederate position and that a second had begun the movement from the city, only to return on the expectation of a Federal attack.[23]

The opposing pickets, to this point at least, had carried out their respective tasks in a rather friendly manner. A member of Company E, Thirty-fourth Mississippi Regiment, Walthall's brigade recalled:

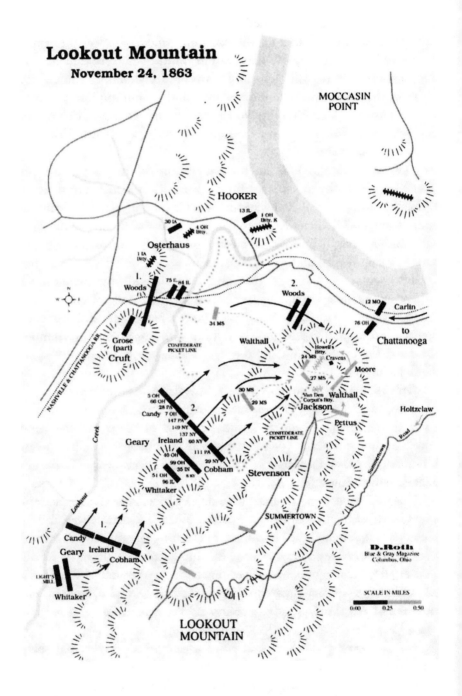

Lookout Mountain
November 24, 1863

MOCCASIN POINT

HOOKER

30 IA
4 OH Bty

13 fl
1 OH Bty. K

Osterhaus

1 IA Bty

1.
Woods

75 IL 84 IL

2.
Woods

34 MS

12 MO
76 OH

Carlin

to
Chattanooga

Grose (part)
Cruft

CONFEDERATE PICKET LINE

Walthall

Howell's Bty.
24 MS
Cravens
Moore
27 MS

NASHVILLE & CHATTANOOGA RR

5 OH
66 OH
28 PA
Candy   7 OH
147 PA
149 NY
137 NY
Geary   Ireland   60 NY

2.

30 MS
29 MS

Van Den Corput's Bty.
Jackson

Walthall

CONFEDERATE PICKET LINE

Pettus

Holtzclaw

Creek

40 OH
99 OH   111 PA
35 IN   29 NY
51 OH   8 KY
96 IL   Cobham

Whitaker

Stevenson

Summertown Road

Lookout

SUMMERTOWN

Candy   1.
Geary   Ireland
Cobham

D. Roth
Blue & Gray Magazine
Columbus, Ohio

LIGHT'S MILL

Whitaker

SCALE IN MILES
0.00   0.25   0.50

LOOKOUT
MOUNTAIN

"We had been stationed on the northwest slope of old Lookout for some two weeks doing picket duty. Our line was down near the base of the mountain, nearly half a mile from camp, and it extended quite a distance to the west and north. Chattanooga Creek, a small stream, flowed between us and the Yankee pickets. We were on very friendly terms with each other, and exchange of canteens, tobacco, coffee, etc., occurred daily. It was understood along the picket-line that if either side received orders to advance they would give a signal, so the enemy could have time to get back to their breastworks ... our company was on picket near where the Nashville and Chattanooga railroad crosses the creek. Everything was quiet, the pickets were in plain view, and neither thought of shooting without giving notice. That night about twelve o'clock the pickets were relieved, Company F, taking our place. Picket posts were always relieved at night."[24]

Sherman moved his troops across the river in full view of the Confederates atop Lookout Mountain. The Federal troops gained concealment using the hills on the north side and would only be seen again when ready to strike the bank of the river. General Howard, in full view of the Confederates, took his troops from the north side and moved to the south side, giving the illusion that his troops were actually those of Sherman. The latter was then able to move into position without detection.[25]

On the morning of the twenty-third, Thomas moved his troops to the foot of Fort Wood, located on a hill east of town. At two o'clock that afternoon, an advance began on the position, and clouds that had concealed the movements earlier in the day lifted to reveal to the Confederates the foe that awaited them. The Confederate pickets were quickly driven back upon the main guard before it too fell to the Union advance. The costly advance placed the Federal line one mile from where it stood that morning. The Federal casualties were approximately 1,100 killed and wounded, with similar estimates for the Confederates.[26]

Such actions caused confusion in the Confederate ranks, a point easily understood when examining the words of a recipient of the Federal assault:

"The Federal batteries in the valley between the mountain and Missionary Ridge [opened up], and kept it up until dark. It was believed that this bombardment was a feint to cover Grant's retreat from Chattanooga as many troops were seen crossing the river on pontoons and going west, but in this view the Confederates were misled, as the movement of Federal troops west of the Tennessee River was for the purpose of making an attack on the mountain at daylight … They attacked Walthall's Brigade … many of them came through … General John C. Moore's [brigade] which was about five hundred yards in rear of Walthall's."[27]

Brigadier General John C. Moore, Cheatham's Division, wrote:

"no serious effort had been made to construct defensive works for our forces on the mountain. It is true some of the timber in front of Walthall's Brigade had been cut down and a narrow, shallow, but worthless, line of trenches, unworthily called rifle pits, extended from Walthall's left to the Craven house, and from the extremity of a short line of stone fence at this point to the mouth of Chattanooga Creek a still more abortive pretense had been made."[28]

Moore continued his elaboration of disgust, "Up to the hour of assault I had never received a word of instruction as to the disposition of my command or the proposed line of defense, if any had even been determined, in case of attack."[29]

Recollections of confusion on the part of the Confederate commanders showed in the reminiscences of one who wrote:

"The day preceding Gen. Hooker's assault on our lines we could see from our mountain perch great activity among the Federal forces on the open plain in front of Chattanooga, large bodies of troops apparently forming in masses, deploying in single, double, or treble lines of battle … They also planted a battery on an Indian mound situated on what had been treated as neutral ground lying between the Confederate and Federal picket lines … we noticed that everything seemed perfectly quiet among the Federal forces north of Lookout Creek. These conditions led me to believe that preparations were being made to attack Gen. Bragg's lines on Missionary Ridge, but subsequent events proved that the whole movement was made as a feint to mislead us as to the intended point of attack, Lookout Mountain."[30]

Generals Thomas and Grant, standing atop Orchard Knob on the twenty-fourth, witnessed the Federal advance. Hooker's movement received assistance from Geary's division as they moved, under cover of mist, to cross Lookout Creek. By 11 o'clock, a bridge was completed over the creek, and Hooker's advance completed the Union line, making it continual. The side of Lookout Mountain Hooker faced "was rugged, heavily timbered, and full of chasms ... difficult to advance with troops."[31]

Though a heavy fog limited Grant's vision of Hooker's movements "except at moments when the clouds would rise," the continual sound of muskets and cannon confirmed the ferocity of the action.[32]

Hooker's advance had captured more than forty Confederate pickets at Light's Mill without firing a shot. Hooker was used as a diversion, as Sherman was to cross the Tennessee River that morning for an afternoon attack. Hooker used his knowledge of the Confederate breastwork layout to his advantage, for he knew the limited preparations had been made for an uphill attack. Instead, Hooker made his assault from the south, along the side of the mountain, negating any advantage the Confederates could have had in using their works.

A Confederate wrote:

> "about sunrise, we heard several musket-shots ... assuring us that friendly relations had ceased ... a messenger came from the picket-line, calling for two companies from our regiment. By the time those two got to the front another messenger came, calling for the balance ... Lieut.-Col. McElwaine ... deployed the entire regiment as skirmishers. Had we remained in that position, the battle ... might have resulted very differently, because the line of pickets covered nearly all that part of the western base of the mountain, and could not have been successfully assailed by the enemy ... in a few minutes the whole regiment was

assembled near where the railroad crosses the creek ... the western face of the mountain being thus left unguarded ... the enemy had nothing to do but march up and find Walthall's Brigade lying around with their guns stacked ... Walthall got his men in line promptly and checked the enemy's advance ... our regiment was at the foot of the mountain, cut off from the rest of the brigade ... We fell back slowly, as the mountain was very steep and rugged. In all my war experience, I never passed through just such a bombardment. It seemed that every battery in the Federal army was pouring bombshells and solid shot into the side of that mountain. The shells burst, knocking off thousands of pieces of rock and scattering them hither and thither. The whole face of the mountain was lurid with bursting shells and seemed to belch smoke from every crevice, while the mountain itself seemed to howl and shriek as if a million demons had been aroused in its caverns. Slowly climbing and struggling up through all that awful storm of iron and smoke, we at last reached our former camp, to find it literally covered with Federal troops between us and our brigade ... In a moment our flag was down, and the Thirty-Fourth Mississippi Regiment had surrendered."[33]

Gen. Walthall added:

"by nine o'clock ... Batteries on the hills beyond Lookout Creek and several pieces in the valley opened fire on my position ... soon my command was under a heavy fire in front and pressed on the left flank by a force of more than three times its own number ... Gen. Thomas ... says, 'the resistance was obstinate' and Gen. Bragg ... that it was 'desperate' ... That the entire command ... was not captured may be ascribed to the rugged field ... When ... troops reached the ridge running down the northern slope of the mountain the guns on Moccasin Point soon rendered any further resistance impossible, and they made their way in confusion past Craven's house under a sweeping artillery fire ... passing Craven's house about four hundred yards they were reformed in a strong position at a narrow point on the east side of the mountain ... At nightfall the Confederates were still on this line, which covered the Summertown Road, the only avenue of communication between the troops on the top of the mountain and the main army and were never driven from it ... During the night Bragg withdrew all troops from the mountain ... in the morning the United States flag was floating at Lookout Point."[34]

Another Confederate, H.H. Sturgis, company H, Forty-fourth Alabama, wrote:

"We were driven from our insecure breastworks ... we were greatly outnumbered. Twice we recovered our works and drove them down the hill ... Once when we recaptured our works a Federal and a Confederate were seen with their left hands in each other's collar, grasping their guns with their right hands, neither being willing to surrender. A lieutenant, seeing the predicament, ordered the Yank to surrender, which he refused to do, when the deadlock was broken with a bullet ... I saw a man roll down the mountain side, started by a ball from my gun when only a few feet distant from its muzzle. He had the first shot at me, his ball passing through my hat."[35]

J. Earl Preston, Moore's brigade, added:

"It was almost 8 a.m. when Moore's Brigade was ordered forward, engaged the enemy, and held them where Walthall's Brigade left them until about 3 p.m., when, becoming much exhausted, we were relieved by Clayton's Brigade ... Clayton was relieved by Pettus ... and the fight continued until about midnight, when firing ceased. About 2 a.m ... .an order was received from Gen. Bragg to evacuate, and thus ended the fight on Lookout Mountain ... At sunrise we reached the base of Missionary Ridge, and were halted to partake of an elaborate breakfast of cornbread and raw, fat bacon. The bread was three days old and the bacon of uncertain age."[36]

One of the most significant areas leading to the Federal success came with Sherman's attack on a railroad tunnel. The Fifth Iowa had made a forced march from Memphis to Chattanooga, a distance of 400 miles, to assist in relieving the besieged Federals. The regiment fixed bayonets and positioned themselves in a spot of trees, relatively hidden from the Confederate cannon fire, and made an advance against strong resistance and cannon fire. Splintered fence rails "shrieking ... cannon-balls and bursting ... shells" met the Union attackers, many of whom fell captive to the Confederates in a superb counterattack. Eventually, Thomas led others up Missionary Ridge, but those Federals captured here were herded to Andersonville, where untold hardships awaited them.[37]

Confederate brigadier general John K. Jackson remembered the Confederate withdrawal from the mountain and noted that after crossing south of Chattanooga Creek, the bridge spanning the creek was burned. An infantryman also recalled that the next night he and his comrades used a narrow footpath to exit the area and head toward Knoxville. Another wrote, "Next morning ... it was found that nineteen, out of about seven hundred" of his regiment had escaped captivity and a trip to a Northern prisoner-of-war camp.[38]

In his official report, General Grant wrote that the Federal losses were 757 killed, 4,529 wounded, and 330 missing, for a total casualty figure of 5,616. He also noted that the Confederate losses should have been less, as they were entrenched while the Federals were advancing upon a fortified position. In addition, Grant claimed that he had gained 6,142 prisoners, of whom 239 were commissioned officers. Forty pieces of artillery, sixty-nine artillery carriages and caissons, and seven thousand small arms were also noted as being gained in the struggle.[39]

Confederate reports showed that Pettus's brigade had a total of fifty-six men killed, wounded, and missing. Of an effective force of 1,205, Moore's brigade listed 251 casualties. Walthall's brigade reported 99 killed and wounded, with 845 missing from an effective force of 1,489. The total Confederate number reported killed was 361; wounded stood at 2,180; and 4146 missing, for a total of 6,687.[40]

The battle produced opposite outcomes for the commanders of the opposing armies at Chattanooga. Ulysses S. Grant was given the leadership of all Union armies, a move that increased his popularity nationwide and resulted in his eventual election to the presidency. Braxton Bragg, on the other hand, resigned after his defeat at the mountains around Chattanooga and slipped into basic obscurity.

Visitors today to Lookout Mountain and Chattanooga will find the area has grown tremendously since the days of 1863. Lookout Valley is the location of a number of establishments, including trailer parks and strip malls. Chickamauga and Chattanooga National Military Park has a number of sites that remain from the battle. Captured cannon, the site of the Union soldiers' scaling of the Palisades to bring about the end of the battle, and an excellent overview from the park are points of interest.

More than 900,000 tourists come to the park each year to see where the Confederacy's doom and the advance upon Atlanta were made official. The park, the largest of its type, is the first established after the war, created in 1890, and became the symbol of reconciliation for a number of veterans of both armies. The railroads that served as a lifeline for the industries of the area are still a major part of the city's economy, as is the war itself. A number of area attractions center on the battle, and lure tourists from all around the world.

The Craven house and other structures have been rebuilt or restored to provide visitors a real sense of the battle's structures. Monuments to soldiers from Iowa, Ohio, New York, and Illinois, along with informational markers, dominate the Craven House grounds. A walk of four-tenths of a mile results in an encounter with Confederate rifle pits atop Lookout Mountain. Park trails, many atop those used by soldiers during the battle, take visitors to locations such as Point Park that allow interpretation and beautiful vistas. Private drives and residences dot Lookout Mountain, providing a minor challenge for visitors to the area. The narrow and curvy road to the Craven House is without guardrails, and necessitates the skills of a heads-up driver. Open every day but Christmas, the park is a must for Civil War enthusiasts, but it also shows how areas of a battlefield succumb to urbanization.

Post-battle view of Moccasin Bend. Courtesy of Confederate Veteran.

Modern view of Moccasin Bend. Photo by author.

View of Chattanooga from Garrity's Alabama Battery located in Point Park atop Lookout Mountain. Photo by author.

The Craven house. Photo by author.

The road to Point Park contains several signs such as these with limited access and visibility. Photo by author.

Along Brown's Ferry Road in Lookout Valley, businesses, traffic, and a variety of signage make it practically impossible to locate the state markers related to Brown's Ferry and the battle of Wauhatchie. Photo by author.

CHAPTER FIFTEEN

FORT PILLOW

Military Necessity or Massacre?
April 12, 1864

Fort Pillow was originally built in 1861-62 as a Confederate river fort, intended to retard the Union's westward advance. Situated forty miles north of Memphis on the Mississippi River and at the mouth of Coal Creek, the installation was named for Major General Gideon J. Pillow, a veteran of the Mexican War. The fort would remain in Confederate hands until a series of events led to their June 1862 evacuation. The struggles of the early days of Fort Pillow's existence are significant, as numerous articles have acknowledged. Events occurring nearly two years later in April 1864 are the incidents that routinely provide a sense of infamy and source of controversy to the location and for the Confederate soldiers and their leader who attacked the establishment.

Originally built to comprise a five-mile circumference including a river battery along the bluffs, the fort had an outer breastwork line in a U-shaped fashion. Trees had been cleared to a distance of approximately one-half mile around the perimeter. Inner breastworks had been built under the orders of Confederate brigadier general J.B. Villepigul, who determined the outer breastworks too long to defend.

By early April of 1864, Union troops occupied the fort, consisting only of a 125-yard-long dirt parapet. Six feet thick at its most-concentrated point, the eight-foot-high structure was surrounded by a twelve-foot-wide and six-foot-deep ditch on the land-ward side. The fort was open to the river.[1]

A superb description of the area explained that the Federal works were built upon the highest part of the bluff and enclosed a northwest angle that was formed by the river and Coal Creek. To the east, a gradual slope from the crown next to the river for as much as sixty yards led into a gorge that combined with hills and ridges to allow "well-covered approaches for an enemy to within thirty to one hundred yards of the interior intrenchments." On the outside of the works, four rows of cabins and tents lay to the left of a rifle pit.[2]

One participant added, "Fort Pillow was the muddiest fort, or any other place, that I ever saw and [had] the meanest water on the continent."[3]

Five hundred fifty-seven Union troops manned this location on April 12, 1864. Two hundred ninety-five white troops, many of whom were termed as "Tennessee Tories" or "home grown Yankees" from West Tennessee and North Alabama joined two hundred sixty-two African Americans inside the fort.[4]

The precise make-up of the Federal army was the First Battalion, Thirteenth Tennessee Cavalry, Major William F. Bradford commanding, 10 officers and 285 enlisted men; First Battalion, Sixth U.S. Heavy Artillery, colored, 8 commissioned officers and 213 enlisted men; and 1 section Company D, Second U.S. Light Artillery, colored, 1 commissioned officer and 40 men.[5]

Approximately 1,600 of Nathan Bedford Forrest's Confederates arrived at Fort Pillow before dawn on April 12. The group had left Jackson, Tennessee on the morning of April 10, marching seventy-two miles in two days. Brigadier General Frank J. Chalmers was under orders from Forrest to attack upon arrival, in order to surprise the Union defenders. Chalmers deployed Col. Tyree Bell's Brigade to the fort's north and east sides; Col. Robert M. McCulloch's Brigade moved to the south of the fort.[6]

General Forrest and Major Charles Anderson had stopped in Brownsville, Tennessee for a few hours' rest, while Chalmers proceeded toward the fort. Approximately eight miles from Fort Pillow, the duo and an escort under the command of Lt. Col. Wisdom heard cannon fire,[7] quickening the group's approach toward the sound of battle and Fort Pillow.

Meanwhile, the action at Fort Pillow had been quick and decisive. Despite the delay the terrain had caused on the Confederate movement, the advance guard of the Confederates had captured a group of Federal pickets, one of whom managed to escape and return to the fort. A Confederate participant recalled that the "very slight resistance" was rapidly subdued and that at 8 o'clock that morning, the fort was under heavy fire from artillery and infantry.[8]

Union major L. F. Booth, commander of Fort Pillow, fell victim to a sharpshooter's aim near 9 o'clock. His adjutant stood at his side and was also killed. Major William F. Bradford, Thirteenth Tennessee Cavalry,[9] gained control of the besieged garrison.

Booth had divided four of his companies and placed two each at the guns and in the rifle pits. Two ten-pound Parrott rifled guns, two twelve-pound howitzers, and two six-pound rifled-bore field pieces added strength to the infantry's firepower. Booth saw his men repel two Confederate charges and challenged his command to "never surrender" moments before falling to his fatal wound.[10]

Near 10 o'clock, General Forrest arrived at the fort and assumed command from Chalmers. The latter informed Forrest that the Union troops were positioned within the rifle pits and an attempt to capture the position would result in heavy losses. Forrest and Major Anderson then "made a rapid circuit around the land side of the fort from the Federal horse lot to Coal Creek." The Federals fired several shots at the officers, wounding Forrest's horse and killing a second from underneath him before he made a complete survey of the area.[11]

Forrest soon spotted a ravine that encircled a majority of the fort's perimeter. He noted that sharpshooters could take positions on the surrounding high ground and, from these locations, command most of the fort's interior and enfilade its retreating angles, making the occupation of them exceedingly hazardous. The superb Confederate general also acknowledged that gaining possession of the ravine would offer his troops a great deal of protection and place them in a position in which only the earthworks separated the two armies.[12]

Forrest ordered Chalmers to advance his line in stating "move up," reportedly Forrest's favorite phrase in such situations. Bell's brigade moved forward, gaining shelter on the right of the fort, extending southward from the mouth of Coal Creek. McCullough's brigade carried the entrenchments on the highest point of a ridge to the left, extending northward and from the ravine below the fort northward. McCullough's right joined Bell's left abreast the fort.[13]

The Federal gunboat Number 7, *New Era*, under the command of Captain James Marshall, had, during the Confederate advance, in the words of General Forrest, "Kept up a continued fire … without effect."

The Confederate sharpshooters had drawn closer to the fort; the Federal occupants were surrounded on all sides. Two companies of the Thirteenth Tennessee Cavalry were sent from the fort to offer opposition to the attackers, but soon returned to the confines of the fort as Confederate sharpshooters steadily fired while holding positions behind high knolls, trees, and logs.[14]

Four rows of buildings stood to the front of the fort; Booth, in the minutes preceding his death, had ordered them burned to prevent them from falling into Confederate hands. The possibility of the Confederate capture of these buildings for use as snipers' nests or as staging areas for an assault upon the fort weighed heavily upon the mind of the commander. Unfortunately for the Federal occupants of Fort Pillow, only the row of buildings closest to the fort were able to be destroyed prior to Forrest's sharpshooters gaining control of the buildings and using them for the purpose Booth so feared.[15]

At 3:30 PM, General Forrest, confident of his position, sent Captain Walter A. Goodman, Lt. Frank Rodgers, and Captain Thomas Henderson under a flag of truce to demand the Union surrender of Fort Pillow. Forrest reported, "being confident of my ability to take the fort by assault, and desiring to prevent further loss of life, I sent ... a demand for the unconditional surrender of the garrison."[16]

Major Charles Anderson recalled:

> "Gen. Forrest ... knew the place was practically in his possession, as the enemy could not depress their artillery so as to rake the slopes around the fort with grape and canister, and the constant and fatal fire of our sharpshooters forced the besieged to keep down behind their parapets. He believed the Federal commander fully recognized the situation, and that he would accept an offer to surrender in preference to an assault by a force much larger than his own, and in full view. Bugles were sounded for a truce and a parley, and a white flag sent forward with a demand for the immediate and unconditional surrender of all the Federal troops at Fort Pillow."[17]

The Confederate trio delivered a written demand that effectively stated:

"As your gallant defense of the fort has entitled you to the treatment of brave men, I now demand an unconditional surrender of your force, at the same time assuring you that they will be treated as prisoners of war. I have received a fresh supply of ammunition, and can easily take your position. N.B. Forrest"[18]

There was reportedly a foreboding in the note's ending, wherein Forrest said he would not be responsible for the fate of the command should the surrender demands not be met. Captain Goodman recalled that a conversation erupted over the contents and questions were given as to whether or not the terms applied to the entire garrison, black and white, being treated as prisoners of war. The reply from Forrest and Chalmers was positive[19] in that the directive was inclusive of all the fort's defenders.

The futility of the situation for the Federals was clearly evident. General Forrest had issued the demand for surrender from a hill upon which he sat as the note's delivery was made. From there, he held a full view of the fort's interior. The Confederates held such a tight position around the fort that before the flag of truce had passed the point of the line held by the left side of McCullough's Brigade, it had to be stopped; there the meeting described above took place.[20]

Major Bradford replied to Forrest's declaration by asking for an hour to consult with his officers before making his decision. Bradford had also signed the name of the recently deceased Major Booth to his reply, evidently desiring that the Confederates remain ignorant of Booth's death. Bradford noted to General Forrest that a time of communication with the officers of the *New Era* was desired. Forrest's subsequent note, explaining that the surrender of the fort and garrison was sought, not that of the gunboat, was amended to state that the timeframe for surrender was twenty minutes, not an hour, as had been requested. Forrest also emphasized the point that he could not be responsible for the consequences should the fort be stormed. Bradford, a West Tennessee native, was certainly aware of the strained relationship between the two armies facing one another at Fort Pillow. Forrest directed Captain W.A. Goodman, under a flag of truce, to personally wait for a reply or for the expiration of time.[21]

Forrest saw Goodman's delivery of the demand and the presentation of the reply. With the latter incident occurring, General Forrest rode forward to receive the answer.[22] The response would set the stage for one of the most controversial incidents of the entire war.

General Forrest reported:

> "The answer was handed me, written in pencil on a slip of
> paper, without envelope, and was, as well as I remember,
> in these words: 'Negotiations will not attain the desired
> object.' As the officers who were in charge of the Federal
> flag of truce expressed a doubt as to my presence, and
> had pronounced the demand a trick, I handed them
> back the note, saying, 'I am General Forrest; go back
> and say to Major Booth that I demand an answer in
> plain, unmistakable English: Will he fight or surrender?'
> Returning to my original position, before the expiration
> of twenty minutes I received a reply ... 'We will not
> surrender.'"[23]

During the truce period, three Federal steamers rapidly approached
the fort. Leading the approach was the *Olive Branch,* which one witness
described as being "crowded from forecastle to hurricane deck with Federal
soldiers and the lower guards filled with artillery." The ship appeared
to be headed toward shore; but the Confederates opened fire upon it,
necessitating its turn toward the far bank. The *Hope* and *M.R. Cheek*
followed the *Olive Branch* to the river's west side, all three vessels passing
the position of the gunboat *New Era,* now located just above the fort. [24]

The appearance of the steamers caused General Forrest to dispatch
Captain Charles W. Anderson, his aide-de-camp, to lead a squadron of
McCulloch's Brigade into the old trenches the Confederates had dug
two years earlier. From this position under the bluff at the river, above
the mouth of the ravine, and just below the southern face of the works,
Anderson ordered the above-mentioned shots to be fired at the *Olive
Branch.*[25]

This movement has caused debates for generations. The repositioning of
the soldiers took place under a flag of truce; this is indisputable. However,
both Major Bradford and Captain Marshall were among the Federal
occupants of the fort and saw the motion, offered no objections, nor
attempted to resist or check it.[26] Likewise, the approach of the gunboats
was the action that reportedly created this controversial realignment.

Captain Anderson made an interesting discovery on this foray and
recorded it years later. He wrote:

"The bugler of the Thirteenth Tennessee Federal Cavalry had taken advantage of the truce to recover his trappings from his horse ... I discovered him, with his back to me, busily engaged in securing his gum cloth and coat. I waited quietly until he turned to regain the fort. His astonishment and trepidation can well be imagined at finding a six shooter leveled at his face and an able bodied 'Reb' behind it. Ordering him to hand me his carbine butt end foremost, and then to untie his horse and lead him out ahead of me, I rode down ... to the General's position."[27]

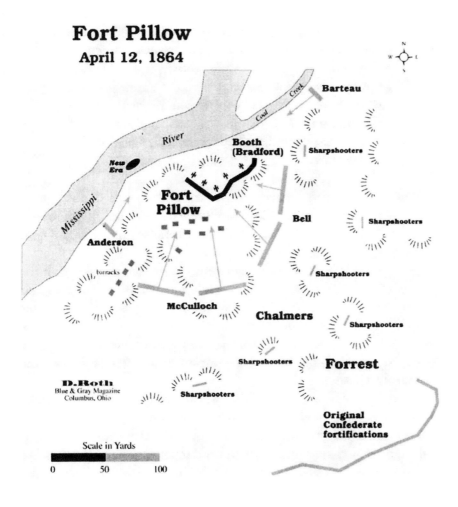

Fort Pillow
April 12, 1864

Barteau

Coal Creek

River

New Era

Booth (Bradford)

Sharpshooters

Fort Pillow

Mississippi

Bell

Sharpshooters

Anderson

barracks

Sharpshooters

McCulloch

Chalmers

Sharpshooters

Forrest

Sharpshooters

D. Roth
Blue & Gray Magazine
Columbus, Ohio

Sharpshooters

Original
Confederate
fortifications

Scale in Yards

0   50   100

Anderson returned to General Forrest with relevant news. In his own words:

> "I ... communicated to him the position of the gunboat, also that two large empty barges were cabled to the shore in rear of the fort, which might be utilized by the garrison ... as a means of escape. I was equally particular in impressing upon him the hazardous position of the detachment on the face of the bluff, out of sight of, and entirely separated from, the balance of the command, and that in the event of any failure to carry the works by assault, a sortie from the south entrance of the fort in their rear, with the gunboat and its cannon and marines in their front, their destruction or capture would certainly follow. He fully recognized their isolated and exposed position ... he directed me to return to my position at once, to take no part in the assault, but to prevent any escape from the garrison by barges or otherwise, to pour rifle balls into the open ports of the *New Era* when she went into action, and, to use his last expression, 'fight everything blue between wind and water until yonder flag comes down.'"[28]

Union troops had doubted the presence of General Forrest, yet a detachment confirmed his close proximity to the fort. Black troops recognized Forrest and proclaimed the fact while the white troops of both sides began a verbal assault upon one another.[29]

A response to Forrest's note demanding surrender returned with the aforementioned reply that surrender would not take place. Forrest stood surrounded by his staff and other officers, informing them to prepare for an attack upon the garrison. He returned to his earlier position upon the hill from which he held a complete view of the fort's interior. Just before moving up, he challenged his troops to plant their battle flags upon the parapets they'd soon be attacking.[30]

Captain Anderson recalled, "This was the situation as taken in while anxiously awaiting the sound of Gan's well-known bugle. It soon came; was repeated along the line, and at once followed by the yells of our men, and a terrific discharge of the batteries and small arms of the fort."[31]

General Forrest also reported that during this initial advance, the earthworks surrounding the fort were "carried without a perceptible halt in any part of the line." Another individual stated that the Confederates "crowning the parapet, poured over, on all sides, into the works. Leaping headlong into the ditch, these agile, hardy young men found it a feeble barrier, and helping each other ... over the breastworks ... opening from its crest a fearful, converging fire, from all its faces, upon the garrison."[32]

The entry of Forrest's men caused the majority of Federals inside the fort to retreat toward the river. Perhaps by an earlier arrangement, the blue-clad warriors, firing at the Confederates, ran toward the presumed safety of the riverbank. Forrest assumed that this was an attempt to signal the gunboat to release canister upon the Confederates while Bradford's Federals lay safe between the river and the fort. Captain Marshall confirmed Forrest's intuition, later explaining that the signal had been given for a Union retreat and that the time had arrived to fire upon the Confederates.[33]

Captain Anderson, to the left, with another detachment to the right, opened fire on the Federal rear. General Forrest explained that this volley provided many retreating Federals, with the first evidence of the Confederate presence at the rear. The Federals at this point appeared "panic-stricken, almost decimated."[34]

Anderson added:

> "a portion of the garrison rushed down toward the river, and upon them we opened a destructive fire. The yells of our troops as they mounted the parapets could be plainly heard above the din and rattle of musketry, and in a moment more the whole force of the garrison came rushing down the bluff toward the water with arms in hand, but only to fall thick and fast ... This fire ... was, for the few moments it lasted, most destructive and deadly. The moment the Federals' colors came down, I ordered firing to cease at once, and it was promptly done. Directing the commanding officer to bring his men out of the pits ... I dashed into the south entrance of the fort. Everything was in confusion and the dead and wounded were lying thick around, but there was no firing anywhere."[35]

At this point, controversy again abounds. Many Union accounts depict the Confederates shooting down Federal survivors, yelling, "No quarter, no quarter," in addition to a host of racially loaded phrases. Some stated the men in blue had thrown down their guns and raised their arms to surrender, only to be shot or bayoneted, hunted down and butchered, with no regard to pleas for mercy.[36]

Lt. Col. Tom J. Jackson, commander of the black troops at Fort Pillow, reported that the Confederates, upon entering the fort, began "an indiscriminate slaughter of both whites and blacks ... they would not surrender ... they could not disobey the order of Major Booth ... men never fought more brave than did the colored soldiers at Fort Pillow."[37]

The Confederate viewpoint differs, as Forrest reported:

> "some of our men cut the halyards, and the United States flag, floating from a tall mast in the center of the fort, came down. The forces stationed in the rear of the fort could see the flag, but were too far under the bluff to see the fort, and when the flag descended they ceased firing ... so near were they to the enemy that few, if any, would have survived unhurt another volley ... many rushed into the river and were drowned, and the actual loss of life will perhaps never be known, as there were quite a number of refugee citizens in the fort, many of whom were drowned and several killed in the retreat from the fort."[38]

Anderson explained:

> "I met the General [Forrest] between the flagstaff and the entrance, and his first words were, 'Major, we drove them right to you, and I cut their flag down as soon as I could get to it.' No one under such circumstances could accurately give the time of these transactions, but I am satisfied in my own mind that it was less than fifteen minutes from the time our bugles sounded until their colors came down, and less than two minutes from the time they were lowered until firing had ceased, and I had joined the General inside the works."[39]

The gunboat, meanwhile, had given no aid to the Federals. They ran from the fort, followed closely by the Confederates. Captain Marshall later reported that he felt the Confederates intended to place hundreds of men on one of the steamboats and attempt to capture him.[40]

Of the intended capture of the *New Era,* Anderson noted:

"Gen. Forrest ... could have opened fire at long range ... but instead ... directed me to take Capt. Young, the Federal provost marshal, and a white flag, and endeavor to open communication with her, with a view of delivering the Federal wounded and securing surgical aid for them ... we followed her up the river bank, waving her to stop ... She paid no attention ... Doubtless her commander thought our flag a ruse to effect his capture."[41]

Details began removing the dead and wounded from the fort. Confederates joined many of the captured Federals in this grisly duty. With the task completed near dark, the earlier intentions of the retreating Federal soldiers became less certain.

A Confederate participant in the caring of the wounded recollected:

"When the wounded and dead had been removed from the face of the bluff, a detail of our own men was sent down to gather up all the small arms thrown down by the garrison. I went with this detail ... inspected and handed over to our ordinance officer two hundred and sixty-nine rifles and six cases of rifle ammunition, all of which were gathered up on the face of the slope from the fort to the water's edge. The six cases of cartridges were piled against the upturned roots of an old tree, with their tops removed, ready for immediate distribution and use."[42]

Along with the large amount of weapons, a number of barrels of whiskey and beer were found within the fort. Dippers were attached to the barrels, many of which were nearly empty, leading to speculation that intoxication of the Federal troops, black and white, contributed to the factors of the fort's final bloody moments.

Forrest left Fort Pillow late that evening and spent the night approximately eight miles away. The next morning, as he prepared to move to Jackson, Forrest and his staff heard cannon fire in the direction of Pillow. Major Anderson, under Forrest's orders, returned to the fort along with Captain Young, now a prisoner of war. Reaching the fort, the group found that Union gunboats were shelling the positions occupied by Confederates, attempting to assist the wounded of both sides.[43]

Anderson hoisted a white flag and the bombardment ceased; in turn, the *Silver Cloud*, previously shelling the area, moved toward the bank. The ship, after some coercion, also raised a flag of truce. Anderson boarded the ship and "in a short time an agreement was made for a truce from 9 a.m. to 5 p.m. All stragglers were to be removed from the area of the fort; only surgeons and their assistants remained.[44]

Possession of Fort Pillow again belonged to the Union army. Almost immediately, the steamer *Platte Valley* began receiving wounded troops. One Union soldier's wife, desperate to learn her husband's fate, was allowed to visit with and bid farewell to her spouse as he awaited his journey to a prisoner-of-war camp.[45]

An interesting situation then took place, courtesy of civilians aboard three nearby boats. A witness observed, "Permission was given to all the passengers on the three steamers to visit the fort, and all of them did so, many of them bringing back in their hands buckles, belts, balls, buttons, etc., picked up on the grounds."[46]

Not only civilians, but military personnel as well, took advantage of the truce to forgo the hostilities. A Confederate officer reminisced, "when my duties were over a couple of lieutenants of the Federal army ... insisted on my taking a parting glass with them at the bar of the steamer, which I, of course, did."[47]

As five o'clock approached, Major Anderson notified Union captain Ferguson of the *Silver Cloud* that upon the end of the truce period, the fort's remaining buildings left standing for the housing of wounded Federal soldiers would be burned. Assurance was given to the steamers that no Confederate forces stood within two miles of the fort and that they could proceed, unmolested, from the area.[48]

A member of the group responsible for burning the buildings recorded the following words:

> "The men with me were dismounted, and set to work scattering and distributing loose straw, hospital beds and bunks through all the buildings ... the torch was applied and ... the last buildings left at Fort Pillow burst into flames. We then mounted our horses and bade Fort Pillow a lasting adieu."[49]

With the battle over and a Confederate victory attained, the controversies surrounding the battle swelled. The first and foremost of these is the alleged Confederate massacre of Federal soldiers. It is a fact that Forrest's men acknowledged the tenacity of the black soldiers' fighting skills. Of the 557 Federal occupants of Fort Pillow, 231 were killed; another 100 seriously wounded. Additionally, 168 white troops and only 58 black soldiers were taken prisoner. The racial situation of the time, added to the presence of Tennessee Unionists, certainly provided just cause in the eyes of the Confederates.

One Federal soldier explained his feelings in writing:

> "The rebels began an indiscriminate slaughter, sparing neither age nor sex, white nor black, soldier nor civilian. The officers and men seemed to vie with each other in the work. Men, women, and even children were deliberately shot down, beaten, and hacked with sabers. Some of the children, not more than ten years old, were forced to stand and face their murderers while being shot; the sick and wounded were butchered without mercy, the Rebels entering the hospital and dragging them out to be shot, or killing them as they lay unable to offer resistance. Numbers of our men were collected in lines or groups and deliberately shot. Some were shot in the river, some on the bank, and the bodies of the latter, many yet living, were kicked into the river. The huts and tents where the wounded had sought shelter were set on fire, both that night and the next morning, while the wounded were still in them, and those who tried to get out were shot. One man was fastened to the floor of a tent by nails through his clothing and then burned, and one was similarly nailed to the side of a building and then burned. These deeds were renewed the next morning, when any wounded who still lived were sought out and shot."[50]

In addition to this situation, accusations abounded regarding the manner in which Confederates and Union prisoners of war, under forced means, possibly buried wounded Federal troops. In fact, a number of black troops testified in a Congressional Committee's report that they had escaped from the grave, placed there among other wounded and the dead.[51]

The controversial Confederate victory was not gained without a cost. Fourteen officers and enlisted men were killed, another eighty-six wounded. Among these figures were Lt. N.B. Burton of the Fifth Mississippi, Capt. W.R. Sullivan and Lt. Ryan of Willis's Texas Battalion, and Captain J.C. Wilson of Russell's regiment of Bell's brigade.[52]

In addition to Capt. Wilson, Lt. George Love of Russell's regiment fell at Fort Pillow. A popular officer, the commander had predicted his death in the hours preceding the attack. He gave directions for the disposal of his horse and possessions, and wrote a letter to his orphan sister. At 11 o'clock, a canister shot hit and killed the young officer. Col. Wiley M. Reed, Sixth Mississippi, fell within eighty yards of the breastworks at Fort Pillow. Shot three times, the thirty-seven-year-old officer was moved to Jackson, Tennessee, where he was given the best surgical skills and medical care available. Reed, also an ordained Presbyterian minister, slowly succumbed to his wounds on April 30, 1864.[53]

Today, Fort Pillow is a well-preserved 1,600-acre member of the Tennessee State Park System. It is considered as possessing "a low threat" on the Civil War Preservation Trust's scale of endangered battlefields. The facility, located in Henning, Tennessee, commemorates the casualties and events of April 1864 and provides insight into the events prior to and following that controversial battle. Restored fortifications, an informative museum, trails, and signs combine with seasonal living-history encampments to assist visitors in gaining a deeper appreciation for the site.

Nathan Bedford Forrest. Courtesy of Confederate Veteran.

Wartime sketch of Fort Pillow's main water battery. Courtesy of Ft. Pillow State Park.

Gen. Forrest stood on the high point at photo's center on April 12, 1864. This allowed him a clear view of the fort below. Photo by author.

Fort Pillow's earthworks lie in the background of this modern photo. In the foreground stood Federal cabins for white troops and tents with wooden floors for black soldiers. The cabins and tents were destroyed at the battle's conclusion. Photo by author.

In addition to rough terrain, attacking Confederates had to cross this moat before scaling Pillow's steep earthworks. Photo by author.

Modern view of Fort Pillow's interior. The Mississippi River bluff begins on the extreme right of the picture. Photo by author.

This April 30, 1864 Harper's Weekly sketch portrays the "Massacre at Fort Pillow." Courtesy of Ft. Pillow State Park, photo by author.

Col. Wiley Reed was mortally wounded at Ft. Pillow. The Cumberland University graduate and pastor of Nashville's First Cumberland Presbyterian Church died in Jackson, Tennessee on May 1, 1864. Courtesy of Confederate Veteran.

The remains of a bottle that held Dr. J. Hostetter's Celebrated Stomach Bitters, a ninety-four-proof tonic. Such discoveries lend credibility to claims that Federal troops were acting intoxicated at the time of the battle. Courtesy of Ft. Pillow State Park, photo by author.

CHAPTER SIXTEEN

JOHNSONVILLE

The Appearance of Forrest's Navy
November 4, 1864

The November 4, 1864 Confederate victory at Johnsonville, Tennessee marked the only recorded battle in which a cavalry force engaged and defeated a naval force. Though largely submerged today following the Tennessee Valley Authority's 1944 creation of Kentucky Lake, the site of the battle was a town of approximately 2,000 people during the Civil War. Saloons, a blacksmith shop, various merchants, and even a coffin factory catering to Union soldiers were present in the town.[1]

An estimate of Federal strength at Johnsonville at the time of the November 4 engagement was recorded as consisting of the Forty-third Wisconsin Volunteers, seven hundred men; Thirteenth Tennessee Colored Infantry, twelve hundred men; and quartermaster's employees, eight hundred men.[2] This number of troops, in conjunction with the town's residents mentioned previously, created a bustling community on the edge of the Tennessee River.

Around 1800, the community of Johnsonville had begun as Knott's Landing. It was renamed Lucas Landing a few years later and gained the name Johnsonville in 1863 when Andrew Johnson, the military governor of Tennessee, rode the first passenger train into the area, reportedly broke a bottle of wine on the track, and unashamedly named the town for himself.[3] The railroad track would bring about a series of events that secured the location a spot in the annals of history.

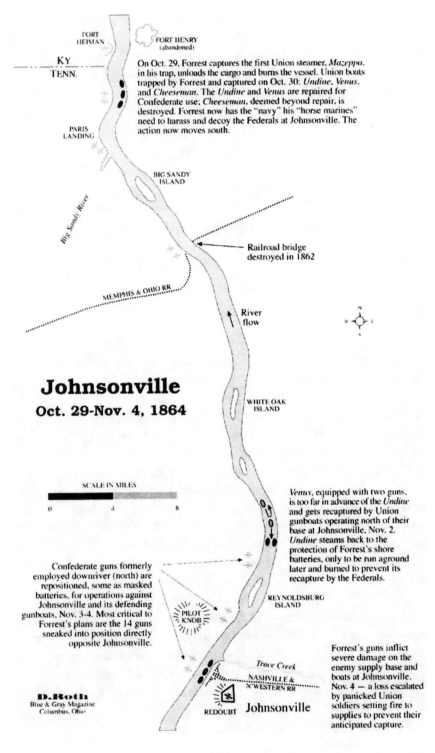

FORT HEIMAN

FORT HENRY (abandoned)

KY
TENN.

On Oct. 29, Forrest captures the first Union steamer, *Mazeppa*, in his trap, unloads the cargo and burns the vessel. Union boats trapped by Forrest and captured on Oct. 30: *Undine*, *Venus*, and *Cheeseman*. The *Undine* and *Venus* are repaired for Confederate use; *Cheeseman*, deemed beyond repair, is destroyed. Forrest now has the "navy" his "horse marines" need to harass and decoy the Federals at Johnsonville. The action now moves south.

PARIS LANDING

BIG SANDY ISLAND

Big Sandy River

Railroad bridge destroyed in 1862

MEMPHIS & OHIO RR

River flow

N

Johnsonville
Oct. 29-Nov. 4, 1864

WHITE OAK ISLAND

SCALE IN MILES

0   4   8

Venus, equipped with two guns, is too far in advance of the *Undine* and gets recaptured by Union gunboats operating north of their base at Johnsonville, Nov. 2. *Undine* steams back to the protection of Forrest's shore batteries, only to be run aground later and burned to prevent its recapture by the Federals.

Confederate guns formerly employed downriver (north) are repositioned, some as masked batteries, for operations against Johnsonville and its defending gunboats, Nov. 3-4. Most critical to Forrest's plans are the 14 guns sneaked into position directly opposite Johnsonville.

REYNOLDSBURG ISLAND

PILOT KNOB

Trace Creek

NASHVILLE & N'WESTERN RR

REDOUBT **Johnsonville**

Forrest's guns inflict severe damage on the enemy supply base and boats at Johnsonville, Nov. 4 — a loss escalated by panicked Union soldiers setting fire to supplies to prevent their anticipated capture.

D.Roth
Blue & Gray Magazine
Columbus, Ohio

By May 1864, the seventy-eight-mile-long Nashville and Northwestern Railroad had been completed, connecting Nashville with Johnsonville, a Tennessee River supply depot. The Federal army relied heavily on this location as supplies had entered here since the completion of the railroad and were then moved to Nashville for shipment to Gen. Sherman in Atlanta. Low water had made the Cumberland River unusable, and regular guerilla activities along the 185-mile-long Louisville and Nashville Railroad made it unreliable, leading the Union army to focus predominantly on Johnsonville as a stop on Sherman's supply line.

General Nathan Bedford Forrest had assembled a number of his Confederate troops at Jackson, Tennessee, where recruiting and gathering of absentees took place in the fall of 1864. On October 26, Forrest sent Brig. Gen. Abraham Buford to Fort Heiman, Confederate earthworks that Federal troops captured in 1862 and subsequently abandoned. This set of works lay just north of the Tennessee-Kentucky state line and was equipped with two twenty-pound Parrotts freshly arrived from Mobile, Alabama for use in the planned raid.[4]

Forrest sent other portions of his artillery to points between Fort Heiman and Paris Landing, enabling him to manage each straight stretch along the west bank of the Tennessee River between these locations. The general's plan was to use these positions to trap and successfully ambush Union ships between any two artillery placements on the river.[5] Having predicted such a move, Union occupants at Johnsonville had cut the timber from the river's west bank opposite the Johnsonville depot during the hot summer of 1864.

Forrest used a local resident to guide him to an area suitable for placing his guns for use in the planned attack on Johnsonville. "Old Man" Jack Hinson had a personal vendetta against the Union army for the execution of his two sons, alleged bushwhackers. Hinson's activities were not limited to guiding Forrest, as his muzzle loader, more than seventeen pounds in weight, was reportedly graced with thirty-six notches, one for each "Yankee soldier" he'd killed in an act of revenge.[6]

On October 29, a division of Forrest's under Buford's command lay well-concealed near Fort Heiman. At 9 AM, the transport steamer *Mazeppa*, full of supplies and towing a barge, entered the Confederate trap. From six hundred yards north of the fort, Morton's Battery of three-inch guns opened fire on the unsuspecting vessel. The steering device was torn apart when hit in the opening volley. In turn, *Mazeppa* drifted to the opposite shore, where the entire crew, excluding the captain, quickly abandoned the craft.[7]

A Confederate soldier then volunteered to enter the river, swim across, and gain possession of *Mazeppa*. The soldier floated the width of the river and accomplished his mission. Aside from these facts, a great deal of controversy exists, primarily over the identity of the Confederate soldier who performed the action.

Pvt. John Allen Wyeth of Alabama served the last two years of the war under Forrest's command. He recorded the naked captor as Pvt. W.C. West of the Second Tennessee Cavalry. Riding a piece of driftwood and using a plank as a paddle, West reached his destination and returned, accompanied by *Mazeppa*'s captain aboard the ship's boat to his comrades, who eagerly cheered him.[8]

Nineteenth-century historians Jordan and Pryor, in conjunction with Gen. Forrest, explained that the distinction fell to Clarksville, Tennessee resident Capt. Frank P. Gracey. They proposed Gracey, of the Third Kentucky, quickly shed his clothing and jumped into the frigid Tennessee River. Using a log as a means of staying afloat, Gracey wore two .44-caliber revolvers around his neck as he approached *Mazeppa*. Labeled as possibly being "the first Rebel frogman," Gracey rode the current and struck land several feet below his intended destination. The wet, cold, and naked soldier strolled to the ship and received the transport's surrender from the captain. Captain Gracey, now re-attired, rowed back across the river. With twenty men and General Buford, the captain returned to *Mazeppa* for its formal surrender.[9]

Gracey recalled that as he approached the grounded *Mazeppa*, he spied three blue-clad soldiers and demanded their surrender while brandishing two wet pistols. The prisoners then helped him in his trip back across the river and in securing the cargo aboard ship.[10]

Capt. Gracey explained:

> "It was a long and fatiguing trip across the river, and I had an abundance of time for reflection before I landed, several hundred yards below the steamer. At times I thought I did not want the stores as bad as I did; but one glance at the supplies would at once renew my patriotism ... I knew my greatest danger was whilst exposed between the water's edge and the timber on the top bank ... Things did look bad. I was on the enemy's side of the river, alone, with

two pistols that had been in the river ... for at least an hour ... I charged, they surrendered ... Fortunately, the prisoners ... proved to be old river men ... I ordered the prisoners into a lifeboat ... passed them coil after coil of rope ... fastening one end to *Mazeppa's* cavil, the prisoners proceeded to row across the river ... a thousand hands reached out to draw the boat across."[11]

The loot gained in the capture of *Mazeppa* was tremendous. Included in the estimated 700 tons of cargo were 9,000 pairs of shoes, hardtack, blankets, winter clothing, axes, and practically "everything a soldier could want." General Buford boarded *Mazeppa* and taunted his men, asserting that there was "plenty of meat, hardtack, shoes, and clothes for the boys, but just enough brandy for the general," as he brandished a bottle. By mid-afternoon, the unloaded supplies covered 200 yards of the riverbank.[12]

Three Federal gunboats soon appeared and began shelling the Confederates' position. Seeing little value in keeping the damaged transport, and fearing the possible recapture of its cargo, General Buford ordered the burning of *Mazeppa*. With sundown approaching, the gunboats withdrew and the nightlong removal of the captured supplies to a point of safety further inland began.[13]

The next morning, the *Anna,* a Paducah, Kentucky-bound steamer, unknowingly entered the Confederate trap. The confident Southerners fired at *Anna* and demanded her surrender. The steamboat's captain consented and affirmed that he would "round to at the lower landing," yet kept moving when he reached that point. The shot-riddled boat made good its escape and reached Paducah, warning others of the danger ahead and effectively ending upstream traffic from becoming ensnared.[14]

Confederate shots fired at *Anna* had been heard among Union sailors aboard the gunboat *Undine*, number 55. *Undine* convoyed *Venus* and its two barges. As if by design, the two boats entered the area of the river between the two gun emplacements. Jack Hinson, the gentleman whose sons had been shot as bushwhackers, called out, "Hello there, gunboat." The captain of *Undine* erred in his judgment and turned off his engines. The fray began.[15]

The upper Confederate battery fired upon the gunboat; three-inch rifled pieces sent four shots through the forward casemates, breaking the steam escape pipe, killing four sailors and wounding three. *Undine* moved above Paris Landing after returning fire with eight twenty-four-pound howitzers, well out of range of Confederate artillery. *Undine's* commander, Master John L. Bryant, found hoped-for shelter approximately halfway between the landing and Fort Heiman. The crew of the gunboat used this brief timeframe to attempt repairs and warn other vessels of the danger nearby.[16]

Confederate general Chalmers had Colonel Kelly, leading Forrest's old regiment, to dismount and, using the cover of bushes, move below the gunboat and *Venus*. A rapid fire directed at the vessels entered the portholes, struck a number of sailors, and instilled fear among those targeted. The captain of *Venus* was killed in one of the volleys, yet the transport received little damage.[17]

Confederate howitzers and two ten-pound Parrot guns joined the riflemen. while ineffective canister shots were fired from *Undine*. At 3:45, *Undine's* punctured steam pipe sent scalding water throughout the boiler room. *Undine* ran aground on the river's east bank. A few of its occupants attempted escape as those aboard *Venus* surrendered. Among the latter were ten members of the Thirty-fourth New Jersey Volunteers, a squad of infantry aboard ship at the time. Following the *Undine* captain's 4:00 striking of his colors, a shell was fired at the gunboat, knocking out the captain. He soon emerged, joining the surrendering crewmen on the bank. The vessel itself had suffered four men wounded and three killed.[18]

During this series of events, *J.W. Cheeseman*, another Federal steamer, entered the trap and ran aground, suffering just one wounded man. Returning from Johnsonville, the transport was virtually empty; yet it provided a few small boats the Confederates used later in emptying *Venus* and *Undine*. Coffee, candy, and nuts[19] were also found and gave the Confederates, long reliant on crude army rations, a brief respite.

Capt. W.W. Tucker had jumped from the bank to the gangway of *Cheeseman* in an attempt to be the first Confederate on board. He fell into the river and, after going under the vessel, returned safely to shore. Only one Confederate had been wounded in the struggle; the Union participants failed to fare as well. Forty-three Federals had been captured in addition to eight being killed and eleven wounded.[20]

Forrest reached the location on October 31 and analyzed the situation. He determined *Cheeseman* to be beyond repair, and ordered its contents of coffee, candies, and nuts removed and shared between the troops and area residents.[21]

The boat itself was then burned. The renowned cavalry officer employed several of his veterans in repairing and trying their hands at operating *Undine* and *Venus*. The men were hailed as "horse marines" and received cheers when they raised the Confederate flag over the boats, a first such encounter for the newly recruited sailors. Frank Gracey of the Third Kentucky Cavalry had served as a steamboat captain prior to the war's beginning and was given command of *Undine;* Lt. Col. Dawson led the crew of *Venus.* After repairs were made, Forrest's flotilla spent two hours of "exceedingly shaky" maneuvers and target practice.[22]

In a letter to Capt. Gracey's son, Capt. John Morton wrote:

> "I personally conducted the fire on ... *Mazeppa* ... It was by my suggestion that your father ... was placed in command of the *Undine* ... Gen. Forrest ordered me to take command of the gunboat, with a detachment from my different batteries to man her. I protested, mildly, mind you, thanked him for the honor, told him I was not familiar with fighting artillery on water, but that Capt. Gracey, a gallant and efficient officer and familiar with managing a boat, was at Fort Heiman ... The General assigned him to the command of the gunboat ... We found that two of her three guns had been knocked out of position by our fire. These we readjusted ... and ... reported to Gen. Forrest that his navy was ready to 'move on the enemy.'"[23]

Lt. Col. Dawson guided the newly formed fleet as it moved slowly upriver. The progression was limited in that the fleet was to advance in tandem with artillery and cavalry of Chalmers and Buford marching on the river's west bank.[24] The undergrowth along the river, added to the muddy trail the artillery and cavalry followed, resulted in numerous stops along the way.

The weather turned cold and rainy, adding to the misery of the marches. Friendly wrangling between the troops on the banks and Forrest's "sailors" granted temporary tranquility to each group. The conditions those on land faced affected their current outlook, yet the sailors knew their true test lay ahead in an encounter with actual sailors.[25]

Aboard *Undine*, troops busied themselves in preparing the eight howitzers for action. Federal attempts to sabotage two of the guns were negated; a third had a shell jammed into its muzzle and was also mended. The fleet anchored for the night near a bluff on the river's west bank; the site of the onetime Memphis & Ohio Railroad Bridge at Danville served as the campsite for the land dwellers.[26]

A heavy rain fell throughout the night, slowing the troops even more and creating a gap between the two groups. As the two riverboats approached the river bend near Davidson's Crossing on November 2, *Venus,* loaded with many of the supplies captured on board *Mazeppa,* was brazenly moving ahead of *Undine.*[27] This error would soon prove costly for Forrest's "navy."

At the bend, *Venus* inadvertently came in contact with three Federal gunboats: *Tawah, Elfin,* and *Key West* and, as one participant stated, "an immediate animated collision ensued." The gunboats fired at *Venus* and almost immediately caused damage. One shot hit the machinery, the tiller-rope was cut, and the vessel, for all practical purposes, became unmanageable. The two Parrott guns aboard *Venus* were no match for the well-armed Federal crafts. Dawson ran *Venus* ashore; his men abandoned the vessel and made their escape into the woods. *Venus,* the two Parrott guns, two hundred rounds of ammunition, and a host of other sorely needed supplies were recaptured by the Federals.[28]

Undine arrived on the scene as Union lieutenant LeRoy Fitch's six additional gunboats appeared. Realizing the futility of the situation and not wanting to risk the loss of additional supplies or the ship itself, *Undine* moved back. On the third of November, *Undine* stood boldly against the nine Federal gunboats armed with some 100 guns. "Doomed when the fight began," the *Undine* approached Reynoldsburg Island, two miles from Johnsonville. Union lieutenant E.M. King ordered the gunboats under his command to fire upon the vessel. The Confederate occupants of the gunboat "far better accustomed to the headlong charge and unhampered warfare of the trooper or dismounted rifleman, than to being cooped up in the narrow gun-room of a ship-of-war" became demoralized.[29]

Undine was struck several times. Confederates aboard the craft set fire to oil-soaked mattresses and abandoned ship; *Undine* burned to the water line. Gracey and his men sought cover in the canebrakes, where they hid until dark. That night, Forrest's "sailors" used makeshift rafts and logs to float across the river[30] and join the general, who was now poised for an attack on the Federal depot at Johnsonville.

While Forrest appeared to have been beaten and perhaps driven off, the loss of *Undine* had, in fact, cost the Federals a great deal as well. The *Key West,* number 32, the flagship of the group attacking on the third, had been hit by ten shells on the upper works, the hull had been struck twice;

the deck was pierced seven times. Another of the Union gunboats, *Tawah*, had been found to have the wrong caliber ammunition on board. The two boats, along with *Elfin*[31] had returned to Johnsonville, where safety presumably greeted them.

Union telegraphs noted that Forrest's presence in the area was known and that an attack on the depot was likely. Yet, late on the morning of the fourth, "business as usual" best described the activity in and around Johnsonville. Just across the river, some 800 yards wide at the location of the hamlet, Forrest's 3,000 men[32] readied for action.

From concealed positions, Forrest used binoculars as he scrutinized the area around the depot. The 2,000-plus Union soldiers worked on loading two freight trains; ten-foot stacks of supplies awaited their labor. At the docks sat three gunboats that earlier attacked the *Undine*, as well as eighteen barges and eleven transport steamers. On the docks of the gunboats, crewmen busied themselves washing clothes. Passengers awaited their call to board. Most milled about the area, many talking, a few smoking. A few ladies joined the crowd, moving toward the steamers, gathering steam for an early departure.[33]

The continuing rain added a sense of eeriness to the settlement's appearance. A historian noted:

> "The town ... was ... nothing more than a railroad spur ... a group of supply buildings, levees, and a few frame houses. The terrain at Johnsonville sloped upward from the river, about eighty yards wide, at that point, to form a high plateau some distance above the warehouses. On this high ground, the Federals had constructed breastworks, where they had placed a remarkably heavy battery." [34]

Forrest's artillery was located at such an angle to the river that the gunboats, if deployed in time, would be unable to strike them at a close distance and, if fired from Johnsonville, the shells would safely pass over the Confederate emplacements.

In the early 1900s, one participant explained, "On the western side the bank rises twenty feet above the water and drops back abruptly to a bottom, thus forming a natural earthwork, at that time heavily timbered and overgrown with cane."[35]

The citizen employees at Johnsonville that day strolled around the depot, an area one historian explained as being no more than "four ...

acres of open storage." Hoisting machines, poised for use, sat unattended.[36] A less-suspecting foe Forrest could not find.

Among the Union soldiers and equipment present at Johnsonville that day were the aforementioned troops and equipment. The First Kansas Battery had been stationed in nearby Waverly for months, and several members had grown rather fond of some of the local girls. At the war's end, a few of the men returned to the area, married the girls, and lived the rest of their lives in and around Waverly.[37]

One writer of the period stated of the Federal troops in the town:

> "the opposite shore presented an inspiring panorama. The Federals thought that Forrest had been turned back by the loss of his boats and was ... in retreat. The day was dreary and misty; but the men had been very busy for the past few days preparing for the expected attack ... The ladies came down the hill to stroll along the streets of the town. Along the path from the boats to the redoubts lounged soldiers, both white and black.[38]

Captain John Morton waited on the west bank of the Tennessee River at Pilot Knob for the command to fire. His guns, as were those of Thrall's battery, were sunk into the wet soil, but other Confederate artillery sections remained free to pursue any vessel attempting escape. The ten pieces, largely comprised of three-inch ordnance rifles [39] would soon earn a distinction in history.

At 2 o'clock, the ten Confederate guns fired simultaneously. The intent was to initially target the gunboats; this conception proved highly successful. The heavy volley, recalled by one observer to have been a thunder-like roar, made a number of direct hits. Steam poured from the gunboats as the boiler aboard one was punctured, scalding to death several of its crewmen. The ladies standing on the riverbank screamed and ran in the direction of the fort. Civilian passengers pushed one another from the gangplanks and into the river.[40]

Within forty minutes of the initial cannon fire, the Confederates had driven the occupants from the three, only one of which returned fire. The *Key West* and *Tawah* attempted to leave the town's docks, but in a river bend above the town, Rice's battery disabled the boats. Both erupted in flames, each side claiming credit for such. Soon afterward, *Elfin* was ablaze. The Federal commander felt assured that as many as forty cannon were bombarding his position. Forrest himself took a turn firing cannon, though few saw the feat as impressive. The Union redoubt erupted in defensive fire of percussion shells, but, as Forrest predicted, it proved nonproductive.[41]

Shells from the Kansas Battery found the range of the Confederate gun placements, yet sank deeply into the muddy soil around them before exploding, in turn causing little damage. While one-third of the Kansas Battery members were veterans, these shots are recorded to be the first the battery fired in anger since their arrival in Johnsonville.[42]

More than 100 shells aboard *Tawah* exploded, while a number of barges and transports were swallowed in the growing blazes. Lt. King ordered the others burned to eliminate the Confederates gaining their possession. Morton now focused on the land batteries, annihilating them in a matter of minutes; the targeting of the warehouses came next. Burning haystacks and crates along the river[43] created a virtual inferno in the village.

The smell of burning bacon, corn, and coffee filled the air, but the sight of blue flames along the hillside caught the attention of many Confederates who had recently been on half rations. Barrels of whiskey had been placed in one of the warehouses, and their burning sent a host of Confederates to the river's edge, shouting to the Union soldiers to save some for them.[44]

Capt. James Dinkins wrote:

> "Soon barrels began to burst, and the burning liquor ran in torrents of livid flame down the hillside, spreading a flame in its course toward the river, and filling the air with blended fumes of burning spirits, coffee, meat, and sugar. A hundred barrels of whiskey burst with ... explosions ... As night came on, the burning spirits ran down the river, making a livid light that seemed most uncanny."[45]

Trace Creek, north of the redoubt and with the Nashville and Northwestern Railway between, undoubtedly contained its share of the burning liquor.

It was recorded that "Thousands of bushels of grain, tons of hay, barrel upon barrel of spirits and oil, hundreds of thousands of pounds of meats, and numerous other stores fed the fury of the flames. The whole river became a veritable wall of fire, and in one hour the great depot was destroyed."[46]

The defenders of Johnsonville began a hasty retreat. Four hundred Union soldiers boarded a freight train that made its retreat from the inferno. C.H. McNabb, the train's engineer, felt the weight of the withdrawing men in blue was slowing down his own attempt to reach safety and decoupled the cars from the locomotive twelve miles from Johnsonville. The men left behind, soldiers and sailors, began looting the cars, taking anything conceived as being of value.[47]

A young civilian named Chris Young reportedly lost his mule, hitched to a post near the depot, to three African-American soldiers.[48] Shouting alarm at the presence of Forrest, perhaps in response to the well-publicized incident at Fort Pillow, other men of color made a rapid retreat from the area. The celebratory mood of the Confederates was dampened as each realized the torched depot and its surrounding stores held the means of relief to their hunger. As darkness approached, Forrest led his victorious force from the area.

While the Confederates abandoned the scene, a regiment of African-American soldiers left their cover and began shouting insults and gesturing toward the victors. Throwing off their coats and shaking their fists, the Union soldiers made evident their disgust of the day's events. In response Brigg's guns, not yet withdrawn from their position and supported by Col. E.W. Rucker's sharpshooters, opened up on the men in blue. The group quickly scattered, but not without leaving several wounded and dead comrades on the bank of the river.[49]

A Confederate participant observed, "A regiment of negroes who had been hiding behind the redoubts emerged ... they filled the air with their arsenal of explosives and offensive epithets ... [we] turned two ... guns upon [them] ... and the howling, capering crowd scampered in the wildest confusion."[50]

Continual rain and mud greeted Forrest's men as they made the way toward Perryville. The next morning, Forrest, Morton, Chalmers, and Buford returned to the river in an attempt to discern the overall situation. Forrest looked at Morton and said, "John, if they'd give you enough guns and me enough men, we would whip old Sherman off the face of the Earth." Within minutes of arriving and determining their action of the previous day to have been a complete success, they returned to their commands.[51]

Forrest's losses had been minimal, with only two men dead and nine wounded. It has been explained that these numbers reflect the casualties of the entire expedition, and that the only Confederate death at Johnsonville occurred when a falling limb shot from a large cypress fell upon a soldier. Forrest had taken a massive store of shoes and other items badly needed for his troops. His opposition reportedly suffered eight casualties and lost one hundred fifty men as prisoners of war.[52]

Uniquely, the true effect of Forrest's raid on Johnsonville can not be measured in casualties, but in the value of the destruction inflicted upon the area. With estimates as high as $7 million in losses, the Federal setback was tremendous. Johnsonville's depot would be of little use to the Union army for the duration of the war, and for weeks after the raid, Union detachments were placed on alert for the possibility of another assault from the elusive Forrest.

A writer of the period exclaimed:

> "There was nothing too desperate or daring for the great 'wizard of the saddle' to attempt if the shadow of success lay beyond it. One of the most brilliant exploits of his military career was his Johnsonville campaign, where he captured and destroyed millions of dollars' worth of Federal army supplies, including the steamer *Mazeppa* loaded with stores of all kinds, the gunboat *Undine* and the transport *Venus*."[53]

Sherman's proclamation that the "devil Forrest" had wreaked havoc in the Johnsonville area seems to have been a self-motivational comment. The Federal officer would make his march to the sea and into the pages of history despite the efforts of Forrest and his gallant navy.

A smallpox epidemic befell a host of remaining Federal soldiers in Johnsonville soon after the Forrest raid. The Tennessee Valley Authority dealt the town its final blow in 1944 when Kentucky Lake was filled, submerging most of the town and its surrounding area. Today two redoubts and lines of rifle pits mark the location of the residences and workplaces of many of the depot's defenders. An unused but attractive visitors' center stands near the upper redoubt, where Osage orange trees line the parking lot. A summer 2007 purchase of fifteen acres for the site of a more modern visitor's center should serve as a significant plus for the battle's interpretation.

The hulls of vessels were seen and explored in the fall of 1925, a time at which the low level of the Tennessee River permitted such activity. Two residents of the area reportedly found rifles, shells, cases of whiskey, canned goods, coffee beans and other items filling the remaining portions of the ships. In late 1990, a video crew recorded the remains of a gunboat while conducting research for Raise the Gunboats, Incorporated. Subsequent dives have led to the locating and retrieval of artifacts from the battle. The significance of these efforts remains to be seen.

Fred Prouty of the Tennessee Wars Commission has explained that only days after the incident at Johnsonville, a Federal salvage vessel removed most of the articles that would tend to be sought by relic hunters or other "treasure seekers." Artillery, outdeck plating, engines, and a host of other articles were taken from the vessels and placed into service on other U.S. ships of war.[54]

As has been explained in numerous writings of the Battle of Johnsonville, in the overall concept of the war, it stands as only a minor point. Yet to Forrest, his men, and the Southern citizens of the period, it provided a boost of morale and provided hope; hope that would disappear in the spring ahead.

Forrest's men improvised a song during their march from Johnsonville. Heartily sung, the tune was to "Columbia, Gem of the Ocean." One stanza ran:

Forrest Artillery Battalion,
Morton, Rice, Ed Walton, and Thrall,
Set fire to their gunboats and their transports,
Nor ceased till they burned them all.[55]

Wartime photo of Johnsonville. Courtesy of Reed Dreaden.

Wartime photo of Johnsonville. Courtesy of Confederate Veteran.

Another view of Johnsonville during the war. Courtesy of Confederate Veteran.

Johnsonville from the air in the Twentieth century. Courtesy of Reed Dreaden.

A safe recovered in 1974 from the wreck of the steamer J.W. Cheeseman. Courtesy of Nathan Bedford Forrest State Park. Photo by author.

Hardtack recovered from the wreckage of the Undine. Courtesy of PanAmerican Consultants and the Tennessee Wars Commission.

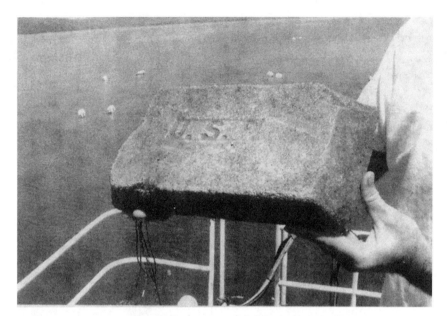

Plate from the Undine. Courtesy of PanAmerican Consultants and the Tennessee Wars Commission.

State marker for Forrest's battery placement at Paris Landing, Tennessee. Photo by author.

Remains of Johnsonville redoubt. Photo by author.

Remains of Johnsonville depot. Photo by author.

Reed Dreaden, Humphreys County Historian, at Johnsonville rifle pits. Photo by author.

View of Pilot Knob, the highest point in West Tennessee, from the remains of Johnsonville. Photo by author.

Monument atop Pilot Knob in Nathan Bedford Forrest State Park. Photo by author.

CHAPTER SEVENTEEN

SPRING HILL

"... deep mortification and shame for the blunder."
November 29, 1864

It has been proposed that the high number of casualties suffered by the Confederates at Franklin and their subsequent defeat at Nashville could well have been avoided if General Hood's forces had capitalized on the opportunity presented them at Spring Hill. On the night of November 29, 1864, hours before the butchery at Franklin, the Federal army, virtually ensnared in the community of Spring Hill, escaped unmolested to entrench themselves in a victorious and impregnable set of defenses. As with the vast majority of losses by either army during the war, Spring Hill would become the subject of analysis, blame, and debate through today.

On November 21, Hood's army began crossing the Tennessee River from Tuscumbia to Florence, Alabama. Many of the Confederates held a high level of enthusiasm over the prospect of driving the Federal army from the borders of Tennessee.[1] The destruction brought to the state's towns and cities as a result of confrontations with the invading Union forces and the knowledge of Nashville having been the first Confederate capital to fall into enemy hands certainly increased the determination of Hood's soldiers to exact revenge.

With the approach of night on November 27, the Federal army abandoned Columbia after a day of heavy skirmishing, and moved to a strong position on the north side of the Duck River. More than seven thousand cavalrymen under General James H. Wilson spread out eastward for approximately ten miles, watching the flank of the Federal army and guarding the fords of the Duck. Wilson's subordinates included the well-trained and experienced cavalry leaders Hatch, Harrison, Coon, Croxton, Capron, Johnson, and Garrard.[2]

That same night, Hood made known his plan of a flank movement to the right of Columbia, to be followed by a rapid march upon the Federal communication line sixteen miles to the north near Spring Hill. Thus began a series of movements as great as any of the war. Confederate advancement would soon pass the Federal flank and rear, reaching the Union artillery, ordnance, and supply trains guarded by only one division of fewer than 5,700 men.[3]

Hood's attacking Confederate force of two army corps and one division of infantry as well as a corps of cavalry had an aggregate number of more than 25,000 men. This force, on the morning of November 28, was on the opposite side of the Duck River from the Union army. The first Confederates to arrive at the location were members of Forrest's Cavalry late on the night of the twenty-seventh. Forrest's men had come to the Duck River after portions of Hood's infantry had relieved them from the skirmish line on Fountain Creek, five miles southeast of Columbia. The 5,500 troopers in the three divisions of Buford, Chalmers, and Jackson, with a small command of Biffle's were well-mounted and equipped.[4]

On the morning of the twenty-eighth, Forrest's three divisions moved rapidly in an easterly direction south of the Duck toward several fords selected for the crossings. Bridges were missing and recent rains had greatly swollen the river to the point that Union general Wilson abided by the opinions of local citizens that the fords were unserviceable. Forrest, renowned among other things for being undeterred in crossing swollen streams and rivers, had two divisions across the river by 4 PM. Chalmers had crossed at Carr's Mill, seven miles east of Columbia; Jackson had done so at Lillard's Mill, east of the Lewisburg and Franklin pikes.[5]

Reinforcing Wilson's cavalry was Major General Schofield. With the addition of his infantry, Schofield brought the number of Federal troops in the vicinity to approximately 28,500. By the morning of the twenty-ninth, Schofield's command would consist of the divisions of Kimball, Wagner, and Wood, comprising the Fourth Corps; and Cox and Ruger, the latter lacking one brigade on detached service, of the Twenty-third Corps.[6]

The third division of Forrest's, that of Buford, had attempted to ford at Hardison's Mill, the crossing of the Lewisburg and Franklin Pike, and was met by Capron's Brigade of 1,800 men. The skirmish delayed Buford's crossing until nightfall. Jackson's force that forded the river at Lillard's Mill—an old mill site four miles above—had been able to move rapidly to Capron's flank and rear, just south of Rally Hill. One Federal company and some wagons were captured, but most of the Union troops retreated toward Franklin, leaving four regiments totaling 1,500 men cut off at the ford. Major J. Morris Young of the Fifth Iowa Cavalry led his regiment and the remaining three, the Fourteenth and Sixteenth Illinois and the Eighth Michigan, in charging through a force of 576 Confederates and escaping toward Franklin. Buford was then able to cross and join the bulk of Forrest's command.[7]

At approximately the same time of night on the twenty-eighth, General Wilson had learned enough about Hood's movement that he sent a message, in triplicate, with the details. Three couriers were sent by different roads to Schofield, informing him:

> "I have a prisoner who came with General Forrest from Columbia. Forrest himself left Columbia at 4:30 p.m. The whole of Hood's infantry were then expecting to march. They were building three pontoon bridges just above Huey's ... expected to be ready by 10 o'clock tonight. I think it is very clear they are aiming for Franklin, and that you ought to get to Spring Hill by 10 a.m. Another prisoner confirms the above. Get to Franklin without delay."[8]

All three couriers reached Schofield's headquarters, the first arriving at 3 AM on the twenty-ninth. General Thomas, in Nashville, sent Schofield a message at 6 AM ordering Schofield to fall back to Franklin and leave "a sufficient force at Spring Hill to contest the enemy's progress until you are securely posted."[9]

By 3 AM, the Confederates were making their bold move. Gen. Cheatham's corps led, with the divisions of Cleburne, Bate, and Brown, followed by Stewart's corps with the divisions of Loring, Walthall, and French. Johnson's division of Lee's corps brought up the rear as the units moved rapidly toward Spring Hill.[10]

General S.D. Lee remained at the river bend opposite Columbia, from which position he began to bombard the Federal position maintained by Cox's division. Col. J.M Dedman's Twentieth Alabama Regiment fired from the right flank and soon cleared away the Federal skirmishers. By 4 PM, three regiments of Pettus's brigade had crossed Col. Ramsey's pontoon bridge and formed under cover of the Thirtieth Alabama under Col. J.K. Elliott on the southern bank. Pettus charged the Federal outposts under Reilly and drove them northward several hundred yards.[11]

Forrest reached Spring Hill around noon, dismounted part of his command, and prepared to attack. Forrest's troops formed in line east of and in front of Spring Hill and pushed forward. Armstrong's brigade and part of Buford's division moved on either side of the Mount Carmel Road from the east and northeast.[12]

Union General D.S. Stanley, corps commander of the Fourth Army Corps, led Wagner's division forward to challenge Forrest. This action very well saved the Federals from defeat at Spring Hill, setting the stage for future encounters.

A member of the Sixty-fourth Ohio wrote:

> "Schofield was so deeply infatuated with his self-imposed delusion as to Hood's intention that, disregarding the orders of Thomas, the advice of Wilson, and the reports of Post, he cherished it until after four o'clock when he heard from Stanley that Hood was attacking at Spring Hill. Wagner's advance, double quicking through Spring Hill at noon and deploying just beyond on a run, arrived barely in time to head off the approach of Hood's cavalry ... a few minutes later, he would have found Forrest in full possession at Spring Hill."[13]

C.C. Hulet, Company A, Fortieth Indiana, recorded his memories of the time as well:

> "As we approached Spring Hill we were met by an excited cavalryman with the report that Forrest's Cavalry was about to take possession of the town and pike. We were at once ordered forward ... as we came into line we opened fire on the enemy, who were advancing across an open field east of the pike in battle order. Forrest's men were soon driven from our front, but soon after made an attack on a wagon train on the road a short distance north of us and shortly afterwards a dash on the depot

... As fast as our men arrived they were formed in line, facing southeast and east from the depot north of town to the pike below ... we rested undisturbed for about two hours, when Hood's infantry began to appear and form line of battle in our front. They soon attacked the advanced brigade on the knoll and after two attempts they succeeded in driving them from their position in some confusion ... Cleburne's Division was struck in the flank by an enfilade fire from our batteries ... they retired in disorder ... long lines of the Confederates were forming in front of our troops ... strung out in a long, thin line, with no supports or reinforcements near enough to help us ... The Confederates continued massing in our front ... Forrest on or near the pike in our rear, the situation looked decidedly bad for us. We could see that we were greatly outnumbered. The artillery firing at Columbia convinced us that we could expect no help from that direction ... we realized that the salvation of our army depended on our holding our position until the troops could march past the enemy we were facing ... Skirmishers were thrown out in front and demonstrations made, which, with Cleburne's repulse, doubtless deceived Hood as to our strength and made him cautious."[14]

The deployment of soldiers from Wagner's division, namely the brigades of Joseph Lane and Emerson Opdycke, evidently led Hood, Cheatham, and Forrest to determine erroneously that a large Federal force lay to their front. To their surprise, though, only 5,500 men stood between Hood's 25,000 and control of Spring Hill.[15]

From the Federal viewpoint, the two remaining hours of daylight coupled with Schofield's delayed decision at 3:30 that Hood intended to gain the Federal line of retreat at Spring Hill rather than attack in force at Columbia,[16] spelled certain defeat for the men in blue.

This late perception on the part of Schofield may have been brought about by an incident on the pike bridge. Elias Bartlett, Thirty-sixth Illinois, was on picket duty at the bridge a half mile south of Spring Hill. Schofield approached the sentry, stating that he felt all was captured at Spring Hill. A Confederate hiding nearby heard the entire conversation and fired on the general, who quickly rode away.[17]

Captain John K. Shellenberger commanded Company B, 64th Ohio Regiment, Bradley's Brigade, Wagner's Division, at Spring Hill. His exciting personal experience and following deduction of the situation were vividly recalled decades later:

> "A bullet ... passed through my overcoat, buttoned up to the chin, in a way to take along the top button of the blouse underneath the coat. That big brass button struck me a stinging blow on the point of the left collar bone. Clasping both hands to the spot, I [became] ... fully convinced that a bullet had entered there, and had inflicted a serious and possibly fatal wound. It was not until I had opened the coat to make a closer investigation that I found I was worse scared than hurt ... about half past three ... the situation of our army had become so critical that nothing short of grossest blundering on the part of the enemy could save it from a great disaster, and ... destroying it."[18]

Wagner's Division confronted overwhelming numbers and was strung out on a line about three miles long. The property assigned to this unit's protection extended from the railway station, nearly a mile northwest of Spring Hill to the Columbia Pike on the southwest. A vast array of ambulances, artillery carriages, and wagons, an estimated eight hundred vehicles, sat behind this long line, filling the village streets and adjacent fields.[19]

Between 3 and 4 o'clock, confusion entered the Confederate command. Cleburne's division moved close to the woods, where Forrest's men and the Sixty-fourth Ohio were fighting. Cleburne halted and fronted into a line facing west toward the Columbia Pike. It has been proposed that Cleburne intended to cross over the pike and advance toward Spring Hill astride the pike. The Irishman's death the following day eliminated any report on his part, but General Bate reported to have received orders to cross the pike and sweep down it toward Columbia. Cleburne's orders from Hood would have likely then been as proposed above. Hood had established his headquarters at the Thompson farmhouse, two miles south of Spring Hill and remained there until the following morning.[20]

At four o'clock, apparently in an effort to save time, Cleburne, with Bate to his left, started to march across the pike. With Cleburne were three of his four brigades: Lowrey's on his right, with Govan in the center and Granbury to the left. Lowrey's right side, when emerging from the aforementioned woods, received enfilading fire from the Forty-second Illinois posted behind a high rail fence. In the woods, Federal infantrymen had used stumps, rotten logs, and stones to build barricades. In the area around the Forty-second Illinois, the Sixty-fourth and Sixty-fifth Ohio soon arrived with the Thirty-sixth Illinois, Opdycke's only reserve, hurried from the other side of Spring Hill to support two guns posted to sweep the fields in front of the Forty-second.[21]

Lowrey's right passed within range of the Forty-second Illinois, causing the latter to open fire as did the two guns at the pike. The Sixty-fourth ran forward, intermingling ranks with the Forty-second, and poured fire into the Confederates. Witnesses noted a number of men in gray "pulled down the rims of their hats over their eyes, bent their heads to the storm of missiles pouring upon them, changed direction to their right and ... came sweeping through the gap between the Forty-second and the pike" and made a swing to the Federal rear.[22]

Cleburne and Forrest rode in the rear of Govan's troops at the Confederate center and joined Govan during the charge, personally directing it with swords drawn. Lowry and Govan made a half wheel to the right, conforming to the right flank of Bradley's command of the Forty-second Illinois and Sixty-fourth Ohio. Bell's Brigade halted at the fence where the Sixty-fourth had been and fired into Bradley's front. Bradley's right wing crumbled and was driven back with only the Seventy-ninth Illinois remaining. The Sixty-fourth and Sixty-fifth Illinois joined the Fifteenth Missouri as well as the Fifty-first Illinois in fleeing to the outskirts of town, where they were rallied by Wagner and Stanley and reformed under the cover of eighteen guns.[23]

Capt. John Shellenberger joined his command of the Sixty-fourth Ohio in the retreat, graphically recording its events:

> "The regimental commanders gave the reluctant order to
> fall back. The contact was then so close that as the men on
> our right were running past the line closing in on them,
> they were called on with loud oaths, charging them with a
> Yankee of canine descent, to halt and surrender. When the
> call was not heeded, some of the men were shot down with
> the muzzle of the musket almost touching their bodies ...
> the four regiments in the woods ... were attacked ... by

> Forrest in front, and by Cleburne on the right and rear,
> and were speedily dislodged ... In falling back, we had to
> cross the valley of a small stream. As we descended into
> this valley, we uncovered our pursuers to the fire of the
> battery posted at the village ... firing over our heads ... not
> less than eight guns opened fire ... Cleburne encountered
> this fire, he hastily drew back out of sight ... Bradley's
> men stopped running and walked back to the vicinity of
> the battery ... a new line was formed."[24]

General Bradley reported a loss of 190 men in his brigade; he suffered a broken arm himself. Command of the brigade fell to Col. Conrad of the Fifteenth Missouri. Elsewhere, command of the Sixty-fifth Ohio went to nineteen-year-old Brewer Smith, perhaps one of the youngest regimental commanders of the war.[25]

The tenacity of the Seventy-ninth Illinois led General Lowry to fear being flanked, a point he made to Cleburne. Cleburne then moved with Govan against the Seventy-ninth, finally dislodging them. Granbury moved to Lowry's left and encountered the Thirty-sixth Illinois and two gun sections of Battery B, Pennsylvania Volunteers, at Bradley's right rear. Granbury moved further left from the distance of the guns.[26]

During this phase, Cleburne's horse was struck by a shell and the general momentarily received a message from Col. Bostick of Cheatham's staff to halt until receiving further orders. Adjutant General Mangrum of Cleburne's staff later stated that had Bostick not delivered the message, Cleburne would have been in possession of Spring Hill in less than ten minutes.[27]

General Bate entered the pike north of the Col. Nat Cheairs home, and used Major Caswell's sharpshooters to lead an attack that drove the Twenty-sixth Ohio from the area. Bate soon received Cheatham's order through Lieutenant Schell to form on Cleburne's left, where he fronted northward and camped for the night. General Johnson's division was moved from the Rutherford Creek crossing westward and fronted the Columbia and Franklin Pike and served as an extension of Bate's left brigade.[28]

In a number of instances, Confederates offered their reminiscences of the day at Spring Hill. The order to cease the advance serves as a common link of indignation among their comments. Frank Stovall Roberts of Cheatham's corps recalled:

"All the corps seems to have gotten well around in the neighborhood of Spring Hill by three or four o'clock that afternoon except our brigade, Gen. S.R. Gist's; which did not arrive until nearly dark. After wading a creek near the Cheairs house two or three times, we were ordered to bivouac, but to build no fires, as it was not desired to let the enemy know our position. So we lay down, wet and hungry, and went to sleep."[29]

Sgt. Major Shapard of a consolidated regiment composed of the Nineteenth, Twenty-fourth, and Forty-first Tennessee regiments added:

"When my regiment reached the vicinity ... of Spring Hill, it was at once hastened forward to within two hundred and fifty yards of the pike on the east side and there halted ... about sundown. There was not even a skirmish line between us and the fleeing Federals on the pike, who were plainly visible ... Our command was surprised at being halted, believed it to be only temporary, and was eager, impatient to make a charge ... The men in the line needed no command to make a charge. They only wanted permission to do so. The result could not have been in doubt. The flight of the Federals indicated that there was no fight in them."[30]

W.W. Gist of the Twenty-sixth Ohio confirmed Shapard's claim in declaring that when he was ordered to help form a line of resistance to defend a portion of Federal artillery, only a dozen or so men joined him. The resistance, feeble as it would have been, was not necessary as darkness fell without the detachment firing a shot.[31]

General Stewart's command returned from Rutherford's Creek only to receive an order to halt and form a line facing the Columbia and Spring Hill Pike. This order was later revoked and called for him to move toward Spring Hill. A witness noted Hood's assailing of Stewart and his failure to attack at Spring Hill as the latter approached the former on the road side. Stewart later stated that his inclination was to question Hood's failure to personally see the attack carried out, yet he chose to not ask, seeing such conduct as being disrespectful. Stewart did ask Hood why he had stopped

Stewart's command at Rutherford's Creek, to which Hood replied that Schofield might have tried to get out that way.[32]

Elsewhere, the waiting game started. C.C. Hulet of the Fortieth Indiana was sent forward on the night of the twenty-ninth to determine the location of the Confederate skirmish line. His encounter that night evokes fear in any reader:

> "I had gone some distance toward the enemy's camp when I smelled tobacco smoke ... nearing a little bunch of bushes a short distance from the fence row ... I caught sight of a faint glow of light against the bushes and another whiff of the tobacco smoke. Instantly I realized the situation. Doubtless the skirmish line was along the fence row ... I had nearly crawled into the arms of one of them. If he had not been violating the regulations by smoking on his post, I could not have detected his presence until too late ... I was flat on the ground, not fifteen feet from a soldier with a loaded gun ready to shoot on the instant ... My first impulse was to get away from there instantly, but I knew it would be almost impossible to get to my feet and get away without causing an alarm ... He looked to be about twelve feet tall and seemed to be looking directly at me. I expected to see his gun go to his shoulder and to hear his challenge ... I resumed my crawfish movement to the rear ... "[33]

During the night, Hulet joined the rest of the Federal army in a virtually uncontested move toward the town of Franklin. It is not the purpose of this text to analyze or place blame for such an incident. It must be noted, though, that the ability of the Union army to escape the snare without a significant Confederate attack is a mystery to this day.

An unconfirmed and somewhat controversial tale arose forty-eight years after the Federal escape from Spring Hill. J.D. Remington, Company I, Seventy-third Illinois, claimed that seven times during his career, he entered the Confederate lines as a spy, the last time occurring at Spring Hill. Remington claimed to have received orders from Opdycke to enter the Confederate position clad as a Confederate captain, complete with saber, revolver, and horse. Remington stated that he met with Hood, Cheatham, Cleburne, and their staffs and informed them that an entire corps of Federal soldiers was in Spring Hill, and later told Hood that the soldiers were making camp in the town and showed no signs of leaving. To the latter lie, Hood, according to Remington, said, "Gentlemen, there may be a skirmish here in the morning, but there will be no battle. It will just be a surrender!" Numerous doubters arose with a host of unanswered questions related to Remington's claims. One pointed question asked how Hood would have taken action based upon the statement of a strange Confederate captain and acted upon it.[34] The story seems to have been largely disregarded through the years as a plausible explanation for the largely unchallenged Federal withdrawal.

After midnight, troops were heard moving on the pike. Capt. R.T. English of Granbury's staff noticed the sounds and stepped forward to learn the reason for such movement. Members of the Twenty-third Michigan, deployed on the right flank of Ruger's Division, almost captured English. The Federals had unknowingly moved within a short distance of Granbury's line, but Granbury failed to have any of his command fire on the column. His death hours later at Franklin negated any report and understanding for the choice to avoid doing so.[35]

Bate's men encountered and attacked Strickland's Third brigade of Ruger's division, inflicting minor wounds. Bate received orders to halt, and moved northeastward, where he guarded his flank from an assault. This enabled the Union soldiers to move along the pike without additional interruption.[36]

One Confederate remarked:

> "We stood there in line until night came and darkness shut from our sight the fleeing Federals, but did not then despair of an order to charge … when … we knew there was to be none, the deep mortification and shame for the blunder could be seen in the bowed head of every one, for this is the only instance coming under my observation in the war where a false movement was so apparent as to be recognized by every soldier of the line … the consequence … the bloody battle of Franklin … "[37]

Another stated, "We could hear the tramp, tramp of the men and the rumble of artillery and wagons until nearly daylight. What a golden opportunity was lost!"[38]

A Federal soldier on the retreat remarked:

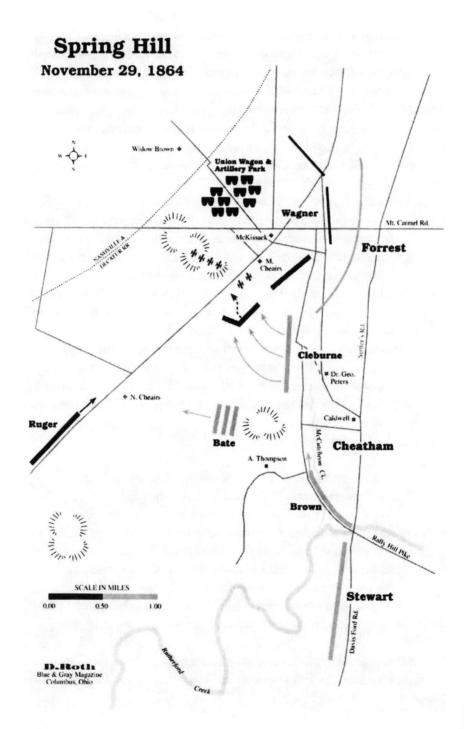

Spring Hill
November 29, 1864

Widow Brown

Union Wagon &
Artillery Park

Wagner

McKissack

Forrest

Mt. Carmel Rd.

NASHVILLE &
DECATUR RR

M.
Cheairs

Settler's Rd.

Cleburne

Dr. Geo.
Peters

N. Cheairs

Caldwell

Ruger

Bate

McCutcheon Ck.

Cheatham

A. Thompson

Brown

Rally Hill Pike

SCALE IN MILES

0.00   0.50   1.00

Stewart

Davis Ford Rd.

D. Roth
Blue & Gray Magazine
Columbus, Ohio

Rutherford
Creek

"For more than two hours our troops marched by almost under the light of the Rebel camp fires ... The enemy in battle order, with their batteries in position, lay quietly a few hundred yards from the road ... we ... felt immensely relieved when the last company had passed ... daylight began to break ... Fortunately for us, with the coming of daylight a dense fog overspread the land, completely hiding us from the eyes of our foe ... "[39]

Another Federal remarked:

"Wagner's Division was the last to leave Spring Hill ... we could hear ... the rumble of the wheels as the artillery and the wagons were pulling out, and ... the dull tramp of many feet and the clicking of accouterments ... There was no other sound, not even the shout of a teamster to his mules or the crack of a whip ... we could see the glow on the sky made by the encircling bivouac fires of the enemy ... with men about them cooking something to eat ... Every minute of those anxious hours we were expecting that they would awake to the opportunity that was slipping by and would advance and open fire on the congested mass of troops and trains that choked the pike ... It brought almost unspeakable relief when, just as daylight was beginning to dawn, our column finally got away in rapid motion for Franklin ... "[40]

During the retreat, as noted in Confederate reports, large amounts of military equipment were discarded. A member of the Fortieth Indiana proclaimed that aside from an occasional brush with Forrest, the only delay his regiment encountered took place in burning disabled wagons on the roadside. A Confederate explained that evidence of the hasty Federal movement was seen all along the route to Franklin. The Confederates used the sight of such wasteful disposal as a source of renewed confidence and expected to soon overtake the Federals and gain a decisive victory.[41]

Frank Roberts, a member of Gist's brigade, ate sweet corn in an effort to supplement his day's rations of "three little biscuits and a small piece of meat." His recollection of the journey toward Franklin included seeing loaded wagons with broken spokes, mules shot or knocked in the head with axes, their bodies still warm when discovered by the close pursuers.[42]

Roberts's battalion, Second Georgia Sharpshooters, would serve as skirmishers during the pursuit, and encountered Federal skirmishers outside Franklin.[43] The events to transpire that day, November 30, would forever alter the concept of General Hood and lessen the effectiveness of his army. The number of casualties suffered by either army at Spring Hill is generally grouped with the figures pertaining to Franklin.

Regarding General Hood, an early historian wrote, "Triumph was in his grasp, but failure came"; another used these words in describing the outcome: "... was Providence, not strategy, which saved the Union army that night."[44]

The battle itself is perhaps best evaluated in the words of a participant who recorded these thoughts thirty years after the war:

> "Hood had outgeneraled Schofield ... marched by his flank to his rear and until he encountered the force at Spring Hill, his movement was completely successful ... had Hood succeeded in throwing his forces across Schofield's line of retreat, the Union army would have been destroyed ... it is doubtful if Hood could have been checked south of the Ohio River ... "[45]

Today the area of Spring Hill has transformed from a rural to a growing suburban area, thus basically erasing the landmarks of the battlefield. In another manner, the encounter itself is largely forgotten in the context of the war. The Spring Hill battlefield has recently received a set of interpretive signs and a trail to add more understanding than was available from the state-supplied road signage. A nine-stop driving tour covers sites along U.S. Highway 31, the Columbia Pike in 1864, and a series of winding back roads. However, with the continued urban encroachment and rising cost of land in the area, the battle to preserve additional hallowed ground is quickly coming to an end, with a probable loss for preservationists.

Rippavilla, the Spring Hill home where Hood lashed out at his staff. Photo by author.

View of field at Spring Hill. Photo by author.

Another view of field at Spring Hill. Photo by author.

CHAPTER EIGHTEEN

FRANKLIN

" ... let us die like men." Patrick Cleburne
November 30, 1864

The Confederate failure to grasp victory at Spring Hill on November 29, 1864 infuriated General Hood. Union general John M. Schofield had led his troops from the snare Hood's troops controlled and had moved to Franklin, a distance of a dozen miles. Amid accusations of being intoxicated, Hood was bent on revenge, a state of emotion resulting in actions that would haunt the Confederate officer the remainder of his life.

Schofield's command marched throughout the night, arriving in Franklin near dawn on November 30. With neither a suitable wagon bridge over the Harpeth River, nor a ford unaffected by the swollen river, the Federal troops were detailed to accomplish three distinct tasks. A footbridge for the infantry was to be constructed; the planking of a railroad bridge was begun; and on the southern end of town, along the Columbia-Franklin Pike, breastworks were to be erected for use in the event of a Confederate attack. A mile from the Union line lay Fort Granger, situated on a high river bluff. Federal artillery was positioned there for additional protection.[1]

Hood held an early-morning meeting at Rippavilla, the Spring Hill home of Major Nathaniel Cheairs, where he "lashed out viciously" with accusations of incompetence toward his staff and was "beside himself with rage" at the situation his army now faced.[2] Hood's orders were clear, in that the Confederate Army of Tennessee would follow and attack Schofield's Federal command.

Captain Joseph Boyce, First Missouri, noted that during the march, "the citizens, nearly all old people or boys too young for military service, and any number of enthusiastic young ladies lined the fences, cheering us and crying out, 'Push on boys; you will capture all of the Yanks soon. They have just passed here on the dead run.'"[3]

Leading Hood's army in its pursuit of Schofield was Lt. Gen. Alexander P. Stewart. Maj. Gen. Stephan D. Lee's Corps brought up the Confederate rear as it approached Franklin. Following closely behind the rear guard, the Confederates arrived in Franklin and, by 2 PM, the Federal soldiers saw the gathering foe on the hills south of Franklin.[4]

The day had broken on that beautiful November morning with the sun "bright and glorious" as one participant recalled. By mid-afternoon, the temperature was forty-five degrees. A Federal soldier proclaimed, "There was nothing to suggest that we were standing on a spot that was soon to become historic" or that "the bravest of the brave were to end their careers there ... cut down as stalks before the sickle ... blown away ... as chaff before the wind."[5]

Hood and his generals used the clear sky of the day to survey the Union breastworks in Franklin. A required meeting occurred at the home of William Harrison one-half mile south of Winstead Hill. Forrest, Cheatham, and Cleburne spoke against a frontal assault. From Winstead Hill, a "cedar-covered rise" some two and a half miles away, all officers but Hood expressed reservations over a frontal assault covering "more than two miles of open ground against such strongly held and formidable fortifications."[6]

H.P. Figuers, a young Franklin boy at the time of the battle, remembered seeing General Hood and his staff ride some 100 yards from the Columbia Pike, a position that gave the officers a clear view of Figuers's Hill, located north of Franklin and serving as the Federal artillery's location. Figuers also noted that only two regiments were seen on Winstead Hill at that point, a sight Gen. Schofield easily distinguished from his location in Fort Granger. From this point, the Union general planned a troop movement across the Harpeth River after dark.[7]

Hood obviously noted the Harpeth River and its northern envelopment of Franklin. The Columbia Pike ran north and south and almost centered the open ground across which the Confederate advance would take place. Carter's Creek Road and Lewisburg Pike, to Hood's left and right respectively, also led to the community.[8]

Franklin

November 30, 1864

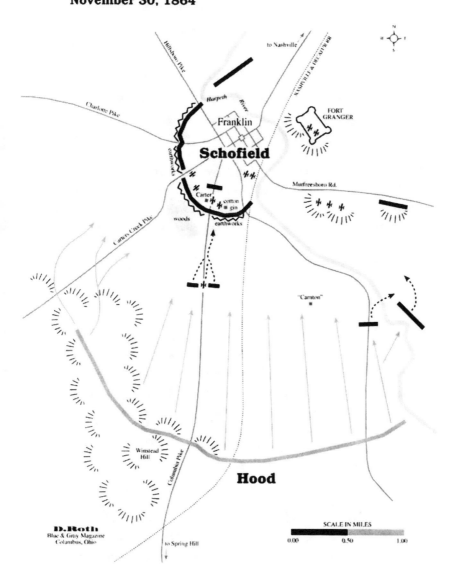

Approximately one-half mile from town, the Fountain Branch Carter family owned a house and cotton gin. The brick house had been built in 1830 and was roofed with hand-split cedar shingles. Facing the turnpike toward the east, the home had a long frame "L" running from the north end. To the south end sat a brick smokehouse. A small frame office stood next to the smokehouse and a well. The gin was a short distance away in the rear of the last Federal works across the pike.[9]

The Union deployment, left to right on their line, was as follows: Stiles, Casemate, Reilly, Strickland, and Moore, totaling some 17,000 troops of the Fourth and Twenty-third Infantry corps. Wagner's 3,000-man Fourth Corps of Lane and Conrad's brigades were placed to the front and center to serve as skirmishers.[10] Opdycke's brigade, the last Federal unit to arrive, was placed in reserve. This decision would prove highly beneficial to the Union army in the coming hours.

The Federal soldiers had "worked like beavers, using houses, fences, timber, and dirt in their works." When the Confederate arrival was first disclosed, a large number of the tired and hungry Federals were resting safely within their breastworks. In many places, the works were six to eight feet high, but five feet was more common along the Federal line that stretched for two and a half miles in length, resembling a backward capital J. The left rested on the Harpeth River and the line ran through the Carter property until the shank of the line again rested on the river north of town.[11]

The town had been the scene of earlier occupations and skirmishes, thus in many places the breastworks simply needed minor repairs. Gen. Cox, of Schofield's command, oversaw their strengthening. Planks from a number of the Carter buildings as well as eight plows were used in the construction of the breastworks. The line also included abates made from a locust grove as well as a battery of artillery to the right of the Carter House, near the line's center and the strongest portion of the line.[12]

An eyewitness described the breastworks as:

> "high enough to protect the soldiers and had head logs on top, so that the Federals could be reached only when the Confederate bullets entered the cracks between the head logs and breastworks. Every few yards along short arms, fifteen or twenty feet in length, were constructed at right angles with the breastworks to prevent enfilading ... in

front of the main breastworks a second line of earthworks was constructed of less importance."[13]

This "less important" series of earthworks lay about a half mile to the front of the main Federal line as the intended deterrent to a Confederate assault in the event of an attack. Within this position was Capt. John K. Shallenburger, commanding Company B of the Sixty-fourth Ohio Regiment, Conrad's brigade, Wagner's division, and Fourth Corps. His recollection of the construction of this position was:

> "we all supposed it would be temporary, but soon an orderly came along the line to give instructions to the company commanders ... the orders were to hold the position to the last man; to ... fix bayonets, and to instruct my company that any man, not wounded, who should attempt to leave the line without orders would be shot or bayoneted ... Four of Conrad's regiments had ... drafted men ... none of them had been with their regiments more than a month ... each company took two spades ... in a large cotton field not under cultivation that year ... our only resource was the earth thrown by the few spades we had ... the men eagerly relieved each other in handling the spades. Whenever a man showed the least sign of fatigue, a comrade would snatch the spade out of his hands and ply it with desperate energy."[14]

Taking in the situation his command now faced, General Hood hastily surveyed the Federal line. Slapping down his field glass and ignoring the suggestions of his subordinates, Hood exclaimed, "We will attack!" Staff officers began galloping from the group, carrying orders to the troops to form for an assault.[15]

Hood's foe at Franklin, General John Schofield, was a fellow 1853 West Point graduate. Of the fifty-four members of the class, Schofield had finished seventh, Hood forty-fifth.[16] The thirty-three-year-old Hood may have been annoyed at this fact and perhaps less than sympathetic to the pleas of his staff due to his own injuries. Hood had to be strapped into his saddle following the amputation of a leg after a wound at Chickamauga, an event preceded by the loss of the use of an arm at Gettysburg.

Walking to the line and preparing for the advance, John M. Copley, Company B, Forty-ninth Tennessee, saw a number of "torn and perforated regimental colors" along the Federal lines and knew the test his company soon faced would be a difficult one.[17]

The Confederates began assembling for the attack on the day "as soft and balmy as spring." Stewart's corps was sent to the right and occupied a line east of the Federal works. In Stewart's corps were the divisions of Loring, Walthall, and French. Quarles's brigade stood at the center of Walthall's division and, as such, the center of the corps. James H. McNeilly, a chaplain in Quarles's brigade, stood with the attacking forces, drawn up in the beautiful bluegrass pasture of John McGavock. McNeilly noted that the lot "sloped gently to a little spring branch, and beyond the branch the ground rose to a heavily wooded tract."[18]

At 3 PM, Caroline McGavock noticed the family livestock stampeding. The wife of John McGavock, Caroline was the mistress of Carnton, an eight-room mansion with two sitting rooms, built years earlier by her deceased father-in-law, Randal McGavock. The house was designed as McGavock's retirement home after serving as Nashville's first elected mayor.[19] The antebellum dream home would become an everlasting symbol of the battle of Franklin.

To the left of Stewart's corps, Cheatham's corps extended across the Columbia Road westward on a line south of town. Cheatham was thus assigned to the center of Hood's force, with General Brown's division to the left of the pike and General Cleburne's to the right.[20]

General Patrick Ronayne Cleburne was a thirty-six-year-old Irish-born son of a doctor. After immigrating to the U.S., Cleburne had settled in Helena, Arkansas and practiced law. Well-liked among his command, Cleburne had graying hair, prominent features, and "whiskers worn on the lip and chin" that became his distinguishing marks. The general was also engaged to be married to twenty-four-year-old Susan Tarleton.[21]

General Walthall sat atop his horse and appeared ready to lead the Confederate charge when General Loring rode up and addressed Walthall roughly. An eyewitness to the incident wrote:

> "It seems there was some confusion in placing the two
> divisions … there was a sharp colloquy between the
> two … Walthall said, 'General Loring, this is no time
> for a personal quarrel. When the battle is over, you will
> know where to find me.' … Loring galloped back to his

command and very soon was in that deadly charge where mere personal quarrels were forgotten amid the awful carnage ... "[22]

General Nathan Bedford Forrest's cavalry was divided and placed on each wing to capture escapees should the frontal attack prove victorious.[23] The choice of Hood to divide Forrest's command would prove to be one of his several errors at Franklin.

The moment for the attack approached. A Federal participant noted, "The ground appeared to us as level as a floor ... After considerable delay, the army ... was in position. It was a beautiful sight. As far as the eye could see it beheld troops moving into line for the attack."[24]

The two-mile-wide Confederate line contained some 17,000 men. Between 5,000 and 8,000 of the troops were shoeless on that balmy day. Their recent daily rations had consisted of three fist-sized biscuits, half of which was sawdust filler. As the temperatures cooled down that afternoon, one of the shortest days of the year, the condition of the Confederates could have only deteriorated.[25]

A Union officer in the skirmish line recalled his observance of the Confederate preparation:

"looking up the valley on our left front was a wide expanse of cleared fields. In these fields we had a good view of ... part of Stewart's Corps ... deploying on double quick from column into line. As fast as the troops could be hurried up from the rear, Stewart extended his lines over toward the pike. We could see all their movements so plainly while they were adjusting their lines that there was not a particle of doubt in the mind of any man in my vicinity as to what was coming."[26]

Four Missouri regiments under General Francis Marion Cockrell joined French's Confederate division to the right of the Columbia Pike. At the request of Col. Elijah Gates, a former brigade commander, the Missouri Brigade band burst into music. Eyewitnesses recalled that the playing of "Dixie" was overshadowed only with the cheers from thousands of throats shouting with "enthusiasm and volume." A moment of silence prevailed and then the Federal band, located at the Carter House, played "Hail, Columbia." The Federals likewise replied with a "vigorous shout of defiance." A Franklin resident added, "While the two armies were in sight of each other, they were nearly two miles apart; but every soldier knew that a great battle was imminent."[27]

A controversial move to this day, General French elected to stay behind while his command marched forward. His conclusion that a great sacrifice of life would be required to drive the veteran Federals from their lines defended with dozens of brass artillery pieces shining in the sun,[28] most likely led to his practice of self-preservation.

Near 4:00 PM, a signal flare was fired and "the march was commenced toward the Federal breastworks—and death." Personifying the sun, a member of the First Missouri wrote, "The sun was going down behind a bank of dark clouds, as if to hide from sight the impending slaughter. His slanting rays threw a crimson light over the field and entrenchments in front, prophetic of our fate."[29]

Carter House historian and curator David Fraley explained that though the attack began at 4:00, sundown took place only thirty-four minutes later. By 5:15, it was completely dark. A large number of the battle's survivors estimated that as many as 90 percent of the casualties of that day took place in the first twenty to thirty minutes of action. One can only imagine the sounds as some 38 cannon, 39,000 muskets, and 40,000 screaming men projected their sounds in unison.[30]

A boy watching the action recalled the Federal guns on Figuers's Hill opening on the attackers as they advanced. The men in gray, the boy exclaimed, had faced the situation before and showed little fear. He added, "no braver army ever stood in line of battle. With great courage and steady step they braved the flying shot and shell and, at the command of their officers, marched into battle ... they pressed in so close upon the heels of the outer lines of the Federals ... the long-range, heavy artillery had to cease firing."[31]

A member of the First Missouri proclaimed, "General Cockrell gave orders to march straight for the position in quick time and not to fire a shot until we gained the top of the works ... 'Shoulder arms! Right shoulder shift arms! Brigade forward! Guide center! Music! Quick time! March!' and this array of hardened veterans ... moved forward to our last and bloodiest charge."[32]

The members of General George D. Wagner's Federal skirmish line atop a slight rise a half mile to the front of the main line began to question their deployment. The first contact with Wagner's men came from Cleburne's and Brown's troops, and caused the skirmish line to break for the main line.[33]

A Union soldier serving in Wagner's skirmish line detailed the event:

> "The opinion was ... universal that a big blunder was being committed in forcing us to fight with our flank fully exposed in the midst of a wide field, while in plain sight in our rear was a good line of breastworks with its flank protected by the river. The indignation of the men grew almost into a mutiny ... Even the green men could see the folly of our position ... The regiment contained a number of men who had not reenlisted when the regiment had veteranized. Their time already had expired and they were to be mustered out as soon as we got back to Nashville. With home so nearly in sight, after three years of hard service, these men were especially rebellious. First Sergeant Libey, of Company H ... a nonveteran ... twice got up from our line and started for the breastworks, vehemently declaring that he would not submit to having his life thrown away ... A little later the sergeant was killed while we were retreating to the breastworks."[34]

A Missourian recorded the opening phases of the attack:

> "The enemy instantly opened heavily with musketry and artillery in front and an enfilading fire from a battery on our right ... we fired not a shot in return. Men commenced dropping fast from the start. The distance we marched ... to the enemy's works was ... about nine hundred yards. In that space our flag fell three times."[35]

A witness to the Confederate advance praised the sight in writing:

> "Hood's army, with perfect line and steady step, moved across the open field ... while the Federals stood in their breastworks ... The flying flags and martial music on both sides were distinctly in evidence and added to the spectacular effect. The Confederate generals were at the heads of their commands, and many of them were speaking words of encouragement and cheer to their men."[36]

The Federal breastworks had transformed from what was described as a "silver thread in the evening sun" into a line of burning fire and rising smoke. Cheatham and Stewart's corps followed the retreating skirmish line as it fell back. One survivor of the skirmish line stated to his comrades that he and his fellow members of the Sixty-fourth Ohio had seen the entire rebel army face-to-face.[37]

Chaplain James McNeilly of Quarles's Brigade remarked:

> " ... our lines rushed forward in the charge ... suddenly one of General Loring's brigades came rushing back in confusion. They had attacked at a point where an Osage orange hedge had been cut down, and its thorny branches formed an impenetrable abatis. They had been repulsed with heavy loss ... General Loring was riding among them trying to rally them ... From spur to plume he seemed a star of chivalry ... for more than a minute he sat perfectly motionless ... he seemed to court or defy death ... he cried out in anguish 'Do I command cowards?' ... Then he ... reformed them."[38]

J.N. Beach was a member of the Fortieth Ohio and stood on the extreme right of the principal Federal line. Playing no major role in the struggle, Beach nonetheless saw the long gray line advance over the fields and mass on the Columbia Pike. Beach referred to "the great wave" that rolled on "pushing away our advanced position ... and ... poured throughout our line of works."[39]

French's division had in fact come abreast of Cleburne's division just to the right of the Columbia Pike. The two commands "raised the glorious old yell, and rushed upon the main works a frantic, maddened body with overpowering impulse to reach the enemy and kill, murder, destroy." The ground to the Confederate's rear was covered with the bodies of their comrades, yet men such as those remaining of the First Missouri moved into the "murderous parapet ... with empty guns, the bayonet now their only trust."[40]

Among the dead Missourians were a number of musicians who had chosen to join their fellow statesmen in the Confederate assault. Federal shot and shell ended the lives of most of the band's members on the gory field. Men like Simeon Phillips, Harmon Kapp, and Benjamin Franklin Hickman fell near the Federal earthworks. So few members of the band survived that it ceased to exist after the battle at Franklin.[41]

Leading their troops and fighting as privates, officers of all ranks accounted for a large number of the Confederate casualties. Cockrell's Missourians were the first to experience this, for they had rushed ahead of all others and received an enfilading fire from three sides. A member of the Sixth Missouri remarked that the air was filled with red and blue flames screeching and howling everywhere.[42]

General Cleburne had two horses shot from under him, but led his men forward on foot, waving his hat in the air. One of Cleburne's brigade commanders, General Daniel Govan, had earlier remarked that there would be few of them—for Govan was a fellow Arkansan—to return home. Cleburne's reply, now a primary quote from the Franklin deathtrap, was, "Well, Govan, if we are to die, let us die like men." Cleburne was stuck by a minié ball below his heart and fell at the head of his division, yards from the Federal line. Additional accounts have the Irishman almost reaching or actually scaling the Federal entrenchments. General Gordon proclaimed that Cleburne was on horseback, running at full speed, when "rider and horse both fell, pierced with many bullets." When his body was recovered the next day, Cleburne's boots and personal effects had been stolen.[43]

T.H Stevens was a member of Casemate's Brigade and a defender of the Federal position. He remembered the right of Cleburne's division lapping the right of Casemate's position and Cleburne falling in front of the Sixty-fifth Indiana. Stevens stated that, "it looked ... as though the whole South had come up there and was determined to walk right over us."[44]

General Otho French Strahl, a native Ohioan and Dyersburg, Tennessee lawyer, bravely met his fate as did Cleburne. Before the battle had started, Strahl had given his mare, Lady Polk, to Bishop Quintard, chaplain of the First Tennessee Infantry. Seven months earlier, Quintard had baptized Strahl, and on the day of the assault at Franklin, the general "evidently felt that the approaching battle was to be his last—with many tender words" he bade the chaplain farewell.[45]

Strahl stood in a ditch at the Federal earthworks, firing at the occupants. S.A. Cunningham stood near the general and recorded his mortal wounding:

> "He turned to me, and though I was several feet back from the ditch, I rose up immediately, and walking over the wounded and dead, took position with one foot upon the pile of bodies of my dead fellows, and the other upon the

embankment, and fired guns which the General himself handed up to me until he, too, was shot down ... Indeed but few of us were left alive. It seemed as if we had no choice but to surrender or try to get away; and when I asked General Strahl for counsel, he simply answered, 'Keep firing.' But just as the man to my right was shot, and fell against me with terrible groans, he, too, was shot."[46]

General Strahl was shot two more times before dying. He had crawled near one of his subordinates, Colonel Stafford, and was in the process of being removed from the field when he received the fatal shots. Stafford was killed minutes later in a hail of gunfire that ended the lives of many around him. When the sun arose the next day, Stafford's body was discovered with his feet wedged within the pile of those falling across and under him. He fell in such a position that left his body half standing "as if ready to give command to the dead." Stafford would be one of 286 members of A.H. Bradford's regiment to become casualties at Franklin.[47]

Brigadier General John Adams, an 1835 West Point graduate and a native of nearby Nashville, received a serious arm wound in the Confederate advance. Adams refused to seek attention and chose instead to lead his troops into the Union position. A defender explained that he and his fellow Federals felt admiration for Adams, riding atop his horse as luck seemed to be at his side. He wrote, "Gen. Adams no doubt felt encouraged as he was so near our line. He spurred his horse and made the last heroic effort to carry his line forward and drive us out of our line, but he was shot down with his faithful horse, both falling together on top of the slight entrenchment." When Adams's body was found later in the trench, his mount's forefeet were on the Union side of the palisade, his rear on the Confederate side.[48]

Other Confederate generals met their destiny at Franklin, bringing the total to six who were killed or mortally wounded on November 30, 1864. States Rights Gist, the son of a former South Carolina governor, was killed near the Federal breastworks. Native Mississippian and Texas judge Hiram B. Granbury fell near Cleburne. Mortally wounded, former lawyer John Carpenter Carter lived until December 10, dying just three miles from the battlefield, in the Harrison home.[49]

Granbury commanded his Texas soldiers to move forward, noting that it should never be said "that Texans lag in the fight." A minié ball hit

Granbury's cheek, exiting the back of his head. His body was discovered the next morning.[50]

In addition, Generals Scott, Quarles, Manigault, Gordon, Brown, and Cockrell were severely wounded during one of the seventeen attacks upon the Federal position. All told, some fifty-three regimental commanders would be killed, wounded, or captured at Franklin. Sixteen generals and sixty-nine colonels would join ten thousand enlisted men of both sides as casualties at Franklin. As historian David Fraley has stated, the battle was off the charts for savagery, and for the moments and hours and numbers engaged, it is America's bloodiest battle.[51]

General Cockrell was wounded twice, but successfully led his Missouri Brigade to the works. Though not fatally wounded the general was knocked off his horse as three minié balls riddled his body. In the Fifth Missouri, Capt. Canniff was knocked from his horse when a ball hit his right shoulder, breaking bones and ripping his flesh. His blood pooled around his body and he propped himself on his elbow, attempting to either rally his troops or seek assistance. A bullet struck him in the face, ending the life of another Irish immigrant who, like Cleburne, had been noted by his peers for his courage.[52]

The Confederates overcame the relentless fire of the Federals to enter the earthworks. Captain Joseph Boyce, First Missouri, described the short-lived occupation:

> "As we crossed the rifle pits our line was delayed ... I cried out, 'Who is going to stay with me?' Lieutenant A.B. Barnett, Dick Saulsbery, Robert Bonner, and Denny Callahan dashed up, flag in hand, and we led the regiment up on the Federal works, where we all went down together. I made a stroke at a bluecoat, felt my leg give way, and fell on top of the works ... In another second our men were on top ... The enemy's fire ceased ... finding I could walk a little I started back to hunt for a surgeon, but ... I fell. Two ... men of the 5th Missouri ... placed me in an ambulance of General Quarles."[53]

Col. Elijah Gates's Missouri Regiment had been "cut up so badly" in crossing the open field that they were unable to hold the earthworks. They scaled them near the cotton gin and the men grabbed shovels, picks, muskets, and sabers in attempts to permanently dislodge the defenders.

Seventeen-year-old Thomas Jefferson Neese scaled the Federal works and
began swinging his musket like a club. He was pulled into the Federal side
of the works when a bullet shattered his left arm just below his shoulder.
One Federal infantryman took sympathy upon the lad, shielding him
from others seeking to run him through with a bayonet. The kind-hearted
Federal soldier placed the youngster upon a blanket and covered him.
Neese's brother found him there the next day and helped in nursing him
back to health.[54]

Bledsoe's Missourians had followed General Strahl down the pike,
pulling their artillery as they progressed. After their horses were shot, the
determined assailants pushed their guns forward by hand.[55]

Bledsoe, far from the only participant at Franklin to do so, most likely
killed many of his fellow Confederates when his cannonballs plowed
through the ranks from the rear and struck the front of the Federal works.
Bledsoe's one-time enemy and later confidant, J.K. Merrifield, added,
"Bledsoe told me as late as 1880 that he told General Hood he was firing
on their men, and that General Hood told him he was mistaken and to
keep on firing; but I know he was right."[56]

Captain John Shallenburger had successfully retreated from Wagner's
skirmish line to the temporary safety of the foremost Federal works. The
Confederate assault resulted in panic among some of the Union defenders.
Shallenburger wrote:

"Their advance was so rapid that my company had fired
not more than five or six rounds when the break came ...
beyond our left ... the opposing lines met in a hand-to-
hand encounter. Our line, overwhelmed by the weight of
numbers, quickly gave way ... I was looking toward the
pike when the break first started ... I instantly sprang to
my feet and looked to the front. They were coming on
a run, emitting the shrill rebel charging yell ... the rear
was open and a sense of duty ... constrained me to take
what I believed would be the dangerous risk of trying to
escape. I shouted to my company, 'Fall back' ... and gave
an example of how to do it by turning and running for
the breastworks."[57]

The Union troops in the primary earthworks had delayed firing into the
advancing Confederates as long as possible, in order to avoid shooting their

own men. As a result, the Confederate advance had overtaken a number of Federal troops who became prisoners, a situation that Shallenburger saw as unbearable, having heard of the horrors of "rebel prisons." With each of the estimated seventeen attacks made along the Federal line, Confederate casualties mounted in each assault.[58]

One Confederate, John Copley, Forty-ninth Tennessee, explained that the Federal "hurricane of combustibles" that left "ruin and destruction in its pathway" undoubtedly killed friend and foe alike.[59]

George W. Leavell was a private in Company B, Forty-first Mississippi, Sharp's brigade. Held in reserve, with Edward Johnson's command, until the later stages of the battle, Leavell watched the carnage with fear and disbelief. "From the hills ... we had an unobstructed view of the battle ... the enemy's earthworks ... bristling with their artillery, was belching flash and flame of lurid fire, and smoking like the crater of a volcano ... we had seen our brave men in solid lines march into the dismal scene and seem to disappear as though they had gone down into the crater."[60]

On the Union side of the works, Col. Emerson Opdycke's reserve brigade of Illinois, Wisconsin, and Ohio troops rushed forward to fill the breach in the Federal line. J.K. Merrifield, Eighty-eighth Illinois, recalled:

> "A ... solid shot ... rolled straight down the pike between many of the men in our brigade ... our colonel, George W. Smith, called out to fall in ... Gen. Opdycke ... took the lead and called out, 'Forward to the works' ... we saw the Confederates inside ... a Confederate with the butt of his gun [was] striking a 16th Kentucky soldier and knocking him down. Another of the 16th Kentucky then clubbed the Confederate with his musket and knocked him down ... the ... soldier who was knocked down was up and put a bayonet on his musket ... and plunged the bayonet in the Confederate ... "[61]

The fight inside the works became vicious as one participant noted:

> " ... there one of the severest struggles that falls to the lot of any men but once in a lifetime took place ... even Gen. Opdycke picked up a gun and clubbed with it. We had Capt Barnard, of Company K, in the 88th Illinois, who

used a little four-barrel pistol and even a hatchet ... At last the Confederates who were inside the works surrendered ... another line charged ... in this charge the color bearer ... of the Mississippi Brigade, came to the top of the works with his flag. As he was shot he pitched forward. I grabbed the flag, took it off the staff, and put it in my pocket. Then another line charged ... Gen. Cockrell's Missouri Brigade ... I noticed a flag and a large, fine-looking man ... They melted away ... I jumped over the works ... and got the flag ... this fine-looking officer ... asked me to pull a dead man off his leg ... He then asked me for a drink of water ... asked me to unbuckle his sword belt. I did so, and at that time firing commenced ... I made a run for the works."[62]

The Confederate officer Merrifield had shown mercy toward was Colonel Hugh Garland of the First Missouri. The St. Louis native, often described as "brave and daring in battle," was found dead on the battlefield the next morning by those left of his command. Garland had fallen about fifty feet in front of the outer ditch of the works. His wound was to the knee, probably not fatal, but in the Confederate charges that followed, he was to receive his mortal wound.[63]

A member of Opdycke's brigade added to the understanding of the charges by stating:

"like a thunderbolt out of a clear sky ... we saw the line breaking in front of us ... and retook the works in the most desperate fighting we ever saw ... we succeeded in retaking the works with considerable loss ... it is always estimated that four men are wounded to one killed, so the loss must have been terrible ... never in the history of the world's wars did so few men save an army as Opdycke's Brigade did at Franklin."[64]

Opdycke's rally had quite possibly saved the day for the Federal army at Franklin. In addition, his troops captured General Gordon and some seventy men of his command. Hand-to-hand fighting, a rarity in most battles, took place on an unprecedented scale at Franklin. Opdycke himself, as he later proclaimed, allegedly for the purpose of a promotion, broke the grip of his revolver over the head of an unfortunate aggressor after having fired all the bullets from its chamber.[65]

The numerous "what-ifs" related to the possibility of Opdycke's failure to mend the Federal line are startling. A Union soldier wrote:

> "if Opdycke's brigade had been out with the brigades of Conrad and Lane, as was contemplated by Schofield's order, the onrushing charge of the enemy would not have been stopped, the break would have been rapidly widened to right and left until it had involved all of Cox's line, and with the river in rear to check retreat, the day would have closed with utter rout and ruin of the four divisions of infantry south of the river … Cox met Opdycke on the field … took him by the hand and fervently exclaimed, '..that charge saved the day.'"[66]

The effect of Opdycke's counterattack and the rallying of other union troops led to a situation that one Confederate stated as "our triumph was very short." Capt. Joseph Boyce, First Missouri, noted that with neither officers nor ammunition and troops out of breath, the thin line he was part of rested briefly before being subjected to a second Union assault. "A solid wall of blue infantry advanced at the double-quick and poured in a volley … our brave fellows came out of the works as quick as they entered them."[67]

First Lieutenant Francis M. Posegate was the regimental quartermaster of the 175th Ohio Regiment at the time the Battle of Franklin occurred. He had taken a small detail across the Harpeth River when word of the Confederate approach arrived. The swiftness of their advance is shown in the fact that Posegate had returned to the Carter House to report to General Cox only moments prior to the Confederate breakthrough. He watched as Major Ed Mullenix led the 175th in a full charge toward the breach, where they assisted Opdycke in securing the line.[68]

From his point of reserve, Pvt. George Leavell joined his comrades of the Forty-first Mississippi in their advance toward the Union lines:

> "Now … came our time … Our final approach was almost from the westward. The shadows of coming night had settled heavily … and nerved ourselves for the charge. We were ordered to omit the usual yell, conceal

our approach under cover of the darkness, and make a spirited dash for the works. My own path lay through the north edge of the famed locust grove. Our progress was retarded by the brush which had been cut down ... we ... crawled under on hands and knees as best we could. We reached the works just a little to the left of the Carter brick dwelling ... when we came to the works we found the enemy there ready to greet us. At once there was a fierce struggle across the embankment as to which should hold the ground ... we were within thirty paces of the enemy's works when the darkness was lighted up as if by electric display. Then our brave men gave the yell and dashed into the works."[69]

Twice the flag of the Forty-first Mississippi topped the Federal earthworks. A participant recalled standing only yards away from the enemy as each side fired into the other. He added:

"We were at a point where the works made a slight deflection to the north ... forming an obtuse angle ... the other side of the ditch was filled with bluecoats just a few yards from us. Being on the outside of the angle gave us the advantage, as we could shelter under the works and pour an enfilade fire down their line ... we poured our deadly fire down their line, we could distinctly hear the death groan and agonizing cries of the wounded above the din of battle."[70]

Captain Spooner of Macon, Mississippi, regarded by many of his comrades as the coolest and most fearless man of the war, miraculously survived the battle and the war. Somehow avoiding wounds at Franklin, Spooner walked up and down the top of the Federal breastworks, yet drew little fire or attention from the enemy.[71]

In some instances, muzzles pointed downward toward an enemy soldier who stood only a few feet away. Guns would be knocked away by an enemy's barrel; men received wounds to their hands as they were the lone visible body parts of those in such close proximity.[72]

Sam Watkins, First Tennessee, explained his feelings of the battle in stating:

"I made up my mind to die—felt glorious ... I got to their works ... the scene lit up by fires that seemed like hell itself ... I ran up on the line of works ... dead men filled the entrenchments. The firing was kept up until after midnight ... We passed the night where we were ... when the morrow's sun began to light up ... we looked over the battlefield ... It was a grand holocaust of death. Death had held high carnival that night. The dead were piled the one on the other all over the ground. I never was so horrified and appalled in my life. Horses, like men, had died ... on the gory breastworks."[73]

Darkness slowly brought an end to the onslaught, yet periodic shots continued. A Confederate remembered that:

"our wounded ... their cries for help and for water could occasionally be heard; but no one could reach them, and they were gradually silenced by the fire from that awful parapet. After midnight the enemy gradually withdrew, leaving his dead and severely wounded in our possession. Following the custom of Federal authorities in similar battles, this might be claimed as a Confederate victory. I can safely say that just two such victories will wipe out any army the power of man can organize. Surely the path of glory leads but to the grave."[74]

The possession of the field, as David Fraley has noted, is usually regarded as denoting the victor of a conflict. Therefore, despite suffering 73 percent of the casualties at Franklin, the Confederate army, holding the field at the battle's end, can legitimately claim a victory. The Federal army had, in fact, left during the night, using blankets on the wagon and cannon wheels to lessen the noise and possibly avoid detection.[75]

A member of the Forty-first Mississippi held this recollection of the night after the battle:

"Late along toward midnight ... a bright flame broke out down in the town. We supposed they were evacuating and burning what they could not carry away. We used this light to good advantage while it lasted. Every object was brought distinctly to view ... I saw a fellow pushing down a cartridge, saw the ramrod. I leveled my rifle till the outline darkened the sight and fired ... During all these long and dreadful hours, covered in the darkness of night, it was impossible for us to know what was going on any distance from us ... The coming of daylight revealed a gruesome sight. Our men who ... bravely sacrificed their lives lay thick about the works and entangled in the locust brush. On the enemy's side to our left, where they had encountered our enfilade fire, their dead lay in a heap."[76]

Captain J.M. Hickey, Company B, Sixth Missouri, was more fortunate than many of those wounded around him. He lay approximately six feet from Colonel Garland when he received his last drink of water, and witnessed the colonel die from a second shot while prostrate on the ground. Hickey stated that years after the battle, the reading of any narrative on Franklin "makes my heart thrill with emotion and brings to mind so vividly the awful, heart rendering, and bloody scenes witnessed by me and other wounded soldiers ... on that battlefield."[77]

Hickey had been shot in his right leg, a wound that necessitated the limb's amputation the next day on the field near the Carter House. Unable to crawl or get away, Hickey had spent the night of November 30 to December 1, 1864 on the ground with "Many other Confederates ... shot all around me ... weltering in their own blood." Several of the men in Hickey's proximity died awaiting attention; he was shot in the forearm while waiting for help to arrive, the ball shattering both bones. Before sunrise, Hickey was shot again, this time in his left shoulder.[78]

Edward Hayward, a member of the Eighty-eighth Illinois of Opdycke's Brigade, provided one of the numerous acts of kindness found among the bloodbath. He noted, "I helped a Confederate major over the breastworks into the cotton gin that night after the fight. I made a bed of cotton for him and gave him a drink of water. He expressed his gratitude beautifully ... I think he belonged to the 45th Georgia."[79]

Confederate General William Bate had an aide named Theodrick "Tod" Carter, whose father's home sat at the center of the Union lines and was a place the Twentieth Tennessee captain hadn't visited in three years. Inside the basement of the home, Tod's sixty-seven-year-old father and some twenty other people sought shelter from the battle. The home was serving as Union general Cox's headquarters, and young Tod, an escaped prisoner of war from the Battle of Chattanooga, was given the opportunity to forgo participation in the Confederate charge. The young officer, a practicing lawyer at the age of eighteen and a war correspondent known as the Mint Julep, refused the offer of safety.

Captain Tod Carter summoned his men to go with him in declaring, "Follow me boys, I'm almost home." Atop his horse, Carter joined the attack that centered on the enemy positioned around his childhood home. Informed by General Thomas B. Smith of his son's presence on the field, Fountain Branch Carter, assisted by three of his daughters and a daughter-in-law, found Captain Carter 200 yards southwest of his home, where he lay mortally wounded.

A local girl visited the Carter home to show her respects for young Tod. She wrote of the visit:

> "As we approached ... Carter's house, we could scarcely walk without stepping on dead or dying men. We could hear the cries of the wounded, of which ... Carter's house was full to overflowing. As I entered the front door, I heard a poor fellow giving his sympathetic comrades a dying message for his loved ones at home. We ... were shown into a little room where a soft light revealed all that was mortal of the gifted young genius, Theo Carter ... Bending over him, begging for just one word of recognition, was his faithful and heartbroken sister ... that active brilliant brain had been pierced by one of the enemy's bullets."[80]

Young Carter lay in the same room and same bed where he had been born some twenty-four years earlier. He had been shot a total of nine times, and woke only twice to speak. The first time he said, "I recognize you all, but it hurts me to talk." His last words came just before his death as he proclaimed, "Home, home, home." Tod Carter died on December 2, 1864.[81]

For the rest of the Confederate army, sunrise on December 1 enabled the observation of the carnage of the previous day's struggle. Of the fewer than 20,000 effectives Hood possessed at the conflict's beginning, 6,252 casualties had been inflicted upon the Confederates; 1,750 were dead. The Confederates suffered more battle deaths at Franklin than did their enemy at Fredericksburg, Chickamauga, Chancellorsville, Shiloh, or Murfreesboro. Schofield's Federal forces, the "defensive unit" in this struggle, had losses of 2,326, with more than 1,200 killed or wounded. One thousand Union soldiers had been taken prisoner.[82]

While not a complete account, the casualties among some units were particularly high. The Thirty-fifth Alabama had 150 men killed and wounded, approximately half of its fighting force. The Thirty-first Mississippi had 45 troops killed and almost 100 wounded from a total of almost 250 men engaged at Franklin. In addition, ten of its color bearers fell in the series of assaults. Another Mississippi group, Company B of the Eighth Mississippi, sent twenty-seven men into action at Franklin; ten were killed, seven wounded, and four captured. The Missouri Brigade, the unit that saw its band decimated, was the smallest brigade numerically at Franklin. Some 419 of its 696 members were casualties of the battle, a rate of over 60 percent.[83]

The aftermath of the battle was sickening. The Carter House and its grounds served as a hospital, with the amputated limbs tossed outside and reaching the window's lower sill. The burial details took three days to complete their tasks. A Union private in the Thirty-sixth Illinois who joined in the Union countercharge that led to the preservation of the Federal line wrote to a paper that the blood flowed so deeply in a ditch that it entered the tops of his shoes. Doubting his story, the newspaper only printed the story when eleven other members of the Thirty-sixth Illinois endorsed the private's statement as true.[84]

Having invested the town around 2 AM, the Confederates viewed the full impact of the battle. A member of Company I, Fourth Florida, wrote that at 10 AM on December 1, blood still flowed four to six inches deep in the ditches around the Carter House.[85]

One Confederate captain had been shot in the throat sixty yards south of the Carter House. Left for dead, the officer lay on the field throughout the frigid night and, unresponsive from loss of blood, was being placed into a mass grave. One of the members of the burial party noticed a pulse still existed in the captain's body. The captain, surnamed Keller, was nursed back to health and later fathered Helen Keller, one of the most prominent leaders for handicapped rights in American history.[86]

Shot in the shoulder, chest, and knee, a twenty-year-old Federal lieutenant colonel, Arthur MacArthur, a regimental commander just out of his teens, was left for dead. He was also nursed back to health and later fathered his son, Douglas MacArthur.[87]

Three future Tennessee governors, John C. Brown, William Bate, and James Porter, all fought around the Carter House. Two of these were wounded, one in the head. Lawrence Ross, a future Texas governor and president of Texas A&M, also became a noted veteran of the Battle of Franklin. No fewer than fifteen men who survived the savagery of the battle later became senators or congressmen.[88]

Other participants of the battle were far less fortunate than these. Balthazar Grisselle, a Frenchman who served in the Forty-fourth Illinois Infantry, Opdycke's brigade, received a gunshot wound to the forehead, losing his nose and both eyes. It is unimaginable to think that in this condition, the soldier lived until January 6 before dying from his severe wound.[89]

Additional immigrants killed included German-born Hermann Fehrmann of the Forty-fourth Illinois and Lt. Col. Porter Olson of the Thirty-sixth Illinois, Opdycke's brigade. Olson was killed on November 30, serving the nation he called home. There is some dispute as to whether Olson was born in Norway or in New York to Norwegian parents. Charles Chon, a private in Company K, Twenty-fifth Texas Cavalry, died near Orasta Papera of the same company. Chon was a native of Shanghai, China and is buried in grave number 66 in the Texas section of McGavock Cemetery. Papera was born in Madrid, Spain.[90] These gentlemen joined others such as Patrick Cleburne in meeting their fate fighting for the cause in which they so strongly believed.

One of the more poignant stories of the battle involves two Yugoslavian brothers who were found embraced in death in the area of the field now designated as the parking lot of the Carter House. While these brothers and the men above died at Franklin, other immigrants such as Lt. John Ozanne of the Ninth Tennessee Sharpshooters, a native Frenchman, and Hungarian-born U.S. brigadier general Frederick Kneffler, would live to fulfill the memory and dreams of others like them.[91]

At Carnton mansion, bloodstains remain today in the home where soldiers of both sides were treated and cared for in all but one room of the house. The bodies of generals Cleburne, Adams, Granbury, and Strahl were allegedly placed on the porch prior to burial. The McGavock family established a cemetery on the grounds of the farm; it serves today as the resting place for almost 1,500 victims of the battle.

Visitors to Carnton and the McGavock Cemetery may view the final resting places of the brave Confederates who fell at Franklin. From the following states, the number of corresponding graves is present: Arkansas,

104; Alabama, 129; Georgia, 79; Louisiana, 18; and South Carolina, 51. In addition, Texas has 89 soldiers represented; Missouri, 130; North Carolina, 2; Florida, 4; Kentucky, 60. Two hundred thirty Tennesseans are buried at Carnton, having died defending their home state. Most notable on the grounds are the graves of 424 Mississippi Confederates entombed at the site. Sadly, 225 bodies rest in graves simply marked as unknown.

As historian David Fraley has explained, the number of superlatives used by veterans and civilian witnesses to the Battle of Franklin are overwhelming. Today the buildings on the Carter House grounds are the most heavily war-damaged structures on the North American continent. More than 1,000 bullet holes can be seen on the house and surrounding buildings.[92]

Historian Thomas Cartwright of the Carter House has explained that in Franklin being denoted as the bloodiest hours of the entire war, one need only to look at the carnage surrounding the house itself. Using the Carter House as ground zero, 4,000 men were killed or wounded within 450 yards of the home. Within 650 yards of the Carter House, 6,000 men became battle casualties; 8,000 men within 1,100 yards.[93]

People viewing the site after the battle were consistent in their description of the destruction. Young Frances McEwen wrote:

> "we passed on to a locust thicket, and men in every conceivable position could be seen, some with their fingers on the triggers ... On the left of the pike, around the old gin house, men and horses were lying so thick that we could not walk ... Our house was full as could be, from morning until night we made bandages and scraped linen lint with which to dress the wounds, besides making jellies and soups with which to nourish them."[94]

Young H.P. Figuers remembered his tour of the field the day after the battle:

> "The first dead person I found was a little Yankee boy, about my own age, lying in the middle of the street with his hands thrown back over his head ... Inside of the breastworks were the dead and wounded Yankees; outside and for a long distance back were the dead and wounded Confederates ... Men, shot and wounded in every part of

the body, were crying out for help ... From the Lewisburg Pike ... as far as the Columbia Pike ... the dead and wounded were so thick upon the ground that it might be said without exaggeration that one could walk upon the dead and never touch the ground. A pit or ditch ... was full of the dead ... piled on one another several deep ... you would find a man with his head shot off ... I remember seeing one poor fellow ... whose whole under jaw had been cut off by a grape shot, and his tongue and under lip were hanging down on his breast ... a locust thicket ... the trees had been set out about ten feet apart ... and averaged from four to six inches across the stump. These trees were stripped of their bark ... many were struck by so many bullets that they fell of their own weight. I distinctly remember seeing General Hood riding down through the streets of Franklin ... I ... was much disappointed in his appearance ... The Federals were not buried until the following Saturday after the battle was fought on Wednesday. They were buried generally just as they had fallen by pulling dirt from the breastworks on them. Many of them had been stripped of their clothing by living soldiers who were almost naked. On Saturday it began to rain ... in the ditch where so many soldiers were killed the water was literally running blood. Right in front of the Carter House ... A Yankee soldier standing behind this tree was shot through the head, instant death and rigidity followed ... he was standing ... dead."[95]

The participants in the battle of Franklin largely agree on the fact that Franklin was the most deadly conflict of the war, considering its duration of some five hours, from 4 to roughly 9 PM.

Chaplain James McNeilly of Quarles's brigade wrote:

"The regiment went into action with one hundred and eight muskets and twenty officers. We had twenty-six killed ... we lost ninety-two muskets and eighteen officers ... a captain was in charge of the brigade ... The men seemed to realize that our charge ... would be attended with heavy slaughter, and several of them came to me with watches, jewelry, letters, and photographs ... I had to decline as I was going with them ... the next morning ... every one who made this request of me was killed."[96]

Captain Joseph Boyce, First Missouri, added, "Our army was a wreck ... So many hearts were stilled forever."[97]

Pvt. W.L. Shaw, Tenth Mississippi, recalled, "I have always thought that Franklin without doubt was the bloodiest ... most severe and hardest contested battle of our Tennessee Army."[98]

Tillman H. Stevens of Casemate's Brigade remarked, "To my mind, the battle of Franklin was the most disastrous ... in the great war."[99]

Captain J.M. Hickey, Second and Sixth Missouri, noted, "Franklin, Tenn ... was the worst slaughter pen and the most bitterly contested of all our battles."[100]

S.C. Walford, a Federal survivor, wrote, "I served three years in the 97th Ohio ... and was in all the battles from Stone's River ... and back to Franklin and Nashville ... I consider Franklin the hardest fought of any I was in."[101]

Isaac Sherwood, also a Federal veteran and later a Congressman, exclaimed, "Ever since the battle of Franklin, when I saw thousands of men torn by shot and shell, I have hated war."[102]

Civilian Moscow Carter, in a letter published in the *National Tribune* on September 9, 1882, remarked:

> "In this yard ... I could walk from fence to fence on dead bodies, mostly Confederates. In trying to clear up, I scraped together a half bushel of brains right around the house, and the whole place was dyed with blood ... I spent the whole of that Christmas day hauling seventeen dead horses from this yard."[103]

Since the end of the war, the residents of Franklin—particularly those desiring preservation of the battlefield—have seen another struggle, one against urbanization. Largely lost during the late twentieth century, the fight to regain lost portions of the area has seen recent success.

The Carter House, the center of the struggle, is well-preserved and greets each visitor with well-manicured grounds and extremely courteous and knowledgeable guides. Carnton, once on the verge of succumbing to years of neglect, now beckons visitors to step back in time to the era of elegance and revel in the situation of November and December of 1864. Standing on the same porch Nathan Bedford Forrest used as an observation post, walking the grounds of McGavock Cemetery, or viewing the area that held the bodies of valiant Confederate officers are impressive points to Carnton.

For years, two pizza parlors with paved parking lots sat on the site generally accepted as the location of General Patrick Cleburne's death. In late 2005, through the combined efforts of Franklin's Charge, a preservation group, and the Tennessee Wars Commission, one of the establishments was purchased to be torn down.[104]

It is sad to realize that Cleburne's death site is only a few yards away from a trash dumpster. Within fifty yards of this dumpster, nine Congressional Medals of Honor were won on the Franklin battlefield.[105] This in itself should be a wake-up call to concerned Americans willing to save what is so frequently referred to as hallowed ground.

Millions of dollars have also been raised to purchase more than 100 acres of land along Lewisburg Pike and Carnton Lane, the eastern flank of the battle. Private donations, the Civil War Preservation Trust, and the City of Franklin have also purchased a local golf course that joins the grounds of Carnton and is separated from the cemetery by a fence.[106]

Sixty-three percent of individuals surveyed in Franklin desire to see the land transformed into a national battlefield park, a sentiment expressed among participants of both armies more than 100 years ago. Franklin's battlefield, though largely overtaken by homes and businesses, has a few bright spots for future visitors.

Perhaps participant Sam Watkins of the First Tennessee best summed up the battle and the hope for the preservation when writing:

> "We shed a tear for the dead. They are buried and forgotten ... We meet no more on earth ... But up yonder ... where the Almighty and Eternal God sits ... we will meet again and see those noble and brave spirits who gave up their lives for their country's cause that night at Franklin, Tennessee ... "[107]

Modern-day view of Winstead Hill. The hill served as Hood's observation post and today contains a number of monuments, a cannon, covered kiosk, and the Brigadier's Walk. The latter serves as a memorial to the men who advanced "into certain death that November afternoon." Photo by author.

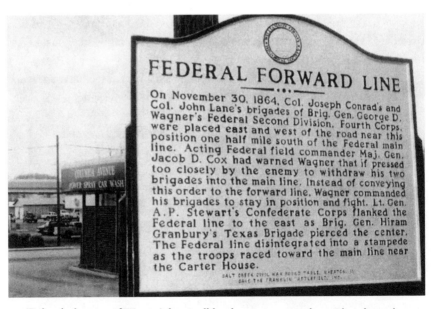

Today the location of Wagner's line is all but lost to commercialism. Photo by author.

Fort Granger's Cavalier or "fort within a fort," the strongest area of the location. Capt. Giles J. Cockerill's Battery D, First Ohio Light Artillery fired 163 rounds from here on November 30, 1864, inflicting heavy damage on the Confederates' right wing. Photo by author.

The Carter House as seen from Columbia Pike. Photo by author.

The basement windows of the Carter House served as the only contact with the outside world for those individuals seeking shelter there on the night of the battle. The home served as a post-battle hospital, with amputated limbs reaching the windowsill of the window to the extreme left. Photo by author.

The back of the Carter House, "ground zero" of the battle. The Union breastworks were to the right, just out of the picture. Photo by author.

On the right is the Carter farm's office. This has the distinction of being the most battle-scared building still standing from the war. The smokehouse on the left bears significant damage as well. Photo by author.

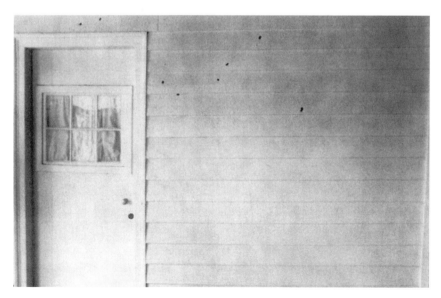

Inside this door located on the back porch of the Carter House and surrounded today by bullet holes, Tod Carter was born and died. Photo by author.

Tod Carter. The young officer remains one of the war's most touching tragedies. Courtesy of the Carter House.

The markers for the Federal entrenchments and the death site of Gen. Adams basically become lost within urban sprawl. Photo by author.

Cleburne's death site. At the time of the battle, the Carter gin sat some forty to fifty yards away. Today, businesses and dumpsters dominate the terrain. Photo by author.

McGavock Cemetery. Photo by author.

The Carnton house. Photo by author.

Inside Carnton, bloodstained footprints remain in a room where soldiers received medical attention. Courtesy of Carnton Plantation.

The Visitor Information Center in Franklin served as a hospital following the battle. Photo by author.

Pvt. Thomas Hansford, Twelfth Kentucky Infantry, was mortally wounded on November 30, 1864. His burial place in unknown. Courtesy of the Carter House.

Capt. Addison Dunn, Fifty-seventh Indiana Infantry, was killed at Franklin and is buried at an unknown location. Courtesy of the Carter House.

Col. Noel Nelson commanded the Twelfth Louisiana Infantry, Scott's Brigade, Loring's Division, Stewart's corps and was mortally wounded at Franklin. He is buried at McGavock Cemetery. Courtesy of the Carter House.

Dr. Fielding Pope Sloan of the Fiftieth Alabama was wounded on November 30 and endured the agony of his wounds until his death on June 19, 1865. Sloan is buried in Franklin's Rest Haven Cemetery. Courtesy of the Carter House.

C.S.A. General William Bate survived a near-fatal wound and served as Tennessee's governor after the war. Confederate Veteran.

The Tennessee monument in McGavock Cemetery. Note the abandoned tennis court in the background. Photo by author.

CHAPTER NINETEEN

NASHVILLE

"Gen. Thomas ... crushed the backbone of the rebellion at
Nashville." Gov. Brownlow
December 15-16, 1864

General Hood's failure to capture the Union forces at Spring Hill
and the Union infliction of heavy casualties on the Confederate Army of
Tennessee at Franklin had left Hood's command obliterated. Following the
Federal withdrawal to Nashville, Hood and his troops followed, perhaps
in an attempt to either gain revenge or "save the day" for the Confederacy
in Tennessee.

General Stewart's Corps of Confederates left Franklin the second day
after the murderous fight at Franklin, their army in mourning. Hood's
troops arrived in the Tennessee state capital on December 2 and began
entrenching itself approximately one mile from the Federal positions
located around the city.[1] Both Hood and Union general Thomas's Army
of the Cumberland would receive criticism until the present day for failing
to initiate a battle before the elapsing of two weeks, yet a number of
skirmishes evolved in the area, focusing on outposts and locations of less
significant military value.

Nashville lacked the industrial facilities that had and would create
battles for a number of other cities and towns, North and South alike,
during the war. Besides holding value though as Tennessee's capital,

Nashville served as a valuable southern transportation hub, with river and railroad traffic, as well as a significant number of roads serving the city.

Arriving at almost the same time as the Confederates, a variety of inclement weather, notably rain, sleet, and snow, and an occasional mixture, fell in torrents for ten days. One Confederate simply recorded that "the surface of the earth was covered with ice" during this period. The weather affected each army differently, for the Union soldiers were reportedly well-clad and fed and living inside comfortable quarters. In contrast, the Confederate soldiers were scantily clad, many without shoes or hats, residing in poor facilities, short on rations, and lacking anything but green timber to burn, as fence rails within a reasonable distance had been consumed. Thousands of Confederate soldiers at Nashville lacking shoes found the rocky ground, covered in many locations with briers and a thick growth of prickly pear, added greatly to their hardships.[2]

Estimated to have had as many as 72,000 men at the onset of action at Nashville, Thomas had begun receiving reinforcements as rapidly as transports could bring them to the city. While other reports place the Federal effective force at 50,000, they nonetheless heavily outnumbered Hood's Confederates with slightly more than 23,000 troops to meet an enemy twice their number.[3]

The Federals had two permanent lines of breastworks with the inner line running from Fort Negley, their strongest fortification, in a northeasterly direction to the Cumberland River. From Fort Negley and in the opposite direction, the Union lines ran to Fort Casino, just west of the Franklin Pike, northwest to Fort Morton, and to Fort Gillem in north Nashville and again to the river. The outer line started at Fort Casino and utilized a series of southwesterly, westerly, and northwesterly turns to include Belmont Heights before reaching the Cumberland River. Temporary breastworks, erected before and during the battle, were situated south of the city.[4]

Confederate deployment, according to a report of Lieutenant General S.D. Lee, was as follows:

> "one mile from the Union entrenchments ... Cheatham's Corps being on the right and extending across the Nolensville Pike and resting on the railroad from Nashville to Murfreesboro, and extending west almost to the Franklin Pike. Lee's Corps occupied the center, covering the Franklin Pike and extending almost to the Granny White Pike. Stewart's Corps was on the left, covering the

Granny White and Hillsboro Pikes, leaving on Hood's left to the river on the west an open space ... more than equal to the front occupied by his entire army, from the Hillsboro Pike to the river and through which ran the Harding and Charlotte Pikes ... covered by one brigade of cavalry under Gen. Chalmers, about 1,000 strong, and for a little while one brigade of infantry under Gen. Ector on the Harding Pike. Gen. Hood had strengthened his right flank by a redoubt on Rains Hill, near the Nolensville Pike, and some smaller works near the railroad, and his left flank by five redoubts on both sides and to the west of the Hillsboro Pike, also by a strong line of rifle pits on Montgomery Hill ... two of these redoubts west of the pike were from a mile to a mile and a half from the left of Gen. Stewart's Corps, and occupied by artillery and small garrisons of from 150 to 200 men."[5]

For several days prior to the battle, the Confederate soldiers in their entrenchments a short distance from the Federal outer lines were constantly under fire. Prior to the battle, General Hood's headquarters were at Travellers' Rest, the home of Col. John Overton. Hood would move his command center as the battle progressed. Gen. Cheatham and his staff spent the nights before the battle at the Wesley Greenfield home, one-quarter of a mile to the rear of the Confederate line.[6]

General George "Pap" Thomas had his Federal headquarters in the old St. Cloud Hotel at the corner of Sumner and Church streets. Prominent Nashville residents regularly questioned the Union general as to whether and when they should move their families from the city. Thomas would usually reply kindly that he would give due warning to do so when the time arrived. Orders from Washington strongly encouraged Thomas to attack, but he replied that an engagement with the Confederates would begin only when he felt prepared. If this decision was found to be unsatisfactory, Thomas stated, another commander must be chosen.[7]

General John Logan was ordered to Nashville to replace Thomas, but failed to arrive in the city prior to the battle. The Tennessee state legislature would honor General Thomas after the war in presenting him a gold medal.[8]

General Thomas was a Virginian by birth and a West Point classmate of Robert E. Lee. The belief that he owed his allegiance to his nation rather than his home state distinguished Thomas from Lee, whose stance was just the opposite. Like Lee, Thomas was well-liked among his troops and took a personal interest in their comfort and welfare. After the war Thomas would be given the honor of selecting the site for the national cemetery in Nashville.[9]

A lengthy list of Tennessee soldiers defended their capital city as the Battle of Nashville approached. They included Cheatham's corps, Maj. Gen. B.F. Cheatham; James D. Porter, chief of staff and assistant adjutant general. Field's brigade, Col. Hume R. Field commanding; Fourth, Sixth, Ninth, and Fiftieth Tennessee, Lt. Col. George W. Pease; First and Twenty-seventh Tennessee, Lt. Col. John F. House; Eighth, Sixteenth, and Twenty-eighth Tennessee, Col. John H. Anderson. Strahl's brigade, Col. Andrew J. Kellar; Fourth, Fifth, Thirty-first, and Thirty-eighth Tennessee, Col. L.W. Finley; Nineteenth, Twenty-fourth, and Forty-first Tennessee, Capt. D.A. Kennedy. Gordon's brigade, Col. William M. Watkins; Eleventh and Twenty-ninth Tennessee, Maj. John E. Bins; Twelfth and Forty-seventh Tennessee, Capt. C.N. Wade; Thirteenth, Fifty-first, Fifty-second and 154th Tennessee, Maj. J.T. Williams. Bate's division, Gen. William B. Bate; Second, Tenth, Twentieth, and Thirty-seventh Tennessee, Lt. Col. W.M. Shy. Cleburne's division; Thirty-fifth Tennessee, Col. B.J. Hill, detached. Lee's corps, Gen. Stephen D. Lee; Palmer's brigade, Gen. J.B. Palmer; Third and Eighteenth Tennessee, Lt. Col. William R. Butler; Twenty-third, Twenty-sixth, and Forty-fifth Tennessee, Col. Anderson Searcy; Thirty-second Tennessee, Col. John P. McGuire, at Murfreesboro. Stewart's corps, Quarles's brigade, Brig. Gen. George D. Johnston; Forty-second, Forty-sixth, Forty-ninth, Fifty-third, and Fifty-fifth Tennessee, Capt. A. M. Duncan; Forty-eighth Tennessee, Col. William M. Vorhies.[10]

In addition, two Tennessee regiments would actually fight one another in the struggle at Nashville. Col. George Spalding's Twelfth Tennessee U.S. Cavalry would meet Col. Ed Rucker's Confederate Twelfth Tennessee Cavalry. In the struggle, Rucker was captured after exchanging blows with Captain Joseph Boyer. Shot in the arm, Rucker fell from his horse and lost his sword, although the latter would be returned to him years later.[11]

The ice storm mentioned previously had caused delays for the execution of Gen. Thomas's plan of battle and increased the levels of anxiety and tension throughout the ranks. The ice began thawing on December 12, and on the morning of the fifteenth, Thomas used the screen of a heavy fog to move his troops into position for an attack upon the Confederate earthworks. Taking advantage of the unoccupied area on Hood's left and between it and the Cumberland on the left, Thomas began his attack.[12]

Warren R. King was a paymaster's clerk aboard *Carondelet* at the time of the battle of Nashville. His impression of Nashville remained vivid forty years after the battle:

> "the whole face of the country was a glare of ice. The gunboat ... lay about three miles below the city, at the right of our armory ... I shall never forget the terrible uproar and commotion of that conflict. Above the tumult there was, at regular intervals, a thunderous roar that was said to be the hundred-pound guns of old Negley."[13]

Major Gen. James Harrison Wilson, an October transfer from Virginia to Tennessee, would play a significant role in the battle's early stages. The twenty-seven-year-old Wilson had led one of Phil Sheridan's cavalry divisions against Robert E. Lee and soon proved worthy of the numerous accolades received during his two and a half years of service. Wilson was understandably labeled as ambitious, vain, and the possessor of a towering ego.[14]

At 10 AM, Wilson's 12,000 cavalrymen of three divisions under brigadier generals Edward Hatch, Richard Johnson, and Robert Knipe led the attack against the Confederate left. Cannon barrages of the previous days had robbed the Confederates of proper rest, and Wilson's charge brushed away Chalmer's small force. As a diversion, U.S. general Steedman's command, largely composed of African-American troops, hit the extreme Confederate right, while the cavalry constantly swung around the left with A.J. Smith, Maj. Gen. Thomas J. Wood, and Maj. Gen. John M. Schofield following.[15]

The only hindrance to Wilson's advance came from the fact that his cavalrymen were fighting on foot. The wet, swampy ground proved difficult to cross. Redoubts positioned to either side of Hillsboro Pike fell to the advancing blue-clad attackers. These five redoubts along the Confederate line offered little resistance.

Col. W.D. Gale, a member of the Confederate Signal Corps, wrote his wife from Stewart's headquarters in Tupelo, Mississippi and relayed his observations of this stage of the battle. He explained:

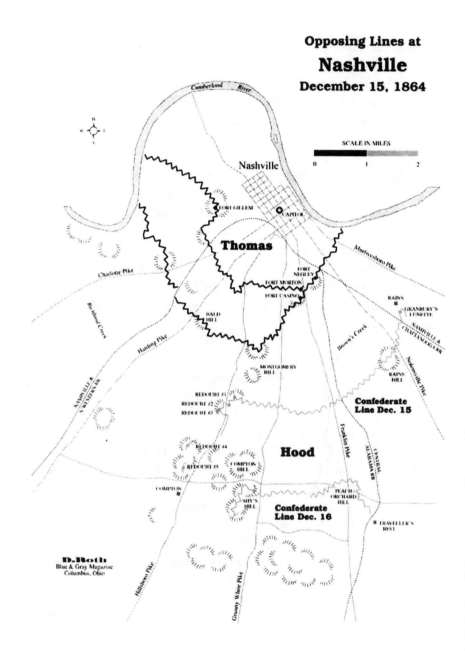

Opposing Lines at
Nashville
December 15, 1864

SCALE IN MILES

0   1   2

Cumberland River

Nashville

FORT GILLEM

CAPITOL

Thomas

Murfreesboro Pike

Charlotte Pike

FORT NEGLEY

FORT MORTON

FORT CASINO

RAINS

GRANBURY'S LUNETTE

NASHVILLE & CHATTANOOGA RR

Richland Creek

BALD HILL

Brown's Creek

Harding Pike

RAINS HILL

Nolensville Pike

MONTGOMERY HILL

NASHVILLE & N.WESTERN RR

REDOUBT #1

REDOUBT #2

REDOUBT #3

**Confederate
Line Dec. 15**

Franklin Pike

GENERAL ALABAMAKER

REDOUBT #4

Hood

REDOUBT #5

COMPTON HILL

COMPTON

SHY'S HILL

PEACH ORCHARD HILL

**Confederate
Line Dec. 16**

TRAVELLER'S REST

D.Roth
Blue & Gray Magazine
Columbus, Ohio

Hillsboro Pike

Granny White Pike

358

"about 9 o'clock it was reported to me that the enemy were advancing in heavy force on the Hillsboro pike and in front of Gen. Loring. Generals French and Walthall had their troops in bivouac along the east side of the Hillsboro Pike ready to move. I informed Gen. Stewart, who mounted and rode to the point ... I had a signal station, and sent dispatches to Generals Hood, Lee and Cheatham, and received others. In a short time the firing began and grew heavier as the enemy advanced. It was soon perceived that his main attack would be here, as his whole army appeared to be in our front. They then stormed and took redoubt 5, our forces being entirely too small to keep them back."[16]

The Federal cavalry soon reached the left and rear of Stewart's corps, gaining a position to the rear of the divisions of Walthall, Loring, and French. The advanced rifle pits on Montgomery Hill fell with the Hillsboro Pike redoubts. Stewart's left, the left of Hood's army and at this stage of the fight, was turned by Thomas's great swing and encircling motion.[17]

Despite the Federal success, it was noon before Wilson's and Smith's lines were fully extended and brought within striking distance of the Confederate works. Post's brigade, in Gen. Sam Beatty's division, lay at the foot of Montgomery Hill, "regarding the works and summit with covetous eyes." Against "a fierce storm musketry and artillery," Post personally led his troops sweeping forward into the Confederate parapet. The guns and massive number of prisoners gained caused havoc in the Federal headquarters, for as they were being marched to the rear, Thomas initially feared the Confederates had rallied and were countercharging. The wild outburst of cheers ringing across the valley relaxed the commander and told a story of complete success.[18]

Reinforcements from Lee's corps arrived after the redoubts to Stewart's left had fallen. The new arrivals initially appeared in a thin line and were rapidly overwhelmed. Lee's troops fell back toward Granny White Pike and took position on the ridges between the Granny White and Hillsboro pikes. The arrival of nightfall was the major factor that prevented Stewart's force from being entirely cut off from their comrades.[19]

Maj. G.W. Garrett was in command of the Twenty-third Mississippi, Adams's brigade, Loring's division, at Nashville. His regiment was stationed southwest of Belmont College with his left resting near the Granny White Pike. The group occupied temporary ditches on the east side of a ridge facing the Union lines. To Garrett's right, his colleagues could be seen, but a ravine eliminated any vision of those on his left. With two pieces of artillery, Garrett received orders to hold his position "at all hazards" to cover the retreat of those who earlier inherited the brunt of the Federal attack.[20]

Garrett recalled:

> "There were three lines of battle advancing in order. When the advance lien came in reach of my artillery, we fired with ball and shell; and when they were closer, we used grape and canister. I read my orders to the men and told them that if we were to be sacrificed for the good of our army and our country we must accept the fate. I told them to remember Franklin and to hold their fire until the enemy came very close, adding, 'I have been with you in many battles, and have ever found you at your places ready for duty as courageous soldiers. Let this day add fresh laurels to the fame of the 23rd Mississippi.' They did their duty, and did it well, as the long line of the enemy's dead and wounded in our front was a solemn testimony. One line after another charged us with desperation ... The men were commanded to fire at will, and the concentrated, galling fire from both cannon and musketry caused the enemy to falter and lie down at this hedge [some seventy-five yards in our front]. They were given one volley after another, until it seemed that no human being could survive. But on came the second and third lines of the enemy, only to meet the same fate ... While they seemed very courageous, their shots were inaccurate."[21]

Col. W.D. Gale maintained his Confederate signal corps station "until the Yankees advanced to within three hundred yards. I then mounted and made my escape ... with my clerks and joined General Stewart."[22]

The retreating Confederates received a plea from Mary Bradford to end their retreat and fight, but the request was in vain. Bradford had met the Confederates days earlier when they entered the city, standing by the road and cheering their appearance. Despite the heavy fire from Union guns, Bradford continued to offer encouragement to the Confederates, yet the retreat continued.[23]

Col. W.D. Gale said of his fellow Confederates that they:

> "seemed utterly lethargic and without interest in the battle. I never witnessed such want of enthusiasm, and began to fear for tomorrow, hoping that General Hood would retreat during the night, cross Duck River, and then stop and fight; but he would not give it up. However, he sent all his wagons to Franklin, which prepared the men still more for the stampede of the next day."[24]

Major G.W. Garrett noticed the Confederates to his right had abandoned their entrenchments, saw Union infantry approaching and soon surrounding Garret and his regiment:

> "Their commanding officer ... ordered me to surrender and to raise the white flag ... He then commanded, 'Go order your men to cease firing, or I will have ... them shot'. My men were not firing; but it was the overshooting of his own men who were in our front ... soon the cannonading ceased, and all was over."[25]

Garrett was marched to Nashville and from there sent to a Northern prison. Years later, he praised his command in writing, "I think I would be safe in saying that the number killed outright in our front was greater than that of my command."[26]

During the night of the fifteenth, Hood formed a new Confederate line one and a half to two miles south of the position held that morning. Cheatham's corps then made its move from the extreme right of Hood's line to the extreme left and formed near the Brentwood Hills to the left of Granny White Pike. Stewart's corps stood to Cheatham's right, and Lee's corps, now resting on Overton Hill on the Franklin Pike, became Hood's extreme right.[27]

Cheatham's right division, under the command of Maj. Gen. William B. Bate, occupied Shy's Hill to the left of Granny White Pike, with Chalmer's cavalry on his left. Stewart's corps was between the Granny White and Franklin pikes. Hood's battle line was almost one-half the length of that he held when the struggle began. His position was critical, for it left the Franklin Pike as his one route of retreat, should disaster strike. On Hood's extreme left, Wilson's cavalry held the important Granny White Pike.[28]

Action of the sixteenth was slow to arrive, with skirmishes and Union deployment comprising the bulk of the activity early in the day. The Union soldiers eventually repositioned in order to confront Hood's army in its new position. Generals Steedman and Wood would face Lee on the Franklin Pike; Lee and Stewart aligned with Wood and Smith between the pikes. Cheatham's corps found themselves in a unique situation as morning maneuvers enabled Thomas's army to envelop Cheatham's position on the Confederate left. Smith and Schofield stood at Shy Hill, surrounding Cheatham, with Wilson's cavalry to Cheatham's left.[29]

Wilson's assignment lay in capturing the Franklin Pike and eliminating Hood's lone escape route. In addition, Thomas desired to crush Hood's extreme right on Overton Hill, to cut off Cheatham and Stewart from the road. Gen. Hood instructed Lee to hold the pike at all costs, with Stewart, in case of disaster, to maintain control of the Franklin Pike at Brentwood until Lee's corps passed to the rear.[30]

A Union artillery barrage began at 9 AM and lasted two hours.[31] The effectiveness of the bombardment would determine the impact of the assault to come.

W.H. Kearney, Sixteenth Tennessee Infantry, recalled the series of events from his Trezevant, Tennessee home on the battle's fortieth anniversary:

> "We were on the left of our army ... on top of a slight hill in the woods ... we saw two Federal officers ride up on top of a high hill in front of us and point to our lines ... A battery soon opened on us ... We could see but a short distance to our right, but we could hear enough to convince us that they were having trouble over there also ... The boys would naturally dodge as they began to get closer to us. Lieut. Col. Harris ... would storm out at us for dodging ... one of the men called out ... pointing to our left and rear, showing an old field full of Yankees marching around us."[32]

Two brigades of white troops of Wood's Corps had joined two brigades of black troops from Steedman's Division in an advance upon Overton Hill on Hood's extreme right. Some of the attacking Federals made it within thirty yards of the Confederate position behind a stone fence. Several times, the attackers advanced, yet each time were repelled as Clayton's division and a brigade of Stephenson's division on Clayton's left fired into their ranks. Lt. Gen. S.D. Lee, to whose corps the defenders belonged, exclaimed, "The assaults were made several times, and so determinedly that one-half the loss of Thomas's entire army occurred in the attempts to carry Overton Hill."[33]

An eyewitness proclaimed, "They came out against us in rather hard style. I do not suppose they had ever been in action before ... They left in disorder, a bad case of disorder." [34]

An account of the incident appeared two days later in the *Louisville Journal*. The report stated:

> "The charge by Col. Thompson's brigade of colored troops and Post's Brigade of Gen. Beatty's Division, was an exceedingly costly one. The losses of those two brigades will amount to five hundred killed and wounded. The eminence assailed is called Overton's Hill. It is just to the left of the Franklin pike, and about four miles south of the city. The enemy had but little time to fortify, but had thrown up breastworks of logs and rails, and, in some places, dirt and stones ... posted on this hill a Mississippi battery of four guns, defended by a brigade of Clayton's Division ... about 3:30 p.m. The enemy reserved his fire until the line was fairly in full view ... two batteries of ours shelled the hill vigorously ... tearing two of the enemy's caissons to pieces and wounding many of the men. A more stubborn conflict is seldom seen. The right of the negro brigade followed their daring young leader, Col. Thompson nobly through the torrent of shot and shell ... losing heavily in killed and wounded."[35]

A Confederate eyewitness added:

> "The attacking column formed near the Rains house. The objective point of attack was a lunette occupied by Granbury's Brigade and a section of Turner's Mississippi Battery, supported by the right of Cheatham's old division.

Cheatham had his field headquarters at the lunette, and gave orders to reserve fire until the assaulting column was in close range. A terrific volley was delivered ... stampeded the whole line and nearly all the men fled from the field. Maj. Gen. Corbin ... was a lieutenant colonel in a negro regiment, and with Shafter ... ran for their lives ... there was no halt until they reached the city."[36]

The black troops who attacked Overton's Hill had never before seen combat. Post received a wound originally thought to be mortal. Many of his command were far less fortunate; 300 men fell in the short duration of the attack. The supporting brigade standing to its left lost 250.[37]

Hood had become so anxious to preserve his right flank that he had ordered Cleburne's old division to move to this position from its previous location on the left. The troops were soon recalled to the left, where devastating results awaited the Confederate defenders.[38]

Union troops had enveloped Hood's left flank, with Wilson's cavalry working over and around Cheatham's left flank. Shy's Hill, on Cheatham's right, just west of the Granny White Pike and near Stewart's left flank at Hood's center, fell into Union hands.[39]

James D. Porter, Cheatham's chief of staff, added:

"Cheatham and I were standing together by a big white oak when a ball passed between us, coming from behind ... Govan was shot down, the colonel next to him was shot down, and the command devolved on a major. Colonel Field, of the 1st Tennessee, in command of what was formerly Maney's Brigade ... was ordered to retake the position on the extreme left from which Govan had been forced. This he did, being joined immediately by Gist's Brigade, under command of Col. John H. Anderson, of the 8th Tennessee."[40]

The Federal troops had passed around Cheatham's left wing, where Bates's division gave way on Shy's Hill. The attackers poured through the gap thus made, cutting the Confederate line in half and isolating Cheatham's division. Stewart's and Cheatham's corps rushed toward the Franklin Pike, and the Federals charged from Granny White Pike toward the rear of Lee's corps. Giving way gradually, Lee's corps and Hood's army were saved when Clayton's division moved forward. Lee formed a second line and successfully checked the Federal advance.[41]

Col. W.D. Gale vividly recalled the assault:

> "What a grand sight ... I could see the Capitol all day, and the churches. The Yanks had three lines of battle everywhere I could see, and parks of artillery playing upon us and raining shot and shell for eight mortal hours ... They made several heavy assaults upon Gen. Lee's lines ... At length, having gained our rear, about 4 p.m. they made a vigorous assault upon the whole line right and left. Bate gave way, and they poured over in clouds behind Walthall ... forced him to give way ... then by brigades the whole line from left to right. Lee held on bravely awhile longer than the center and left."[42]

Another Confederate exclaimed:

> "The enemy, seeing our army cut in two, poured through the gap ... It required very prompt action to save the brigade commanded by Colonel Field ... causing the enemy to fall back, and then the order was given ... for the men to climb the hills in their rear and reach the Franklin Pike. It was done promptly, but was not attended by anything like a panic ... it was impossible to maintain the position we occupied."[43]

General A.P. Stewart backed this proclamation in writing:

> " ... It has been frequently said that when the line gave way at Shy's Hill, a panic ensued and the entire army fled in disorderly rout ... there was no panic. For two days the soldiers in Stewart's Corps had faced an enemy overwhelming in numbers, and with indomitable pluck had met and repelled every assault ... At last the crisis came, anticipated by everybody ... Nobody knew better than the Confederate soldiers in the rifle pits that their line could be no longer maintained, and that only one outlet was open by which to escape the inevitable capture

... the line gave way at Shy's Hill, and served as a signal for a stampede to the Franklin Turnpike. This was done, of course, in great disorder; but if panic was there, I failed to see it ... no cries of terror. The men simply knew ... not because they were panic-stricken, but because it was the proper thing to do."[44]

Another participant added:

"we rode as fast as we could to where I thought Gen. Stewart and Gen. Hood were. They were gone and in their places were the Yankees. I turned my horse's head toward the steep knobs and spurred away ... The first place I struck the hill was too steep for any horse to climb ... Finally I reached a place not so steep ... The bullets began to come thick and fast. Now, I found my saddle nearly off, and was forced to get down, but on I went on foot. All along ... fellows were crying out to me ... some were wounded, and many exhausted from anxiety and over-exertion. On I struggled until I, too, became exhausted ... the enemy had gotten to the foot of the hill and were firing at us freely ... I ... was borne to the top of the hill by the noble animal, more dead than alive."[45]

The attack on Shy's Hill had cost the Confederates dearly. Col. William Mabry Shy, Twentieth Tennessee, was killed during the artillery barrage; his body was left behind during the Confederate retreat. Later recovered, his naked body had been bayoneted to a tree. General Thomas Benton Smith, an alumnus of Nashville Military Institute, fell captive during the attack. A colonel of an Ohio regiment that had lost a great number of soldiers to the guns of Smith's troops repeatedly hit Smith over the head with his saber, exposing his brain. Smith, the youngest brigadier general in the Confederate army, spent the last forty-seven years of his life in a Nashville insane asylum.[46]

The retreat from the Confederate lines and the subsequent withdrawal from the Nashville area are described in this recollection:

"I could see our lines giving way ... I could see the Yankee columns flanking us on our left ... The ground was very muddy, and not a good race track, though we made very good time. The fall of Minie balls, accompanied by shell and grapeshot caused us to increase our speed. I passed our major general, Edward Johnston, who was on foot ... Being corpulent and unaccustomed to running, he was soon far behind ... Just as I reached the Franklin Pike ... some one with a battle flag waved it, crying, 'Halt and rally round the flag, boys!' Soon there were several hundred of us formed in line across the pike, and we began firing at the blue coats in the valley below ... This voluntary attempt to rally did but little good, but it checked the rapidly advancing column for a few moments, and enabled many exhausted Confederates to escape. We fired a few rounds, the last shots fired at the battle of Nashville ... some one cried out, 'It's no use boys, let's give it up, or we will be captured,' and all fell back ... Night was soon on us, and the road was fearfully muddy. We had no rations, and had gotten but little sleep for several nights. Tennesseans never had a more disagreeable night march."[47]

On the evening of the sixteenth, Chalmers's command of Forrest's cavalry and S.D. Lee's infantry served as the Confederate rear guard. Almost-constant fighting with Wilson's cavalry, coupled with foggy, rainy, and cold weather, added to the misery of Hood's army. Chalmers had earlier followed Hood's order to "hold the Granny White Pike," regardless of losses. After gathering some 1,200 men, the order had been followed, despite being outnumbered five to one.[48]

James D. Porter stated:

"Lee covered the retreat ... the attack ... was made on him near Brentwood ... Lee formed a square to receive the charge. The Federal colonel formed his troops in columns the width of a company, and the impetus of the charge carried them right through the Confederate square; but they never got back. It is very difficult ordinarily to break a square properly formed, and that one was properly formed by fine soldiers ... they [Federals] were killed, wounded, and disabled in every way."[49]

Hood reported few desertions during the retreat, a significant fact, considering that many of the Tennesseans would pass near, perhaps within sight of their homes. One private reportedly received permission to visit his mother, yet rejoined his regiment after seeing Union soldiers camping around the family farmhouse.[50]

The poor weather conditions and Confederate fortitude is clearly shown in a passage related to the retreat:

> "We had reached the hilly country ... It had snowed and sleeted the day before, and the ground was as slick as glass ... General Cheatham ... sent word to me to pick out a hundred well-shod men and send them to help push the wagons up ... The fellows soon found out that I was after men with shoes on, and they were highly amused. They would laugh and stick up their feet as I approached. Some would have a pretty good shoe on one foot and on the other a piece of rawhide or a part of a shoe made strong with string made from a strip of rawhide tied around it ... some were entirely barefooted ... I got about twenty or twenty-five men out of that entire army corps."[51]

Hood's 18,742 survivors of his Tennessee campaign reached Tupelo, Mississippi in early January. On January 13, 1865, Hood asked to be removed from command of the Army of Tennessee. His 1,500 lost soldiers were fewer than Thomas's 2,562, but Hood also had some 4,500 of his once-mighty force fall captive at Nashville.[52]

The conditions of Nashville and the weariness of its visitors are reflected in the recollection of Warren King from December 17, 1864:

> "the day after the battle I was at the stockade when the Confederate prisoners were brought in. All about the gateway the mud was about eight inches deep and very thin. A Union soldier brought in a prisoner, turned him over to the proper officer, sank down in that thin mud, and in half a minute was fast asleep."[53]

While criticism of Hood's performance at Nashville exists to this day, his praise for the troops of his command portrays a man who held the utmost honor for the men who had sacrificed so much. He wrote, "The Tennessee troops entered the state with high hopes as they approached their homes. When the fortunes of war were against us, the same faithful soldiers remained true to their flag, and, with rare exceptions, followed it in retreat as they had borne it in advance."[54]

Early in the twenty-first century, Nashville was listed as one of the top ten most endangered battlefields in the U.S. Urbanization has taken over a large portion of the battlegrounds around Nashville, as commercial and residential areas develop at a rapid pace. On December 10, 2004, a major step to preserving a portion of the field was made when Fort Negley—after careful restoration following decades of neglect—reopened to the public.[55] The Civil War Preservation Trust and the Battle of Nashville Preservation Society, BONPS, have combined for this and a number of other success stories in the preservation efforts around the city.

The BONPS holds title to Confederate redoubt #1, one of five small forts overrun on the first day's battle. Portions of Shy's Hill have also been saved, another honor for this group. The Joseph Johnston Sons of Confederate Veterans camp has preserved Granbury's Lunette, where the east flank of the Confederate line offered resistance to the Union advance on the first day. In addition, four buildings that served as headquarters, Traveller's Rest, Belmont Mansion, Belle Meade, and Sunnyside Mansion, stand today as well-maintained relics of the era. A host of churches and a stone University of Nashville building that served as hospitals stand in the downtown area, along with the battle's most prominent structure, the Tennessee State Capitol.[56]

The 300-foot-tall Overton Hill is cut by Harding Place between Interstate 65 and Franklin Road. As the site of more than 1,200 Federal casualties, and the location of one of the earliest battles involving black troops, this site deserves more recognition and interpretive work.

With mixed success, Nashville's preservation efforts stand foremost on the agendas of several organizations that seek to set aside this hallowed ground for future generations.

Traveller's Rest, Hood's Nashville Headquarters. Photo by author.

First Presbyterian Church in downtown Nashville served as a hospital during the war. Photo by author.

The Tennessee State Capitol. Photo by author.

Fort Negley's restored interior. Photo by author.

Fort Negley's restored interior. Photo by author.

Heavy vegetation growth and crumbling exterior of Negley. Photo by author.

Shy's Hill summit. Photo by author.

Shy's Hill access trail. Photo by author.

CHAPTER TWENTY

NOTEWORTHY SITES ACROSS THE STATE

West Tennessee

Memphis

The largely agricultural section of West Tennessee was the location of a large number of conflicts during the first half of the American Civil War. The primary source of military actions of the second half came from cavalry raids, usually masterminded by Nathan Bedford Forrest. With only pockets of pro-Union sentiment, the area and its residents tended to harbor and provide stores for Confederate units in the area, and contributed greatly to the enrollment of the same.

While Shiloh and a select few others garner most of the region's attention directed toward Civil War sites and preservation efforts, a number of others are certainly worthy of acknowledgement and awareness of preservationists.

One of the most noteworthy struggles in West Tennessee took place in Memphis on June 6, 1862. The city itself was a major railroad hub and river port, a prize for either army. Control of Memphis meant controlling another point along what the Native Americans deemed centuries earlier as "The Mother of Waters."

As if expecting a show, thousands of Memphians stood on the bluffs of the Mississippi River awaiting a clash between the eight steamers of the Confederate fleet and the approaching Federal ironclads and rams. What the spectators were to behold was the largest inland naval battle in world history.

A population of almost 23,000 hailed Memphis as home at the time of the war. The bluff city, Memphis was cited as the "Charleston of the West" for its heavy secessionist stance. Its ordnance workshops, machine shops, and foundries had had a limited amount of protection as long as Fort Pillow was in Confederate hands, but its fall to the Federals signaled the beginning of the end for their possession of the pro-Confederate river town. Brigadier General Jeff Thompson, the Confederate commander at Memphis, had no fortifications from which to protect the city from invasion. Thompson would, in fact, watch the struggle for Memphis from horseback, stationed amid a group of onlookers. The Confederate Defense Fleet under Captain James Montgomery would join Thompson's troops as the obstacle to a Federal takeover of the city.

Leaving Island Number 45, just north of Memphis, Flag Officer Charles H. Davis and Colonel Charles Ellet led their Federal fleet toward Memphis early on the morning of June 6. The U.S. gunboats, *Benton, Louisville, Carondelet, Cairo,* and *St. Louis* joined the two rams *Monarch* and *Queen of the West* as they moved into position. The Confederates' *Lovell* fired unsuccessfully at the *Queen;* the ram's response came from a sharpshooter who hit *Lovell's* captain in his head. *Queen* slammed into *Lovell;* the Confederate ship sank in minutes. Only eighteen of the Confederate vessel's crew of eighty-six survived the incident.[1]

Smoke from the struggle of the remaining boats filled the air, ending the ability of the spectators to see all but the smokestacks of the steamers. *Price* and *Beauregard,* two of the Confederate steamers, failed in an attempt to hit *Monarch,* ironically slamming into each other instead. *Little Rebel* suffered a vicious shot and ended up on the Arkansas banks across the river. *Jeff Thompson* received a broadside from *Benton* and exploded moments later.[2]

In a fight ending by 7 AM and lasting no more than an hour and a half, five Confederate vessels had been disabled or sunk, and the city of Memphis was primed for Union occupation. Only *Van Dorn* escaped, a miracle in that Federal shot sent water exploding around her as she moved downriver. Confederate losses were eighty killed and wounded; one hundred fell captive to the Federals.[3]

General Thompson fled for Mississippi, avoiding the surrender ceremony. Memphians took their uneaten meals and headed for home. The Memphis mayor surrendered the city amid protests from the remaining onlookers who lacked a desire to see the Confederate flag on Front Street replaced with the Stars and Stripes.[4]

Not all would go well during the Federal occupation of Memphis. The most famous resistance came from Major General Nathan Bedford Forrest two years later on August 21, 1864. Forrest took 2,000 cavalrymen toward Memphis, leaving 500 along the way, lost to horses with insufficient stamina. Six thousand Union troops stationed in Memphis negated any attempt to recapture the city, but Forrest evidently had multiple purposes in conducting the raid.

W.B. Stewart, a participant in the raid, recalled the assignments and highlights of the day:

> "About 4 a.m. Sunday, August 21, 1864, Gen. Forrest, with part each of Bell's and Neely's Brigades and two pieces of artillery, moved briskly through the hazy twilight in columns of four along the Hernando Road toward Memphis ... Capt. W.H. Forrest moved into the lead with his company, to clear the way of pickets. Our detachment was led by Col. T.H. Logwood, with orders to proceed to the Gayoso Hotel and capture Gen. Hurlbut ... Col. Jesse Forrest was directed to make for Gen. C.C. Washburn's headquarters on Union Street ... one detachment to capture Gen. R.P. Buckland and another to the Irving Block, on Second Street, to release the Confederate prisoners held there ... Forrest ... Bell and parts of Barteau's, Newsom's, and Russell's regiments, and Lt. Sale, with his two pieces of artillery, were to remain in the neighborhood of the State Female College, to cover the return ... A shot was heard, the outmost pickets having been reached and captured ... a few more shots were heard ... the excitement was intense ... Though daylight was abroad, a thick fog enveloped our right, from which a Federal officer was heard trying to rally his scattered men ... We hastened to the Gayoso Hotel, where we found Capt. Forrest with some of his men on horseback in the rotunda of the hotel ... A cigar case in the hotel

was broken ... I got two pipes and a few cigars ... Col. Logwood conscripted a clerk in the hotel, and commanded me to take him in charge and go with him to his room to get his pistol and such other articles as he desired to take with him ... Logwood ... said, 'Turn him loose ... we are going to leave here immediately.' ... Squads of Federals began to gather and fire at us from house corners. Not finding ... Hurlbut ... our mission in that respect was a failure ... At every cross street we were fired at by scattered bands. One or two horses were killed here, and one man wounded ... a large strong woman, a Mrs. Beeth, succeeded in getting the wounded man into her store ... and with an ax successfully kept off some negroes who were anxious to kill him ... Comrade Perkins was killed ... ladies were seen going to where he lay with upturned face. On passing my old home I turned to the gate, where I saw standing my mother, sisters, brothers, and one or two others ... some Federals ... fired across our yard at the passing Confederates, when mother and the others ran toward the house to get out of the way ... I called to my youngest brother, but in the confusion he did not recognize who it was ... After remaining there an hour or so skirmishing, we moved out toward Nonconnah Creek, where we halted two or three hours to communicate with Gen. Washburn in regard to exchanging and paroling prisoners and furnishing the Federal prisoners, four or five hundred, with food and clothing. Many of them were taken in their nightclothes."[5]

In fact, more than 600 Union prisoners had been taken in addition to almost 100 horses and wagons loaded with needed supplies. The plans to capture the Federal officers had failed, as did the intention to release the Confederate prisoners. One goal was successfully achieved, in that Forrest's raid caused the movement of 20,000 Federal troops from Mississippi to Memphis.[6]

The landmarks from the battle of Memphis and the Forrest raid have largely disappeared. Confederate Park, where Memphians watched the naval battle, contains a marker describing the action of June 6, 1862. The park itself has been the topic of various groups emphasizing political correctness and seeking the renaming of the location. The State Female College was torn down many years ago; the Gayoso Hotel burned in the late 1800s and a new building was built in its place. Washburn's Alley has a historical marker noting where Gen. C.C. Washburn escaped capture on August 21, 1864, clad in his nightclothes. Interpretation at the locations of the actions in Memphis are the major asset in the city's link to its military history, yet Memphis and its preservation efforts, as well as the ability to capitalize on its portion of the state's Civil War tourism dollars, are cause for major concern.

Middleburg

On August 30, 1862 and again on December 24, 1862, the hamlet of Middleburg saw heated struggles. In the former, one of the few saber battles between Federal and Confederate cavalry units took place. Confederates under acting brigadier general Frank C. Armstrong intended to go to Jackson, Tennessee and complete a raid on the rail station there, but Union intelligence led to a message being sent to Colonel Marcellus Crocker at Bolivar, informing him of an approaching sizeable body of Confederate cavalry.[7]

Four slaves belonging to Bolivar resident John H. Bills were captured by Union pickets near Bolivar, and their owner was brought in for identification purposes. Through their interrogation, Union officers learned that the rumors of an approaching enemy cavalry was much more than hearsay, a fact that caused Crocker to dispatch Colonel Mortimer Leggett of the Seventy-eighth Ohio Infantry toward Middleburg. The hamlet of Middleburg lay south of Bolivar and slightly north of LaGrange, the town where Crocker's foe camped.[8]

Crocker carried with his brigade two cannon from the Ninth Indiana Artillery in addition to two companies of the Eleventh Illinois Cavalry. Failing to agree with initial reconnaissance reports, Leggett viewed the Confederate detachment as consisting of 6,000 men, much more than the projected 300 to 400. Despite this fact, Leggett's command and the body of Confederates began a struggle that has been reported to have lasted as long as seven hours.[9]

Armstrong felt a movement on his part might break the hold that the Federal force seemed to have initiated. With this in mind, he sent two cavalry regiments, the Second Missouri and the Second Arkansas, toward the enemy. Captain Rock Champion, Company K, Second Missouri, initially led the attack, but became the first casualty of the battle when he was shot through the head.[10]

As Leggett wrote in his official report, the opening struggle took place on ground not suitable for cavalry, and forced the dismounting of his men. Likewise, the Confederates dismounted and appeared in two lines, emerging from a stand of trees. The predicament the Federals had found themselves in was temporarily eased with the arrival of Lieutenant Colonel Harvey Hogg with the Second Illinois Cavalry. Hogg's men moved toward the dismounted Confederates while Hogg ordered his mounted troops to give the Confederates the cold steel.[11]

Hogg entered into a hand-to-hand struggle with Colonel McCulloch of the Second Missouri, one of the most pivotal points of the battle. A shot hit Hogg in the side, and another killed his horse as it entered the animal's forehead. Hogg seemed primed to hit McCulloch with his sword when Tom Turner, a young member of McCulloch's command, shot the Federal officer in the head. Reportedly, after the battle, Hogg's face was being eaten by hogs that had escaped from pens with fences destroyed in the struggle. In addition, the officer's body was reportedly placed atop a nearby rail fence in an attempt to end the animals' desecration.[12]

In Company E, Seventh Tennessee Cavalry, Pvt. John Milton Hubbard acknowledged that in the entire war, no prettier line of battle was seen than that he viewed at Middleburg. A group of Texans established the line that Hubbard praised and later remarked always came to mind when traveling through that part of Hardeman County.[13]

The struggle eventually drew to a conclusion with Leggett ordering a retreat to Bolivar. Armstrong moved northward and encountered a vicious foe two days later at Britton Lane. Reported casualties for the Confederates in the encounter at Middleburg are usually listed as "over 200" while the Federal losses, according to Leggett's report were 10 dead, 18 wounded, and 71 captured.[14]

Today the battlefield at Middleburg is unmarked. No signs, markers, or maps denote its location, the exact spot of which is a subject of debate among locals. The town itself has all but vanished, usually regarded as a mere pullover on Tennessee State Highway 18. For the men who fought and risked all at this unique battlefield, no tribute is present.

Trenton

On Saturday, December 20, 1862, Nathan Bedford Forrest pushed northward from Spring Creek, having divided his force by sending part to Humboldt and another portion to cover Spring Creek and the possible Federal escape route. Upon reaching Trenton around 1 PM, Forrest determined that he would demand the surrender of the town and led his force into the town. The Federal army, under the leadership of Col. Jacob Fry, had prepared for Forrest's arrival in Trenton by placing tobacco barrels and cotton bales around the Mobile and Ohio Railroad depot in an attempt to barricade themselves from the Confederates. With only an available force of 250 men, Fry's success relied heavily on luck. In addition, twenty-five sharpshooters lined the roofs of buildings to possibly shoot Forrest himself.[15]

Forrest's intended target was the railroad, a means by which the Union army received supplies for its further aggression against the people of the South. Upon the Confederates' arrival, a Federal sharpshooter killed a member of Forrest's cavalry; yet the sharpshooter himself was disposed of with a shot to the forehead. Forrest proceeded down Lexington Street and pushed the Federals into the safety of their breastworks, while Major Cox moved to the right, securing the east of town. Only three shots from Captain Strange's cannon were fired toward the depot, three hundred yards in the distance, before white flags appeared "from all quarters of the Federal fortalice."[16]

Demanding an unconditional surrender, Forrest began the process of counting the captured goods: 1,000 mules and horses; 400,000 rounds of small-arms ammunition; 20,000 rounds of artillery; and 100,000 "rations of subsistence, together with a large amount of cavalry equipments, clothing, quartermaster stores, and … soldiers' baggage, in value at least $500,000." Before the inventory was completed, a number of Federal troops broke the truce and set the depot on fire, a feat that proved futile as Forrest ordered its immediate extinguishing. In addition to the supplies, Forrest gained some 1,300 prisoners.[17]

Today, visitors to Trenton are capable of seeing the location of the actions of Forrest and his troops during the December 1862 raid. A complete seventeen-stop driving tour and accompanying guide provide a great understanding of the day's events. While many of the structures themselves have been replaced, the atmosphere of the town maintains a certain quality of long-ago. Some increased maintenance is needed on a few of the tour's stops, but aside from that fact, the memory of the December struggle is well-preserved.

Collierville

The city of Collierville was the site of four battles, largely skirmishes, in 1863 and is today rated as a "highly threatened" battlefield by the Civil War Preservation Trust. On November 3, 1863, Collierville was the location of an unsuccessful attempt by Brigadier General James Chalmers to raid and hamper a Union detachment bound for Chattanooga. Chalmers's approach was detected, and the Confederate general found himself heavily outnumbered by well-fortified Union troops with reinforcements arriving from Germantown. In turn, Chalmers determined a withdrawal to be his most beneficial move. Usual accepted figures for casualties of the event are approximately sixty for the entrenched Union troops and one hundred for the Confederates.

Fort Germantown, built to protect the railroad line from such raids, has portions of its earthen walls that exist still, but on private property. Likewise, Fort Collierville, the location of action in October 1863, also has visible remains, again on private property. Ironically, the day of the October 1863 attack, Sherman left the area for the beginning of his "march to the sea," an effort the attack almost foiled with the near capture of the Union officer. A sign erected in downtown Collierville provides visitors with information needed for a basic interpretation of the incidents in the city.

Preservation-minded individuals who do not mind enduring walks without the benefits of paved walkways can find the remains of a number of earthen structures in West Tennessee. Pocahontas has remains of a Union railroad fort once used to guard the Memphis and Charleston Railroad, as well as the Tuscumbia and Hatchie rivers. In Grand Junction, portions of Fort McDowell, the Union star fort, are still visible. LaGrange, Rossville, and Moscow each has remains of a Union fort, yet in many of these cases, the structures are on private property. In addition, Fort Heiman on the Tennessee River, a Union structure, and Fort Wright in Randolph, once a Confederate redoubt and one of the few in the region, are discernable. Proper budgeting would enable these sites to become more accessible and improve the economic bases of the neighboring communities.

Middle Tennessee

Vaught's Hill (Milton)

On March 18, 1863, Colonel Albert Hall's Union brigade moved from Murfreesboro on reconnaissance, but the troops were intercepted by

John Hunt Morgan's cavalry. On the twentieth, Morgan again caught up with Hall after the latter had achieved a successful withdrawal two days earlier. The ensuing action would bring about approximately 60 Union and more than 350 Confederate casualties. Considered by the Civil War Preservation Trust to have little threat to its preservation, the battlegrounds have practically no public access.

B.L. Ridley recalled that Hall evidently sensed:

> "that Morgan's beehive was stirred up" and attempted to beat the Confederate cavalryman to safety. Ridley recalled, "A hill selected by [the Union] could not have been better; it seemed impregnable ... covered with woodland, including cedar bushes so thick that one could not see a soldier. The line advanced, its flanks barricaded by nature with rugged boulders and undulations ending in sudden gorges ... When we got to the base a volley belched forth from the enemy ... Lt. Cates ... immediately on my right, had his fingers shot off ... A little orderly ... rushed up with orders from General Morgan directing Ward's Regiment to support the battery ... Onward we went, our pieces unlimbered ... The fight became terrific, the enemy in his lair, keeping up a vigorous fire until we were in close quarters ... The whole line was ordered to take trees. All got behind trees but my captain, Charley Cossett and me; we secured protection behind a stump ... The poor fellow got up ... a ball struck him just above the heart and lodged in his lung ... Cossett was bleeding inwardly ... He threw his arm around my shoulder, and the trial of my life was to stay with him ... the whole Yankee line seemed to take us for a target ... I clung to him and brought him off. He ... died that night. The fight lasted three hours, and was hotly contested." [18]

Hoover's Gap

Limited signage today notes the location and events of the battle of Hoover's Gap. A nearby cemetery contains Confederate dead of the battle, one of the events in the Tullahoma Campaign.

A member of the Twentieth Tennessee noted in the late Nineteenth Century that his regiment was sent to Hoover's Gap, about eight miles from

Tullahoma, and located about two miles from the gap on the Manchester Pike. Rain started on June 24 and lasted throughout the night. Surprised by Federal soldiers at the gap, the Twentieth was called to action and met the Federal skirmishers, driving them into the main line.[19]

The soldier added:

> "our line was advancing and it was getting hot. The Federal artillery was playing on our battery in our rear, so that our line of battle was between the two fires ... Major Claybrooke rode up ... and was preparing to dismount when a shell from the enemy's line burst near him, and he fell mortally wounded ... two [others] were killed by the same shell ... In this engagement we fought about five to one, and history will some day record that if Gen. Bate ... had not held in check the great odds, the two wings of Bragg's army at Shelbyville and Tullahoma would have been cut in two."[20]

Additional fighting would persist until midday on the twenty-sixth, when the Confederate forces began pulling back, leading to Bragg's abandonment of Middle Tennessee. While the site of this action lacks the attention it deserves, those who participated in the struggle at Hoover's Gap demanded the preservation of its fields.

Statements such as one from a participant in the struggle provide ample proof of the need to preserve such a location: "In the bloody little fight at Hoover's Gap, we had sixty-two men killed and wounded out of one hundred and fifty in action."[21]

Clarksville

The Montgomery County city of Clarksville contributed a large amount of men to the Confederate army during the Civil War and was an object of occupation for both armies. Its close proximity to Fort Donelson and Nashville, as well as being the center of some 20,000 residents on the Cumberland River, garnished attention. Several historic homes are in the area, but perhaps the most uniquely preserved object from the Civil War is Clarksville's Fort Defiance.

Construction of the fort was started by Confederates in November of 1861, but two months later, Federal gunboats from Fort Donelson found the site deserted. The Seventy-first Ohio Volunteers manned the fort for a short period of time, when, in August of 1861, the Confederates recaptured Clarksville, only to lose it again in September; it remained in Union hands for the remainder of the war. Fort Defiance, which also has recorded references to the name Fort Severe, was renamed Fort Bruce following the Union capture of September 1862.

Preserved battlements of the fort today include trenches, gun platforms, a magazine, and other earthen depressions. Resting on a bluff some 200 feet above the Cumberland, Fort Defiance is open to the public and provides an interesting view of the area's history.

Giles County in southern Middle Tennessee has done an excellent job of making its Civil War sites known. Ten sites are acknowledged on the county's driving tour. and include the site of the Battle of Anthony Hill, the Confederates' last stand in Tennessee, and the site of the capture of Sam Davis, a young man hanged for spying and hailed as a hero for proclaiming, "If I had a thousand lives, I would give them all here before I would betray a friend or the confidence of my informer." More information is available on the Giles County sites in contacting the Giles County Historical Society.

Humphreys, Dickson, and Cheatham counties in Middle Tennessee have combined to provide a thorough driving tour of nine sites related to the lifeline of railroads in the state during the war. With mixed success at preservation, these include Johnsonville Historic Site, a trestle site a half mile east of McEwen, another two and a half miles east of McEwen, stone piers from a bridge in Kingston Springs, stone piers of a bridge located in the Kingston Springs city park, and a redoubt along a trestle at Sullivan's Branch Bridge #2. Others along the route include fortifications from a trestle at Gilliam's or Gillem's Station, now the location of a cemetery; Fort Hill in Waverly, the location of well-preserved earthworks; and a former blockhouse site east of Denver with no existing physical remains. A brochure for these sites is available from any of the three counties' chambers of commerce and will prove to be an enjoyable trek into the past.

East Tennessee

Blountville

In September 2003, the Lt. Robert Powel Camp of the Sons of Confederate Veterans dedicated a marker to the interpretation of the battle of Blountville. The Sullivan County site is regarded by the Civil War Preservation Trust as being too late to save, and thus a lost cause for preservationists. As sad as this may seem, the battle itself on September 22, 1863, also referred to as the Battle of Blountsville, was the site of 192 total casualties, 27 Union and 165 Confederate, in a struggle between the commands of Col. John Foster's U.S. troops and those of Col. James Carter's Confederates.

Beginning at noon and lasting four hours, the battle began when Carter decided to engage the Federal forces and placed his battery east of town. Near a graveyard and on the opposite side of the town, Foster's army—twice the size of Carter's 1,250 soldiers—took position. The headstones of a number of the graves in the cemetery bore the damage inflicted in the battle for years to come.[22]

A shell from the Federal artillery hit the courthouse, setting it and eventually most of the town on fire. Women and children fled for their lives while cavalrymen dashed in and out of the stampeding crowd, endangering the lives and safety of all involved. The Confederates learned that the Federals were attempting a flanking movement, and retired toward Bristol, where several were captured; others fled toward Zollicoffer before being reinforced at Hamilton's Hill by men under Jones. The fire in the town created a rush of returning citizens, some of whom had sought safety a mile and a half outside of town. Their return was hampered by retreating Confederates with faces blackened with powder.[23]

A young female witness of the struggle wrote:

> "Later the ambulance with the wounded followed, and I remembered the groans and moans of the wounded. One ambulance stopped in front of our home and the wounded were begging for water ... The Federals were expecting to be attacked and selected my father's farm for the battle ground and located their artillery on a hill in the rear of the house, but no fighting was done there. One of the Federals advised us to vacate ... we returned [and] found the soldiers cooking in the house and the house ransacked ... The Federals camped on the farm for a few days and lived off our farm products. When the army departed we had nothing to eat except some apples ... they collected all the fence rails and burned them to convey the impression to the Confederates that they were still in camp."[24]

Blue Springs

Another East Tennessee sight is that of Blue Springs in Greene County. In the city of Mosheim, an annual re-enactment is held in October to commemorate the battle that ended the Confederate presence in the largely pro-Union region. With 100 Union and more than 200 Confederate casualties, the significant area is considered to be under some threat to preservation, yet is not pursued diligently, as its results are deemed to have had little effect upon the outcome of the war.

The October 10, 1863 battle pitted Major General Ambrose Burnside's Union troops against Brig. Gen. John S. Williams. Beginning at 10 AM and lasting past dark, the struggle resulted in the fulfillment of Burnside's goal to eliminate the Confederate influence in the area, and capture the salt works in Saltville, Virginia. The Virginia and East Tennessee Railroad also fell to Federal control, points that the Federal commander felt justified the number of casualties in the struggle.

Dandridge

Several skirmishes took place in and around Dandridge in late 1863 and early 1864. Despite this fact, the battlefields of Dandridge are highly threatened by development and hold basically no interpretation or preservation success stories for the general public. The most significant of the struggles in and around Dandridge took place on January 17, 1864, when Confederate forces under Longstreet failed to capture Samuel Sturgis's Federal cavalry. The Federal casualties totaled approximately 150;[25] the Confederate figures are based on pure conjecture.

In the early twentieth century, a movement began to give five dollars to veterans missing a limb. Edward McClendon was one applicant, having lost his right arm above the elbow at Dandridge. Incidents in area locations such as Mossy Creek on December 29, 1863 resulted in veterans claiming in later years "we lost nearly one hundred men and were forced to retreat … which left such a bad taste in my mouth that I have not yet gotten rid of it."[26]

J.W. Minnich, Sixth Georgia Cavalry, remembered arriving at a farm outside Dandridge and encountering "a large force posted … in the open fields west of the road." Following his assistance of a sharpshooter, Minnich entered the Union camps on the morning of January 18, only to find them empty. He proclaimed, "we entered Dandridge, and were informed that the enemy's infantry, artillery, and wagons had passed through early in the night ... numerous fires kept up were but a blind to cover their retirement."[27]

One must ask if such a fate awaits each of us, self-proclaimed enthusiasts and supporters of preservation. Are we to simply read about and fail to act upon the need of saving the fields Abraham Lincoln so eloquently declared as hallowed? The disappearance of these parcels is taking place at an alarming rate all across our state and nation. It has been noted, "saving a battlefield is oftentimes a battle in itself." This struggle is one that can be undertaken and, with the application of financial and personal resources, overcome. Victory over such losses of land is one manner in which each citizen of Tennessee and our nation may honor and preserve the memory of the untold number of ancestors who believed in a cause and put their lives on the line on numerous occasions in towns and cities all across our state for that belief. It must be done.

As organizations related to battlefield preservation are created on a frequent basis, this is a partial list of agencies to contact in order to participate in the process of saving Tennessee's Civil War battlefields:

Tennessee Civil War Preservation Association
    P.O. Box 148535
    Nashville, TN 37214-8535
    www.tcpa.org

Tennessee Wars Commission
    Fred Prouty, Director of Programs
    2941 Lebanon Road
    Nashville, TN 37243

Britton Lane Battlefield Association
    4707 Mill Ferry Road
    Medon, TN 38356

Chattanooga Civil War Roundtable
    Chattanoogacwrt.org

Civil War Preservation Trust
    www.civilwar.org

Davis Bridge Battlefield Association
   c/o Herbert Wood
   1250 Clifft Road
   Bolivar, TN 38008

Nathan Bedford Forrest State Park
   1825 Pilot Knob Road
   Eva, TN 38333
   731-584-6356

Fort Donelson National Battlefield Park
   P. O. Box 434
   Dover, TN 37058-0434
   615-232-5706

Fort Pillow State Historic Park
   3122 Park Road
   Henning, TN 38041
   731-738-5581

Save the Franklin Battlefield
   P.O. Box 851
   Franklin, TN 37065-0871

Johnsonville State Historic Park
   Rt. 1 Box 374
   New Johnsonville, TN 37134
   931-535-2789

Battlefield of Nashville Preservation Society
   P.O. Box 190493
   Nashville, TN 37219

Parker's Crossroads Battlefield Association
   P.O. Box 265
   Parker's Crossroads, TN 38388

Battle of Hartsville Preservation Association
  c/o Gen. Robert H. Hatton camp 723
  P. O. Box 782
  Lebanon, TN 37088-0782

Knoxville Civil War Roundtable
  P.O. Box 313
  Knoxville, TN 37901

Bleak House/Confederate Memorial Hall
  3148 Kingston Pike
  Knoxville, TN 37919

Salem Cemetery Battlefield Association
  367 White Fern Road
  Beech Bluff, TN 38313
  731-424-1279

Shiloh National Military Park
  1055 Pittsburg Landing Road
  Shiloh, TN 38376

Stone's River National Battlefield
  3501 Old Nashville Highway
  Murfreesboro, TN 37129
  615-893-9501

Memphis waterfront in the 1860s. Confederate Veteran.

A stop on the Trenton battle tour. Photo by author.

ENDNOTES

Abbreviations: (See Bibliography for full text titles)

C.V.	*Confederate Veteran*
H.G.	*Hallowed Ground*
J&P	Jordan & Pryor, *Campaigns of Nathan Bedford Forrest*
O.R.	United States War Department, *The War of the Rebellion*
T.H.Q.	*Tennessee Historical Quarterly*

CHAPTER 1. Fort Henry

1. Miller, *Photographic* ... , 182.
2. "Career," 274-75.
3. Griffin, "Famous Tenth," 553.
4. Ibid.
5. Taylor, "Defense," 369.
6. Walke, "Gunboats," 362.
7. Ibid.; Taylor, "Defense," 370.
8. Taylor, "Defense," 370.
9. Bearss, "Fall," 96.
10. Walke, "Gunboats," 363.
11. Taylor, "Defense," 370-71.
12. Walke, "Gunboats," 364; Miller, *Photographic*, 182.
13. Walke, "Gunboats," 364.
14. Ibid.

15. Bearss, "Fall," 100; Walke, "Gunboats," 363-65.
16. Taylor, "Defense," 371.
17. Walke, "Gunboats," 367; Taylor, "Defense," 372.
18. C.V., v. 15, 545.
19. *users.aol.com/greenup1*

CHAPTER 2. Fort Donelson

1. Miller, *Photographic*, 184; J&P, 59.
2. J&P, 59; Walker, "Command," 345-46; Taylor, "Defense," 369.
3. J&P, 60; Miller, *Photographic*, 184.
4. Miller, *Photographic*, 184-86.
5. Wallace, "Capture," 429.
6. Ibid.
7. C.V., v. 38, 16.
8. Ibid.
9. J&P, 62-63.
10. Walker, "Command," 347.
11. C.V., v.5, 285.
12. C.V., v.4, 393.
13. Ibid.
14. Ibid.
15. C.V., v.1, 308.
16. C.V., v.5, 283.
17. C.V., v.38, 16.
18. C.V., v.37, 449.
19. C.V., v.4, 394; C.V., v.5, 624.
20. C.V., v.4, 394; Walker, "Command," 348; Cooling, *Donelson*, 26; Wallace, "Capture," 410.
21. C.V., v.5, 81.
22. C.V., v.4, 395.
23. Ibid.
24. Cooling, *Donelson*, 27.
25. C.V., v.4, 395.
26. Ibid., 396.
27. Ibid.
28. Ibid.
29. Cooling, *Donelson*, 27; C.V., v.4, 397; Miller, *Photographic*, 188; C.V., v.4, 397.

30. C.V., v.4, 397.
31. Ibid., 397-98.
32. Ibid.
33. Ibid., 396.
34. Ibid., 397.
35. Ibid., 396.
36. Ibid., 396-98.
37. Ibid., 398.
38. Nelson, "Curious."
39. Miller, *Photographic*, 189-90; C.V. v.5, 283; Wallace, "Capture," 414.
40. Wallace, "Capture," 415.
41. C.V., v.5, 283-85.
42. Ibid.
43. Ibid.
44. C.V., v.17, 167.
45. Cooling, *Donelson*, 29; Wallace, "Capture," 417.
46. Cooling, *Donelson*, 30; Wallace, "Capture," 420.
47. Wallace, "Capture," 420.
48. Ibid.
49. Ibid.; Cooling, *Donelson*, 31.
50. C.V., v.7, 356-57.
51. Wallace, "Capture," 422-24.
52. O.R., v.11, 333-34.
53. C.V., v.5, 285.
54. O.R., v.11, 333-34.
55. Ibid.
56. Wallace, "Capture," 426-28.
57. Ibid., 428.
58. C.V., v.7, 10.
59. *nps.gov/fodo;* Wallace, "Capture," 428; Cooling, *Donelson*, 39.
60. Ibid.
61. Davis, Questionnaire.
62. C.V., v.5, 15.
63. C.V., v.15, 234.
64. Cooling, *Donelson*, 40; Walker, "Command," 357.
65. C.V., v.3, 110.
66. C.V., v.36, 175.

CHAPTER 3. Shiloh, Day 1

1. Green, Journal.
2. Ibid.
3. C.V., v.25, 71.
4. Martin, *Shiloh,* 24.
5. C.V., v.36, 335; Johnston, 552.
6. C.V., v.25, 71; McDonough, 72.
7. C.V., v.25, 71; C.V., v.25, 146.
8. C.V., v.31, 129-30; Grant 469.
9. C.V., v. 31, 129-30.
10. Ibid.; C.V., v.11, 44; McDonough, Shiloh, 10, Grant, 466.
11. Yadamec, "ripe," 8.
12. Grant, 481; Allen interview
13. Green, Journal.
14. C.V., v.7, 556.
15. C.V., v.31, 130.
16. C.V., v.7, 556.
17. C.V., v.31, 130; Allen interview.
18. Green, Journal.
19. C.V., v.31, 130.
20. C.V., v.25, 71; Johnston, 555-56; Beauregard, 581-83; Jordon, 597.
21. C.V., v.2, 138.
22. C.V., v.31, 131.
23. C.V., v.25, 71; Allen interview.
24. "Bloody Rout."; Daniel, 152.
25. C.V., v.31, 131.
26. C.V., v.25, 71; Allen interview.
27. C.V., v.25, 71.
28. C.V., v.36, 335; Grant, 473.
29. C.V., v.31, 131; C.V., v.7, 556.
30. Beauregard, 587; Allen interview.
31. "Reminiscences."
32. Green, Journal.
33. C.V., v.25, 72.
34. Daniel, 158.
35. C.V., v.25, 72.
36. C.V., v.22, 307.

37. Ibid., 306.
38. Grant, 467; C.V., v.11, 44.
39. C.V., v.11, 44.
40. Ibid.
41. C.V., v.1, 298; Grant, 468.
42. Allen interview.
43. C.V., v.31, 131; Grant, 473-74; Allen interview.
44. C.V., v.6, 311.
45. Beauregard, 588; Johnston, 550.
46. C.V., v.6, 311.
47. C.V., v.6, 66; C.V., v.5, 99; Grant, 483, Johnston, 542.
48. C.V., v.3, 85-87.
49. Ibid.
50. Ibid, McDonough, 153..
51. C.V., v.3, 385-87.
52. C.V., v.6, 313; Daniel, 227.
53. C.V., v.7, 306.
54. C.V., v.6, 313; Daniel, 226.
55. C.V., v.5, 611.
56. C.V., v.6, 66; Daniel, 227.
57. C.V., v.5, 611.
58. C.V., v.22, 314; Beauregard, 590.
59. Reminiscences.
60. Allen interview.
61. Green, Journal.
62. Baker, "Last".
63. C.V., v.25, 73..
64. Green, Journal.
65. C.V., v.10, 316-17.
66. C.V., v.22, 342.
67. C.V., v.19, 72.
68. Yadamec, "Ripe", 8; McDonough, 22..
69. C.V., v.3, 104-05.
70. C.V., v.18, 275.

CHAPTER 4. Shiloh, Day 2

1. C.V., v.9, 21; Watkins, 65-66.
2. C.V., v.10, 163.

3. C.V., v.13, 163.
4. C.V., v.31, 132.
5. C.V., v.9, 166-67; Daniel, 299
6. C.V., v.2, 234; C.V., v.18, 63.
7. C.V., v.9, 167.
8. C.V., v.31, 132; Wyeth, *Devil*, 77-78; C.V., v.2, 32-33.
9. C.V., v.22, 314.
10. C.V., v.9, 532.
11. C.V., v.7, 556; Grant, 485.
12. C.V., v.36, 336; Allen, p.36; Daniel, 265.
13. C.V., v.36, 336; Daniel, 301
14. C.V., v.36, 336; McDonough, 158-59.
15. Grant, 468.
16. C.V., v.36, 336; C.V., v.1, 289, Grant, 468.
17. Green, Journal.
18. C.V., v.9, 21; Beauregard, 591.
19. C.V., v.9, 499.
20. "Reminiscences."
21. Visser, "Bloodbath," 7.
22. Ibid.
23. C.V., v.36, 336.
24. C.V., v.16, 281.
25. C.V., v.19, 452.
26. C.V., v.36, 336; McDonough, 145.
27. Visser, "Bloodbath," 6.
28. C.V., v.36, 336; Grant, 477.
29. C.V., v.22, 343.
30. Martin, *Shiloh*, 179.
31. C.V., v.36, 337.
32. Ibid.
33. Daniel, *Shiloh*, 292.
34. Martin, *Shiloh*, 111-12.
35. C.V., v.36, 337.
36. C.V., v.2, 35; J&P, 79; McDonough, 292.
37. Ibid.
38. C.V., v.2, 35; J&P, 79.
39. "Reminiscences."
40. C.V., v.31, 132; Grant, 479-80.
41. "Reminiscences."

42. Buell, "Shiloh," 535-39.
43. C.V., v.34, 127-28.
44. Ibid.
45. Ibid.
46. Willoughby, "Forgotten."
47. Alderson, "Civil War," 161.
48. C.V., v.13, 254-55.
49. C.V., v.34, 128; C.V., v.15, 498-99.
50. Harrell, "Shiloh," 5.

CHAPTER 5. Island Number 10

1. "Battle … Number Ten."
2. Ibid.
3. Ibid.; Miller, *Photographic,* 218.
4. O.R., Mackall's Report of 8-21-62.
5. Bissell, "Sawing," 463.
6. Hubbard, *Notes,* 28.
7. Bissell, "Sawing," 460; Miller, *Photographic,* 220.
8. Hubbard, *Notes,* 28-29.
9. Miller, *Photographic,* 220.
10. Ibid., 222; Bissell, "Sawing," 460.
11. Bissell, "Sawing," 460-61.
12. Ibid., 462; Miller, *Photographic,* 224.
13. "Battle … Number Ten."
14. C.V., v.9, 295.
15. Hubbard, *Notes,* 30-31.

CHAPTER 6. Britton Lane

1. Brewer, "Britton's Lane."
2. Ibid.
3. Ibid.
4. Roberts, "Battle."
5. Brewer, "Britton's Lane"; Gates, "Britton's Lane"; Alexander, "Armstrong," 40.
6. Ibid.
7. C.V., v.30, 290.
8. *I Marched,* 65.
9. Ibid.

10. Gates, "Britton's Lane."
11. Roberts, "Battle."
12. C.V., v.30, 290.
13. Hubbard, *Notes*, 34-35.
14. C.V., v.11, 442-43.
15. Roberts, "Battle."
16. C.V., v.11, 443.
17. Alexander, "Armstrong," 43; Gates, "Britton's Lane."
18. C.V., v.11, 442-43.
19. Gates, "Britton's Lane."
20. C.V., v.37, 23.
21. Neville, "Woman's Mercy."
22. Neville, "Battle."
23. Ibid.
24. Ibid.
25. Brewer, "Britton's Lane."

CHAPTER 7. Davis Bridge

1. Rogers, "Battle."
2. Roth, "Battle of Corinth," 56.
3. O.R., XVII, 392.
4. "Battle ... Hatchie."
5. Green, Journal.
6. "Battle ... Hatchie"; Cozzens, *Darkest*, 281, O.R., XVII 392-99.
7. C.V., v.18, 468.
8. O.R., Ser. I, Pt. 1, 305.
9. C.V., v.20, 121.
10. O.R., Ser. I, Pt. 1, 305.
11. Martin, "Diary."
12. O.R., Ser. I, Pt. 1, 322.
13. "Battle ... Hatchie."
14. "Confederate Monument"; O.R., Ser. I, pt. 1, 306.
15. "Battle ... Hatchie."
16. C.V., v.20, 120.
17. Ibid.
18. Martin, "Diary."
19. Ibid.
20. "Battle ... Hatchie."

21. Strong, letter.
22. C.V., v.18, 468.
23. Ibid.
24. Richardson, "On the Hatchie," 3.
25. O.R., Ser. I, pt. 1, 403.
26. "Battle ... Hatchie."
27. Martin, "Diary."
28. O.R., Ser. I, pt. 1, 403.
29. Green, Journal.
30. Cozzens, *Darkest*, 288; Ballard, Battlefield.
31. "Confederate monument ..."
32. O.R., Ser. I, pt. 1, 312.
33. "Battle ... Hatchie."
34. Green, Journal.
35. "Confederate monument ..."
36. C.V., v.20, 121.
37. O.R., Ser. I, pt. 1, 307.
38. Green, Journal.
39. "War Spirit."
40. "Twenty-eighth Infantry Regiment."
41. Green, Journal.
42. Hubbard, *Notes*, 44-45.
43. Martin, "Diary."
44. Russinoff dictation.
45. Strong, letter.
46. Hubbard, *Notes*, 45.
47. Wagoner, "Civil War Cannon."

CHAPTER 8. Hartsville

1. *Vidette*, 8/17/1862.
2. Ibid.
3. C.V., v.17, 202.
4. C.V., v.9, 317.
5. C.V., v.7, 431-32.
6. Ibid.
7. "Detailed."
8. C.V., Oct. 1905, 454.
9. Stone, "Repelling," 451.

10. "Detailed."
11. Ibid.
12. "Local Troops."
13. "Battle of Hartsville, Tennessee."
14. "Detailed."
15. Ibid.
16. Ibid.
17. Ibid.
18. Ibid.
19. C.V.; April, 1906; 188-89.
20. "Detailed."
21. Ibid.
22. C.V., May 1899, 278.
23. Ibid.
24. Quisenberry, "The Eleventh Kentucky," 263.
25. Ibid.
26. C.V., April, 1906; 189.
27. Ibid.
28. C.V., Oct. 1902, 271.
29. C.V., v.10, 29-30.
30. Ibid.
31. Ibid.
32. C.V., v.10, 30.
33. C.V., v.19, 424.
34. "Driving Tour"; C.V., v.9, 318.

CHAPTER 9. Salem Cemetery

1. O.R., v.7, 482.
2. Stillwell, *Story*, 114.
3. Engelmann letter.
4. Stillwell, *Story*, 115.
5. Ibid., 116-17.
6. Ibid.
7. Lawrence letter.
8. Engelmann letter.
9. Ibid.
10. Ibid.
11. Roth, "Salem," 62.

12. "Lone Monument"; Coble letter; Coble transcript.
13. Roth, "Salem," 62; Coble letter; Coble transcript.
14. Ibid.
15. Roth, "Salem," 62; Coble letter; Coble transcript.

CHAPTER 10. Parker's Crossroads

1. O.R., v. 17, 579, 580, 586, 588.
2. Ibid.
3. Ibid.
4. Ibid.
5. Corbin letter.
6. Halstead, "Seventh Battery."
7. J&P, 210.
8. Halstead, "Seventh Battery."
9. O.R., v. 17, 579-88.
10. Ibid.
11. Ibid.
12. Ibid.
13. Ibid.
14. Corbin letter.
15. Ibid.
16. Wyeth, *Devil*, 108-09; J&P, 212.
17. Ibid.
18. C.V., Feb. 1907, 55.
19. J&P, 213.
20. Corbin letter.
21. Anderson, "Report," 435.
22. Halstead, "Seventh Battery."
23. O.R., v. 17, 579-88.
24. Ibid.
25. Corbin letter.
26. Ibid.
27. Bearss, "Forrest's West," 46.
28. Ibid.
29. Ibid.
30. C.V., v.16, 108.
31. Ibid.
32. Smith, *Fuller's Ohio Brigade*, 124-25.

33. Ibid., 125.
34. O.R., v.17, 579-88.
35. J&P, 214.
36. C.V., Oct. 1894, 308.
37. Ibid.
38. J&P, 214-15.
39. C.V., Feb. 1908,73; Corbin letter.
40. Corbin letter.
41. J&P, 214-15.
42. *Thirty-ninth Infantry*, 340-41.
43. O.R., v. 17, 579-88.
44. C.V., v.37, 27.
45. O.R., v.17, 579-88.
46. Thirty-ninth Iowa Volunteer Infantry casualty report.
47. Seventh Wisconsin Artillery casualty report.
48. 122nd Illinois Vol. Infantry casualty report.
49. C.V., Feb. 1901, 54.
50. Corwin, "Grave."

CHAPTER 11. Murfreesboro (Stone's River)

1. O.R., v. 20, pt. 1, 201.
2. Kniffin, "Battle," 614.
3. C.V., v.11, 66.
4. Kniffin, "Battle," 614.
5. C.V., Nov. 1912, 519.
6. C.V., v.11, 66.
7. Ibid.
8. C.V., v.31, 341.
9. C.V., Aug. 1908, 391.
10. C.V., Nov. 1912, 515.
11. C.V., v.11, 66.
12. C.V., Nov. 1912, 515.
13. Kniffin, "Battle," 618.
14. Ibid., 618-19.
15. C.V., v.16, 574.
16. Ibid.
17. C.V., v.31, 341.
18. C.V., Aug. 1908, 391; C.V., Nov. 1912, 515.

19. Kniffin, "Battle," 619.
20. C.V., March 1904, 118.
21. C.V., Aug. 1908, 391.
22. C.V., v.31, 341.
23. C.V., v.13, 411.
24. C.V., July 1901, 306.
25. Kniffin, "Battle," 619.
26. Ibid.
27. Ibid.; Cozzens, *Stone's River*, 27.
28. C.V., Feb. 1900, 73.
29. C.V., v.16, 454.
30. Ibid., 64.
31. C.V., Nov. 1907, 263.
32. C.V., Dec. 1896, 439.
33. C.V., v.16, 574.
34. C.V., v.31, 342.
35. Ibid.
36. C.V., Aug. 1894, 228.
37. Pinney display.
38. Dell display.
39. C.V., v.16, 64.
40. C.V., May 1908, 209.
41. Ibid.
42. C.V., v.7, 72.
43. C.V., v.16, 451-52.
44. C.V., Dec. 1909, 581.
45. C.V., July 1907, 335.
46. C.V., June 1895, 162.
47. C.V., March 1899, 119.
48. Kniffin, "Battle," 630.
49. C.V., Aug. 1908, 391.
50. C.V., July 1901, 306.
51. Mitchell, S.R.B. archives.
52. DeVellin display.
53. C.V., v.13, 411.
54. C.V., v.1, 452.
55. C.V., v.11, 67.
56. Ibid.
57. Ibid.

58. Ibid.
59. C.V., v.16, 452-53.
60. Ibid., 453.
61. Ibid.
62. Ibid.
63. Ibid.
64. Ibid.
65. Ibid.
66. Ibid., 454.
67. Ibid.
68. C.V., v.3, 239.
69. C.V., Dec. 1894, 356.
70. C.V., Aug. 1900, 368.
71. C.V., Aug. 1901, 355-56.
72. C.V., Aug. 1896, 264.
73. C.V., Feb. 1908, 73.
74. C.V., Nov. 1893, 333.
75. C.V., May 1911, 220.
76. C.V., Aug. 1903, 376.
77. *Boston Journal*, Jan. 6, 1863.
78. *Daily Sun*, Jan. 11, 1863.
79. C.V., v.13, 411.

CHAPTER 12. Thompson's Station

1. J&P, 231-32.
2. Ibid.
3. Wade, "Thompson's Station."
4. Ibid.
5. *www.williamsoncounty-tn.gov.*
6. J&P, 233.
7. Ibid.; Wyeth, *Devil*, 158.
8. J&P, 234; Wade, "Thompson's Station."
9. McCrea, "Thompson's Station."
10. J&P, 234; Wyeth, *Devil*, 158; *indianainthecivilwar.com*
11. Wyeth, *Devil*, 158-59; O.R., v. 23, pt. 1, 81.
12. Wade, "Thompson's Station"; Wyeth, *Devil*, 159.
13. *indianainthecivilwar.com.*
14. Wade, "Thompson's Station."

15. C.V., v.8, 263.
16. Ibid.
17. C.V., v.21, 487.
18. *indianainthecivilwar.com.*
19. Ibid.; J&P, 236-37.
20. Wyeth, *Devil,* 160; J&P, 236.
21. J&P, 238.
22. Ibid.
23. C.V., v.8, 403.
24. Wade, "Thompson's Station."

CHAPTER 13. Knoxville

1. "Opposing Forces at Knoxville, Tenn.," 751-52.
2. Poe, "Defense," 731-32.
3. Ibid., 732.
4. C.V., v.21, 11.
5. Ibid., 12.
6. C.V., v.30, 340.
7. Poe, "Defense," 737-38; Young, letter.
8. "Brearly ... ."
9. C.V., v.21, 123.
10. Knoxville Civil War Roundtable membership pamphlet.
11. Ibid.
12. Poe, "Defense," 739-40.
13. Kelly, "On they came ... "
14. C.V., v.22, 266.
15. Poe, "Defense," 740-41.
16. Kelly, "On they came ..."; "Battle of Fort Sanders."
17. Poe, "Defense," 742.
18. Ibid., 741.
19. Kelly, "On they came ..."; C.V., Jan. 1910, 24.
20. C.V., Jan. 1910, 24.
21. C.V., v.22, 266.
22. Ibid.
23. Ibid.
24. C.V., Jan. 1910, 24.
25. C.V., v.31, 288.
26. Ibid.

27. C.V., Jan. 1910, 24.
28. Ibid.
29. Poe, "Defense," 743; C.V., v.22, 266.
30. C.V., v.22, 266.
31. C.V., v.18, 468.
32. C.V., v.30, 341.
33. C.V., v. 30, 10-11.
34. Ibid.
35. C.V., Jan. 1910, 24-25.
36. "Battle of Fort Sanders."
37. Alexander, "Longstreet ..." 750.
38. Kelly, "On they came ..."
39. C.V., July 1908, 360.
40. C.V., Jan. 1910, 24.
41. Ibid.
42. C.V., v.22, 266-67.
43. Alexander, "Longstreet ..." 750.
44. C.V., v.30, 341-42.
45. Ibid.
46. Ibid.
47. Knoxville Civil War Roundtable membership newsletter.

CHAPTER 14. Chattanooga

1. C.V., v.6, 564.
2. Ibid., 562.
3. Ibid.
4. Grant, "Chattanooga," 685.
5. Ibid., 680-81.
6. C.V., v.6, 562.
7. Ibid.
8. Ibid.
9. Ibid.
10. Ibid.
11. Fullerton, "... at Chattanooga," 719.
12. Grant, "Chattanooga," 683.
13. Ibid., 683-84.
14. C.V., v.1, 375.
15. C.V., v.6, 426.

16. Grant, "Chattanooga," 685.
17. C.V., v.6, 562.
18. Grant, "Chattanooga," 687.
19. Ibid.
20. Smith, "Comments," 714.
21. Grant, "Chattanooga," 695.
22. O.R., Grant's report, p. 6 of 10 online edition.
23. Ibid.
24. C.V., v.6, 34.
25. Grant, "Chattanooga," 697.
26. Ibid., 698-99.
27. C.V., v.6, 427; C.V., v.6, 110.
28. C.V., v.6, 427.
29. Ibid.
30. Ibid.
31. Grant, "Chattanooga," 703.
32. Ibid., 703-04.
33. C.V., v.6, 110.
34. C.V., v.6, 427.
35. C.V., v.7, 121.
36. C.V., v.6, 110.
37. Grant, "Chattanooga," 704.
38. O.R., Jackson's report, p. 5 of 6 online edition.
39. O.R., Grant's report, p. 9 of 10 online edition.
40. O.R., Jackson's report, p. 5 & 6 of 6 online edition.

CHAPTER 15. Fort Pillow

1. Casteel, "Fort Pillow," 1.
2. J&P., 427.
3. Beckman.
4. Akers, "... still argued ..."
5. J&P, 428-29.
6. Ibid.; C.V., v.3, 322.
7. Ibid.
8. Casteel, "Fort Pillow," 2.
9. J&P, 428-29.
10. O.R., Tom J. Jackson's report.
11. C.V., v.3, 322.

12. Ibid.
13. Ibid., 323.
14. J&P, 430; Forrest's Official Report of 4-24-1864.
15. J&P, 430.
16. Akers, "... still argued ..."; Forrest's Official Report of 4-24-1864.
17. C.V., v.3, 323.
18. J&P, 431.
19. Ibid.; Akers, "... still argued ..."
20. J&P, 432.
21. Ibid.; Forrest's Official Report of 4-24-1864.
22. Ibid.
23. Ibid.
24. Ibid.; C.V., v.3, 323.
25. J&P, 433.
26. Ibid.
27. C.V., v.3, 323.
28. Ibid.
29. J&P, 434.
30. Ibid., 435-36.
31. C.V., v.3, 323.
32. J&P, 437; Forrest's Official Report of 4-24-1864.
33. Ibid.
34. Ibid.
35. C.V., v.3, 323-24.
36. Akers, "... still argued ..."; Casteel, "Fort Pillow," 3-4.
37. Jackson's report.
38. Forrest's report.
39. C.V., v.3, 324.
40. J&P, 438.
41. C.V., v.3, 324.
42. Ibid.
43. Ibid.
44. Ibid.
45. Ibid., 324-25.
46. Ibid., 324.
47. Ibid.
48. Ibid., 325.
49. Ibid.

50. C.V., v.26, 149.
51. Casteel, "Fort Pillow," 6-7.
52. J&P, 441-42.
53. C.V., v.5, 102.

CHAPTER 16. Johnsonville

1. Wyatt, "Johnsonville"; Williams, "Johnsonville," 246.
2. C.V., v.22, 175.
3. Wyatt, "Johnsonville."
4. Williams, "Johnsonville," 246.
5. O.R., pt. 3, 437, 439, 815-817, 870.
6. Slayden, "Months."
7. Cross, "From ... Johnsonville ..." 25; J&P, 591-92.
8. Wyeth, 174.
9. J&P, 592-93; Cross, "From ... Johnsonville," 25.
10. Slayden, "Forrest Moves."
11. C.V., v.13, 567.
12. J&P, 593; Cross, "From ... Johnsonville ..." 25, Perry, "Forrest's Navy," 28.
13. J&P, 593; Cross, "From ... Johnsonville ...", 28.
14. J&P, 594; Williams, "Johnsonville," 235.
15. Ibid.; Perry, "Forrest's Navy," 28; Cross, "From ... Johnsonville ...", 25.
16. Ibid.
17. J&P, 595; Cross, "From ... Johnsonville ..." 25; Williams, "Johnsonville," 236.
18. Cross, "From ... Johnsonville ..." 26; Wyeth, 525.
19. J&P, 596; Williams, "Johnsonville," 236.
20. Garrett, *History*, 104.
21. J&P, 596.
22. Williams, "Johnsonville," 237; Cross, "From ... Johnsonville," 26; Perry, "Forrest's Navy," 28.
23. C.V., v.13, 566.
24. Perry, "Forrest's Navy," 28; J&P, 597.
25. Perry, "Forrest's Navy," 29.
26. Cross, "From Johnsonville," 26.
27. J&P, 598.
28. Ibid.; Cross, "From Johnsonville," 26.

29. J&P, 599; Perry, "Forrest's Navy," 29.
30. Cross, "From Johnsonville," 26; Garrett, *History*, 105.
31. Williams, "Johnsonville," 240; Perry, "Forrest's Navy," 29.
32. Williams, "Johnsonville," 242; J&P, 599.
33. Cross, "From Johnsonville," 27; J&P, 599; Perry, "Forrest's Navy," 28.
34. Cross, "From Johnsonville," 26.
35. C.V., v.22, 175.
36. Garrett, *History*, 106-07.
37. Slayden, "Gunfire."
38. C.V., v.22, 175.
39. J&P, 600-01; Williams, "Johnsonville," 242.
40. J&P, 602; Cross, "From Johnsonville," 26-27; Perry, "Forrest's Navy," 30.
41. Ibid.
42. Ibid.
43. J&P, 604; Perry, "Forrest's Navy," 30; Cross, "From Johnsonville," 26.
44. Perry, "Forrest's Navy," 30; Cross, "From Johnsonville," 26.
45. C.V., v.37, 343.
46. C.V., v.22, 175.
47. Perry, "Forrest's Navy," 30.
48. Garrett, *History*, 107.
49. J&P, 605.
50. C.V., v.37, 343-44.
51. Perry, "Forrest's Navy," 30-31; Cross, "From Johnsonville," 26.
52. Ibid.; C.V., v.22, 175.
53. C.V., v.13, 566.
54. Prouty interview.
55. C.V., v.37, 344.

CHAPTER 17. Spring Hill

1. C.V., v.24, 138; C.V., v.12, 395.
2. C.V., v.16, 25.
3. Ibid.
4. Ibid.
5. Ibid.
6. C.V., v.12, 395; C.V., v.36, 100.

7. C.V., v.16, 25.
8. C.V., v.36, 100.
9. Ibid.
10. C.V., v.16, 26.
11. Ibid.
12. Ibid., 30.
13. C.V., v.36, 101.
14. C.V., v.27, 139.
15. McDonough, "West Point," T.H.Q., 190.
16. Ibid., 191.
17. C.V., v.36, 142.
18. Ibid., 101.
19. Ibid., 101-02.
20. Ibid., 102.
21. Ibid.
22. Ibid., 102-03.
23. C.V., v.16, 31.
24. C.V., v.36, 103.
25. Ibid.
26. C.V., v.16, 31-32.
27. Ibid., 32.
28. Ibid.
29. C.V., v.27, 58.
30. C.V., v.24, 138.
31. Ibid.
32. C.V., v.17, 32.
33. C.V., v.27, 139-40.
34. C.V., v.21, 569-70; C.V., v.22, 60.
35. C.V., v.17, 37.
36. Ibid.
37. C.V., v.24, 138.
38. C.V., v.27, 58.
39. C.V., v.24, 138.
40. Ibid.
41. Ibid.
42. C.V., v.27, 58-60.
43. Ibid.
44. C.V., v.16, 41.
45. C.V., v.27, 138-39.

CHAPTER 18. Franklin

1. McDonough, "West Point," T.H.Q., 192.
2. Farley, "Franklin," C.V., 1993, 35; Crownover, "Franklin," T.H.Q., 10.
3. C.V., v.24, 102.
4. Farley, "Cleburne," 30; Crownover, "Franklin," T.H.Q., 10-11.
5. Cartwright, "Franklin," H.G., 30; C.V., v.11, 165.
6. Farley, "Cleburne," 30; Cartwright, "Franklin," H.G., 28.
7. McDonough, "West Point," T.H.Q., 193; C.V. v.23, 5.
8. Farley, "Franklin," 35.
9. McGann, "Carter House," T.H.Q., 40-44.
10. Ibid.
11. Crownover, "Franklin," T.H.Q., 12; C.V., v.23, 5; Cartwright, "Franklin," 28.
12. Ibid.
13. C.V., v.23, 5.
14. C.V., v.36, 381.
15. Ibid.
16. McDonough, "West Point," T.H.Q., 183.
17. Ibid.
18. C.V., v.26, 116.
19. Miller, "Tragedy."; Jacobson interview.
20. C.V., v.26, 117; Farley, "Franklin," 35.
21. C.V., v.12, 17; Joslyn, "Irish Hero," C.V., 1998, 37-44.
22. C.V., v.26, 117.
23. J&P, 546.
24. C.V., v.24, 102.
25. Fraley interview.
26. C.V., v.36, 381.
27. C.V., v.23, 5.
28. Tucker, "First Missouri," T.H.Q., 26.
29. C.V., v.24, 102; Farley, "Franklin," 38; C.V., v.23, 5; Cartwright, 30.
30. Fraley interview; Jacobson interview.
31. C.V., v.23, 5.
32. Tucker, "First Missouri," T.H.Q., 26.
33. Farley, "Franklin" 36-38.
34. C.V., v.24, 102.
35. C.V., v.24, 102.

36. C.V., v.23, 5.
37. Ibid.; C.V., v.36, 381.
38. C.V., v.26, 117.
39. C.V., v.2, 239.
40. C.V., v.24, 102-03; Cartwright interview.
41. Tucker, "Funeral Dirge," 25.
42. Tucker, "First Missouri," 28.
43. Cartwright, 31; C.V., v.12, 17; C.V., v.11, 165-67.
44. C.V., v.11, 165-67.
45. C.V., v.4, 300.
46. Ibid.
47. Ibid.
48. Crownover, 21; Farley, "Franklin," 40; C.V., v.11, 167.
49. Farley, "Franklin," 40.
50. Ibid.
51. Ibid., 40-42.
52. Tucker, "First Missouri," 28.
53. C.V., v.24, 103.
54. C.V., v.5, 274.
55. C.V., v.1, 339.
56. C.V., v.13, 564.
57. C.V., v.36, 382.
58. Ibid.
59. Ibid.
60. C.V., v.10, 500.
61. C.V., v.13, 563.
62. Ibid.
63. Ibid.; C.V., v.24, 103; C.V., v.24, 551.
64. C.V., v.13, 564.
65. Ibid; Jacobson interview.
66. C.V., v.36, 383.
67. C.V., v.24, 102.
68. Posegate, "Battle."
69. C.V., v.10, 500-01.
70. Ibid., 501.
71. Ibid., 502.
72. Fraley interview.
73. Crownover, 27.
74. C.V., v.24, 103.

75. Fraley interview.
76. C.V., v.10, 501.
77. C.V., v.16, 14.
78. Ibid.
79. C.V., v.16, 14.
80. C.V., v.3, 72-73.
81. Fraley interview.
82. C.V., v.24, 103; Farley, "Franklin," 42.
83. Ibid.
84. Fraley interview.
85. Ibid.
86. Ibid.
87. Ibid.
88. Ibid.
89. Ibid.
90. Ibid; Cartwright interview.
91. Fraley interview.
92. Ibid.
93. *Hallowed Ground* video; Cartwright interview.
94. C.V., v.3, 73.
95. C.V., v.23, 5-6.
96. C.V., v.26, 118.
97. C.V., v.24, 103.
98. C.V., v.17, 221.
99. C.V., v.11, 167.
100. C.V., v.16, 14.
101. C.V., v.16, 14.
102. C.V., v.23, 4.
103. Carter letter.
104. Williams, "Franklin," 1.
105. Fraley interview.
106. Williams, "Franklin," 1.
107. Crownover, 27.
108. C.V., v.26, 116.

CHAPTER 19. Nashville

1. C.V., v.2, 46; C.V., v.12, 269.
2. C.V., v.12, 274.

3. C.V., v.12, 269; Cooling, "Decisive," H.G., 26.
4. C.V., v.16, 17.
5. Ibid.; C.V., v.12, 269; C.V., v.12, 274.
6. C.V., v.16, 17.
7. C.V., v.12, 274.
8. Ibid.
9. Ibid., 25-76.
10. C.V., v.16, 20-21.
11. Keenan, "Fighting," 50.
12. C.V., v.12, 269.
13. Ibid., 276.
14. Fitzgerald, "Clash," 23.
15. Ibid.; C.V., v.12, 269.
16. C.V., v.2, 46.
17. C.V., v.12, 269.
18. Stone, "Repelling," 458-59.
19. C.V., v.12, 269-70.
20. C.V., v.18, 470.
21. Ibid.
22. C.V., v.2, 46.
23. Ibid.
24. Ibid., 47.
25. C.V., v.18, 470.
26. Ibid.,
27. C.V., v.12, 270.
28. Ibid.
29. Ibid.
30. Ibid.
31. Ibid.
32. C.V., v.13, 68.
33. C.V., v.12, 270.
34. C.V., v.16, 18.
35. C.V., v.9, 30.
36. C.V., v.12, 272.
37. Stone, "Repelling," 462.
38. C.V., v.12, 270.
39. Ibid.
40. C.V., v.16, 19.
41. Ibid.; C.V., v.12, 270.

42. C.V., v.2, 47.
43. C.V., v.16, 19.
44. C.V., v.12, 274.
45. C.V. v.2, 47.
46. C.V., v.9, 31; Boyce, *prodigy.net.*
47. C.V., v.7, 154.
48. Fitzgerald, "Clash" 30.
49. C.V., v.16, 19.
50. Ibid., 20.
51. Ibid.
52. Cooling, "Decisive," H.G., 26-27.
53. C.V., v.12, 276.
54. C.V., v.16, 21.
55. C.V., v.16, 21.
56. Zimmerman, "Nashville," H.G., 7.
57. Ibid.

CHAPTER 20. Noteworthy Sites Across the State

1. Newcomer, "Battle," 56.
2. Ibid., 56-57.
3. Ibid., 57; Robbins, "Yankees Held," 28.
4. Robbins, "Yankees Held," 29.
5. C.V., v.11, 503.
6. Ibid.
7. O.R., v.17, pt. 2, 688; O.R., v. 17, pt. 1, 46.
8. Bills diary, August 30, 1862.
9. O.R., v.17, pt. 2, 688; O.R., v.17, pt. 1, 46.
10. C.V., v.30, 290.
11. O.R., v.17, pt. 1, 49.
12. Richards, 79.
13. Hubbard, *Notes,* 33-34.
14. O.R., v.17, pt. 1, 49; Richards, 81.
15. Culp letter and driving tour; J&P, 200-03.
16. Ibid.
17. Ibid.
18. C.V., v.12, 535-36.
19. C.V., v.6, 123-24.
20. Ibid., 124.

21. C.V., v.33, 101.
22. C.V., v.36, 384.
23. Ibid.
24. Ibid., 385.
25. C.V., v.30, 294-97.
26. C.V., v.20, 513.
27. C.V., v.33, 55-57.

BIBLIOGRAPHY

Abbreviations:

B&L: Battles and Leaders of the Civil War
JMCL-TR: Jackson Madison County Library-Tennessee Room
PCBA: Parker's Crossroads Battlefield Association
SRBA: Stones River Battlefield Association
THQ: Tennessee Historical Quarterly
WTHSP: West Tennessee Historical Society Papers

Akers, Merton T. "It's still argued: Was Ft. Pillow a Massacre?" *Commercial Appeal*, April 12, 1964.

Alderson, William T. "The Civil War Reminiscences of John Johnston, 1861-1865. *T.H.Q.* Vol. 13, #2, June, 1954: 156-178.

Alexander, E. Porter. "Longstreet at Knoxville." *B&L:* 745-51.

Alexander, Harbert L. Rice. "The Armstrong Raid including the battles of Bolivar, Medon Station, and Britton Lane." *T.H.Q.* V. 21, #1.

Allen, Stacy. Interview of July 16, 2007 with Randy Bishop.

----. "Shiloh: A Visitor's Guide", *Blue and Gray, 2001.*

Baker, Everard W. "Last Living Soul Who Heard the Roar of Shiloh's Cannon Still." *Adamsville News*.

Ballard, Delores. "Battlefield wins fight for historic recognition." *Jackson Sun*. June 3, 1991.

"Battle of Fort Sanders Fought 43 Years Ago Today." *Knoxville Journal and Tribune*, November 29, 1906.

"Battle of Hartsville, Tennessee."

"Battle of Island Number Ten." Lake County Civil War Centennial Commission. Courtesy of Reelfoot Lake State Park.

"Battle of Murfreesboro." *Daily Reporter*; Selma, AL. Jan. 10, 1863. Courtesy of SRBA.

"Battle of Murfreesboro." *Daily Whig*; Vicksburg, MS. Jan. 13, 1863. Courtesy of SRBA.

"The Battle of Murfreesboro." *New York Tribune*, Jan. 3, 1863. Courtesy of SRBA.

The Battle of Nashville Preservation Society, Inc. Web site: *BONPS.org*

"The Battle of the Hatchie." *Chicago Times*. October 1862.

Bearss, Edwin C. "The Fall of Fort Henry," *WTHSP*, v. 17, 1963: 85-107.

----- "Forrest's West Tennessee Campaign of 1862 and the Battle of Parker's Crossroads." *Blue and Gray Magazine*. V. 20, #6: 6-22, 43-50.

Beauregard, G.T. "The Campaign of Shiloh", B&L, 569-93.

Beckman, Elihu C. "A Good Story." *Melbourne Times*. Sept. 6, 1906.

Bills, John H. "Diary." Hardeman County Library; Bolivar, TN.

Bissell, J.W. "Sawing out the Channel above Island Number Ten." *B&L*: 460-62.

"Bloody Rout of Union Soldiers opens battle." *Jackson Sun*, April 5, 1987.

Boston Journal; January 8, 1863. Courtesy of SRBA.

Boyce, Doris. "The Battle of Nashville: Shy, Smith, and Hood." *Pages. prodigy.net.*

"Brearly, on the experience of the Union soldier during the siege." *Web. utk.edu.*

Brewer, James D. "The Battle of Britton's Lane."

"Britton's Lane: Southern Win?" *The Jackson Sun*; May 29, 1972.

Buell, Don Carlos. "Shiloh Reviewed." *B&L* Castle Books: New York. 1956. pp. 487-539.

"Button clears mystery of unknown boy soldier of Britton's Lane battle." *Bolivar Bulletin. 10-4-1962.*

Byers, S.H.M. "Sherman's Attack at the Tunnel" *B&L*: 712-13.

Carter, Moscow. "Letter." *National Tribune*; September 9, 1882.

Cartwright, Thomas Y. "Franklin: The Valley of Death." *Hallowed Ground*; v.5, # 1:28-31.

----Interview of September 8, 2007 with Randy Bishop.

Castel, Albert. "Fort Pillow: Victory or Massacre?" *American History Illustrated.* April 1974.

The Charleston Mercury. January 3, 1863. Courtesy SRBA.

Coble letter. March 22, 1914. Courtesy JMCL-TR.

Coble transcript. Salem Cemetery File. Courtesy JMCL-TR.

"Coburn's Brigade." *Indianainthecivilwar.com.*

"Confederate Monument is dedicated." *Bolivar Bulletin*; Oct. 16, 1991.

Confederate Veteran magazine: April 1893, June 1893, Sept. 1893, Oct. 1893, Nov. 1893, Dec. 1893, Jan. 1894, Feb. 1894, May 1894, Aug. 1894, Oct. 1894, Dec. 1894, Mar. 1895, Apr. 1895, June 1895, July 1895, Aug. 1895, Aug. 1896, Sept. 1896, Nov. 1896, Dec. 1896, Jan. 1897, Feb. 1897, Mar. 1897, June 1897, Dec. 1897, Jan. 1898, Feb. 1898, Mar. 1898, April 1898, July 1898, Aug. 1898, Sept. 1898, Dec. 1898, Jan. 1899, Feb. 1899, Mar. 1899, April 1899, May 1899, July 1899, Aug. 1899, Oct. 1899, Nov. 1899, Dec. 1899, Feb. 1900, Mar. 1900, June 1900, Aug. 1900, Sept. 1900, Jan. 1901, April 1901, July 1901, Aug. 1901, Sept. 1901, Dec. 1901, Jan. 1902, April 1902, June 1902, July 1902, Oct. 1902, Nov. 1902, Jan. 1903, Feb. 1903, April 1903, Aug. 1903, Oct. 1903, Nov. 1893, Jan. 1904, Mar. 1904, June 1904, Aug. 1904, Feb. 1905, April 1905, May 1905, Sept. 1905, Oct. 1905, Dec. 1905, April 1906, May 1906, Feb. 1907, May 1907, June 1907, July 1907, Nov. 1907, Dec. 1907, Jan. 1908, Feb. 1908, Mar. 1908, May 1908, June 1908, July 1908, Aug. 1908, Sept. 1908, Nov. 1908, Jan. 1909, April 1909, May 1909, Dec. 1909, Jan. 1910, Feb. 1910, June 1910, July 1910, Oct. 1910, Feb. 1911, May 1911, Sept. 1911, Oct. 1911, Mar. 1912, Oct. 1912, Nov. 1912, Feb. 1913, Mar. 1913, Oct. 1913, Feb. 1914, Apr. 1914, May 1914, July 1914, Aug. 1914, Jan. 1915, Feb. 1916, Mar. 1916, Feb. 1917, April 1917, Mar. 1918, April 1918, Feb. 1919, April 1919, Sept. 1919, Aug. 1922, April 1923, Aug. 1923, Sept. 1923, Feb. 1925, Mar. 1925, April 1926, Jan. 1927, March 1928, Apr. 1928, May 1928, Sept. 1928, Oct. 1928, Jan. 1929, Sept. 1927, Dec. 1929, Jan. 1930

Cooling, Benjamin Franklin. *The Campaign for Fort Donelson*. Eastern National, 1999.

-----"The Decisive Battle of Nashville." *Hallowed Ground*. v.5, #1: 21-27.

Corbin, L.B. Letter of 1/4/1863. Used with permission of PCBA.

Corwin, Tom. "Digging the Civil War." *Jackson Sun*. November 29, 1993.

Cox, N.N. "Forrest's Men captured at Parker's crossroads." *Confederate Veteran.* 73.

Cozzens, Peter. *The Battle of Stone's River.* Eastern National, 1995.

----- *The Battles for Chattanooga.* Eastern National. 1996.

-----*The Darkest Days of the War.* The Univ. of North Carolina Press, Chapel Hill. 1997.

Cross, Charles C. "From Fort Heiman to Johnsonville: The Tennessee River Campaign of Nathan Bedford Forrest." *Confederate Veteran*; v. 6, 2000.

Crownover, Sims. "The Battle of Franklin" *THQ*; v. 14, #4: 1-31.

Culp, Fred W. Letter of August 18, 2005 to Randy Bishop.

-----Driving tour of Trenton, Tennessee.

Daily Rebel Banner-Extra. January 2, 1863. Courtesy SRBA.

Daily Sun. Columbus, GA. January 6, 1863. Courtesy SRBA.

----- January 1, 1863. Courtesy SRBA.

-----January 19, 1863. Courtesy SRBA.

Daniel, Larry J. *Shiloh: The Battle that Changed the Civil War.* Touchstone, N.Y., 1997.

Davis, John H. "Questionnaire." Courtesy PCBA.

Davison, Eddy, and Daniel Foxx. "In Search of Forrest at Shiloh." *Confederate Veteran*, v. 2, 1999: 28-37.

Dell Display. Courtesy SRBA.

"Detailed Battle of Hartsville Account."

Devellin Display. Courtesy SRBA.

Dreaden, Reed. Interview of July 29, 2005 with Randy Bishop. New Johnsonville, TN.

"Driving Tour: The Battle of Hartsville, Tennessee."

Englemann, Adolph. Letter of Dec. 26, 1862. Courtesy of Lincoln Presidential Library; Springfield, Ill.

Farley, M. Foster. "The Battle of Franklin." *Confederate Veteran.* May/June 1993: 30-42.

Farley, M. Foster. "Patrick Ronayne Cleburne: The 'Stonewall Jackson' of the West." *Confederate Veteran.* v.38, #3: 16-19, 29-31.

"Fifth Tennessee Regiment." *West Tennessee Whig.* April 25, 1862.

Fitzgerald, William S. "Clash of Genius: Forrest vs. Wilson in the Nashville campaign." *Confederate Veteran.* Jan./Feb. 1992: 23-32.

Foote, J.A. "Shiloh's Bloody Battle." *The Bolivar Bulletin.* April 12, 1929.

"Fort Dickerson." Knoxville Civil War Roundtable pamphlet.

Fraley, David. Interview of March 25, 2006 with Randy Bishop. Carter House, Franklin, Tennessee.

Fullerton, Joseph S. "The Army of the Cumberland at Chattanooga." *B&L*: 719-26.

Garrett, Jill Knight. *A History of Humphreys County, Tennessee.* 1963.

Gates, John W. "Britton's Lane: some interesting facts concerning the battleground." *The Jackson Sun*; August 29, 1897.

Grant, Ulysses S. "Chattanooga." *B&L*: 679-711.

Green, Christopher John Newlon. "The Civil War Journal of Sgt. William Clark Newlon"

Hallowed Ground: Preserving Tennessee's Battlefields. 2001. Tennessee Wars Commission.

Halstead, S.L. "From the Seventh Battery." Used with permission of PCBA.

Harrell, Woody. "Shiloh: America's Best Preserved Battlefield is Getting Better." *Hallowed Ground.* v.4, Spring 2003: 5-6.

Hubbard, John Milton. *Notes of a Private.* R.P. Shackelford. Bolivar, TN. 1973.

Jacobson, Eric. Interview of August 29, 2007 with Randy Bishop.

Johnston, William Preston. "Albert Sidney Johnston at Shiloh", B&L, 540-63.

Johnstone, Alexander S. "Regulars at Stone's River." *Weekly Times*, Philadelphia, PA. April 12, 1884, Courtesy SRBA.

Jordan, Gen. Thomas & J.P. Pryor. *The Campaigns of Lieut. Gen. N.B. Forrest and of Forrest's Cavalry.* 1866.

Jordan, Thomas. "Notes of a Confederate Staff Officer at Shiloh". B&L, 594-603.

Joslyn, Mauriel P. "The Irish Hero of the Southern Army." *Confederate Veteran.* v.6, 1998: 36-44.

Keenan, Jerry. "Fighting with Forrest in the Tennessee Winter." *America's Civil War:* 49-53, 70-72.

Kelly, Dorothy E. "Civil War Knoxville, A Driving Tour." Knoxville Civil War Roundtable.

-----"On they came with a yell" *discoveret.org,* 1988.

-----Interview with Randy Bishop, July 26, 2006: via telephone.

Kniffin, G. C. "The Battle of Stones River." *B&L*: 613-632.

Knoxville Civil War Roundtable membership pamphlet. Courtesy of Jim Lyle.

Lawrence, James. Letter of December 30, 1862. Courtesy of JMCL-TR.

"Letter from Tennessee." *The Daily Sun.* Columbus, GA. Jan. 14, 1863. Courtesy SRBA.

"Local Troops fought with 9th Tennessee at Hartsville battle."

"The Lone Monument." *The Historical News.* v.20, #37-TN: 13.

"Loss of the Fourth Tennessee." *West Tennessee Whig.* April 25, 1862.

"Many years ago." *The Morning Tribune.* Knoxville, TN; Nov. 29, 1896.

Martin, David G. *The Shiloh Campaign: March-April 1862.* Combined Books, Conshohocken, PA 1996.

Martin, John D. "Diary." Courtesy of Davis Bridge Memorial Foundation.

McCrea, John. "Battle of Thompson's Station." *Indianapolis Journal.* March 13, 1863.

McDaniel, Steve. Interview of November 12, 2005 with Randy Bishop. Parker's Crossroads Battlefield.

McDonough, James L. "West Point Classmates—Eleven Years Later: Some observations on the Spring Hill—Franklin Campaign." *THQ.* v.28, #2: 182-196.

----. *Shiloh: In Hell Before Night.* University of Tennessee Press, 1977.

McGann, Will Spencer. "The Old Carter House at Franklin, Tennessee. *Tennessee Historical Magazine*. Ser. II, v. III, #1: 40-44.

McNeil, E.B. "Battle of Britton's Lane." *Jackson Dispatch*. January 25, 1889.

Matthews, W.M. "Middleburg." *Bolivar Bulletin*. January 12, 1940.

Miller, Evan. "The Tragedy at Carnton." *The Jackson Sun*. Jackson, TN; Nov. 10, 1985.

Miller, Francis Trevelyan, ed. *The Photographic History of the Civil War*. New York: Castle Books. 1957.

Minnich, J.W. "The Cavalry at Knoxville." *Confederate Veteran*: 10-13.

Mitchell, Lt. James B. Courtesy SRBA.

"Morgan's Brigade." *The Vidette Extra*. Hartsville, Tennessee. August 10, 1862.

-----August 17, 1862.

Mulket, W.A. "3rd Ga. Cavalry in the fight." *Daily Sun*. Columbus, GA. Jan. 7, 1863, Courtesy SRBA.

Nelson, Ronald L. "A curious Civil War phenomenon." *Springhousemagazine. com*.

Neville, Fonville. "Battle of Britton's Lane was fought for high ideals." *The Jackson Sun*. Aug. 26, 1962.

-----"Woman's Mercy Braved Bullets." Courtesy JMCL-TR.

Newcomer, Lee N. "The Battle of Memphis, 1862." *WTHSP*. V.12, 1958.

New York Tribune. January 8, 1863. Courtesy SRBA.

"Opposing Forces at Knoxville, Tenn." *B&L* New York: Castle Books. pp. 751-52.

Parker's Crossroads Casualty Reports. Courtesy PCBA.

Paul Flower's Greenhouse. *The Commercial Appeal*. Memphis, TN. March 23, 1965.

Perry, John C. "Forrest's Navy: The Raid on Johnsonville." *Confederate Veteran*. Jan./Feb. 1993.

Pinney Display. Courtesy SRBA.

Poe, Orlando M. "The Defense of Knoxville." *B&L*.: 731-45.

Posegate, Francis M. "Battle of Franklin." *National Observer*. 1879.

Prouty, Fred. Telephone interview on July 19, 2006 with Randy Bishop.

Quisenberry, Anderson Chenault. "The Eleventh Kentucky Cavalry, C.S.A" *SHSP*. pp. 259-90.

"Reminiscences of Shiloh." *Daily Evening Traveller*. Boston; October 7, 1862.

Richards, Charles H. "The 'Arme Blanche' In Tennessee: The battle of Middleburg." WTHSP. Vol. XLV, Dec. 1991. pp. 68-82.

Richardson, L.W. "On the Hatchie: How Gen. Ord Struck the Adjutant." *National Tribune* March 25, 1886.

Robbins, Peggy. "When the Yankees held Memphis." *Civil War Times Illustrated*. v.16, #9, 26-37.

Roberts, Bill. "Battle of Britton's Lane." *The Jackson Sun*. March 7, 1976.

Rogers, Margaret Greene. *The Battle of Corinth, 125th Official Souvenir Program*.

Roth, Dave. "The Battle of Corinth and the Fight at Hatchie River (Davis Bridge)." *Blue and Gray.* Summer 2002.

-----"The Battle of Salem Cemetery." *Blue and Gray.* v.XX, #6: 61-62.

-----with Steve McDaniel and Jim Weaver. "Forrest in West Tennessee, 1862." *Blue and Gray.* v.20, #6, Fall 2003: 51-58.

Russinoff, Paul. Dictation related to William D. Price, 53rd Illinois.

Salem Cemetery Web site. Used with permission of Malcolm Wilcox.

"Seek Soldier's Grave." *The Commercial Appeal.* Memphis, TN. March 12, 1914.

Slayden, Van H. "The 1st Kansas Battery." *The News-Democrat.* January 11, 1991.

-----"Forrest moves on Johnsonville." *The News-Democrat.* February 1, 1991.

-----"Gunfire on the river." *The News-Democrat.* Feb. 22, 1991.

-----"Months of Madness." *The News-Democrat.* December 7, 1990.

-----"Ruckus on the River Banks." *The News-Democrat.* March 1, 1991.

-----"The Three Northern Forts in the County." *The News Democrat.* Oct. 26, 1990.

Smith, Charles H. *The History of Fuller's Ohio Brigade 1861-1865.* Cleveland, Ohio.1909.

Smith, William Farrar. "Comments on General Grant's Chattanooga." *B&L*: 714-17.

Stillwell, Leander. *The Story of a Common Soldier.* Franklin House Publishing, 1920.

Stone, Henry. "Repelling Hood's Invasion of Tennessee." *B&L*. 440-464.

Strong, William W. Letter of October 25, 1862. *Winchester* (Illinois) *Democrat*.

Taylor, Captain Jesse. "The Defense of Fort Henry." *B&L*: 368-72.

Thompson, Lt. Heber S. "The Seventh Pennsylvania Cavalry in the Battle of Murfreesboro." *Miner's Journal*. Pottsville, PA. 1/24/1863. Courtesy SRBA.

"Thompson's Station, Tennessee" *williamsoncounty-tn.gov*.

Tucker, Phillip Thomas. "The First Missouri Brigade and the Battle of Franklin." *THQ*. v.46, #1: 21-32.

Tucker, Phillip. "Funeral Dirge in Tennessee: The Decimation of the First Missouri Confederate Brigade's Band at Franklin." v.1, 1995: 22-25.

Twenty-eighth Infantry Regiment—Illinois Adjutant General's Report.

Twenty-seventh Infantry, Co. F, Muster Roll of Nov./Dec. 1862. Courtesy of PCBA.

Users.aol.com/greenup1

U.S. War Department. *The War of Rebellion: A Compilation of the Official Records of the Union and Confederate Armies*. Washington, D.C. 1887.

Visser, Steve. "Bloodbath at Shiloh." *The Jackson Sun*. April 29, 1986.

Wade, Gregory L. "The Battle of Thompson's Station and 140 years later."

Wagoner, Billy. "Was a Civil War Cannon Really left in Hatchie Bottom?" *Wagon Spokes*. October 18, 1979.

Walke, Henry. "The Gunboats at Belmont and Fort Henry." *B&L*: 358-67.

Walker, Peter Franklin. "Command Failure: The Fall of Forts Henry and Donelson." *THQ.* v.16, #4, Dec. 1957: 335-60.

Wallace, Lew. "The Capture of Fort Donelson." *B&L:* 398-429.

"The War Spirit of an Iowa Soldier." Author, date and place of publication unknown.

Watkins, Sam. *Co. Aytch.* Jackson, TN 1952.

The Weekly. Columbus, GA., Jan. 20, 1863. Courtesy SRBA.

Wilcox, Malcolm. Interview of August 7, 2005 with Randy Bishop. Jackson, TN.

Williams, Denise. "Franklin Battlefield Reclaimed." *The Civil War Courier.* v.21, #1.

Williams, Edward F. "The Johnsonville Raid and Nathan Bedford Forrest State Park." *THQ.* v. 28, #3: 225-51.

Willoughby, Earl. "A forgotten regiment." *State Gazette.* Dyersburg, TN. 7/31/2005.

Wyatt, Robert G. "Johnsonville, held by Federals, destroyed in battle." *Johnsonville Times.* Oct. 1967.

Wyeth, John A. *That Devil Forrest.* New York, 1959.

Yadamec, G.J. "A Ripe Heritage." *The Jackson Sun.* April 29, 1986.

"Yankees, Rebels fought to draw at Britton Lane." *The Jackson Sun.* January 16, 1990.

Young, Namui Hale. Letter of August 26, 2007 to Randy Bishop.

Zimmerman, Mark. "Nashville Civil War Preservation." *Hallowed Ground.* v.5, #11: 7.

INDEX

State Line Road 93, 94, 96
Stewart, A.P. 74, 365
Stone's River x, xiv, 167, 171, 172,
    181, 185, 188, 189, 190, 191,
    192, 194, 336, 404, 405, 425,
    427
Strahl, Otho French 321
Strange, John 147
Sullivan, Jere 127
Sunken Road 140

T

Tawah 280, 281, 282, 283
Tennessee Civil War Preservation As-
    sociation x, 25, 107, 122
Tennessee River 1, 2, 3, 4, 31, 33, 48,
    51, 57, 70, 139, 153, 209, 212,
    227, 233, 234, 239, 244, 245,
    273, 275, 276, 282, 285, 295,
    382, 425
Tennessee Valley Authority 224, 273,
    285
Tennessee Wars Commission x, xiv,
    286, 289, 290, 337, 427
Thomas, George H. 167, 171, 235
Thompson's Station 202, 205, 206,
    207, 406, 407, 428, 432
Tilghman, Lloyd 1, 4
Traveller's Rest 369, 370
Trenton xiv, 380, 381, 391, 425
Tyler 2, 10, 16, 61, 62

U

Undine 277, 278, 279, 280, 281, 285,
    289, 290

V

Van Dorn, Earl 62, 93, 201
Vaught's Hill 382
Venus 277, 278, 279, 280, 285

W

Wagner, George 318

Walke, Henry 3, 16, 17
Wallace, Lew 10, 17, 20, 21, 23, 34,
    42, 62, 64, 66
Wallace, W.H.L. 20, 34, 43, 47, 50
Walthall, Edward 233
Watkins, Sam 328, 337
Wheeler, Joe 215, 238
Wilson, James 296
Winstead Hill 312, 338
Wood, Herbert xiii, 107
Wood, Thomas 167

About the Author

Civil War enthusiast and relic collector Randy Bishop teaches history at Middleton High School and serves as an adjunct professor for Jackson State Community College. A six-time recipient of the Teacher of the Year Award, Bishop was recognized in *Who's Who Among America's Teachers*. He is a member of the Sons of Confederate Veterans, Tennessee Civil War Preservation Association, and Parker's Crossroads Battlefield Association. In addition, he has served his community as president of the local elementary- and high-school parent-teacher organizations as well as the community library board. He is the author of Pelican's ***The Tennessee Brigade.***